"I Made Mistakes"

Speaking to an advisor in 1966 about America's escalation of forces in Vietnam, Secretary of Defense Robert S. McNamara confessed: "We've made mistakes in Vietnam ... I've made mistakes. But the mistakes I made are not the ones they say I made." In *"I Made Mistakes"*, Aurélie Basha i Novosejt provides a fresh and controversial examination of Secretary of Defense Robert S. McNamara's decisions during the Vietnam War. Although McNamara is remembered as the architect of the Vietnam War, Basha i Novosejt draws on new sources – including the diaries of his advisor and confidant John T. McNaughton – to reveal a man who resisted the war more than most. As Secretary of Defense, he did not want the costs associated with a new international commitment in Vietnam, but he sacrificed these misgivings to instead become the public face of the war out of a sense of loyalty to the President.

AURÉLIE BASHA I NOVOSEJT is a Lecturer in American History at the University of Kent in Canterbury.

Cambridge Studies in US Foreign Relations

Edited by

Paul Thomas Chamberlin, *Columbia University*
Lien-Hang T. Nguyen, *Columbia University*

This series showcases cutting-edge scholarship in US foreign relations that employs dynamic new methodological approaches and archives from the colonial era to the present. The series will be guided by the ethos of transnationalism, focusing on the history of American foreign relations in a global context rather than privileging the US as the dominant actor on the world stage.

Also in the Series

Greg Whitesides, *Science and American Foreign Relations since World War II*
Hideaki Kami, *Diplomacy Meets Migration: US Relations with Cuba during the Cold War*
Jasper M. Trautsch, *The Genesis of America: US Foreign Policy and the Formation of National Identity, 1793–1815*
Shaul Mitelpunkt, *Israel in the American Mind: The Cultural Politics of US-Israeli Relations, 1958–1988*
Pierre Asselin, *Vietnam's American War: A History*
Elisabeth Leake, *The Defiant Border: The Afghan-Pakistan Borderlands in the Era of Decolonization, 1936–1965*
Tuong Vu, *Vietnam's Communist Revolution: The Power and Limits of Ideology*
Michael E. Neagle, *America's Forgotten Colony: Cuba's Isle of Pines*
Lloyd E. Ambrosius, *Woodrow Wilson and American Internationalism*
Geoffrey C. Stewart, *Vietnam's Lost Revolution: Ngô Đình Diệm's Failure to Build an Independent Nation, 1955–1963*
Renata Keller, *Mexico's Cold War: Cuba, the United States, and the Legacy of the Mexican Revolution*

"I Made Mistakes"

Robert McNamara's Vietnam War Policy, 1960–1968

AURÉLIE BASHA I NOVOSEJT

CAMBRIDGE
UNIVERSITY PRESS

CAMBRIDGE
UNIVERSITY PRESS

University Printing House, Cambridge CB2 8BS, United Kingdom

One Liberty Plaza, 20th Floor, New York, NY 10006, USA

477 Williamstown Road, Port Melbourne, VIC 3207, Australia

314–321, 3rd Floor, Plot 3, Splendor Forum, Jasola District Centre, New Delhi – 110025, India

79 Anson Road, #06–04/06, Singapore 079906

Cambridge University Press is part of the University of Cambridge.

It furthers the University's mission by disseminating knowledge in the pursuit of education, learning, and research at the highest international levels of excellence.

www.cambridge.org
Information on this title: www.cambridge.org/9781108415538
DOI: 10.1017/9781108234108

© Aurélie Basha i Novosejt 2019

First published 2019

Printed in the United Kingdom by TJ International Ltd. Padstow, Cornwall

A catalogue record for this publication is available from the British Library.

ISBN 978-1-108-41553-8 Hardback

For my father, Ydriz Basha i Novosejt

Contents

Figures

Cover: Secretary of Defense McNamara press conference on the withdrawal of troops and units from France, June 16, 1966. (Bettmann/Getty Images.)

Acknowledgments

Every story has a long and short version. The long version of the story behind this book begins in 2002 when I met the man at the center of this research, Robert S. McNamara. Many people, too many to acknowledge here, have contributed to the journey that led to my doctoral work and ultimately to this book. In the shorter version, I am especially grateful to Steven Casey, Andrew Preston and MacGregor Knox. This book would not have been possible without their encouragement, inspiration and mentorship as well as their critical eye. My special thanks also go to Marc Selverstone and Peter Trubowitz, who offered their invaluable comments and perspectives.

I benefited from two particularly collegial and intellectually stimulating summer workshops that shaped the direction of my research: Columbia University's Saltzman Institute for War and Peace Studies' Summer Workshop of Military Operations and Strategy and the University of Texas at Austin's Clements Center's Summer Seminar in History and Statecraft. Special thanks are due to Kori Schake, Elliot Cohen, Mark Atwood Lawrence, Jonas Hagmann and Lisa Karlborg.

Many other colleagues whose work I admire provided important advice and support. They include the late Stanley Hoffmann, Fredrik Logevall and Lawrence Kaplan. John Dumbrell, Mara Oliva and Kasper Grotle Rasmussen were the best co-panelists one could wish for on two occasions. Errol Morris and Daniel Ellsberg were unusually generous with their time and insight. Alex McNaughton and Tom Paulin kindly shared the McNaughton diaries and their time. Diego Ruiz-Palmer made military jargon comprehensible. The Historical Office of the Office of the

Secretary of Defense kindly allowed me to draw on their impressive collection of photographs.

In addition, thank you to Jeremy Schmidt and Tim Holtz at the Gerald R. Ford Presidential Library and to Stephen Plotkin at the John F. Kennedy Presidential Library, who helped to make my research trips as enjoyable as they were. My research would not have been possible without financial support from a Marjorie Kovler Fellowship from the John F. Kennedy Presidential Library Foundation, a George C. Marshall/ Baruch Fellowship from the George C. Marshall Foundation, a Gerald R. Ford Presidential Library Research Travel Grant and a Roosevelt Study Center Research Grant.

I owe a debt of gratitude to my students and colleagues at the London School of Economics. My students sustained my enthusiasm, with a special nod to Shreya Das and Uday Mehra. The LSE100 team provided an exciting intellectual home for many years. My deepest thanks go to Andrea Mason, Diego De Merich, Daniel Strieff, Mahon Murphy, Jonas Gjersø, Tobias Vogelgsang, Jessica Templeton, Jose Olivas-Osuna, Maria Chen, Bryan Gibson, Maria Brock, Dayna Barnes, Taylor Sherman and Maria Kyriakidou.

Debbie Gershenowitz took a leap of faith in backing this book. I am grateful to her and her colleagues at Cambridge University Press for their help in making this book a reality.

Finally, my family and friends provided the perspective and cheer that I needed over the years, including Sarah Basha, Jerry Mitrovica, Laura De Kock, Almudena Suarez-Fernandez, Benjamin Grenier, Talal Salman, Kostas Matakos, Joop ter Harmsel, as well as the Glucksman and van Vollenhoven families.

My son Arendt was born halfway through the process of producing this book and changed everything for the better, except for the quality of my sleep. I am immensely thankful to Cidalia de Pina Macedo for helping me know that he would be happily taken care of while I could get back into my other world. My husband Olivier van Vollenhoven, the love of my life, has been my partner in every sense of the word. And finally, my parents Ydriz and Kimete Basha i Novosejt have been my greatest source of strength and motivation. I dedicate this book to my father, who relished the idea that his daughter was a history teacher as de Gaulle had been but never got to hold these pages in his comforting hands.

Abbreviations

ARPA	Advanced Research Projects Agency
ARVN	South Vietnamese Army Forces
BRIAM	British Advisory Mission to South Vietnam
CBS	Columbia Broadcasting System
C&C	Commissions & Committees Files
CDTC	Combat Development Test Center
CG	Civil Guard
CI	Counterinsurgency
CIA	Central Intelligence Agency
CIDG	Civilian Irregular Defense Group
CINCAL	Commander in Chief, Alaska
CINCPAC	Commander in Chief, Pacific
CORDS	Civil Operations and Revolutionary Support Program
CPSVN	Comprehensive Plan for South Vietnam
CY	Calendar year
DCI	Director of Central Intelligence
DDR&E	Director of Defense Research and Engineering
DIA	Defense Intelligence Agency
DOD	Department of Defense
DPM	Draft Presidential Memorandum
FCO	Foreign and Commonwealth Office, UK
FO	Foreign Office, UK
FRUS	Foreign Relations of the United States Series
FY	Fiscal year
GDP	Gross domestic product
GFL	Gerald R. Ford Presidential Library

GNP	Gross national product
GVN	Government of the Republic of Vietnam (South Vietnam)
GWU	George Washington University, National Security Archive
HASC	House Armed Services Committee
HBS	Harvard Business School
INR	Bureau of Intelligence and Research
ISA	International Security Affairs
JCS	Joint Chiefs of Staff
JFKL	John F. Kennedy Presidential Library
LBJL	Lyndon B. Johnson Presidential Library
LoC	Library of Congress
MAAG	Military Assistance and Advisory Group
MACV	Military Assistance Command, Vietnam
MAD	Mutually Assured Destruction
MAP	Military Assistance Program
MC	Miller Center, University of Virginia
M&M	Meetings & Memoranda Series
NARA	National Archives and Records Administration, College Park
NCP	National Campaign Plan
NME	National Military Establishment
NSA	National Security Advisor Files
NSAM	National Security Action Memorandum
NSC	National Security Council
NSF	National Security Files
NSRB	National Security Resources Board
OH	Oral history
OSD	Office of the Secretary of Defense
PM	Prime Minister
POF	Presidential Office Files
PPBS	Planning, Programming and Budgeting System
PREM	Prime Minister's Files
RAF	Royal Air Force
R&D	Research and development
ROK	Republic of Korea
RSC	Roosevelt Study Center, Middelburg, NL
RSM	Robert S. McNamara
SASC	Senate Armed Services Committee
SEATO	Southeast Asia Treaty Organization
SDC	Self-Defense Corps

SFRC	Senate Foreign Relations Committee
TFX	Tactical Fighter Experimental
USAF	United States Air Force
USAID	United States Agency for International Development
USG	United States government
USIA	United States Information Agency
USMC	United States Marine Corps
USOM	United States Operations Mission
UVAL	University of Virginia Library Archives
VC	Viet Cong
WH	White House

Introduction

Robert Strange McNamara, President John F. Kennedy's restless Secretary of Defense, was flying back to Washington, returning from yet another trip, this time from South Vietnam. The Southeast Asian country was a nuisance, a nagging problem for the Secretary but one that few could predict would eventually tarnish his reputation irreparably and mark US foreign policy for the remainder of the Cold War. That was still a few years off. On this day, October 1, 1963, McNamara worked alongside his assistant, William P. Bundy, to finalize their delegation's trip report.

Despite their fatigue, McNamara did not sleep on the long journey back to Washington but instead parsed over the report. President Kennedy had asked his Secretary to produce a document that would define the government's policy on South Vietnam and, in so doing, bring some order to the chaotic scenes both in Washington and in the field. Over the past week, the US team in South Vietnam had frustrated McNamara, who had observed and disapproved of the bickering between agencies and advisors whose "emotional" attitudes seemed to cloud their judgment.

Now the focus was on the future and moving past these obstacles to produce what the Secretary saw as a coherent and rational policy in the shape of the report. It was his intention to present a document that reconciled disagreements among advisors over their diagnosis of the core problems in South Vietnam as well as their evaluation of the prospects for the existing US policy there. When he was not rolling off statistics, as he was wont to do, McNamara was questioning Bundy's choice of words. McNamara liked precision, in numbers and in words. The Secretary enjoyed poetry and the poet's sparse and attentive choice of words. His plane rides occasionally involved sharing poetry with his colleagues and his rare friends among those colleagues.

The day before he had left for South Vietnam, on September 26, 1963, CBS had broadcast an hour-long interview with the Secretary during which he had recited a poem to illustrate his 980 days in office and to describe relations with the Soviet Union, with whom the prospect of détente was appearing on the horizon. Quoting the dissident Russian poet Yevgeny Yevtushenko, McNamara read:

There's no doubt that it's spring. It's a rough spring, a difficult spring, with late frosts and a cold wind, a spring which takes a step to the left and then a step to the right and then a step back, but which is certain nevertheless to go on and take two or three steps forward. And the fact that winter should hold the earth so desperately in its grip and refuse to give up is also quite in the order of things. But then in the very counter attacks of winter one can sense its growing impotence because times have changed.[1]

As the poem suggested, the Kennedy administration was enjoying an optimistic moment. Over the last ten days, the administration had scored a number of victories with a hitherto uncooperative Congress. The Senate had ratified the nuclear test ban treaty, which McNamara and his team had worked tirelessly to achieve against the objections of many military officials. Despite their disappointment with its details, the product of many compromises, for Kennedy and McNamara, the treaty represented an important first step. Just two days later, the House of Representatives also approved the President's proposed income tax cut, which to the relief of his Keynesian advisors, Kennedy had finally agreed to. His Council of Economic Advisers in particular predicted that it would kick-start the economy and bring down the unemployment numbers that had helped him get elected.

More than South Vietnam, as the Secretary returned to Washington, President Kennedy's focus was on the domestic front. If there was one battlefield that preoccupied the New Frontiersmen during these warm fall days of October, it was on the home front. *Time Magazine*'s cover featured Alabama Governor George Wallace's profile and the headline "Alabama: Civil Rights Battlefield." The administration had faced a stand-off with the Governor as he resisted federal efforts to force desegregation of schools across the country. In a frenzy of southern resistance, white supremacists had bombed a church in Birmingham, Alabama, killing four young black girls as they changed into their choir clothes. In yet another symbol of the domestic tensions that flared around the young

President and his team of New Frontiersmen, on the day that McNamara had left for South Vietnam, a deranged man had crashed the White House gates in a paranoid episode.

However, for the next few days, McNamara and his report took center stage, setting strictly domestic concerns aside for a time. An exhausted William Bundy accompanied McNamara as they went directly from the plane to the White House to present their report to the President before convening the whole national security team in the ensuing days.[2] On October 3, after meeting with all of Kennedy's senior advisors, with the notable exception of Secretary of State Dean Rusk, who was away at a NATO meeting in Europe, the administration produced a press release that summarized McNamara's preferred policy for South Vietnam.

Speaking to the gathered press corps, Press Secretary Pierre Salinger explained: "The security of South Vietnam is a major interest of the United States as of other free nations ... Major United States assistance in support of [the] military effort is needed only until the insurgency has been suppressed or until the national security forces of the Government of South Vietnam are capable of suppressing it. Secretary McNamara and General Taylor reported their judgment that the major part of the United States military task can be completed by the end of 1965." He concluded by saying, "It remains the policy of the United States in South Vietnam, as in other parts of the world, to support the efforts of the people of that country to defeat aggression and to build a peaceful and free society."[3]

By tracing the policy enshrined in the carefully worded press release back to its origins, this book sheds light on McNamara's early decisions on Vietnam and specifically on his plans to withdraw from the country in that period. Although his policy for withdrawal was made public only in October 1963, it originated in the spring of 1962 when McNamara took control of the administration's policy for South Vietnam. During the spring of 1962, McNamara received counsel from a number of people that would shape his recommendations for South Vietnam. In particular, he met with the British counterinsurgency expert Robert G. K. Thompson, who accelerated McNamara's adoption of other advisors' counterinsurgency strategies for South Vietnam. He also met with the economist John Kenneth Galbraith, who drew McNamara's attention to the potential repercussions of a more open-ended or traditional military commitment to South Vietnam.

Although McNamara later explained that war was not amenable to calculation, in these early years he approached the problems in Vietnam with numbers in mind. His calculations were not in terms of "body counts," as they would infamously become later, but in terms of the economic and fiscal impact of overseas military commitments on the US balance of payments position and on the administration's budget. From McNamara's vantage point, the problems in South Vietnam were not entirely unrelated to domestic issues.

The responsibilities of the Cold War had produced a range of defense installations around the world that were producing year-on-year balance of payments deficits, an alarming prospect for Kennedy, who feared that a run on the dollar could undermine all other aspects of US power. President Kennedy weighed on his Secretary of Defense to help him balance the budget and to alleviate pressures on the dollar. The fall 1963 policy for South Vietnam was more economical in both respects.

By looking at McNamara's positions on South Vietnam, in the context not of the broader Vietnam War but of his office, the book provides insight into how the machinery of defense policy had evolved until and then under McNamara's stewardship. Understanding how McNamara defined his job provides some explanation for his preoccupation with economic issues as well as his resistance when Kennedy's successor Lyndon B. Johnson eventually overturned his withdrawal plans. The role of the Secretary of Defense was ill-defined when McNamara joined the Kennedy administration, and its primary focus was inward. Even when the war escalated under Johnson, McNamara scarcely considered the "other side" very much. His inability to factor in Hanoi's motives and the international context, beyond his fears of a Chinese intervention when the United States escalated, were a remarkable oversight.

As Secretary of Defense, McNamara's first concern was with civilian control, both in controlling the impact of the defense budget on economic issues and in ensuring that military tools were best aligned to civilian objectives. Unfortunately, McNamara defined his role too narrowly. Although he recognized the shortcomings, and later the absence, of a strategy for South Vietnam, he refused to step in to fill the void, and instead waited for non-defense advisors to do so. He only belatedly broke out of his self-imposed restrictions.

The received wisdom that McNamara's estimate that the United States would withdraw from South Vietnam in 1965 was based solely on optimism about the situation on the ground is also challenged in the chapters ahead. In reality, from 1962 and into the early months of the Johnson administration, McNamara was pessimistic about prospects in South Vietnam and in particular about the ability of the South Vietnamese to sustain the proposed program both economically and logistically.

Similarly, as the war escalated under President Johnson, he questioned the military value of the bombing campaign and of the introduction of US ground troops, which he publicly recommended. However, McNamara repeatedly self-censored his doubts, at first so they would not detract from his planning and later out of loyalty to the President that he served.

Perhaps the greatest insight of this book is into how important the notion of "loyalty" was to McNamara in the execution of his job. Loyalty trumped even his best judgment. This became especially problematic as he oversaw increasing troop deployments into South Vietnam despite having little or no faith in what those troops could accomplish and despite understanding sooner than most that those deployments could have a crippling economic effect on the United States and, in so doing, on the international monetary system as a whole.[4]

The new insight into McNamara adds to the usual counterfactual question on the early period of US involvement in Vietnam, namely: "What would Kennedy have done if he had lived?" In its stead, it provides other questions that are implicit in each of the chapters that follow. The alternative counterfactuals include: Could the counterinsurgency strategy laid out in the 1962–1963 period have worked if it had been scrupulously applied? Could the war have been prevented if Lyndon Baines Johnson had been less of a spendthrift New Deal Democrat? Could a stronger civilian voice at the State Department or elsewhere have provided alternatives to the application of military force to solve the problems in South Vietnam?

The chapters ahead build on several important histories of the Vietnam War, the Office of the Secretary of Defense (OSD) and of Robert McNamara himself. Andrew Preston's work on the National Security Council under McGeorge Bundy provided a template: he described his work as a "bureaucratic history of the changes in presidential decision-making and a diplomatic history of the origins of the Vietnam War."[5] To paraphrase Preston, this book is a bureaucratic history of the changes in *the* OSD and a history of the early years of the Vietnam War. This approach borrows from political science models and assumes that "where you stand depends on where you sit."[6] The research looks at the OSD to see how "where McNamara sat" had an effect on "where he stood" on Vietnam. At the same time, it suggests that idiosyncratic personalities and human relationships complicate neat analytical models.

The book attempts to recreate McNamara's reality from the vantage point of his office to explain his recommendations for Vietnam. It does not provide a chronological account of the decisions for Vietnam and how these interacted with international events. Instead, it casts a light on how McNamara and his colleagues at the OSD experienced the Vietnam War, focusing on events and factors that mattered most to them. Central to this has been the need to understand how McNamara defined his job and, in so doing, reconcile two historiographies that have largely been treated as discrete, namely the history of the OSD and the history of McNamara in Vietnam. In so doing, another interpretation of McNamara's decisions on Vietnam emerges.

In keeping with trends in the history of the Cold War more broadly, the existing literature on the Vietnam War has gone through a number of waves as new materials emerge and new, often more nuanced, interpretations are provided.[7] For the most part, across these waves, McNamara has been described as one of the war's "villains" albeit for different reasons. Where military authors criticize him for putting far too many restraints on his military advisors,[8] others insist on his role in silencing voices of dissent, especially in the Johnson administration.[9] One possible reason for this consensus among unlikely allies is that McNamara was an iconic figure of the war, the images of his press conference so deeply ingrained in the collective memory of the war. As a case in point, Deborah Shapley's leading biography of McNamara is dedicated: "to the millions who, like me, were born as World War II ended and the cold war began, and whose lives were changed by this one life."[10] A similar, more mournful, interpretation of McNamara's trajectory pervades Paul Hendrickson's *The Living and the Dead*, which describes an aged McNamara as a "ghost, a ghost of all that had passed and rolled on beneath his country in barely a generation."[11]

As time has passed and the polarizing memory of McNamara as the architect of Vietnam has either faded or been replaced by the image of the reflective man in Errol Morris's *The Fog of War*, a different interpretation is perhaps no longer taboo. In areas outside history, and particularly in business management from where McNamara came, he has gone through something of a revival.[12] This sympathetic literature harks back to McNamara's early years before Vietnam when his revolutionary leadership was widely applauded.[13]

The goal of this book is not to try to redeem McNamara but to treat his early contributions without the benefit of hindsight and without the need to fit him into a binary "hawk" or "dove" framework.[14] As new documents have emerged, historians have reassessed other advisors to President Kennedy and Johnson, including McGeorge Bundy, Paul Nitze and to a lesser extent Dean Rusk, but McNamara has largely eluded this treatment. This book is a first attempt at rectifying that oversight.

At a minimum, the book contributes to answering Shapley's question, "Was his choice of war an aberration in his character and career? Or was it inevitable, given his nature?"[15] It also disproves statements that "It is a painful irony that the man who preached the gospel of cost-effectiveness for the nuts and bolts of military hardware failed to comprehend that the Vietnam intervention would become the least effective and most costly military venture in American history."[16] Quite the contrary: this book suggests that economic concerns and relatively accurate predictions about the costs of escalation conditioned McNamara's recommendations for Vietnam. They explain why he led withdrawal plans from 1962 to 1963 and later resisted the introduction of ground troops.

Rather than focus on McNamara as an individual, the book evaluates his role as Secretary of Defense and situates him at the end of a historical process for that office, a young agency still being shaped by incumbent Secretaries. Also, where many historians have tended to treat the Pentagon as a unitary organization or, at best, as an uncertain union between the OSD and the Joint Chiefs of Staff (JCS) separately, this book goes a little deeper in identifying the key centers of power within the OSD for Vietnam decision-making.[17] It traces the key offices that McNamara created to continue the process of enforcing civilian control over the military and how these offices were distinct, if not in outright opposition, to the military services. As Chapter 2 explains, many of the offices that were either created or elevated in importance during McNamara's tenure, for instance Systems Analysis or the International Security Advisor's office, were specifically designed to undercut the Chiefs' budgetary and policy-making roles.

Moreover, diplomatic historians of the Vietnam War have tended to overemphasize the diplomatic and military aspects of decision-making. As a result, the existing literature has relied heavily on archival collections that are more narrowly relevant to Vietnam without placing those decisions in their economic context.[18] This tendency is particularly problematic with McNamara since he was the first to acknowledge that he had very little knowledge of foreign policy coming into his role as Secretary of Defense. His focus was on another dimension of civilian control, namely controlling the economic and fiscal aspects of defense.

In this regard, this research builds on Francis Gavin's work, which places greater onus on issues such as the balance of payments and gold outflow.[19] Economic concerns were central to McNamara's decision for

Vietnam and in determining the timing and shape of withdrawal plans from 1962 to 1963. The change in strategy from the Kennedy to the Johnson administration also hinged on the two Presidents' different appreciation of economic issues and specifically on Johnson's judgment, which he shared with more liberal economic advisors, that Kennedy had been too fiscally conservative.[20]

In addition, the book challenges the tendency to depict a relatively neat upward trajectory in the US commitment to Vietnam.[21] While many studies recognize that 1965 was a watershed moment, they nevertheless rely on statistics of ever-increasing troop numbers, even if they were "just" advisors in the Kennedy years, to describe an almost inexorable process toward the full-scale American war in Vietnam. However, what these troop numbers overlook is that a period of planning for withdrawal led by McNamara in 1962–1963, and underpinned by a strategy for counterinsurgency rather than for conventional war, punctuated this process.

More recently, with the declassification of relevant archival collections, historians have given more credence to "Kennedy's withdrawal plans." These move beyond the early, and often speculative, recollections of Kennedy's colleagues, who affirmed that the slain President was determined to withdraw on the eve of his death irrespective of the situation on the ground.[22]

However, in portraying Kennedy as an isolated clairvoyant, most historians have overlooked McNamara's role in the withdrawal plans. They have glossed over McNamara's interests in pushing for withdrawal and, in painting a picture of him as a mere "implementer," discounted his ability to learn on the job and to seek out experts, in particular on issues like counterinsurgency. Although their approach makes for a consistent reading of McNamara's place in the Vietnam War – as a hawk until later in the Johnson administration – it is at odds with new documentary evidence. Marc Selverstone has provided an invaluable corrective here. As he persuasively argues, Kennedy may have inspired the actual withdrawal plans, but they were closely aligned to McNamara's own priorities for the Department of Defense (DOD) and he was their main architect.[23]

The book confirms Fredrik Logevall's view in his seminal book *Choosing War* that Johnson *chose* war in South Vietnam. By relying more heavily on the presidential recordings during the early months of the Johnson administration, it challenges the opposing view that Johnson was "scrupulous in continuing" Kennedy's Vietnam policy.[24] Instead, as Chapter 7 shows, during the transition, Johnson knowingly changed strategy, abandoning the counterinsurgency strategy that was central to Kennedy's approach to Vietnam and to his withdrawal plans.

Unlike Johnson, Kennedy was deeply immersed in counterinsurgency theory and surrounded himself with formal and informal experts on the issue, most of whom were isolated, pushed out or left under Johnson, notably Roger Hilsman and his brother Robert F. Kennedy.[25] As McNamara explained, "[The] statements and recommendations [about the 1965 end date] were associated with the strategy we were then following in Vietnam. That strategy was subsequently changed; and when it changed, the statements and recommendations made with respect to that strategy were no longer valid."[26] In other words, the withdrawal plans under Kennedy relied on his understanding of counterinsurgency: when the counterinsurgency strategy was dropped, so too were the withdrawal plans.

Johnson's starker views on Vietnam underpinned the shift in strategy. From the outset, he believed in falling dominos more strongly than Kennedy had and was against the idea of withdrawal in any situation short of victory. There had been two lowest common denominators in government under Kennedy (policies that could earn broad administration agreement albeit for conflicting reasons): one was withdrawal and the other was the introduction of troops. Kennedy expressly rejected the latter. Unlike Johnson, he had a somewhat blasé attitude to recommendations for the introduction of troops.[27] By contrast, very early on, Johnson felt that the "sky was the limit" for US support to Vietnam and sought out military advice more often than McNamara himself was inclined to do.[28]

In addition, as Chapter 6 will also show, Kennedy and McNamara placed Vietnam in a broader context of US commitments around the world and were concerned about its impact on the balance of payments. As such, withdrawal from Vietnam did not imply the abandonment of Vietnam, only the creation of a new model of influence around the world – one that need not rely on military tools or a heavy US troop presence. Both Kennedy and McNamara shifted the administration's definition of the problem in Vietnam in a way that would facilitate this view: instead of being an externally driven conflict, it was internal; and instead of being "our" war it was "their" war.

Broader economic considerations did not weigh on Johnson in the same way. Instead, and ironically, as Chapter 8 shows, he seemed more willing to "bear any burden" and criticized his predecessors' concern for balanced budgets as he, in contrast, embraced neo-Keynesianism in the Great Society programs. McNamara, who was reluctant to identify any divergences between his views and those of the President he served, later admitted that he and Johnson had not seen eye to eye on the costs inherent to escalation in Vietnam.

When the transition is seen through the lens of civilian control – namely aligning military tools to civilian-designed strategy and weighing the defense budget against internal constraints, and primarily a sound economic base – McNamara was remarkably consistent as he transitioned from the Kennedy to the Johnson administration. In both instances, McNamara did not design strategy but instead devised the most cost-efficient program to support the President's chosen strategy. Also, McNamara had embraced Kennedy's policy because it promised to reduce the balance of payments deficit and could deal with a congressional attack on the Military Assistance Program that funded Vietnam operations. In the Johnson administration, he pressed harder to reduce defense outlays to compensate for the increase in costs on Vietnam while urging the President to repeal the tax cut that he had inherited from Kennedy.

McNamara was especially consistent in allowing the Presidents he served to make him the public face of a policy that was not his alone: out of a sense of loyalty to the Presidency, first he became the public face of the withdrawal plans and then for escalation. As each of the chapters shows, this was a deliberate decision by both Presidents and by McNamara himself. McNamara sought to protect the Presidents he served because he understood the reputational damages that could be incurred if their policies were unsuccessful. As Chapter 9 shows, he waited a long time to publicly break ranks with the administration. From the fall of 1965 onward, when he understood that his days at the OSD were numbered, he tried to repair his damaged reputation and legacy.

These new findings are possible because the full body of primary materials is now available. They complete what was already a rich set of materials. In a classified oral history for the Historical Office of the OSD undertaken in 1986, McNamara explained why, in office, he had asked his Assistant Secretary of Defense for International Security Affairs, John T. McNaughton, to compile *United States–Vietnam Relations, 1945–1967: A Study Prepared by the Department of Defense*, or what would become more commonly known as the *Pentagon Papers*. He recounted that he told McNaughton: "This is a damn mess. We must insure that those who at some point will wish to study the action and draw lessons from it will have all the raw materials they need. So collect all the raw materials and be sure they are available to historians." He wanted "historians, political scientists, and military experts [to] examine the mistakes in judgment."[29]

Although the *Pentagon Papers* are an important resource for any research on the OSD in Vietnam, especially since they now have been declassified in full, they also do not provide the definitive account of the Defense Department in Vietnam. First, its authors did not have access to "all the raw materials": they drew only on documents that were both directly relevant to Vietnam and that came through the OSD. In addition, the *Pentagon Papers* are essentially a curated selection of documents that are framed in analysis rather than the raw material per se. Their analysis, especially for the Kennedy years, is sometimes off the mark. Daniel Ellsberg was responsible for the Kennedy chapters and, perhaps because he had no contact with Vietnam in those early years, may have overlooked collections or factors that were equally, if not more, relevant to understanding decisions on Vietnam. In the *Pentagon Papers*, Ellsberg dismissed Kennedy's withdrawal plans as premised on optimism and primarily designed for budgetary projections not operational realities. However, in later years, in light of new documents, he revisited that conclusion.[30] Finally, the *Papers* relied only on the written record and, in this, were at a major disadvantage to histories today that have a far richer set of primary documents to draw from, especially the presidential recordings.

On the issue of relying on the written record, McNamara's Special Assistant and later Deputy to McNaughton, Adam Yarmolinsky, explained: "The written record more and more, and even in those days, tends to be defensive and it provides rationalizations rather than reasons. The written record is that – you know, McNamara, the DPMs [Draft Presidential Memoranda] – they were drafts until they were promulgated so that it could never be said that there was disagreement between the Pentagon or the Secretary and the President." When asked specifically what was not on the written record, Yarmolinsky replied, "Probably everything. Almost everything." He also added, "I think [McNamara] realized early on than the record shows that it was a mistake. And he tried in ways that are not apparent to disentangle."[31]

This research has benefited from a number of new resources, material that has either just come to light or was only recently declassified as well as material beyond the written record to provide a more complete picture of McNamara's early decisions on Vietnam.

First and foremost, since 2010, Robert McNamara's personal papers have been accessible at the Library of Congress. These contain

McNamara's notes as he researched his own memoirs, his heretofore classified oral histories for the OSD Office of the Historian and his personal correspondence. In addition, his papers contain his calendar as Secretary of Defense, which has proven invaluable in terms of identifying the people McNamara spoke to as he turned to a policy of disengagement from Vietnam, most notably Robert Thompson and John Kenneth Galbraith.

Second, John Newman has made his material available to researchers at the Kennedy Library.[32] His papers provide an invaluable shortcut as they contain much of the material that has been declassified on Kennedy's withdrawal plans in archives around the United States, including many of the military archives that are less accessible to researchers.

Also, Marc Selverstone and the Miller Center have posted a number of transcribed tapes online that provide fascinating insight into Vietnam decision-making during the Kennedy and Johnson years, and on McNamara in particular. In the Kennedy tapes, more than anywhere else, McNamara is heard dominating discussions on Vietnam and going against the current for escalation instead of leading it. Similarly, the Lyndon B. Johnson Library online collection of presidential recordings has been crucial to contextualizing and explaining the written record during the transition. For the reasons Yarmolinsky described, these recordings underpin the chapters on the Johnson years.

In addition, this research has drawn on oral histories, primarily at the presidential libraries, to understand the context in which recommendations were made and the relationships between people and agencies. Despite their inherent problems, the oral histories on McNamara and his tenure as Secretary of Defense during the Kennedy years provide an interesting perspective into his management style, his relationship with his military advisors and those whom he consulted on Vietnam.

McNamara's oral histories for the Office of the Historian at the Office of the Secretary of Defense, which were declassified in 2010, offer a fresh perspective on the Kennedy administration's withdrawal plans as McNamara is unusually candid in them. Indeed, twice during the interviews he asks for guarantees that they would remain classified. Those oral histories are the only place, for instance, where McNamara unambiguously admits that President Johnson fired him. Moreover, other key oral histories, notably with McNamara's Deputy Roswell Gilpatric, Treasury Secretary C. Douglas Dillon and the Council of Economic Advisers, were recorded in 1964 and thus before the full-scale escalation in Vietnam that could have colored judgments on President Johnson, McNamara or others.

Also, because this research tries to place the Vietnam War in its broader bureaucratic context, it has drawn on the papers of a larger swathe of advisors, not just those directly concerned with Vietnam and national security issues, but also advisors that dealt with economic issues (e.g. Carl Kaysen and C. Douglas Dillon) and organizational issues (e.g. Adam Yarmolinsky) to understand how they perceived Vietnam. For the economic dimensions, a number of online archives, in particular the Federal Reserve Archive, were also helpful.

Finally, the research has benefited from access to collections and documents that are not widely available to researchers. In particular, Alex McNaughton, through Thomas Paullin, the author of a blog on McNaughton, kindly provided a copy of his father John McNaughton's private diary, which gives an unparalleled and unfiltered view onto the private thoughts of McNamara and his closest confidants during the 1966–1967 period.

By using this full set of materials, the book reframes the withdrawal plans in the 1962–1963 period and the military escalation thereafter, as well as McNamara's role therein. It suggests that the decisions for withdrawal were rooted in issues that were less glamorous than Kennedy's vision, namely bureaucratic and budgetary processes. Also, by analyzing the decisions for Vietnam through the lens of the OSD, different lessons emerge about the "mistakes" made. McNamara's eventual disillusionment with the war and his advisors' post-mortem conclusions about the process that led to the war are revealing. While McNamara's reforms had been designed primarily to provide a "checks and balances" function, they had also strengthened the Department of Defense so that it had become a more flexible, well-run, well-funded and "active" organization in contrast to the State Department, which had a "talking shop" role. In so doing, the OSD produced what McNamara's Special Assistant Adam Yarmolinsky called "centrifugal tendencies," where military solutions to international problems were available and easier to deploy. In the end, the same factors that had, until 1963, coalesced into a policy for disengagement from Vietnam made escalation more likely under the Johnson administration.

In some respects, McNamara was a victim of his own success. His ability to implement policy loyally and efficiently and to execute the President's chosen policy faithfully made him the ideal agent for potentially delicate policies. In one presidential recording, President Johnson can be heard saying, "I thought you'd done the best job I've ever seen done. I hope you go on and brag yourself to your wife. I know you won't do it to anyone else."[33] McNamara echoed this theme when he was asked in an oral history why he had become involved in economic issues that were only tangentially relevant to his role as Secretary of Defense. He explained, "I was loyal to the point that he had complete assurance that I would carry through those tactics; and [that I was] skillful and tough enough that there was a high degree of probability that I would carry them out successfully."[34]

While that loyalty served the Presidents he worked for well, the same cannot be said for US efforts in Vietnam. Instead, as the chapters ahead will show, McNamara's conception of loyalty, which he felt served the interest of healthy civil-military relations, became especially problematic during the transition into the Johnson administration. It led him to self-censor his prescient understanding about the economic impact of the conflict in Vietnam and about the lack of an overarching strategy that could justify the increasing troop deployments that he also oversaw.

The History of the Office of the Secretary of Defense, 1947–1961

When Robert McNamara accepted President Kennedy's offer to serve as the United States' eighth Secretary of Defense, the role was still new, a barely decade-old innovation emanating from World War II. As a young agency, the OSD was still defining its place in the national security decision-making landscape and, in so doing, trying to find the appropriate balance of power between civilian and military authorities. President Dwight D. Eisenhower had left the new administration with the Defense Reorganization Act of 1958, a congressionally mandated program for change at the Department of Defense. McNamara recognized its sweeping potential to pave the way for his bureaucratic revolutions as the longest-serving Secretary of Defense.[1] The year 1960 was a propitious moment in the office's history and for a man who by personality as well as professional and intellectual inclination was predisposed to pushing organizational change and centralizing authority around himself.

The history of the OSD and the legacy of McNamara's predecessors provide a context and a framework in which to consider civil-military relations at the time and, ultimately, to understand McNamara's policy recommendations for Vietnam. The framework in the pages ahead breaks with existing literature that has tended to consider civilian control in terms of cultural, sociological or organizational relationships with the military. Instead, the history of the OSD's civilian control until 1960 was essentially the history of two trends: strategic and operational control, on the one hand, and "resource allocation," on the other.[2]

First, civilian control of strategy and of operational decisions has been the traditional focus of civil-military relations literature and has concentrated on the changing relationships and power dynamics between the

OSD, the President, State Department, the National Security Council (NSC) and military services in the articulation of national strategy. The steady progression of civilian control before McNamara's arrival at the OSD was coupled with the gradual reduction of military voices in the upper echelons of decision-making, a process that each incumbent Secretary on the whole supported.

The second dimension is the economic one, or what Samuel Huntington called "resource allocation": civilian control was also about defining the appropriate level of fiscal commitment to military expenditures and balancing defense spending with other domestic or civilian needs. Here, the evolution had been more fitful and controversial. Senator Kennedy had campaigned aggressively for increased defense spending and criticized his opponent's thriftiness. However, despite his campaign rhetoric, Kennedy's transition team recruited a Secretary of Defense with the managerial skills to control the ballooning defense establishment and its costs. Although the defense budget expanded during the Kennedy years and McNamara's tenure, the reforms they engineered were specifically designed to reduce defense expenditures in the long term.[3]

Each Secretary of Defense from the first incumbent James Forrestal to McNamara confronted an in-built cultural ambivalence in the United States about anything that could be construed as extending the reach of the federal government in general and of military authorities specifically. Americans were uncomfortable with the military establishment that they had inherited from World War II. The Pentagon building itself was erected hastily between 1941 and 1942 to coordinate the war but with a stipulation from Congress that it was a temporary structure and that it would be converted into a veteran's hospital "after peace is restored and the army no longer needs the room."[4]

As Ernest May observed, although the US federal government and its military structures were among the "longer-lasting artifacts of the Cold War," they were not preordained in a culture that had resisted permanent structures to organize the country's relations with the world.[5] The Defense Department was a product of necessity, born of battlefield imperatives during the war rather than from deliberate design. All previous and subsequent attempts to centralize and organize a standing military force faced deeply rooted resistance as it raised the specter of a Prussian-style General Staff.[6]

After the attack on Pearl Harbor and the United States' entry into the war, the Franklin D. Roosevelt administration recognized that existing structures were inadequate for a world war and especially for joint operations with British allies. As a result, in February 1942, "quickly and without great fanfare," the existing, more loosely organized Joint Boards between the Army and Navy were replaced with what would become known as the Joint Chiefs of Staff.[7] The latter mirrored the British armed forces as a way to streamline coordination of the Anglo-American Combined Chiefs of Staff that oversaw Allied operations. To provide a counterpart to the British Royal Air Force (RAF), and in recognition of the growing role of air power in this new conflict, the Army's Air Force was given equal status with the Army and Navy and eventually became a third, independent service.[8]

The organizational changes to the services challenged the previous segregation of the Army and Navy which, on the basis of "elemental distinction" between land and sea, had jealously guarded their independence until that point, going as far as to produce separate war plans. Even though the war experience offered a case for the unification of the services, unification did not occur. The Navy, under the stewardship of James Forrestal, attacked the plans. In addition to philosophical fears associated with a centralized, military command, the Navy felt that it had the most to lose with unification: it could lose its air power to the newly created Air Force that seemed destined to play a leading role in the command of atomic weapons, and its Marine Corps could be subordinated to the Army to leave the Navy with a much-reduced role.[9]

By contrast, the Army and Air Force largely welcomed, and even encouraged, the wholesale merger of the armed services. In addition to promising relatively more budgetary security, for the Army, unification provided "a way to deal with a dangerous, rebellious, cocky child, the semiautonomous Army Air Force."[10] For its part, the Air Force supported unification because it relied on greater capital investments that could be siphoned off from the Navy; it "cockily" assumed that it would get a larger share of a unified budget. Its leaders also concluded that equal independence would ensure Air Force dominance because it had succeeded in capturing the imagination of the US public and its congressional leaders by convincing them that air power would be the key to any future war.[11]

In addition to debates on the merits of unification, the new national security infrastructure caused a debate about the appropriate balance between respecting and protecting military expertise, on the one hand, and ensuring civilian control, on the other. Reflecting this climate, in 1957, Samuel Huntington produced his groundbreaking work on civil-military relations, *The Soldier and the State*.[12] Huntington later described the book as an "unabashed defense of the professional military ethic and rejection of traditional liberalism [which] was in itself evidence of this intellectual debate."[13]

Huntington described how the increased complexity of warfare and technology in the nuclear age and the attendant need for specialized military expertise required "institutional autonomy." Washington's civilian leaders should resist the temptation to civilianize the military or interfere with its conduct – what he termed "subjective control" – and instead encourage independent military professionalism, or "objective control." For Huntington, the "requisite for military security [was] a shift in basic American values from liberalism to conservatism"; that is, military values could enrich society rather than vice-versa. Ultimately, Huntington's work was a product of and reaction to the debates of the times and was born of a concern, which was also distinctly American, that overbearing control of the military was a distinguishing characteristic of dictatorial regimes.[14]

Huntington juxtaposed two types of actors – civilian and military – in a neat dichotomy around which the battle lines of civil-military relations would be drawn. Barring emblematic civil-military clashes such as the MacArthur controversy over the Truman administration's policies in Korea, the situation in practice was more complicated. Also, Huntington assumed that military institutions were or could be apolitical, which ignored the fact that from the 1940s onward, military authorities had become intensely political as they became more savvy at competing for resources and influence in Washington.[15]

Instead of a battle between two sets of actors, the creation of the national security infrastructure had created tensions across several, interlocking axes, including between services themselves, between coordinating bodies such as the NSC and the State Department, between the legislative and executive branches, and between the JCS and the OSD.[16] As the Defense Department's budget expanded, many were concerned about the growing focus of military power on the projection of US power abroad and the OSD's growing prominence over the State Department. The relationship between the State and Defense Departments and between the Secretaries in defining national security strategy troubled each incumbent pair; more often than not the issues were resolved through personal rapport rather than any enduring bureaucratic solution.

The JCS/OSD axis was equally salient because it hinged on who should be the leading military advisor to the President, the Commander-in-Chief. For General Taylor, Eisenhower's Army Chief and later Kennedy's Chairman of the JCS, the JCS should be a non-political body that could transcend agency needs and provide advice on the best way of fulfilling civilian-set objectives.[17] At the same time, he agreed with two of McNamara's civilian advisors who later suggested that "meaningful professional advice" from the JCS was "difficult" if not impossible because of the individual Chiefs' "channelized thinking." As he noted, each Chief was still embedded in his service, and as a result, the JCS's advice was "largely the product of bargaining" between the services.[18]

The manner in which each President defined the JCS's role had a direct bearing on the type of Secretary of Defense he sought, namely in determining if the Secretary's role should be a policy-making one or a managerial one primarily concerned with organizing the budgetary process.[19] During these key decades, the OSD expanded its responsibilities along both lines, often to the detriment of the Joint Chiefs of Staff.

The first President to grapple with these bureaucratic and intellectual challenges was Harry S. Truman. Thrust into the role of President in the closing years of the war, he oversaw the defining moments of the Cold War. During the closing months of the war, the Truman administration also faced the challenging task of demobilization. However, confronted with new threats and international obligations, not least of which was the occupation of Germany and Japan, the United States retained a force that was four times that which had existed in 1939. This was the first time that the United States had a substantial military force in a time of peace. With it came a five-fold increase in defense allocations from $1.8 billion in 1940 to $10 billion in 1948, representing 14 percent of the US GDP by the end of the Truman administration.[20]

Events including the Berlin airlift in Europe, McCarthyism at home and, above all, the Korean War dashed Truman's earlier hopes to reap a "peace dividend," or a major reduction in this new defense budget. Instead, the rivalry between the United States and the Soviet Union emerged as the defining characteristic of international relations. Responding to new international realities and responsibilities, Truman presided over the expansion of the national security state. His four Secretaries of Defense – James Forrestal, Louis Johnson, George Marshall and Robert Lovett – each grappled with the President's inclination to compromise among stakeholders, to "satisfice" in setting up often flawed national security structures and to give them contradictory objectives. In particular, President Truman urged each of his Secretaries of Defense to keep the military budget down even while he expanded the United States' worldwide commitments.[21]

The founding act for the Department of Defense, the "compromise National Security Act of 1947," as one scholar has called it, created most of the principal structures for national security decision-making without settling underlying issues that plagued inter-service relations and their relations with the civilian authorities.[22] As the historian John Lewis Gaddis has critically noted, "preoccupied as they were with maintaining support for containment within the bureaucracy, the Congress, the informed public, and among allies overseas," the administration chose political expediency over efficiency: the "price of administrative effectiveness can be strategic shortsightedness," and, in this instance in particular, "process triumphed over policy," where policies and structures that were feasible were chosen over those that were desirable.[23] Moreover, many of the structures and especially the OSD were structurally weak, with a notable gap between their formal authority, which was relatively broad, and their substantive authority.

Principally for economic reasons, Truman was initially favorable to the wholesale merger of the services. However, faced with congressional resistance, he compromised and proposed a program of legislative reform whose "overall purpose was to erect an integrated structure to formulate national security policy at the uppermost level of government."[24] The National Security Act created the NSC, which was designed to advise the President on national security issues and provide strategic direction as the country's international obligations expanded. The NSC's Chairman was the President and its members included the Secretary of State as well as representatives of three new agencies: the National Security Resources Board (NSRB), the Secretary of Defense and the Central Intelligence Agency (CIA). The CIA, the successor agency to another World War II innovation, the Office of Strategic Services (OSS), became the NSC's main source of intelligence, although other intelligence agencies scattered across government, including in the military services, continued to operate in parallel. Crucially, each of the Service Secretaries was on the NSC. As a result, defense representatives held four of the seven seats on the NSC in its founding years.[25]

In addition, the National Security Act created the OSD to oversee the National Military Establishment (NME), later renamed the Department of Defense. The Secretary of Defense was designated as the President's principal advisor on military affairs and, as such, provided "general direction" to the Secretaries of the Army, Navy and new Air Force. However, in practice, his supervisory responsibilities were limited and, more often than not, undermined by the President himself. Furthermore, the act created three civilian "special assistants" to support the Secretary. These included a Comptroller, who was responsible for harmonizing the service budgets into one annual military budget.[26] In addition, the Secretary oversaw two new boards that concerned all military services: the Munitions Board and the Research & Development (R&D) Board.

Despite these reforms, the Service Secretaries retained most of their power, notably by keeping a direct line of communication to both the President and the Bureau of the Budget. The position of the Chairman of the Joint Chiefs of Staff was a shallow one even if his announced responsibility was ambitious. Officially, he was charged with providing strategic direction to the military forces, preparing plans, establishing unified commands and reviewing materiel and training requirements. In practice, however, he had no power over the Chiefs and instead acted primarily as a liaison with the White House. General Eisenhower was appointed as the first Chairman on a temporary basis in November 1948, but since he continued in his capacity as President of Columbia University, he spent scarce time on his JCS duties. It was not until August 1950, with the appointment of General Omar Bradley, that the JCS had an official Chairman. Moreover, from the start, the Chairman of the Joints of Chiefs and the individual Chiefs were in an unhappy tension with the Secretary of Defense: although they reported to the Secretary of Defense, they were also rival military advisors to the President, NSC, State Department and Congress.

As a result, In August 1949, the act was amended to clarify the respective roles of the Secretary of Defense and the JCS. The powers of the Comptroller were reinforced with a view to creating a first unified budget in fiscal year (FY) 1950. Although the amendments strengthened the Secretary of Defense's position on the budget, they weakened him by limiting his role to that of "principal assistant to the President in all matters related to the Department of Defense" rather than to defense policy more generally.[27] Similarly, since the Service Secretaries no longer chaired in the NSC, they were forced to consolidate their views through one representative, the Chairman of the JCS. In so doing, the latter's role was strengthened.

In addition, in a move that would frustrate successive administrations, the amendments allowed members of the JCS who were designated as the "principal military advisors to the President and the Secretary of Defense" to disagree with the administration's policy and to raise their disagreements in Congress "on [their] own initiative, after first informing the Secretary of Defense."[28] The Chiefs' independent advisory role to

Congress, to the President but also to the NSC and the State Department further politicized them and arguably paved the way for public spats with each administration, most notably over the Truman administration's strategy in Korea, which culminated in the MacArthur controversy.[29]

The first Secretary of Defense, in office from September 1947 to March 1949, was former Secretary of the Navy James Forrestal. A central figure in the creation of national security structures during and after the war, Forrestal was also credited with coining the phrase "national security" when, during a congressional hearing, he had explained that "our national security can only be assured on a very broad and comprehensive front. I am using the word 'security' here consistently and continuously rather than 'defense.'"[30] At the Navy, Forrestal had also been a leading opponent of President Truman's plans to support the unification of the services. In his first week on the job, he wrote in his diaries, "My chief misgivings about unification derived from my fear that there would be a tendency toward overconcentration and reliance on one man or one-group direction. In other words, too much central control."[31] As a result of his "misgivings," Forrestal was more responsible than most for the compromises that had resulted in the OSD's structural weaknesses. Yet despite a personal relationship that would continue to be ambivalent, Truman chose him as his first Secretary of Defense.

Forrestal was given a near impossible task riddled, as it was, with conflicting goals and stakeholders. Truman extended the United States' responsibilities but imposed low force and budgetary ceilings on Forrestal, which he then had to communicate to and enforce on the Chiefs. In an effort to assuage inter-service issues, the administration insisted on balanced forces, or an equal distribution of resources across the three services. This was counterproductive and resulted in heated debates about strategy among the services. The perceived unfairness of balanced forces played a part in the bitter battle between the Navy and the Air Force about who should be the custodian of atomic weapons.[32]

The Secretary's lack of executive power over the Chiefs was almost immediately apparent: the Chiefs ignored his proposed national strategic concept that was designed to guide their military assessments as well as Truman's budgetary ceiling.[33] Instead, they presented him with separate positions and budgets as the Chairmen of the JCS, Eisenhower and then Bradley sidestepped their official responsibility for coordinating the Chiefs' views. Truman further undermined Forrestal's authority by regularly bypassing him and reaching out to the Chiefs and the Service Secretaries directly. Perhaps the only relationship that was comparatively smooth during Forrestal's tenure was with the State Department where he benefited from his friendships with Secretary of State George Marshall and his Undersecretary, Robert Lovett. Their relationships did much to smooth collaboration between the two departments.

Eventually, the stresses of the office began to take their toll on Forrestal, who was unable to control the NME. Aides observed that "part of his scalp had become irritated from continued scratching" as he began to retreat into a state of increased isolation and paranoia.[34] By reaching out to Thomas Dewey, Truman's opponent in the 1948 election, in a bid to remain in office whoever won, Forrestal effectively ended his career. Within three months of resigning from office and after at least one previous attempt, Forrestal committed suicide, by throwing himself from the window of his hospital room at Bethesda Naval Hospital where he was recovering from "nervous exhaustion" that his doctors and friends traced back to the unification debate and to "excessive work during the war and post-war years."[35] The last person to see him recalled him "copying lines from Sophocles' chorus about the warrior Ajax, worn by the waste of time."[36]

James Forrestal's experience would cast a long shadow over each of his successors and especially on McNamara's colleagues in the Kennedy and Johnson administrations, many of whom had begun their careers in government under him. For some, the relationship with Forrestal was very personal. Michael Forrestal at the NSC was James Forrestal's son and was unofficially adopted by one of his father's closest friends, Averell Harriman at the State Department. Townsend Hoopes, a Forrestal mentee and later McNamara's Deputy for International Security Affairs, wrote a biography of Forrestal in which he described the latter's death as "towering loss" and a "profound personal tragedy."[37] Secretary of the Treasury C. Douglas Dillon's father had chosen Forrestal to succeed him at the head of his investment bank Dillon, Read & Co. where Forrestal also worked with the younger Dillon and Paul Nitze. In later years, Forrestal offered Dillon his first job in government.

Forrestal's failure to mold already entrenched service interests, or what Samuel Huntington termed "servicism,"[38] and other resistances most haunted his successors. McNamara kept a large portrait of Forrestal above his desk (see Figure 1.1). In one telling exchange with President Johnson after several years in the job, the President complimented McNamara's ability to maintain a stronger team than had existed in "Jim Forrestal's time." McNamara responded, "He wouldn't have killed himself that's for sure."[39] Forrestal's failure to create unity

FIGURE 1.1 Secretary of Defense McNamara sits down for an interview with CBS, September 19, 1963. A painting of former Secretary of Defense James Forrestal hangs in the background.
(OSD photograph collection: OSD Historical Office.)

primed McNamara's tight control over and high expectations of loyalty from his subordinates.

In a similar vein, during McNamara's confirmation hearings as Secretary of Defense, the Chairman of the Senate Armed Services Committee (SASC), Richard Russell, wryly commented: "In the past, there have been partly humorous suggestions that being named Secretary of Defense merits condolences instead of congratulations; and, of course, it is true that any person who successfully discharges the duties of this position needs all the cardinal virtues, a double portion of fortitude, and some others."[40]

The experience of Louis Johnson, Forrestal's immediate successor, who served from March 1949 to September 1950, was hardly more encouraging. A lawyer by training, Johnson had been Assistant Secretary for War from 1937 to 1940, during which time he oversaw the wartime industrial mobilization. After the war, he had been a major fundraiser for Truman. Promising to "knock a few heads together," Johnson announced that he would succeed where Forrestal had failed, particularly in achieving greater unification and keeping the budget in line with, if not below, the President's wishes.[41]

However, by trying to make a reputation as a "great economizer," Johnson made enemies who subsequently made him the scapegoat for the Truman administration's humiliation when it was caught off-guard and unprepared at the outbreak of the Korean War. His decision to focus relatively more on strategic air power, which he considered a cost-effective investment in security, alienated the Navy, who staged a major protest that became known as the "Revolt of the Admirals." In general, his inclination to ignore the advice of military colleagues meant that they remembered him as "probably the worst Secretary of Defense."[42] His relationship with the State Department was no better: he feuded with his counterpart, Dean Acheson, who described him as "mentally ill" in reference to a brain operation Johnson had undergone to remove blood clots.[43] At first, Johnson was philosophical about the criticisms aimed at him: "A public official, of course, must expect a good deal of criticism, particularly when he must take a stand on a controversial issue."[44] Nevertheless, he was eventually dismissed.

Johnson's discharge came at a time when NSC 68, with President Truman's approval, was gaining momentum across government and in the midst of the Korean crisis. Both created pressures for increased military spending to meet expanded worldwide commitments. In particular, NSC 68, the joint State–Defense document that Paul Nitze at the Policy Planning Staff in the State Department had primarily drafted, called for a "substantial increase" in military forces and for vast investments to match the growing Soviet threat.

Within two months of taking office as the third Secretary of Defense, George Marshall, the Army war hero and retired Secretary of State, championed a changed defense posture. In a nod to his predecessor, he explained:

Always there has been a drive to find scapegoats to shoulder the blame. The basic error, however, has always been with the American people themselves. The fault has been with their refusal to sanction an enduring posture of defense that would discourage aggression, and, if war came, would reduce the casualties, the sacrifices, the excessive costs and the needless waste.

Echoing an argument James Forrestal had made, he criticized the "emotional instability" of the American people and their legislators who pushed for massive demobilization (a "violent dip") after the war despite being "in the midst of a dangerous world."[45]

When Marshall left, he insisted that his Deputy, Robert Lovett, succeed him as Secretary of Defense. A banker before the war, Lovett had directed the buildup of US air power during the war as Assistant Secretary for Air in the War Department, after which he had worked on the Marshall Plan. He shared Marshall's view about the American tendency to neglect defense, explaining that "we seem to have had only two throttle positions in the past: wide open when we are at war and tight shut when there is no shooting."[46]

Lovett oversaw the Korean buildup and, more than any Secretary of Defense, played a central part in raising the United States' level of military readiness to respond to the Cold War and the growing potential of limited war. Echoing a rhetoric that would become commonplace and that would justify a growing defense budget throughout the Cold War, he explained: "We must make an effort to get the only insurance that works – strength. We tried peace through weakness for generations, and it didn't work."[47] At the same time, as a progressive Democrat who understood that defense drew on finite governmental resources that could instead be earmarked for domestic issues, he explained how a longer-term level of preparedness would be cheaper in the longer term: that "less money annually, but steadily, can accomplish much more than huge sums today and nothing tomorrow."[48]

Although his tenure was relatively smooth and free of controversy, Lovett closed the Truman administration's chapter for defense policy by raising concerns about the organizational arrangements for defense, warning his successor that the 1949 Amendments had not solved inherent tensions between the Secretary of Defense and the JCS and that the budgetary process was still not efficient and economical enough.

At this critical juncture in the history of the OSD, General Eisenhower was elected as President, an exceptional presidency in many respects especially for defense policy. In addition to promising a prompt end to the Korean War, Eisenhower campaigned on the pledge to restore fiscal responsibility to government. As one of the most decorated generals in US history and as the first Chairman of the JCS, Eisenhower had a keen interest in defense policy. Although he had three Secretaries of Defense during his two terms, in reality, Eisenhower was his own Secretary. Moreover, as someone who had commanded or served with many of his Chiefs and senior military officers, Eisenhower was a special President and could more easily overrule his military advisors, something he did repeatedly.

Having been consulted at various points in the Defense Department's nascent years, Eisenhower was quick to identify and act on its structural problems. He was inclined to support greater unification because of his experience as Supreme Allied Commander in the war and at NATO, while his fiscal conservatism moved him to act on more efficient budgeting practices. As he explained to a friend shortly before his inauguration in 1953, Eisenhower's attitude to defense and to security was grounded in this attitude to federal spending: "The financial solvency and economic soundness of the United States constitute the first requisite to collective security in the free world. That comes before all else."[49] In practice, although he set up a number of structures and reforms aimed at reducing expenditures, his budgets "were never as austere as he made out."[50]

Still, in a spirit of managerial reform, in his first year in office, Eisenhower asked the banker David Rockefeller to chair the "Committee on Methods of Reorganizing the Executive Branch for the Federal Government," which also included Robert Lovett and General Bradley. Among its recommendations, many of which would inform the administration's congressional moves, the committee suggested centralizing authority at the OSD with respect to research, logistics and procurement decisions, and at the level of the Chairman of the Joint Chiefs of Staff.

Perhaps Eisenhower's most important innovation was to strengthen the NSC as a way of enforcing his fiscal discipline and bringing defense expenditures down. The NSC was expanded to include the Secretary of the Treasury and the Bureau of the Budget, which participated in spelling out a Basic National Security Policy that was meant to inform the military department's budgets within an overall ceiling, although Eisenhower tactfully called them "targets" instead.[51]

If Truman's last Secretaries of Defense lamented the lack of investment in defense, Eisenhower's first Secretary of Defense, Charles Wilson, swung the pendulum decidedly in the other direction. Coming from General Motors, which he had led for over a decade, Wilson controversially quipped during his confirmation hearings that "What's good for General Motors is good for the country." In addition to being the largest US corporation at the time, General Motors had been a major supplier of military equipment during the war. The comments exacerbated criticism leveled against the Eisenhower administration that out-of-touch businessmen dominated it or, as one critic put it, that it was an administration with "seventeen millionaires and one plumber" with Secretary Wilson as the "businessman *ne plus ultra*."[52]

Wilson ruffled the most feathers as he searched for savings. He drastically cut appropriations without consulting the Chiefs as he presumed they would continue to ask for much more than could be realistically appropriated. Within four months of taking office, he cut 40,000 civilian employees in the Defense Department. In addition, he designed the administration's new strategy, "the New Look," with the NSC and not with the JCS. The New Look focused heavily on nuclear weapons and thus prima facie favored the Air Force. The Army, which had historically supported unification, now, under the stewardship of Maxwell Taylor, turned decidedly against it in a confrontation that the *New York Times* dubbed the "Revolt of the Colonels."[53] All in all, in his steadfastness to achieve savings and his inability to communicate constructively with the Chiefs, Wilson's tenure was an acrimonious one.

In October 1957, the industrialist and former President of Proctor & Gamble, Neil McElroy, replaced Wilson. During his two years in office, and under the impetus of Eisenhower, McElroy oversaw the most important legislative reform of defense organization since the war: the Department of Defense Reorganization Act of 1958. The act gave President Eisenhower virtually all he had asked Congress for and laid the groundwork for McNamara's changes to the department. It placed defense policy and notably the budget in civilian hands in order to balance each of the service's needs while keeping in mind administration-wide fiscal priorities. As the act read, it aimed "to provide for the establishment of integrated policies and procedures for the departments, agencies, and functions of the Government relating to the national security." Reflecting the administration's concern about the role of the defense budget in federal spending, it sought "to provide more effective, efficient, and economical administration in the Department of Defense."[54]

Overall, the Secretary of Defense's power was substantially increased. The act "provide[d] a Department of Defense, including the three military Departments of the Army, the Navy (including naval aviation and the United States Marine Corps), and the Air Force under the direction, authority and control of the Secretary of Defense" and increased the staff at the OSD and the JCS. The Chairman of the JCS was given voting rights on the JCS, changing his role to one with clearer executive responsibility. The services themselves were changed from departments that were separately *administered* to departments that were separately *organized* under the authority of the Secretary of Defense. In other words, the services now reported to the President through the Secretary of Defense. However, in spite of McElroy's objections, the act preserved the right of the Service

Secretaries and Chiefs to make recommendations and to express independent opinions to Congress; it maintained the "legislated insubordination" that had troubled him and every other Secretary before and after.

Finally, as Eisenhower had suggested, the act "provide[d] for the unified strategic direction of the combatant forces, for their operation under unified command, and for their integration into an efficient team of land, naval, and air forces." By setting up a new system of unified commands under the direction of the Secretary of Defense and the President, the act cut the Chiefs' authority across horizontal lines as well.[55]

The first Secretary of Defense to benefit from these changes, although he did not act on them in any significant way, was Thomas Gates. A former banker and Secretary of the Navy, Gates had hoped to return to banking until the untimely death of Deputy Secretary of Defense Donald A. Quarles, who was on track to replace McElroy, forced him to reconsider his plans. In many ways, Gates' tenure was a caretaking one but one during which the tone was set for the arrival of McNamara. Gates passed the Defense Reorganization Act and turned attention to the growing salience of limited wars in the nuclear age.

Building on an intellectual and legislative context that was open to questioning the Defense Department's position and structures, Eisenhower took two final steps before leaving office. First, in 1960, he appointed New York Governor Nelson Rockefeller to review the organization for defense and to present his findings before the Jackson Subcommittee on National Policy Machinery. In his report, Rockefeller recommended greater centralization around the office of the President and presented an ideal Secretary of Defense as a "management specialist" who could faithfully implement presidential directives through "active management."[56] The report also suggested one of the reforms that would make McNamara famous, namely that the defense budget should be organized according to themes and defense functions rather than by services.[57]

Second, Eisenhower's departure speech was decidedly pedagogical and warned Americans of the dangers that their new defense establishment could represent to the country's economic health. He reminded the public that the "conjunction of an immense military establishment and a large arms industry is new in the American experience" and had been "compelled," and he warned of the "potential for the disastrous rise" of "unwarranted influence, whether sought or unsought by the military-industrial complex" in "the councils of government."[58] The speech went on to expand on a related theme, namely the danger that federal spending could increase to a point that it would crowd out private entrepreneurial efforts in science or indeed in any field. He explained that "It is the role of statesmanship to mold, to balance, and to integrate these and other forces, new and old, within the principles of our democratic system – ever aiming towards the supreme goals of our free society."[59]

Eisenhower's successor, John F. Kennedy, demonstrated a lively interest in defense policy during his campaign. He had set up a Special Committee during the transition to study "how to strengthen the Defense Department and make it more responsive to the needs of our time" and chose Senator Stuart Symington as its Chairman. A one-time competitor for the Democratic nomination, Symington converged with Kennedy on the issue of a possible "missile gap" that Eisenhower had allowed to open by emphasizing fiscal prudence over military strength.[60] Symington, who had been the first Secretary of the Air Force under Forrestal, turned to his old friends and associates from the Truman administration.[61] The Committee's final report reiterated many of the positions that Symington had championed since his days at the Air Force. These included recommending the unification of the services under a single chief of staff and the wholesale reorganization of the armed services into functional commands, for instance with one concerned solely with nuclear weapons and another with limited war. The report was greeted with predictable hostility in the services and much of the Congress, and the incoming administration privately deemed it "not feasible."[62] Publicly, Kennedy's reaction to the 5,000-page report was more diplomatic: he told the waiting press that it was "an interesting and constructive study which I know will be carefully analyzed by the Congress and the incoming Administration."[63]

Within the transition team, Richard Neustadt, the famed political scientist of presidential power, echoing the Army and Secretary Gates' response to the Symington report, wrote to the incumbent President that he should focus on the "far-reaching potential"[64] of Eisenhower's legislative legacy. He wrote that "27 months after the passage of the 1958 Act," the Defense Department was in a "transitional period" and explained to the President that "steps towards unification have been made necessary" by two imperatives: "One, to bring better business management to the massive operations of the Defense Department and thereby to effect efficiencies and prevent waste in the activities that have come to consume more than half the Federal expenditures and, two, to accommodate military strategy and operations to the technological revolution in warfare that has marked the past two decades." The challenge for the administration was to organize the defense establishment in the "most economical and efficient manner possible . . . in a framework of responsible civilian control."

Although Neustadt favored making the most of the 1958 act as a first step, he nevertheless proposed a number of bureaucratic steps and changes that went well beyond the act as a sort of menu for the incoming administration. These steps included converting Secretaries of the military departments into Undersecretaries of Defense or abolishing them altogether, and getting rid of the Chiefs' dual responsibilities to their departments and the JCS. Neustadt also reiterated many of Symington's recommendations, including "restructuring the military departments into functional organizations" and creating a single chief of staff, even while he accepted that the latter "is the most controversial step" and that the wholesale merger of the services "the most controversial of all . . . a most extreme degree of unification." All in all, although Neustadt and his colleagues in the transition team accepted that the 1958 act had established a framework for reforming the Defense Department, they did not exclude further and more aggressive moves.

As far as staffing arrangements at the OSD were concerned, Neustadt explained, "The main present need is not further legal structural changes but improvements in the programming, budgeting, another decision-making processes and in the staff arrangements to get on top of the remaining difficult problems." The administration needed a first-class manager of people and processes. He suggested to the new President that key bureaucratic changes were needed at the OSD, whose "central defect" was the "lack of civilian advisors." A Secretary of Defense aided by civilian advisors should work toward a "fundamental overhaul of the Department's budgetary processes to achieve a sound management framework."[65]

Robert Lovett, who had served as Truman's last Secretary of Defense and who was initially offered the job but declined, suggesting Robert McNamara in his place, shared Neustadt's views. Together with Charles Wilson, Eisenhower's first Secretary of Defense, Lovett counseled the transition team and described the ideal candidate. He argued that the Pentagon needed an "analytical statistician who can tear out the overlap, the empire building."[66] He later explained his choice of Robert McNamara to fill these shoes by saying that there were "very few people who were competent to deal with the basic problems in the Pentagon which was getting into the unnecessary duplication and the over-layering which had grown up under our system of operation. I felt that there should be a really careful analysis of the Department and that statistics should be developed which might help in pointing a way to a solution."[67]

Both Neustadt and Lovett's remarks illustrate how ill-defined the role of the Office of the Secretary of Defense was and just how much in "transition" it was when McNamara came to Washington. As one of McNamara's predecessors, Lovett had first-hand experience of the problems that would confront the new Secretary. The administration needed a candidate with the managerial and budgetary vision to implement Eisenhower's reforms and to deal with the inevitable and ongoing bureaucratic resistance.

Neustadt and Lovett also implied that achieving "civilian control" would depend on appointing a manager who could be completely loyal to the President and who could, in turn, inspire the loyalty of his own advisors. Moreover, the transition team counseled that the ideal Secretary would come from the private sector, bringing managerial experience, but without appearing to be part of the military-industrial complex that Eisenhower had spoken about. The Kennedy campaign latched onto criticism of the Eisenhower team, and his Secretaries of Defense in particular, as being an administration dominated by business people. In later years, McNamara was explicitly compared to his predecessors in this respect: one wrote, "Mr. McNamara is not subject to the family, socialite and public-figure consciousness of Neil McElroy ... Nor is he subject to the Ivy League inhibitions and investment-trust dignity of Thomas Gates ... Mr. McNamara simply isn't susceptible to any pressures – social, military, intellectually, or editorial."[68]

As the British Foreign Office observed at the time, appointments in the Kennedy administration put a greater "emphasis on a professional or professorial background" with "strikingly few connections with big business."[69] Although McNamara came from the Ford Motor Company, he also captured the spirit and tone of the New Frontier and became one of its iconic figures. As the journalist David Halberstam described, "Bob McNamara was a remarkable man in a remarkable era."[70]

Much has been made of McNamara's intellectual qualities, in particular of his quantitative logic and cold rationality. While his statistical skills made him stand out to people like Robert Lovett, for John Kenneth Galbraith and Adam Yarmolinsky (who with Kennedy's brother-in-law Sargent Shriver led the staffing task force of the transition team), it was McNamara's sense of public service that distinguished him most.[71] On paper, McNamara's professional journey was one that fit the stereotype of the quantitative-minded manager. However, his CV belied a greater degree of intellectualism and interest in public service. As Halberstam put it, "challenges fascinated him, but not worldly goods or profit as ends in themselves."[72]

Born in San Francisco to a modest family, McNamara attended public schools and the state university at Berkeley before going on to Harvard Business School (HBS) for a Master of Business Administration degree. After spending a year at the Price Waterhouse accounting firm, he returned to HBS as its youngest assistant professor where he taught a course on planning and control from August 1940 until January 1942. In so doing, he contributed to the school's groundbreaking work on the application of statistical methods and quantitative data for the purpose of management. Newly married, McNamara described living in Cambridge "more happily than we had ever dreamed possible."[73]

He left Harvard on unpaid leave to join the war effort and apply his work in academia to public purposes. He worked for Robert Lovett, then Assistant Secretary of War for Air, in the Army's Department of Statistical Control under Charles B. "Tex" Thornton reviewing the Army Air Force's bombing campaign, and eventually served under General Curtis LeMay in the Eighth Air Force.[74] McNamara and his team of "whiz kids" applied the statistical methods they had developed at HBS to strategic bombing and, in so doing, improved both the efficiency and lethality of the air strikes.

After the war, McNamara hoped to return to Harvard and to the intellectual excitement that he had enjoyed there. However, when he and his wife Margaret contracted polio, their "very, very expensive"[75] medical bills forced him to choose a more profitable path. Although he was not particularly drawn to business – in fact, his first response to Thornton's suggestion to go into the corporate world was an "unequivocal no"[76] – the "whiz kids" including McNamara brought their skills to the Ford Motor Company and overhauled the company in the ensuing decade. Building on his course at HBS, McNamara became director of planning at the company.

However, at Ford, McNamara chose a lifestyle that was more academic than it was corporate: he described himself as "a motor company executive who seemed an oddball for Detroit."[77] Whether or not his intellectualism was "self-conscious,"[78] the McNamaras chose to live in the university town of Ann Arbor rather than Detroit and preferred local book clubs to golf clubs. In his job as well, McNamara did not fit the typical model of the corporate leader: he was instrumental in improving the cars' security record and in pushing social responsibility measures at time when they were rare, as well as in building up the Ford Foundation in its formative years.[79]

On November 9, 1960, the day after the election, McNamara was promoted to become the first President of the Ford Motor Company who was not a member of the Ford family. As McNamara later explained, he "was one of the highest paid industrial executives in the world, not wealthy, but in a position to become so."[80] Although he declined the administration's first offer to serve as Secretary of the Treasury, it was not long before he accepted to serve as Secretary of Defense even while he admitted that he only "followed defense matters in a rather superficial way through the press."[81] Despite his "deep loyalty to [the Ford family] and to the Ford Motor Company," McNamara explained, "I could not let their interests outweigh my obligation to serve the nation when called upon."[82]

In addition to providing a platform for public service, the OSD provided an intellectual challenge. McNamara told a *New York Times* reporter: "I think each large organization goes through a period of evaluation when the patterns of the future are formed, when the intellectual framework for decisions is established, when the administrative techniques are sharpened, when the organization structure takes shape[;] I believe that the Department of Defense is in such a period today."[83] After successive leaders' attempts at "trimming," McNamara was determined to press on with bottom-up reform.

McNamara accepted Kennedy's offer on two conditions, both of which were largely met. First, that he "would have the authority to organize and staff the Defense Department with the most competent men [he] could find without regard to political affiliation or obligation." Barring some Service Secretary positions, this condition was largely upheld. McNamara's second condition spoke to the campaign and transition team's intellectual approach to the department. Although McNamara agreed with "the premise" of Symington's report, he "felt that it was extremely unlikely that the report, or any significant part of it, could be implemented politically."[84] As a result, he asked that "during at least the early part of my term (i.e., approximately the first year), I would not be obligated to undertake a major reorganization of the Defense Department of the type recommended in the Symington Report."

A final and implied third condition was his "belief that the Secretary of Defense, in order to succeed, must have the closest possible, personal working relationship with the President and must receive the President's full backing and support so long as he is carrying out the policies of the

President."[85] Just as his success at the Ford Foundation rested on his personal loyalty to the Ford family, his loyalty to Kennedy determined his efforts to bring military bureaucracies and power under civilian and presidential control.

The congressional leaders who had pushed through the 1958 act welcomed the arrival of a Secretary who was prepared to deliver on its promise. Richard Russell applauded McNamara's efforts, saying: "It is gratifying to note that the Secretary is making use of the authority the Congress has vested in him to streamline the Defense Establishment as it has been the position of this committee that the Secretary of Defense needs no additional authority to accomplish desirable changes but need only exercise the authority given him by the Congress. It is hoped that such changes as have been made and others yet to be accomplished will go far to eliminate many of the examples of wasteful duplication and competition between the services which have all too frequently come to the attention of the committee."[86]

In a similar vein, his counterpart in the House, Carl Vinson, added, "He's a genius, the best who's ever held the job."[87] While both Chairmen were Democrats, admittedly southern conservative Democrats, McNamara also provided a measure of protection from Republicans. Even the most conservative members of the committees, including Barry Goldwater, appreciated McNamara, who had been a nominal Republican although he had voted for Kennedy. Republicans were generally satisfied with his skills as a manager and only later became frustrated when he cut into R&D projects in their constituencies or in ways that they felt could undermined the US position vis-à-vis the Soviet Union.[88]

Looking back on his arrival at the OSD, McNamara remarked that the two most pressing needs that he confronted were to align policy and strategy to force structure and to integrate the different parts of the department. He recognized that his predecessor, Thomas Gates, had been moving in that direction, "but the linkage between foreign policy and the defense budget was totally lacking."[89] Instead of following the rather more political avenues that Symington had suggested, McNamara chose Neustadt's recommendation to capitalize on Eisenhower's reforms and centralize authority around his office, notably through the budgetary process, as "a substitute for unification of the services and the establishment of a single chief of staff."[90]

As this brief history of the OSD has shown, by the time McNamara entered the Pentagon, the nature of civil-military relations had evolved on two fronts. First, civilians had progressively implemented greater control over their military counterparts in designing policy and strategy. Through various permutations, the power relationship between the JCS and the Secretary of Defense had become clearer and leaned decisively in the OSD's favor. Second, the defense establishment and its budget had become a central part of the federal government. Yet the debate about "how much is enough" raged on, especially in determining the exact process by which civilian objectives and service budgets could be reconciled.[91]

McNamara's revolution at the OSD in the 1960s intensified this process on both fronts. In the spring of 1962, McNamara proudly submitted his first budget for FY63, the first budget that demonstrated his transformation of the budgetary process and that showcased his "tearing into" the inefficiencies at the Department of Defense. He could proudly look forward to cost savings in the coming years. At about the same time, the issue of Vietnam landed on his desk as President Kennedy leaned on his "dynamo" of a Secretary to bring order to another messy challenge for the administration.

Too often, historians have evaluated McNamara's contributions to Vietnam through diplomatic and military lenses and in binary terms, along neat dove/hawk lines that obscure an arguably more informative lens, namely how Vietnam might have been perceived from the vantage point of his office at a special time in its history. The bureaucratic influences on McNamara worked in contradictory and at times paradoxical ways. However, McNamara favored withdrawal and then resisted the growing US commitment to South Vietnam because of, not in spite of, being Secretary of Defense. By mapping how McNamara defined his job, his policy recommendations on Vietnam begin to make much more sense.

2

Civilian Control

Since the end of World War II, the balance between civilian and military voices in the formulation of national security policy had leaned decisively in favor of the OSD and its civilian authorities. In its early years, military voices dominated the NSC, but with the Defense Reorganization Act of 1958 and then McNamara's tenure, these voices were ever more distanced from the process of setting national security strategy. McNamara reduced his own office to one primarily concerned with managing defense agencies and aligning military tools and resources to the President's overarching strategy. He positioned the office as a pivot for foreign policy in a way that derived from his particular conception of his job as Secretary of Defense and of what he, as well as the administration, considered to be the appropriate nature of civil-military relations. For McNamara, the Secretary of Defense served the President, and the services were there to provide tools, and not policy guidance, in the execution of foreign policy. McNamara favored "subjective control": he implemented processes and rules that were designed to reinforce civilian authority and to erode the institutional autonomy that the military services had heretofore enjoyed.

McNamara's changes within the Defense Department came at a time when President Kennedy began dismantling the NSC structures that his predecessor had built up for foreign and defense policy. Together with McNamara's personal influence on the President, these changes paved the way for the OSD to become ubiquitous on many foreign policy issues and eventually on Vietnam. Paradoxically, although McNamara's reforms were designed to limit the role of the Defense

Department in national policy formulation, they resulted instead in his office becoming far more influential.

McNamara came to office with a reform agenda that his predecessor, Thomas Gates, had essentially already laid out for him. Above all else, the Defense Reorganization Act of 1958 was concerned with centralizing control over strategy and operations in the hands of the President and his civilian advisors. In time, each of the act's objectives were, albeit imperfectly, implemented through what became McNamara's landmark reforms. As the act had anticipated, McNamara and his Deputy, Roswell Gilpatric, centralized authority in their hands in an unprecedented manner.

The act called for "integrated policies and procedures" in national security policy. To achieve this objective, McNamara introduced Draft Presidential Memoranda (DPMs) that provided strategic guidance on which force levels were planned for. Finally, it called for economies and efficiency gains. To this end, McNamara introduced systems analysis and the Planning, Programming and Budgeting System (PPBS) that "rationalized" the budgetary process in a groundbreaking way.

Each of McNamara's reforms was concerned with aligning civilian and military objectives. Much like Eisenhower before him, McNamara believed that in order to achieve this alignment, the administration needed a guiding grand strategy and civilian "security intellectuals." The latter could inform defense policy in a way that allowed the Secretary of Defense to "avoid becoming a captive of the Chiefs and the Joint Staff and the Generals," and what McNamara saw as their parochial bureaucratic interests.[1] McNamara acknowledged that while Eisenhower and Secretary Gates had made some progress in producing an overarching strategy, they had failed to produce a detailed strategy that could usefully serve as a basis for long-term defense planning and budgeting.[2]

Informed by the Defense Reorganization Act, McNamara also felt that the President should have greater control over the formulation of national security policy to the detriment of military voices. Charles J. Hitch, McNamara's Comptroller and a leading "security intellectual" in his department, recalled that "Robert S. McNamara made it clear from the beginning that he intended to be the kind of Secretary that President Eisenhower had in mind in 1958."[3] McNamara explained what this "kind of Secretary" was: "I believed, for example, that there must be a definite integration of defense policies and programs with State Department policies. Military strategy must be a derivative of foreign policy. Force structure is a derivative of military strategy. Budgets are a derivative of force structures. So in a very real sense, a defense budget, in all of its detail, is a function of the foreign policy of the nation."[4] McNamara was to be the civilian manager who executed this neat alignment.

McNamara moved to cut back the Chiefs' power in designing national security policy in part because he sought neat alignment with foreign policy objectives but also because both he, and arguably the Kennedy administration as a whole, lacked respect for the Chiefs, who were deemed out of step with their times. Many of the administration's senior advisors had also served in some capacity during the war, and according to the in-house historian Arthur Schlesinger, "The war experience helped give the New Frontier generation its casual and laconic tone, its grim, puncturing humor and its mistrust of evangelism."[5]

Although McNamara had served under General Curtis LeMay in the US strategic bombing campaign during the war, once he came to office and with the General now Chief of Staff of the Air Force, whatever respect he had had seemed to evaporate. The young Secretary felt that neither of his Generals "got it" and seemed especially irritated with his old boss, who needed a hearing aid and did not reflect the tenor of the New Frontier either physically or intellectually.[6] For his part, the President mirrored this chasm: he always referred to the Chairman of the Joint Chiefs of Staff Lyman Lemnitzer as "General," a mark, as one colleague remembered, "that he didn't like him."[7]

Very quickly, the administration neither gave the Chiefs' views a central role nor valued their intellectual contributions. McNamara remembered, "It never bothered me that I overruled the majority of the Chiefs, or even occasionally the unanimous recommendations of the Chiefs. It didn't bother me in the slightest."[8] McNamara's will to impose his authority and his condescending attitude toward military institutions and leaders drove his attitude. For instance, McNamara refused to speak at military colleges, telling his friends, "These are not worthy academic institutions, and I will not lend my presence to them."[9]

From an organizational point of view, McNamara became dominant in the administration and loomed large across the board on Kennedy's foreign policy but especially on Vietnam for a number of reasons. First and foremost, he centralized authority around his office. Making good on Eisenhower's reforms, the JCS now reported to him rather than directly to the President. In turn, this centralization of authority meant that McNamara could come to the President with one, clear position for his department. Given that Kennedy's dismantling of the NSC structures had resulted in somewhat chaotic decision-making in the administration, this clarity gave McNamara enormous power. Finally, his personality and bullishness, if not authoritarianism, coupled with his personal connection to Kennedy gave him an advantage over other actors involved in national security decision-making.

McNamara's changes to the budgetary process also reflected a move to impose "subjective control" over the Chiefs. This ultimately strained relations with congressional leaders as well. One flash point in these deteriorating relations occurred during what came to be called the "muzzling hearings." McNamara's Special Assistant, Adam Yarmolinsky, had asked that all senior military officials' public statements be sent to his office for clearance in order to remove "color words." As McNamara later explained, the administration was "annoyed" that military leaders "were exaggerating the [Communist] threat, treating it as monolithic," whereas the administration did not feel "it should be simplified to the extent of an ideology." He also added, "I wasn't an expert of the Soviet Union but I did recognize that a degree of paranoia existed in certain parts of our Republic."[10]

The administration's frustration with the politicization of military leaders came to head with its dismissal of General Walker from the 24th Infantry Division in Germany in 1961 after it emerged that he had distributed John Birch Society material during the election campaign and that he had questioned the patriotism of then-Senator Kennedy, of Harry Truman and of Eleanor Roosevelt in an effort to influence his troops' voting.[11] General Walker, who was a World War II and Korean War hero, later became a figurehead for radical right groups in the South and made a bid for the governorship of his home state, Texas.[12] Walker's allies in Congress, who included Senator Strom Thurmond, accused Assistant Secretary of Defense Arthur Sylvester of being "taken in" by anti-military propaganda and used the confrontation to resurrect a complaint that dated back to the 1950s when he had lobbied for a preemptive strike against the Soviets and against containment as a "no win foreign policy."[13] For both Walker and Thurmond, civilian oversight of military officials' public statements implied a "retreat from victory" as it imposed a conciliatory foreign policy that was inconsistent with their preferred "victory ethos of the military."[14]

The administration's directive and the confrontation with Walker ultimately led to a furor in Congress, which accused the OSD of attempting to "muzzle" the military and which insidiously suggested that Yarmolinsky was a Communist infiltrator.[15] McNamara, defending his assistant, insisted to the Chairman of the SASC, Richard Russell, that while the Chiefs had a right to share their frank opinions with Congress "as provided by the National Security Act," it was the "long-standing policy of the Department [that] military and civilian personnel of the Department should not volunteer pronouncements at variance with established policy."[16] Former Secretary Lovett also stepped into the fray and testified at the hearings, explaining that it was fundamental to the process of national security decision-making in the US system of government that civilian authorities should control foreign policy and that military subordination and obedience to this civilian authority was legally mandated. On the issue of troop indoctrination, he added that the absentee ballot had been granted to troops stationed abroad on the sole precondition that base commanders should not influence their vote.[17]

Although these issues, in retrospect, may seem minor or inconsequential, in 1962 they contributed greatly to the souring of relations between McNamara, the services and key members of Congress. Writing in 1963, a columnist noted how quickly McNamara had fallen from grace. Formerly "the greatest thing to come off the Ford assembly line since the Model T," he was now decried as a "dictator and a bum."[18] McNamara persevered despite the many headlines, one of which read "Kennedy Fights the Generals," and in spite of the climate of mutual distrust if not outright hostility.[19]

Outside the OSD, Kennedy made a move that further undermined the authority of the Chiefs. In April 1961, the administration acted on a CIA-led plan that it had inherited from the previous administration to invade Cuba at the Bay of Pigs with a group of CIA-trained paramilitary groups composed of Cuban exiles. Unfortunately, the operation ended in a debacle, which left the administration humiliated only months after coming to office. Publicly, President Kennedy took full responsibility for the failure and saw his public ratings paradoxically shoot up as a result. In private, he was furious at the Chiefs and the CIA for their lack of candor and their flawed advice.

As a result, he commissioned Maxwell Taylor to produce a report to identify failures and lessons. Taylor had an impressive background, notably as Superintendent of West Point and as Eisenhower's Army Chief of Staff. During the Eisenhower years, he had openly criticized the New Look strategy and published two best-selling books that had contributed to the intellectual foundations of flexible response. He was widely respected as a soldier-scholar and eventually became very close to both Kennedy brothers.[20] In his final report, Taylor was especially scathing about the Chiefs and their failures to highlight predictable operational weaknesses of the invasion plan. When Kennedy subsequently kept him on as his personal Military Representative, the Chiefs quietly seethed. The position was unprecedented and effectively went even further in undermining the Chiefs' advisory role to the President.

In 1962, Taylor was promoted to become the Chairman of the JCS. On one level, this meant that Kennedy and McNamara had an "agent" among the Chiefs. Taylor explained that he informed McNamara that he "would never take a black snake whip to try to drive unanimity between the Chiefs," but then that "It was amazing how few splits we had. Why? Because they knew that I was very close to McNamara, that I would never bring a paper that the Secretary wouldn't support. So I had a great advantage versus the Chiefs."[21] However, Taylor was tactfully pushed out as he began to show his "limits." In the months leading up this "promotion," Taylor had repeatedly taken hawkish stances on a range of issues, notably in suggesting the introduction of troops to Vietnam, leading to suspicions that, in practice, he really was more of a soldier than a scholar.[22]

Two offices within the Defense Department were especially concerned with matching defense resources with strategy. These were the Deputy Secretary of Defense's office, whose incumbent, Roswell Gilpatric, McNamara described as his "alter-ego," and the Office of International Security Affairs (ISA). A lawyer by training and protégé of former Secretary of Defense Lovett, Gilpatric had a long career in and around the Defense Department, including as Undersecretary of the Air Force and more recently as a member of the Symington Committee. As for ISA, it became a central unit for adapting defense policy to the administration's new thinking: McNamara described it as "one of the two or three most significant posts in the department."[23]

ISA was set up in the fall of 1949 to help administer the Mutual Assistance Program. Although the military aid program remained one of its core functions, during the Eisenhower administration and in a reflection of the United States' growing international responsibilities, the unit grew and became known as the "little State Department." It was the principal vehicle through which the department coordinated its policies with other agencies concerned with foreign policy, principally the State Department.[24] Among its new and more visible responsibilities, ISA also oversaw NATO affairs.

However, the office really came into its own with the Kennedy administration's expanded interest in the developing world and with McNamara's efforts at aligning defense tools to foreign policy. As one Foreign

Office report at the time put it: it was "one of the main instruments through which Mr. McNamara has affected his considerable changes in the Pentagon."[25] For McNamara, the Secretary of Defense was "a servant of the foreign policy of the country, and therefore I conceived Dean Rusk as superior to me."[26] This hierarchy was reflected in the budgetary changes with the introduction of PPBS: the President and Secretary of State established missions and objectives that informed military strategy and eventually budgets.[27] By definition, this meant that McNamara needed a team within the OSD that could develop security policy independently from military advice. ISA fulfilled this function and became the key unit for the implementation of flexible response and for a very broad set of foreign policy challenges including Vietnam.

At the same time, ISA's growing role in coordinating policy did not necessarily mean that it favored "defense answers" to problems or even that it played a greater part in designing policy. McNamara slammed, and eventually removed, the first head of ISA, Paul Nitze, largely because he tried to fill in the policy void that Dean Rusk had left and because he had advocated more aggressive steps during both the 1961 Berlin Crisis and the 1962 Cuba Missile Crisis. When Nitze overstepped his office's prerogatives, McNamara angrily told him "just keep your sticky fingers out of foreign policy."[28] For McNamara, the head of ISA needed to align with foreign policy objectives, not set the policy himself. McNamara "handpicked" each of its incumbents who were all men he trusted. They included William Bundy, Paul Warnke and John McNaughton; the latter became one of McNamara's closest friends and a notable skeptic in the later years of US involvement in Vietnam (see Figure 2.1).

Ultimately, the centralization of authority within the Defense Department had important repercussions for the role of the OSD in national security decision-making and in the administration as a whole. McNamara ran a tight ship and had gathered an impressive group of experts, most of whom reflected the Kennedy administration's ethos. They were "men in the same age bracket as the President, ... tough and highly-trained specialists"[29] who were impatient and decisive. McNamara described them as the "finest group of associates of any Cabinet member, possibly ever."[30] Collectively, they guaranteed that the Defense Department maintained one stance on all the key issues, however forced the consensus might be.

In the *New York Times* in 1964, McNamara explained how he managed the potentially unruly defense structure: "It goes without saying, perhaps, that once a decision has been made, we all must close ranks and

FIGURE 2.1 Secretary of Defense McNamara (right), swears in Secretary of the
Army Cyrus R. Vance (left) and Defense Department General Counsel John
T. McNaughton (middle), July 5, 1962. He described his appointees as the "finest
group of associates of any Cabinet member, possibly ever" and the two men
would become confidants.
(OSD Photograph, John T. McNaughton family collection.)

support it."[31] However authoritarian the process might have been, it
meant that McNamara could report to the President with one "defense"
position that fit into the President's worldview. In this, he had a marked
advantage over the State Department, which the much gentler Dean Rusk
led at the time.

Kennedy may have deliberately chosen a weak Secretary of State
hoping to carve out a central role for himself in the articulation of the
administration's foreign policy, much like Eisenhower had done with his
Secretary of Defense. However, the result was that, faced with a more
improvised national security decision-making style, many junior State
Department officials reported directly to the President. Even while this
improvised decision-making process guaranteed access for some State
Department officials, more often than not it resulted in the Defense
Department taking responsibility for many issues "by default, because
neither the State Department nor [US]AID seemed to zero in on the
problem."[32]

Kennedy's decision to replace existing NSC working groups that had dominated decision-making under the Eisenhower administration with ad hoc interdepartmental task forces, designed to address crises, favored the Defense Department. Defense Department staff, Deputy Secretary Gilpatric and Paul Nitze, led the administration's first two task forces on Laos and Cuba, respectively.[33]

Part of the problem was also that the State Department was historically a "talking department" as opposed to the Defense Department, which was an "operating department."[34] Arthur Schlesinger wrote: "Other departments provided quick answers to presidential questions and quick action on presidential orders. It was a constant puzzle to Kennedy that the State Department remained so formless and impenetrable." The State Department seemed riddled with "intellectual exhaustion" and seemed always to fall short of Kennedy's ambition to have it act as an "agent of coordination."[35]

Moreover, the same junior State Department officials that benefited from direct access to the President complained that because Rusk did not defend them or a "State" position in NSC meetings, McNamara inevitably overpowered them. One of the staff members observed: "So it went by, with Rusk not taking a strong stand and McNamara interrupting anybody less than the President and the Secretary of State so there wasn't much I could do."[36] The implication was that the Defense Department dominated national security decisions by the sheer force of McNamara's personality, which contrasted starkly with Dean Rusk's reserved demeanor. The Director of the State Department's Bureau of Intelligence and Research (INR) Roger Hilsman, who played an important role in the Vietnam decisions, sarcastically described one NSC meeting where the Director of Central Intelligence (DCI) John McCone "got two sentences out and McNamara interrupted him because Man Namara had been in that part of the world only 15 hours before he knew more than the CIA by a long shot."[37]

Kennedy's more informal arrangements tended to favor personal rapport. Here too, McNamara was at an advantage. He enjoyed a special relationship with the President, who often remarked that McNamara was his "most versatile member of Cabinet."[38] Listening to the Kennedy presidential tapes, McNamara is the only official who ever interrupted the President. According to Robert Kennedy, "it was a more formal relationship than some but President Kennedy liked and admired him more than anybody else in the Cabinet,"[39] while Jacqueline Kennedy recalled that "the McNamaras" were the only couple, aside from "the

Dillons," that the President interacted with socially and added that the President "loved and admired" him.[40]

Aside from personal amity, President Kennedy appreciated McNamara's proven loyalty, a core value in choosing associates for both the Kennedys and McNamara. Kennedy's associates recall how McNamara fought through Kennedy's projects as if they were his own: "He's got his marching order and he doesn't walk away because he's being beaten on the head. I've never seen a man more willing to take so much abuse, sometimes for a position I know he's already taken the opposite position for. He continues to be loyal beyond his congressional testimony, even into his most private remarks."[41]

The concept of loyalty was central to the way that Kennedy managed his administration and McNamara the OSD. The most loyal members of Kennedy's administration, men such as McNamara, were rewarded with the power of proximity to the President in a sometimes unstructured decision-making process (see Figure 2.2). Loyalty provided organizational coherence and order by guaranteeing a unity of purpose: subordinates applied the directives of their bosses. Recalling the atmosphere at the OSD, Daniel Ellsberg described a "feudal concept of loyalty to the king," that loyalty was "the number one value." As McNamara himself suggested, it was a particular kind of loyalty: to the boss rather than to the country.[42]

Each of McNamara's policy decisions, and particularly those on Vietnam, needs to be understood in the context of his loyalty to the President and not to his office per se and with his definition of the job of Secretary of Defense in mind. McNamara came to the issue of Vietnam, as he did with all issues, with his biases and blind spots, and with his particular understanding of what the role of Secretary of Defense should be. He changed the Defense Department to match the foreign policy direction that the White House laid out and, in keeping with this, moved toward capabilities for counterinsurgency that played a central role in Vietnam during the Kennedy years.

The net result of McNamara's policy reforms was that, whereas in 1947, the OSD had been limited to coordinating war plans that were produced in each military service, by 1962, the latter had little input on setting strategy in Vietnam or indeed elsewhere. On the budgetary side, the evolution of the OSD's role historically had been more erratic, while McNamara's changes were sweeping and enduring. Since 1947, each successive administration had tried to reinforce civilian control of the budgetary process but with only limited success. The 1958 Defense

FIGURE 2.2 President John F. Kennedy with Secretary of Defense McNamara outside the Oval Office, October 29, 1962.
(Cecil Stoughton, White House Photograph Collection, JFKL.)

Reorganization Act asked that the OSD "provide more effective, efficient, and economical administration in the Department of Defense," and McNamara's immediate successor, Thomas Gates, defined the outlines of an action plan to this end but without substantially acting on it. With McNamara, this too changed.

McNamara's predecessors were divided between those who were great economizers, such as Eisenhower's Secretary of Defense Charles Wilson, who put a primacy on fiscal balance, and those who were "defense-first-ers," such as Truman's last Secretary, Robert Lovett. In 1961, the incumbent President seemed to fall into the latter group: a central theme of his campaign was that Eisenhower had been dangerously concerned with budgetary balance and thus had allowed a "missile gap" to emerge. Moreover, Kennedy reached out to figurehead "big spenders" in the transition, including Symington and Lovett. He tried to bring Lovett into his administration, offering him either his old job or the Secretary of the Treasury post. However, despite the campaign rhetoric and after Lovett turned down the offers, Kennedy filled both positions with Republicans with more conservative attitudes toward the budget.

As Secretary of Defense, McNamara erred on the side of fiscal prudence and developed a reputation for cost-cutting while he recognized, and at times was alarmed with, the pressures to increase spending on defense projects. The pressures were those that had troubled his immediate predecessors, particularly the services' defense of their budgets and the congressional leaders' defense of the services and related jobs in their constituencies. At the same time, with a Congress that dragged its feet on most of the administration's proposed social programs, McNamara and his colleagues recognized the Keynesian potential of the defense budget and pushed through programs, including the civil defense program, that were as much defense projects as they were about upgrading civilian infrastructure.

Ultimately, McNamara's core "revolution" on implementing civilian control came to the budgetary process, principally in the shape of systems analysis and PPBS. More than the changes to the reporting lines, these changes became a "substitute for unification of the services and the establishment of a single chief of staff" as they forced the services to produce one overarching budget in keeping with national, shared objectives.[43] In addition to the analytic rigor they brought to defining the United States' goals and aligning resources to those ends, they gave McNamara a privileged overview of the department's economic impact.

Having been given a free hand to hire the team he desired, McNamara brought in his "whiz kids," primarily analysts from RAND or other security intellectuals, many of whom had a background in economics, to radically overhaul what they saw as an archaic way of organizing the defense budget. They brought a culture of "rational" thought from RAND and the techniques of systems analysis to existing "irrational planning and budgeting practices."[44]

The key office for this agenda was the Comptroller. McNamara chose Charles Hitch. Their first meeting "was reported to be 'love at first sight.'"[45] Before coming into government, Hitch had been the head of the Economics Division at RAND and, together with his colleague Roland McKean, had written the "bible of defense economics,"[46] *Economics of Defense in the Nuclear Age*, which spelled out PPBS, his main innovation in office.[47] As his Deputy Alain Enthoven later wrote in an obituary for his mentor, "'Hitchcraft,' as it was affectionately known, was the most important advance in public administration of our time."[48]

While Hitch was known as the "father of defense economics" and of PPBS in its precise form, similar ideas circulated already both in and outside the US Defense Department. At its core, systems analysis was a method of reducing otherwise political and fungible issues to numerical values that allowed a more "objective" assessment of costs and benefits. This approach chimed with McNamara's work at HBS, the Army Air Force and Ford where he encouraged the use of statistics to improve policy. Ultimately, Hitch's ideas reflected a bipartisan consensus that the defense budget, as it drew on a growing share of federal resources, should become more transparent and accountable.

First applied to the 1963 budget, PPBS was essentially a planning tool to define national security objectives and to break these objectives into missions and functional areas (through so-called DPMs). Before, the budget had been allocated on a yearly basis and according to service-specific inputs, for instance, personnel or logistics costs. Under the new system, services budgets were allocated according to their ability to achieve the stated objectives in the most cost-efficient way and were calculated over a five-year period in order to capture the total cost of programs, which invariably spread over many years. When McNamara presented his first budget in the spring of 1962, newspapers recognized the transformative nature of the changes and noted that McNamara had "virtually abolished separate budgets and it was he and not the Joint Chiefs of Staff who explained the new military strategy to Congress."[49]

By placing ultimate budgetary authority in the hands of civilian agencies of the Defense Department, namely with the Comptroller, rather than the services, PPBS further eroded the services' power. PPBS required that each service submit its budget through its Chief rather than its Secretary, which de facto stripped the Service Secretary positions of their power and made them organizationally redundant. As a result, Service Secretary positions became "parking lot" positions for Kennedy's friends. Secretary of the Navy Paul B. Fay, for instance, was mostly remembered for his time on the golf course.[50] When he left, he was replaced with Paul Nitze as a way of short-circuiting Nitze's long-term ambition to replace Gilpatric as Deputy Secretary of Defense.[51]

In principle, under PPBS, the budget was open-ended and not bound by the set budgetary ceilings that had capped the budgets of McNamara's predecessors. In practice, the reforms were designed with a cost-cutting agenda at their core and forced civilian authorities, mainly the President, to be more modest in setting strategies and national ambitions. Enthoven and Smith explained, "A frequently stated but mistaken view of setting strategy and force requirements is that the process is one of starting at the top with broad national objectives and then successively deriving a strategy, force requirements, and a budget. It is mistaken because costs must be considered from the very outset in choosing strategies and objectives."[52]

The whole system of forward planning and budgeting was designed to align the Defense Department's resources and planning more effectively with the rest of government. As a result, the budgetary process was coordinated with the Bureau of the Budget, whose director, not surprisingly, praised the first budget. He noted that it made "enormous advances in concept, clarity and logic" that were "literally revolutionary." He added, "there is much more to be done, as Secretary McNamara knows better than any of us, but the improvement in the degree of rationality which can be applied to military planning and budgeting is already tremendous."[53]

However, as they were implemented further, the steps to rationalize and reduce defense expenditures ruffled many feathers, not least in the services. The services were the principal target of cuts, and the reforms challenged their authority most. The State Department was also often unsupportive. Looking back on this period, Paul Nitze asserted that if McNamara's "belief in forward planning, in particular time phased logistic and financial planning was close to absolute," it also sometimes lacked "tactical and broad judgmental vision."[54]

For the services and the Defense Department, cost-cutting first came in the shape of the 1962 Defense Department Cost Reduction Program, which included standardizing logistics and procurement and especially military base closures.[55] To support his effort, McNamara created a set of dedicated offices within the OSD, including the Defense Supply Agency, which was responsible for procurement, and the Defense Contract Audit Agency. Base closures were especially complicated politically because many of the senators in the SASC, which was ultimately responsible for allocating the defense budget, were also from states that hosted major bases and defense-related operations, and so, if nothing else, base closures involved job losses for their constituents.

McNamara's relations with the congressional Armed Services Committees were just as ambivalent on budgetary issues as they were on defense policy issues. On the one hand, Richard Russell, had pushed through the Defense Reorganization Act of 1958 and thus welcomed the reforms that McNamara promised to implement. On the other, like many on his committee, he was prone to adding wasteful projects to the defense budget for political, rather than operational, reasons.

In an oral history, McNamara described some of the tensions that blighted his congressional relationships. He explained that the members of the Armed Services Committees in the House and Senate at the time "were not representative of the people" and "were disproportionately Southerners," where many military installations were located. He added, "Southerners, as we all know, have had a different view of the military requirements of the nation and the national security of the nation, and how it might best be achieved, than have the rest of the people." Moreover, the committees were "dominated by reserve officers," who were "spokesmen for military interests as opposed to the national interest. They saw things through the narrow parochial views of the military." He ended on one of the main points of contention in his congressional relations, namely that they got in the way of his cost-reduction programs: "There was at that time a situation difficult for many people to imagine today: a desire in the Congress to spend far more than the Secretary of Defense and the President wished to spend on defense."[56]

McNamara's remarks raised many issues but especially Eisenhower's concern about the "iron triangle" between industry, the military and congressional leaders, or what the President had called the "military-industrial complex." Ironically, Eisenhower's remarks were in part a reaction to Kennedy's and Symington's accusations during the campaign that he had been "weak on defense"[57] and reflected not just on the failures of congressional oversight but also on the novelty of a major military establishment in the US experience. In later years, McNamara's colleagues, including Yarmolinsky, echoed Eisenhower's views and complained about the "military-industrial-labor-congressional complex." Yarmolinsky wrote that Congress "since World War II" had "to a considerable extent abdicated" its oversight role of the armed services in part because of the growing complexity of military issues and programs but also because of "self-interest in major contracts" which produced "wasteful development and procurement procedures."[58]

Nevertheless, from McNamara's vantage point, PPBS coupled with the sheer strength of his character could be enough to short-circuit congressional manipulations that would undermine an efficient allocation of federal resources to clear defense purposes. He claimed not to "share Eisenhower's concerns" and suggested that the "influences" could affect national security policy only "to the extent that the President and/or Secretary of Defense wants to be influenced."[59] In office, he did not shy away from following through with the logic of PPBS and overruling the services' military judgment on costly procurement decisions for new weapon systems, precisely the kind of program their allies in Congress tended to defend.

However, this led to more acrimonious arguments between the OSD and the Senate and services, most famously over the so-called Tactical Fighter Experimental (TFX) fighter jet. On McNamara's insistence, the Air Force and Navy were meant to jointly procure and operate the jet. Despite reservations from both services, the OSD pushed the program in an effort to pool resources, encourage inter-service cooperation and, in so doing, cut costs and apply the logic of PPBS more effecitvely. The OSD also chose General Dynamics over Boeing to build the jet, a choice that overruled the services' recommendations. The whole program became even more controversial as cost overruns dented McNamara's effort to showcase its cost-efficiency logic and when the Senate openly challenged McNamara's competence by initiating an investigation into his decision.

The TFX incident was emblematic of relations between McNamara and the services and their allies in the Senate. It highlighted their resistance to McNamara's reforms. Within the OSD it crystallized a confrontational attitude toward the Chiefs and the Senate and further contributed to the deterioration of trust and goodwill between the two.

Writing about the incident to President Kennedy's Special Counsel Theodore Sorensen, Gilpatric was angry:

> The only feasible method of handling this situation as far as the Defense Department is concerned is to shift the basis for the debate. Every effort must be made, of course, to establish the facts. But this will not do the job that must be done. Somehow, the debate must be shifted from a question of merits (which the public is incapable of deciding) to a question of whether the military, in conjunction with large weapons systems producers, will be able to dominate the responsible officials of our Government who, under our Constitution, are supposed to be in charge ... What we are really dealing with in the TFX investigation is the spectacle of a large corporation, backed by Air Force Generals, using the investigatory powers of Congress to intimidate civilian officials just because it lost out on a contract.[60]

Gilpatric's letter betrays both the extent to which the OSD, by 1963, was in a confrontational relationship with the services and their friends in the Congress and the extent to which McNamara and his colleagues saw themselves as serving the public interest in spite of, if not against, them.

The battle lines in this confrontation were actually between the executive, through the President's advisors, and the military and legislative branches of government. In the short term, the confrontation hinged on the latter's resistance to any cuts in the defense budget. In the longer term, it reflected a deeper rift over McNamara's attempts to break through their entrenched interests in the status quo and, more broadly, his efforts to move foreign and defense policy-making into civilian and specifically the President's hands.

While the Armed Services Committees were relatively spendthrift, the same was not true across Congress, especially after 1962 when Kennedy announced his intention to pass a personal and corporate tax cut to kick-start the ailing economy. In the wake of the Berlin Crisis in 1961, Kennedy had planned on proposing a tax increase to match increases in defense spending, but his economic advisors, including Sorensen and Walter Heller, the Chairman of the Council of Economic Advisers, convinced him otherwise. By the summer of 1962, when Kennedy finally settled on the tax cut, he met with almost immediate resistance from Republicans in the House and conservative Democrats in the Senate who wanted to force the administration to match the proposed tax cuts with cuts to federal expenditures.[61]

The administration's decision to push for a tax cut and increases in defense spending rather than spend directly on social programs, as Kennedy's more Keynesian advisors would have preferred, hinged on issues of political feasibility. Kennedy concluded that it was "probably easier, given the mood of Congress and the country, to obtain the necessary economic stimulus through tax reduction than through expenditure increases."[62] Similarly, given the relative invulnerability of the defense budget to cuts, the Kennedy administration concluded that "spending for national security, with its remarkable sanctity from attack by pressure groups, including business[, should take] the place of massive public works."[63]

Whereas Eisenhower had added $7 billion to federal spending between 1953 and 1961, Kennedy added $17 billion in three years. Three-quarters was allocated to defense,[64] but the Defense Department's funds were also used for social purposes. In addition to creating jobs, the ill-fated civil defense program morphed into a civilian infrastructure project and McNamara spearheaded civil rights issues in the Defense Department specifically to compensate for the lack of congressional action.[65] McNamara also used the department's clout over industry to intervene in the domestic economy. For instance, when in 1961 steel companies flouted the administration's suggested price guidelines that were designed to stem inflation, McNamara threatened to change the department's steel providers, forcing them to back down. Overall, Kennedy's liberal critics failed to appreciate the way the defense budget was used, albeit as a second-best option, to influence the domestic economy and to push social spending through a resistant Congress.

At the same time, Kennedy's liberal critics were correct in their suspicion that he was more fiscally conservative than they would have liked. Even before his decision to pass the tax cut, Kennedy sought to balance the budget. In fact, the CEA remembered his "bombshell" just after the inauguration when he agreed with leaders of the Democratic Party in both houses to balance his budget as soon as feasible. He would have achieved a balanced budget as early as FY63 were it not for weak economic indicators in 1962.[66]

Moreover, he chose Republicans to fill two of the most important positions for federal spending, namely Treasury and Defense. C. Douglas Dillon, with his background in finance at his father's investment bank, Dillon, Read & Co. where the late James Forrestal had also begun his career, and McNamara were both nominal Republicans disposed to balanced budgets. The Council of Economic Advisers, which was filled with Keynesian economists, complained about Dillon's influence on the President.[67] Although Dillon later explained that in Kennedy's view the Treasury and Defense positions should be apolitical, he also described himself as Kennedy's "Chief Financial Officer" and accepted that he usually had the last word on most economic issues.[68]

In addition, Kennedy gave both Dillon and McNamara operational control of his attempts to limit federal spending. In an effort to reduce expenditures across the board and on defense in particular, Kennedy charged Dillon with a government-wide cost-cutting drive. Dillon's principal ally in this campaign was McNamara, who enthusiastically supported the agenda against both the State Department and the advice of the services. As one of National Security Advisor McGeorge Bundy's deputies, Carl Kaysen, observed at the time, McNamara used "the pressures Dillon . . . generated as a means for pushing through various reorganizations that he had in mind in any event."[69]

McNamara enthusiastically jumped on Dillon's bandwagon for a number of reasons but especially because Defense Department expenditures had increased exponentially since the end of World War II and were at the heart of expanding federal expenditures. One of the President's notes on the budget and debt from January 1963 put it simply: in response to "what causes the budget deficit?" it answered, "first, the cost of national security."[70] According to official estimates, by 1963 the defense budget represented approximately 50 percent the federal budget,[71] but national security expenditures generally, including space, raised that number to over 70 percent.[72] In other words, if the administration was going to cut federal expenditures and especially expenditures abroad, the first and most obvious place to begin was the Defense Department.

Kennedy had campaigned on a platform that suggested that he would overturn Eisenhower's fiscal conservatism, with respect to both the federal budget and the defense budget in particular. However, much to the chagrin of his more liberal advisors, he was far more fiscally conservative than they had anticipated and chose Republicans for both the Treasury and Defense positions. Even if defense expenditures increased in absolute terms in the short term, McNamara's reforms were geared toward economies in the longer term. To a large extent, his professional reputation at the OSD was built on his abilities as a cost-cutter.

McNamara sought to align Defense Department resources to civilian objectives and strategies, but this was also true in the economic sense. As envisaged in the Defense Reorganization Act, McNamara's major reforms, including PPBS, were aimed at matching the department's resources in the most cost-efficient way possible and with domestic, economic concerns in mind. At the same time, McNamara confronted entrenched interests in the status quo, including from the services and Congress, which made defense spending easier to access. As a result, the administration drew on the defense budget to support programs that were only tangentially relevant to it, for instance, on civilian infrastructure projects and eventually in Vietnam.

The two conflicting types of pressures played a part in McNamara's policies for Vietnam. On the one hand, the ready availability of resources propelled McNamara and his department into a leading role on Vietnam. On the other, Kennedy's, Dillon's and McNamara's fiscal conservatism, as well as McNamara's concerns about the costs associated with Vietnam, explain why he favored a more modest commitment.

3

Continuity and Change

Coming off the back of an electoral campaign, each new administration tends to overplay its "break" with its predecessors and to emphasize the aspects that represent change rather than continuity. In few transitions was this truer than when Kennedy replaced Eisenhower: the New Frontier and its youthful President, the first one born in the twentieth century, replacing the "old" guard with a new vision for the projection and use of American power in the Cold War.[1] In his inaugural address, Kennedy picked up on this generational theme in announcing, "let the word go forth from this time and place, to friend and foe alike, that the torch has been passed to a new generation of Americans – born in this century, tempered by war, disciplined by a hard and bitter peace, proud of our ancient heritage."[2]

The journalist Theodore White captured the mood of expectation in describing "an impatient world wait[ing] for miracles" from the new President, who "had been able to recognize and distinguish between those great faceless forces that were changing his country and the individuals who influenced those forces. For if it is true that history is moved on by remorseless forces greater than any man, it is nonetheless true that individual men by individual decision can channel, or deftly guide, those impersonal forces either for the good or to disastrous collision."[3]

However, for all its promise of change, many of the ideas that Kennedy articulated for economic and foreign policy in an "impatient world" predated his arrival in the Oval Office. Just as the bureaucratic "revolutions" that McNamara undertook at the OSD fell within a lineage of change, a gradual process of bureaucratic transformation that preceded his tenure, so too did many of the Kennedy administration's foreign policy ideas. On economic policy as well, a great deal of continuity existed between Eisenhower and Kennedy. Even if the administration had brought in prominent left-wing economists, leading some to conclude that, "Kennedy's economic advisors ... were Keynesian expansionists, committed to full employment and economic growth, less concerned than their Republican counterparts about budget deficits and inflation,"[4] in reality, the President was cautious and reluctant to move on their recommendations.

Moreover, although Kennedy had chastised Eisenhower for "putting fiscal security ahead of national security"[5] during the election campaign, once in office, he too was concerned that international responsibilities were beginning to weaken the economic foundations of the United States. World War II and the ensuing Cold War created new treaty obligations and defense installations across the world that produced persistent balance of payments deficits. As a result, a central but overlooked part of Kennedy's foreign policy and, in turn, of his defense policy was that other countries should bear a greater share of the burden for their own security.[6] Economic concerns conditioned his, and McNamara's, strategic choices in Vietnam and elsewhere.

Notwithstanding a high degree of continuity and the fact that President Kennedy's views on national security and defense policy evolved in office, a number of philosophical threads underpinned the new administration's defense policy and differed in emphasis from its predecessor's. First and foremost, Kennedy shifted away from a policy that focused on nuclear forces and toward flexible response, which allowed for a broader foreign policy view and the deployment of both military and non-military tools to allow cross-government, coordinated interventions on a broader spectrum of international situations, especially in the developing world. The administration pledged to experiment with new ways of projecting US power after decades during which the projection of US power had become increasingly defined in military terms.

The inaugural address set the tone and ended on a measured note, a message to other countries that they had to make sacrifices and share the burdens of protecting their freedom. Contrary to popular belief, the speech was not "bellicose and filled with soaring hubris,"[7] and when President Kennedy said that "we shall pay any price, bear any burden ... in order to assure the survival and success of liberty," the operative *we* was not just the American people but also the people of the world.[8] Although he suggested a clear focus on providing aid to the developing world and to the "peoples in the huts and villages of half the globe," Kennedy alerted that the administration would merely "help them help themselves." Furthermore, while he accepted the logic of nuclear deterrence, Kennedy cautioned that both the Soviet Union and the United States were "overburdened by the costs of modern weapons" and threatened by the danger that "science [might] engulf all humanity in planned or accidental self-destruction."[9]

Nevertheless, the address established a revised intellectual framework, new priorities for and a redefinition of international security. As a result, it spurred drastic changes at the OSD, which moved to align defense capabilities to meet the new objectives. Where Vietnam was concerned, this included the Special Group on Counterinsurgency, ISA at the OSD and McNamara's private office. Each played a preeminent role in the articulation of Vietnam policy and eventually in the withdrawal plans initiated in the spring of 1962.

If Kennedy was keen for allies to pick up a greater share of the costs associated with their defense, it was also because he had set in motion a shift away from nuclear power that, in the short term, was inevitably very expensive. Paradoxically, as Yarmolinsky later explained, it was precisely because the budget was expanding for a time that the administration could push through its necessary reforms. Cutting force levels and the budget at the same time was unfeasible – it "tend[ed] to freeze attitudes and to heighten institutional jealousies" – even if, in the longer term, a significant budget cut was "highly desirable."[10]

Strategically, two ideas inspired the move away from Eisenhower's national security policy, which was centered on nuclear deterrence. First, although they were reticent to make these ideas public, Kennedy and several of his closest colleagues believed that nuclear weapons and their use were inherently immoral. Second, reflecting the mood of the times, they felt nuclear deterrence specifically, and the Cold War competition more generally, had created conditions in which lower-level conflict had become more likely. Accordingly, defense policy was overhauled to respond to a broader set of contingencies and particularly situations of low-level, guerrilla-type conflict in newly independent states where the Communist threat seemed on the rise, notably in Laos and Congo. The Defense Department played a key role in coordinating relevant tools across government for these types of conflicts, principally by expanding the administration's aid program and strengthening its own capabilities, including by reinforcing the Army's Special Forces.

From the outset, the administration adopted a moralistic tone about nuclear weapons.[11] In September 1961, once again building on the rhetoric of his inaugural address, Kennedy spoke to the issue of nuclear disarmament at the UN General Assembly, saying that nuclear weapons threatened to turn the "planet into a flaming funeral pyre" and that "weapons of war must be abolished before they abolish us."[12] At other times, religious undertones pervaded his speeches on the issue. For instance, in his June 1963 commencement address at the American University, he argued for a relaxation of the arms race, saying, "For, in the final analysis, our most basic common link is that we all inhabit this small planet. We all breathe the same air. We all cherish our children's futures. And we are all mortal." Using quasi-biblical language, he implicitly confronted the reluctance of the JCS to begin disarmament talks,[13] by adding: "Surely this goal is sufficiently important to require our steady pursuit, yielding neither to the temptation to give up the whole effort nor the temptation to give up our insistence on vital and responsible safeguards."[14] Privately, Kennedy held even stronger reservations and questioned whether nuclear weapons could ever be useful or if they could ever achieve what were ultimately political objectives.[15]

Similarly, in April 1963, Alain Enthoven, a key figure in the formulation of nuclear policy, wrote an article in a Jesuit publication describing how the administration's shift in policy fit within the moral codes of the just war tradition. Enthoven wrote: "Now, much more than in the recent past, our use of force is being carefully proportioned to the objectives being sought, and the objectives are being carefully limited to those which at the same time are necessary for our security and which do not pose the kind of unlimited threat to our opponent in the Cold War that would drive them to unleash nuclear war."[16] In other words, by developing a more flexible force structure, the administration was laying the groundwork for a more proportional and discriminate response to political crises than a posture relying primarily on nuclear weapons allowed.

McNamara echoed the President's views in his own speeches, but in a way that reflected both the practical steps that his department had undertaken to lessen the United States' reliance on nuclear weapons, and his concerns that allies, especially France, were increasing the likelihood of nuclear escalation by developing their independent nuclear force. McNamara made two particularly controversial and landmark speeches: one on May 5, 1962, to the NATO Ministerial Meeting in Athens and a distilled version of the same speech the following month in Ann Arbor, Michigan.

Both speeches outlined the administration's general approach to nuclear strategy, but whereas the former was classified and only for NATO Defense Ministers, the latter was a public address aimed at "talking to [unresponsive] NATO Allies through the press."[17]

In Ann Arbor, McNamara said, "Surely an Alliance with the wealth, talent, and experience that we possess can find a better way than extreme reliance on nuclear weapons to meet our common threat." He reiterated the idea set out in the inaugural address that the projection of US power had to rely on more than military power, let alone nuclear power. He explained that "military strength is a necessary, but not sufficient, condition for the achievement of our foreign policy goals" and added that "military security provides a base on which we can build free world strength through the economic advances and political reforms which are the object of the President's programmes, like the Alliance for Progress and the trade expansion legislation."[18]

Moreover, one of the main ideas in McNamara's speeches and in Enthoven's article was that the United States had enough, even perhaps too many, nuclear weapons.[19] Although the administration, and the JCS in particular, had many reservations about the viability of disarmament talks and the 1963 Nuclear Test Ban Treaty, McNamara nevertheless argued that it was important "to lay groundwork" and that the administration could "never know [how useful these initial steps would be] in future."[20]

McNamara and his colleagues' speeches were drafted in a way that reflected the delicate nature of the changes within the Defense Department and with an eye toward their inevitable international impact. According to his main speechwriter, "we began each talk of this kind by pointing out our enormous superiority" before moving on to presenting the potentially controversial policy changes.[21] The primary purpose was not to reassure the allies but the Chiefs. The administration was declaring that in spite of the shift in policy, it would not cut their nuclear arsenal drastically. Yarmolinsky recalled that the Chiefs had framed "the terms of the debate" in such a way that such cuts were impossible.[22]

Overall, as they did with many of McNamara's changes, the Chiefs lodged wholesale resistance to almost every aspect of the reforms to nuclear strategy. They resisted disarmament talks and the test ban treaty on the basis that they lacked adequate verification systems. More alarmingly, they refused to share their main nuclear contingency plan, the so-called Single Integrated Operational Plan, or SIOP 63, with Defense Department staff or even with the President himself, offering only to brief

McGeorge Bundy on its contents.[23] They also resisted Defense Department efforts to integrate flexible response thinking into their planning.[24] Even Maxwell Taylor resisted reform once he became Chairman of the Joint Chiefs of Staff in October 1962. In a taped conversation with President Kennedy in December 1962, he stated, "As you know, in the past I've always said, we probably have too much ... But sir, I would recommend staying with the program essentially as it is."[25]

By 1962, faced with resistance from the Chiefs as well as from European allies who were reluctant to invest in the conventional forces required for a more flexible nuclear strategy, the administration discretely settled on a policy of mutually assured destruction (MAD). In part, the policy was a logical corollary of McNamara and his colleagues' conclusion that "nuclear warfare itself was suicidal" and therefore that the United States needed a "nuclear component sufficient to serve only as a deterrent."[26] Above all, it was the product of economic concerns. The administration toyed with nuclear policy alternatives, notably by investing in civil defense projects and by studying the possibility of a counterforce strategy, namely attacking Soviet nuclear sites before they could launch missiles. Both were designed to limit damage to the United States and thus increase survivability in the event of a nuclear exchange. McNamara ultimately considered both to be cost-prohibitive and so they were eventually axed. As one scholar has noted, "the downward revision of strategic goals was ... motivated in large part by a desire to put a lid on defense spending."[27]

In reality, Kennedy's nuclear policy was not radically different from Eisenhower's, which is not to say that flexible response was, as some have contended, entirely a "myth."[28] The prospect of nuclear war repulsed both Kennedy and Eisenhower, but for Kennedy, this implied the need to reshape defense policy and its tools so that the United States could respond to conflicts across the spectrum of violence from the lowest level up to and including nuclear war.

The idea that the United States should be prepared for lower-level conflict, especially in the developed world, had intellectual precedents in the Eisenhower administration.[29] Maxwell Taylor, Eisenhower's Army Chief, had fallen out with the administration over the New Look strategy and had provided much of the intellectual foundation for flexible response in his book *The Uncertain Trumpet*, which was published with great fanfare in 1960.[30] Elsewhere, others such as then Undersecretary of State for Economic Affairs C. Douglas Dillon recalled that, in the last two or three years of the Eisenhower administration, he and his State

Department colleagues had "push[ed] hard" for limited war capabilities. However, not until Kennedy's election did his "minority view," which the new President shared, take center stage.[31]

The Kennedy administration was predisposed to take the contingency of US involvement in lower-level conflicts seriously, but this gained a sense of urgency in January 1961. At that time, Chairman Nikita S. Khrushchev made his landmark "national wars of liberation" speech in which he predicted that local insurgencies in the developing world were more likely in a thermonuclear world and where he stated that Marxists had "a most positive" attitude toward "such uprisings."[32] Khrushchev's speech made a deep impression on the Kennedy administration: one joint State-Defense report from December 1961 noted that the administration recognized "changing political conditions around the world, shifts in the nature and probability of threats" and especially that the "likelihood of indirect aggression seems much greater during the 1960s than that overt local aggression."[33]

McNamara, in an address to the National Bar Association in February 1962, described Khrushchev's speech as possibly "the most important statement made by a world leader in the decade of the 60's." In a lengthy analysis of Khrushchev's words, he explained: "What Chairman Khrushchev describes as wars of liberation and popular uprisings, I prefer to describe as subversion and covert aggression. We have learned to recognize the pattern of this attack. It feeds on conditions of poverty and unequal opportunity, and it distorts the legitimate aspirations of people just beginning to realize the reach of the human potential. It is particularly dangerous to those nations that have not yet formulated the essential consensus of values, which a free society requires for survival."[34]

In responding to this threat, Kennedy argued that the United States' image abroad needed an overhaul and recommended a full set of strategies ranging from appropriate military interventions to well-designed aid and development efforts.[35] To this end, delivering on a campaign promise, he established the Peace Corps under the leadership of his brother-in-law Sargent Shriver in March 1961 and, in October 1961, the United States Agency for International Development (USAID) under David Bell, "one of his closest associates."[36] Responding to congressional criticism, USAID consolidated existing and scattered aid programs to encourage a longer-term and more strategic approach to existing aid efforts. The creation of USAID also embodied the administration's belief that "foreign aid [was] a relatively cheap way of preventing Communist encroachment."[37]

In keeping with these changes, McNamara argued before Congress that "a dollar of economic aid is as important as a dollar of military aid,"[38] and behind the scenes, he coordinated the Defense Department's overseas programs closely with USAID, notably in Vietnam, where their budgets were practically fused. Paradoxically, McNamara's ability to think of his office within the larger scope of government rather than downward to the military services and other bureaucratic interests meant that he weighed heavily on a number of relevant government-wide structures.

At the time, one of the most important cross-government offices for the administration's stated desire to respond to "wars of national liberation" was the Special Group Counterinsurgency (CI). According to National Security Action Memorandum (NSAM) 124, which set up the Special Group in January 1962, its purpose was "to ensure proper recognition throughout the US government that subversive insurgency ("war of national liberation") is a form of politico-military conflict equal in importance to conventional warfare" and to ensure the "adequacy of resources" and "interdepartmental programs" to "prevent and defeat subversive insurgency."[39]

To this end, the group included a number of military, OSD, NSC and State Department representatives, the director of the CIA and the director of USAID.[40] Maxwell Taylor, first as the President's Military Representative and then as Chairman of the JCS, together with Attorney General Robert Kennedy, headed the group. Although, from a bureaucratic perspective, the Attorney General was an unusual choice for this role, his presence was designed to send a strong signal that the President was the "driving force behind this effort."[41] Roswell Gilpatric, who usually represented the Defense Department on the Special Group (as it was not McNamara's "dish of tea") remembered that, "You know, [Kennedy had] read some Marine magazine about Green Beret type of activity, and he felt that when you got away from strictly conventional military or intelligence of State Department activities, there wasn't any well-coordinated, cohesive direction. And that's when I think he told his brother he wanted to get him into this thing."[42]

At any one time, the group oversaw efforts in a dozen or so countries spread across Latin America, the Middle East, Africa and Asia.[43] Asia had always been its first focus: Thailand, Laos and Vietnam had been founding countries in its portfolio, although Latin America superseded them by 1963.[44] For each of these countries, the group prepared quarterly

Internal Defense Plans, which were a kind of progress report on each country's efforts to suppress domestic insurgencies or unrest. The group reviewed and assessed the work of relevant US agencies' work in each of the countries, usually USAID, United States Information Agency (USIA) and civic action programs, which included efforts at building up local military and policing capabilities. Although the most visible aspects of the group's work were on military and paramilitary capabilities, its focus was primarily on civic action programs. Civic action was a murkier aspect of US foreign policy and had been regarded as marginal within government before the Kennedy administration.[45] It involved projects on the boundaries of the different agencies.

The Special Group was particularly active throughout 1962, but by January 1963, after Taylor's move to the JCS,[46] it seemed to fall into disuse, much to the chagrin of Robert Kennedy, who complained that "there are a lot of things that could be done under the proper auspices," whereas "our present CI operation is most unsatisfactory."[47] His colleagues were even more pointed in their criticism and bemoaned that the State Department could not pick up where Taylor had left off. One wrote: "I assume that the Department of State is still not ready (I am not prepared to say unable) to assume this leadership role."[48]

Robert Komer, the NSC's representative to the group,[49] was slightly more positive in his assessment and felt it "performed a real service in pushing, needling, prodding and coordinating" counterinsurgency efforts across the administration.[50] Yet by July 1962, he too became frustrated at the State Department's lack of leadership: "A case could be made that [the Special Group] has already performed its main service, i.e. to get the town moving on CI in the way JFK wants. But I fear that if we scratch the Group now everything will sink back into the usual bureaucratic rut. State, which should be monitoring the CI show, is simply not set up to do it."[51]

The Kennedy administration's counterinsurgency agenda had important budgetary and bureaucratic repercussions for the Defense Department that aggravated its already strained relationship with the services. Marine Corps General Victor Krulak had the frustrating task of overseeing the services' progress on building counterinsurgency expertise and capabilities and adjusting their doctrines. They reported to Krulak, who was based out of the JCS Staff, and he, in turn, reported to McNamara and occasionally directly to the President. He also participated in the Special Group (CI), sometimes sitting in for Taylor or Gilpatric. Later he recalled that most of the time, despite impressive statistics and a service-wide *Joint*

Counterinsurgency Doctrine, progress was "more volume than value" and "mostly they weren't doing much."[52]

The services resented yet another OSD-led reform agenda but were compelled to go along given the administration's public commitment to counterinsurgency. Most senior military officials dismissed these efforts as "faddishness" and considered themselves more than prepared to respond to any contingency.[53] In part, as far as the Navy and Air Force were concerned, resistance was also rooted in suspicions that the administration's interest in counterinsurgency was essentially designed to strengthen the Army, which itself had initially resisted involvement in counterinsurgency operations.[54] If Eisenhower's New Look had favored the Air Force and to a lesser extent the Navy budget, it was clear that flexible response favored the Army. Both services regularly lamented the administration's perceived "Army bias" particularly after the arrival of Taylor, and the administration's fascination with the Special Forces puzzled them.

In many ways, this early period of the Kennedy administration's involvement in Vietnam was a "coming of age" period for the Special Forces. Although the Special Forces had been activated in 1952 at Fort Bragg in North Carolina, they were largely dismissed as an esoteric bunch until Kennedy came to power. Their numbers almost tripled between 1961 and 1963.[55] The administration's first budget specifically foresaw "a substantial contribution in the form of forces trained" for guerrilla warfare (see Figure 3.1).[56]

In addition, the administration maintained a high level of publicity around the Special Forces. The columnist Joseph Alsop, an administration insider, writing just weeks after Kennedy's inauguration, described an NSC meeting where Kennedy praised the Special Forces as "equal to the nuclear deterrent."[57] Both Kennedy brothers went out of their way to raise the profile of the Special Forces: President Kennedy decreed that they be given their iconic green berets as a "symbol of excellence, a badge of courage, a mark of distinction,"[58] and Robert Kennedy famously kept a green beret on his desk.

In his address to the National Bar Association in February 1962, McNamara singled out the Special Forces, though not by name, as a key tool to deal with "wars of national liberation," which he described as "often not wars at all." He warned that dealing with these types of situations "requires some shift in our military thinking" and that the Defense Department was "used to developing big weapons and large forces," whereas it now needed to train "fighters who can, in turn, teach the people of free nations to fight for their freedom."[59]

FIGURE 3.1 Secretary of Defense Robert McNamara visits the 82nd Airborne Division at Fort Bragg, North Carolina, October 12, 1961. McNamara favored light and mobile Army units, prompting the other services to accuse the administration of having an Army bias.
(Cecil Stoughton, White House Photograph Collection, JFKL.)

In a speech delivered at the Special Forces training school in Fort Bragg that was initially intended for McNamara, Yarmolinsky explained how the Special Forces fit into flexible response and the need to have forces "across the full spectrum" of conflicts. He explained their special value in the face of guerrilla warfare and subversion, where they had "taken on an importance that was virtually undreamed of only a decade ago." Significantly, one line was removed from his speech at the last minute that might have had special resonance with Vietnam: "We have no desire to, and few countries would want us to, send large scale American troops to their

nations to deal with problems of terrorism and subversion and guerrilla
warfare. Nothing could be more inappropriate."[60]

In private, Yarmolinsky, who as a leading member of Kennedy's
presidential campaign had been instrumental in creating the idea of the
"New Frontier," went further and explained how "these people are
properly New Frontiersmen as much as any Peace Corps volunteer or
[US]AID mission member. In a world where force is still necessary, they
can make the necessary use of force both understandable and justifiable to
the uncommitted people of the world."[61] Thomas Hughes, who became
director of INR in 1963 and who worked closely on Vietnam, also saw
the Special Forces as a preeminent symbol of the New Frontier and
Vietnam as their first project. He explained, "A new breed of Americans,
right out of Kennedy's inaugural address, was being tested in Vietnam."[62]

From a bureaucratic perspective, the Special Forces fit tidily into the
types of cross-government work that the administration wanted to experiment with and from the Defense Department's view, with a more cost-
efficient strategy whereby the United States could rely on airlift
capabilities and rapid reaction forces instead of forward positioning to
deal with crisis situations across the world. Yarmolinsky described how
"not numbers but quality" mattered most and that the Special Forces
showed how a "relatively small body of superbly capable and superbly
trained men can provide, and I am sure will provide, an enormous
contribution."[63] In addition, capabilities such as the Special Forces held
a distinct appeal because they were so adaptable and had a much lighter
logistic and support base, and because the Defense Department did not
have to finance them entirely.

The Special Forces in Vietnam represented the type of bureaucratic
innovations that the Kennedy administration pursued through its Special
Group (CI). The Special Forces were deployed under CIA command and
ran projects in remote villages where ethnic minorities lived, notably
the Montagnard communities. The latter were discriminated against in
Vietnamese society and were therefore reluctant to embrace either the
Ngo Dinh Diem regime in Saigon or the North Vietnamese communists.
Working with other agencies in Vietnam, the Special Forces combined
seemingly anodyne activities such as running clinics and offering job
training with psychological and propaganda operations as well as programs to arm and train local militias. As one CIA history explained, "they
were more than soldiers; they were, in a way, community developers in
uniform."[64] From a bureaucratic perspective, the most interesting aspect
of these activities is that the executive authority over the Special Forces

and civic action programs was not with the Army but with the CIA, in coordination with the ubiquitous ISA.[65]

The administration's interest in Special Forces and counterinsurgency was a response to objective international realities about the changing shape of conflict but was conditioned by economic concerns. The same pressures that had encouraged McNamara to settle on a nuclear policy premised on MAD also informed his interest in counterinsurgency programs over traditional military deployments.

Kennedy entered the White House with a sense of economic vulnerability that continued throughout his time in office and colored many of McNamara's defense decisions. Part of this vulnerability stemmed from slow growth in the US economy and nagging unemployment figures that coincided with Premier Khrushchev's own economic plan that threatened to overtake the US economy by 1970.[66] But especially it came from the balance of payments problem and the threat it posed to the dollar as the international reserve currency. As Kennedy's economic advisor Seymour Harris explained, "We have now become like all other nations – a nation that has to watch its balance of payments. We were free of that particular responsibility for a long time."[67]

Confirming Francis Gavin's work, and contrary to the conventional wisdom that the balance of payments and gold outflow would not surface as an issue until much later in the decade, the economic historian Barry Eichengreen used data mined from official documents to show that balance of payments concerns had a greater level of saliency in the 1962–1963 period than at any other point, including the "crisis years" of 1968 and 1971 when the Bretton-Woods system eventually collapsed.[68]

Eichengreen has also shown that the first dollar crisis occurred not at the end of the decade as scholars have traditionally assumed, but at the end of 1960 just as the Kennedy administration prepared to take office. Two related trends converged to undermine the dollar at that moment. First, in that year, the traded value of an ounce of gold on the open markets shot up to $40 whereas the dollar converted at $35, a moment the Kennedy's Council of Economic Advisers later described as "the gold flutter."[69] Galbraith wrote to Kennedy in October of that year that the increase had been "unprecedented" and that the "counterpart of this is a weakening of the dollar," which could precipitate a devaluation of the dollar.[70] Second, the period of 1958–1960 was the first period since 1945 during which the United States experienced a balance of payments deficit, which would persist for the remainder of the decade, and a gold outflow of $1.7 billion in 1960 alone. As a result, 1960 was the first year where dollar claims exceeded the United States' gold reserves. As foreign holders of US dollars, primarily Western Europeans, began to trade in their dollars for gold, fears about an eventual run on the dollar spread.

The recollections of Kennedy's colleagues suggest that gold loss issues were not just salient across government but had a special impact on President Kennedy, who feared that by undermining the role of the US dollar as a reserve currency, gold losses posed a direct threat to US power. According to Carl Kaysen, who was the main point man on these issues in the NSC staff, "The President was occupied, and in the judgment of some of his professionally knowledgeable advisors, over-occupied with the problem of balance of payments and gold for the whole of his term in office."[71] Similarly, Paul Nitze, from the vantage point of the Defense Department, recalled that "President Kennedy ... felt that this was one of the most important things that had to be controlled; that if we didn't control this gold outflow, there could be a run on the dollar and this would be a disaster, forcing us to currency control and all kinds of things which were unattractive."[72]

For many, the specter of the 1933 Banking Crisis loomed large: facing similar circumstances, the Democratic Roosevelt administration was forced to devalue amid a major financial crisis that many blamed on a lack of clear government policy.[73] Kennedy's first State of the Union address made it clear that the administration would not devalue and that it would address the deficit head on. He explained: "This Administration will not distort the value of the dollar in any fashion. And this is a commitment. Prudence and good sense do require, however, that new steps be taken to ease the payments deficit and prevent any gold crisis. Our success in world affairs has long depended in part upon foreign confidence in our ability to pay."[74]

Kennedy sought to reassure key stakeholders with a message of prudence and of continuity on the economic front. Secretary Dillon's recollections are interesting on this subject because they explain the nature of Kennedy's concern just as they elucidate why he might have selected Republicans as Secretaries of Defense and Treasury, key posts at the intersection of foreign and economic policy. In addition to his background in finance, Dillon had served as Eisenhower's Ambassador to France at a time when France was disengaging from Indochina and offloading the war's costs onto its ally, the United States. In addition to his experiences in the State Department, as a member of the establishment, Dillon was a close personal friend of the Rockefeller brothers and

FIGURE 3.2 Secretary of Defense McNamara (right) with Secretary of the Treasury C. Douglas Dillon (left), August 5, 1964. Dillon encouraged President Kennedy's fiscal conservatism and was frustrated with President Johnson's economic policies.
(OSD photograph collection: OSD Historical Office.)

many others in the business world, which gave him valuable access to a Democratic administration and to a young President under pressure to prove his economic credentials (see Figure 3.2).

Dillon explained Kennedy's "particular" concern over the balance of payments and the offer of the Treasury position: "He was afraid that there was a lack of confidence in the US and that nobody knew what the new policies would be. He said that I could render substantial assistance because I was known in Europe and was known to believe in the maintenance of the value of the dollar and in a sound dollar, which he very much believed in himself."[75] In and of itself, a balance of payments deficit was not a problem, and as the administration itself explained in a press release in February 1961, "early deficits in our balance of payments were, in fact, favorable in their world effect" since they had stimulated growth and thus new markets, especially in Europe.[76] The danger came if dollars were converted into gold, which would threaten the stability of the dollar as the international monetary system's reserve currency.

From the outset, the administration was alerted to "speculative fears concerning the future of the dollar"[77] and especially, as Galbraith suggested to Kennedy, the risk that "Republican bankers" might seek to "embarrass the administration" by provoking a run on the dollar.[78] Since devaluation was not an option for a President who had pledged to "maintain the value of the dollar," Kennedy chose to reassure those who might initiate a speculative attack.[79]

As a result, Dillon became the administration's envoy to the business community, whose confidence was needed but which was suspicious of an administration considered too liberal and intellectual for its liking. The administration had "started afoul" with business, clashing, as it had done in 1961, over steel prices and making staffing choices that accentuated fears. In the Eisenhower administration, 36 percent of appointments were from the business community; in Kennedy's, only 6 percent were.[80]

Dillon reached out, among others, to his friend David Rockefeller, whose advice to the new President was that "the only way to achieve a solid solution to our balance of payments problem ... is through time honored methods," namely an expansion of exports, manipulating interest rates and, crucially, "through maintaining confidence (both here and abroad) in the soundness and integrity of the dollar." He ended by explaining to the President that confidence could be encouraged with "more effective control of expenditures and a determined and vigorous attempt to balance the budget."[81] Rockefeller's letter suggests that the administration's fiscal prudence was not just an intellectual preference but also the product of real and perceived constraints, not least of which was the specter that the US business community could use underlying economic weaknesses to embarrass it.

In time, the administration acted on each of Rockefeller's suggestions, but it could not detract from the fact that it was defense installations and not trade that drove the balance of payments deficit. In fact, trade had expanded as European economies recovered in the preceding decade and the United States ran a "very substantial, unusually large, export surplus."[82] Instead, services drove the deficit. More specifically, as a Federal Reserve report at the time concluded, over 38 percent of the deficit could be traced back to "services in connection with the maintenance of installations abroad."[83]

During the presidential campaign, in a speech on the balance of payments delivered in Philadelphia in October 1960, then Senator Kennedy explained that the "first" contributor to the balance of payments was the "heavy commitments abroad for military and economic aid, and for the support of our own overseas military forces."[84] Newspapers at the time echoed his remarks and warned that "the cost of preserving American's world-wide defense commitments, particularly the lavish establishment in

Europe, has been a major cause of the outflow of gold and foreign currency, now threatening the stability of the dollar."[85]

Given McNamara's background as an economist and his focus on economical defense as well as his efforts to align defense resources and capabilities to national priorities, he turned to the issue of the balance of payments with vigor. It shaped his approach to ruthless cost cutting in all operations abroad and especially on Vietnam. In 1962, a number of factors converged to produce McNamara's disengagement plans from South Vietnam. First and foremost, many of the economic and budgetary issues that troubled the incoming administration became especially acute just as Kennedy charged his trusted Defense Secretary to bring order to South Vietnam policy. At the same time, civilian advisors at the State Department and elsewhere produced a strategy for South Vietnam that reflected the ethos of the New Frontier and its interest in lower-level conflicts and counterinsurgency. More than that, their strategy seemed to kill two birds with one stone: it provided a possible answer to South Vietnam's problems and a solution for McNamara's economic and budgetary concerns.

4

Taking Charge of Vietnam Policy

In some respects, McNamara became the victim of his own success. Although he had always been on the sidelines of the Special Group (CI)'s work, he was made responsible for implementing the administration's counterinsurgency agenda in its first major test case, South Vietnam. The administration's interest in counterinsurgency provided the intellectual bedrock for the Comprehensive Plan for South Vietnam (CPSVN), the administration's plan to disengage from the country. In keeping with McNamara's notions of civilian control of policy-making, the plan was predicated on a strategy emanating from civilian advisors primarily at the State Department, and he limited his role to aligning military resources to best serve the defined strategy. He did not comment on the strategy's substance but focused instead on the organizational and military requirements required to meet its objectives. His enthusiasm for the strategy was rooted in the fact that it dovetailed with and complemented his own managerial priorities at the Defense Department.

Vietnam seemed a perfect place for the Kennedy administration to "take a stand" and test its abilities to wage limited wars in the developing world. As General Taylor enthusiastically wrote, "A victory for us would prove that our people can live in the village with Asians and help them. That underdeveloped nations can defeat 'wars of liberation' with our help, strike a telling blow to the mystique of the 'wave of the future.'"[1] Many historians remember the Kennedy administration's involvement in Vietnam against this militant and hopeful backdrop. They have depicted a linear and uninterrupted upward trajectory toward a deepening United States' commitment and increasing number of troops that culminated in the full-scale "American War" in Vietnam. However, the trends in increasing troop numbers belie the fact that a period of planning for withdrawal in 1962–1963 punctuated this otherwise steady trajectory and that McNamara was the leading force behind those plans.

In the spring of 1962, after months of disorder in the field and in Washington, the Defense Department finally "zeroed in" on Vietnam policy just as it had already done on many of the administration's other more complex problems. Although this initially seemed to presage a deeper and more militarized presence in Vietnam, the administration instead turned to a policy of disengagement. In July 1962, McNamara formally instructed the JCS to draft what became known as the CPSVN and which posited as its goal a relatively swift US withdrawal by 1965. As the CPSVN emerged as the most effective tool for a general "winding down"[2] of the in-country presence and became embedded in the OSD's budgetary calendar, it created a momentum and imperatives of its own.

The October 1963 NSC meetings, which took place after Taylor and McNamara's trip to Vietnam, enshrined the CPSVN in a public and administration-wide policy of disengagement from Vietnam. The transcripts of the October NSC meetings reveal the motivations of the various decision-makers in accepting the policy and in making it public. Together with McNamara's trip notes, the transcripts also shed particular light on his role in pushing for withdrawal.

McNamara's understanding of where the Defense Department stood in relation to other agencies in government – namely as an implementing rather than a policy-setting office – together with his own short-term bureaucratic priorities explain his support for withdrawal. His approach was more mechanistic than visionary: he implemented rather than articulated strategy and was more concerned with the economic and budgetary issues than any grand strategy per se. Historians have largely ignored the period in part, perhaps, because it fits poorly with the conventional view of McNamara as one of the most prominent and explicitly hawkish architects of the war.

Roger Hilsman, a former colleague and main strategist for Vietnam in the State Department, perhaps overstated McNamara's intelligence but not his forcefulness in describing how McNamara had the "imagination to push views even farther down the line of their logical development, and ... the will for strong leadership."[3] In the months leading up to McNamara's instructions to the JCS to draft the withdrawal plans, he received a number of overlapping views on Vietnam from Kennedy and his counterinsurgency advisors. Specifically, the advisors felt that US policy in Vietnam had become excessively reliant on military force.

Historians have long debated "Kennedy's withdrawal plans." When they accept that these plans were more than contingency plans or a public relations stunt, they tend to assume that the plans flowed from President Kennedy's vision. John Newman, for instance, has written about secret understandings and meetings where President Kennedy instructed McNamara to begin plans to withdraw after he realized that military advisors in the field had deceived him.[4] However, when asked about this, McNamara said he had "absolutely no recollection of any such conversation" and insisted that *he* initiated the planning rather than the President.[5] Ultimately, the decisions to move toward a policy of disengagement on Vietnam were largely above board and fit neatly with McNamara's own bureaucratic priorities at the OSD.

Also, just as the war itself later came to be known as "McNamara's war," the withdrawal plans were also closely associated with McNamara. In Washington, in 1963, they were known as "his" plans.[6] Furthermore, just as President Johnson played a key role in the branding of the war as "McNamara's," and to some extent hid behind his Secretary of Defense, Kennedy too let McNamara become the public face for plans with which he was at least complicit.

During the crucial October 2–3, 1963, meetings where McNamara and Taylor's report from Vietnam was discussed and after which his disengagement plans were publicized and agreed on as administration policy, President Kennedy asked McNamara a number of probing questions as if he was discovering the material for the first time. However, they had met alone for two hours on the morning of October 2, 1963, following McNamara's return from Vietnam to review the draft report.[7] After meeting with the President, McNamara had spent about two hours with William Bundy, finalizing the report in time for the NSC meeting in the late afternoon. Given the importance of "loyalty" in McNamara's understanding of his job, he would most likely not have supported such a high-profile policy if it did not have presidential approval.

Also, it was not unlike McNamara to change the policy he defended after meeting with the President, arguing the exact opposite of what he privately or at least initially supported. McNamara might have shifted from being relatively aggressive on Vietnam to being the leading advocate for disengagement because he wanted to loyally represent the President's secret views. However, his own priorities at the OSD and the fact that, until 1962, he and many in the administration had not really given Vietnam their full attention also explain his change.

Although Kennedy had created a Task Force on Vietnam in his first month in office,[8] the administration turned its attention there only in the spring of 1961. Before this time, the administration's main focus in Southeast Asia had been Laos, a candidate for military intervention until Kennedy settled on negotiations and eventually neutralization. However, both Kennedy and McNamara rejected French President Charles de Gaulle's and later Senator Michael Mansfield's idea that Vietnam should be neutralized as well.[9]

With Vietnam coming to the fore, in May 1961, Kennedy dispatched his Vice President to reassure South Vietnamese President Diem and to assess the regime's ability to withstand an intensifying Communist insurgency. On his return, Johnson expressed alarm at the situation but applauded Diem's leadership qualities – calling him the "Churchill of Asia" – and proposed that with greater US support, he could provide a "pole of attraction for the countries of Southeast Asia."[10] Kennedy greeted Johnson's suggestion that intervention was needed "with a great deal of impatience" even while he expanded US assistance to Vietnam.[11] At the time, McNamara supported robust backing of the Diem regime and explained to the House of Representative's Committee on Foreign Affairs, "You ask how much effort should we put in to stem the flow and march of Communism in that area and I would reply whatever effort is required."[12]

To some extent, McNamara's strong statements were a product of the administration's lack of strategy for Vietnam. The Vietnam problem had not preoccupied the administration and so it had chosen instead to follow the path of least immediate resistance, namely to continue to define the conflict in Vietnam in terms it had inherited from Eisenhower.[13] The commitment to President Diem and South Vietnam's independence went unquestioned, and, just as Eisenhower had described in his landmark "domino theory" speech, the conflict was defined principally as one of Communist aggression.[14]

However, even as US assistance expanded, the situation on the ground continued to deteriorate. Within the administration, a consensus was emerging that the Defense Department should prepare for a more active military role for the United States. In this context, in November 1961, Kennedy sent two more advisors to Vietnam: Maxwell Taylor, who was then still the President's military advisor, and Walt Rostow, McGeorge Bundy's deputy at the NSC and a noted economist and modernization theorist. Kennedy's instructions for them reflected the administration's ambivalence over Vietnam: on the one hand, he asked them to consider "how we organize the execution of this program" while also asking "is the US commitment to prevent the fall of South Vietnam to Communism a public act or an internal policy decision of the US Government?"[15] In other words, the trip's objective was two-fold: to ascertain whether the administration should commit itself to the fate of South Vietnam and, separately, what it could do in either scenario to improve the situation on the ground.

From the outset, Kennedy and Sorensen expressed reservations over a stronger military role. Sorensen wrote that "we need to think" before sending combat troops, including about "whether US troops can accomplish much more in the mud and the mountains than Vietnamese troops (who could be better trained, supported and directed)."[16] Similarly, Taylor noted that Kennedy's instructions were that he "should bear in mind that the initial responsibility of the effective maintenance of the independence of South Vietnam rested with the people and the government of that country. This was not something that the United States should take over and deal with unilaterally."[17]

Despite this note of caution, Taylor and Rostow returned from Vietnam with a host of recommendations for improving and expanding the assistance program, including replacing Ambassador Frederick Nolting with someone "like [veteran diplomat Averell] Harriman," expanding the defoliation program, deploying more air support and, crucially, introducing troops using the cover of floods that had been battering the country.[18] The Commander of the Military Assistance Advisory Group (MAAG) Lt. General Lionel C. McGarr in Vietnam and the Commander in Chief of the Pacific Command (CINCPAC) Admiral Harry D. Felt had first suggested the floods as "excellent opportunity to minimize adverse publicity" for introducing troops.[19] At the same time, knowing the President's reservations, Taylor reassured Kennedy that "this force is not proposed to clear the jungles and forests of VC [Viet Cong] guerrilla. That should be the primary task of the armed forces of Vietnam from which they should be specifically organized, trained and stiffened with ample advisors down to the battalion level."[20]

Although McGeorge Bundy had warned Taylor not to share his views publicly, "especially those relating to US forces,"[21] he and others in the administration were receptive to the idea of troops. Bundy himself told the President, "I believe we should commit limited US combat units, if necessary for military purposes (not for morale) to help South Vietnam," and agreed with Rusk and McNamara that a "military man" rather than a civilian ambassador should be put in charge of the country team.[22]

The State Department agreed. Deputy Undersecretary of State U. Alexis Johnson wrote that the government should "take the decision to commit ourselves to the objective of preventing the fall of South Vietnam" knowing that the introduction of "US and other SEATO [Southeast Asia Treaty Organization] forces may be necessary to achieve that objective."[23]

McNamara initially supported the conclusions of the report and suggested that the administration should send a "strong signal to the other side," even if introducing troops threatened to create greater commitments down the road. He even estimated that this could balloon into as many as 205,000 troops.[24] However, by November 11, he made a revealing volte-face and instead agreed with the President that troops should be only a last resort.[25] Where some see a "vacillation"[26] on McNamara's part, it is more likely, as the *Pentagon Papers* have suggested, that presidential instructions or nudging explain his change of opinion. McNamara turned around in order to defend the President's view or at least a view Kennedy wanted represented within the bureaucracy.[27] Nitze's notes from the meeting where the Taylor report was discussed are informative. In them, Nitze wrote that Kennedy commented, "Don't say we commit. Don't want to put troops in."[28]

In the months that followed, and as he assumed a leadership role on Vietnam policy, McNamara pushed this view more aggressively throughout the bureaucracy. By December 1961, he was redacting Kennedy's letters to Diem to ensure that no open-ended commitment was provided for the remainder of the Kennedy administration. For example, a key line that promised "the needs of your embattled nation will be met" was deleted.[29]

As he had done within the OSD, McNamara took charge by also changing organizational structures and the people that staffed them. Some of the staff changes were under his control; others were part of a broader administration reshuffle. Two advisors were sidelined because they were considered to be too close to the Diem regime and associated to past, failing policies. The first was Edward Lansdale, a former OSS officer in Vietnam and friend of Diem's who had been active on the Task Force on Vietnam. He was also eclipsed because McNamara "did not like him."[30] The second was Ambassador Nolting, who was sidelined before Henry Cabot Lodge eventually replaced him in 1963.[31]

Lodge was an interesting choice as he had been Kennedy's political opponent for the Massachusetts Senate seat in 1952 and again as vice presidential candidate on the Nixon ticket in 1960. Although the administration insisted that Lodge's appointment did "not have political significance" and that Rusk alone had made the decision, neither is likely.[32] McGeorge Bundy's notes from a later meeting when problems in Vietnam became particularly acute suggest that Lodge provided useful political cover against Republican criticism: "put it on Lodge," Bundy wrote and underlined several times.[33]

Moreover, in November 1961, in a government reshuffle dubbed the "Thanksgiving Massacre," key hawks were removed from positions of influence on Vietnam as the administration moved to "bring more people who understand the Kennedy policies and believe in them."[34] Walt Rostow, the Deputy National Security Advisor, who had sparked a governmental debate by proposing the introduction of ground troops to Vietnam, became head of the State Department's Policy Planning Council.[35] At the CIA, John McCone replaced Allen Dulles and immediately worked on improving cooperation with the OSD. Averell Harriman, who as Ambassador at Large had overseen negotiations on Laos, became Assistant Secretary for the Far East. Later, Arthur Schlesinger described how the notoriously overpowering and impatient Harriman "gave Far Eastern policy a coherence and force it had not had for years [and] rapidly became the particular champion of the New Frontier within the State Department."[36]

On the military side, things also changed rapidly. First, the Taylor–Rostow report provided added impetus to McNamara's support for creating a command rather than the MAAG, a more technical and informal arrangement, that currently existed. Acting on other recommendations in the report, McNamara increased assistance programs including Project Farm Gate, which aimed to use air power for guerrilla warfare including through defoliation. Second, Rostow added to growing criticism of McGarr's ability to manage the mounting US presence. He wrote to President Kennedy that he "believe[d] that all the choppers and other gadgetry we can supply South Vietnam will not buy time and render their resources effective if we do not get a first class man out there to replace McGarr."[37] By February 1962, the MAAG and McGarr had been replaced with the Military Assistance Command – Vietnam (MACV) led by General Paul Harkins, a Maxwell Taylor protégé. McNamara pitched Harkins to Kennedy arguing that the "JCS consider him an imaginative officer, fully qualified to fill what I consider to be the most difficult job in the US Army."[38]

Kennedy's civilian advisors understood the risk inherent in creating MACV with a designated four-star general at its helm and in incrementally strengthening its powers. With troop numbers rising from an early low of 3,000 in 1961 to more than 12,000 by 1962, the organizational change could be perceived, as Admiral Felt described it, as a "theater buildup for the entire Southeast Asia."[39] Civilian advisors worried that military commanders might view the creation of MACV as a concession to their plans to "be ready for whatever action they may decide it necessary to take."[40] The embassy in Saigon warned that "this is essentially a political job in the broadest sense, and should be organized and run as such" and cautioned that the "vigor in the Department of Defense in this situation needs to be matched by equal vigor in the non-military aspects if the proper proportions are to be maintained in our total effort there."[41]

The civilian advisors were also concerned that by centralizing authority under MACV, US strategy in Vietnam might shift toward a conventional military position. In April 1962, for instance, Robert Komer wrote to McGeorge Bundy and Taylor questioning whether the Defense Department was well suited to assume responsibility for policing functions and counseled that the United States should "guard against over-militarizing our counterinsurgency effort." He added that the military had "no greater expertise than cops recruited by [US]AID/CIA, indeed less," and that putting these activities under DOD control "risk[ed] the same thing that occurred in [US]AID – the program is so small compared to the main function of the agency that it gets lost in the wash." He concluded, "We don't want a bunch of colonels running programs in which they have no particular expertise."[42] Rufus Phillips, the head of USAID in Saigon, who was also a former CIA official in the country, had in fact threatened to resign over these concerns: he worried that DOD command produced inefficiencies, delays and impeded the necessary flexibility for counterinsurgency.[43]

However, by January 1962, it was the JCS, not McNamara, who were encouraging the introduction of ground troops and a more conventional reading of the conflict in Vietnam. The JCS argued for "all actions necessary to defeat communist aggression" and warned that losing South Vietnam could lead to "communist domination of all of the Southeast Asian mainland" and that "SEATO [would] cease to exist." Crucially, whereas he had been receptive to ground troops requests in the past, McNamara now forwarded the recommendations to the President with a cover letter that said that he was "not prepared to endorse" it.[44] McNamara sounded more like Komer and Phillips. In a speech delivered in February 1962, as MACV was being established, he struck a note of caution, saying, "Combating guerrilla warfare demands more in ingenuity than in money or manpower."[45]

By early 1962, McNamara's attention turned to counterinsurgency strategies coming from the field and Washington that promised to achieve the two objectives that President Kennedy had laid out after the Taylor–Rostow report, namely limiting the US government's commitment to South Vietnam and avoiding the introduction of ground troops. As the number of troops grew, it became all the more urgent to define what exactly these troops could or could not do and what their exact objective was; in other words, to develop a strategy.

Concurrently, the administration matured in its organizational arrangements for counterinsurgency, most notably with the creation of the Special Group (CI). In its first month of existence, the Special Group received a document that Hilsman had drafted, entitled the "Strategic Concept for South Vietnam." The paper was specifically designed to produce a counterinsurgency strategy for Vietnam as an alternative to the application of military force. Hilsman, a West Point–educated counterinsurgency expert, had been with the OSS behind enemy lines in Burma and later had become a speechwriter for Senator Kennedy. Together with Harriman, his mentor, who had been promoted with the "Thanksgiving Massacre," Hilsman tried to regain State control of Vietnam policy in the early months of 1962.

At the OSD, ISA replaced Gilpatric in coordinating Vietnam policy and eventually oversaw each successive draft of the CPSVN from 1962 to 1963. From McNamara's bureaucratic vantage point, the administration's Vietnam policies were now beginning to work as they should: strategic guidance was coming from the State Department and the White House, and ISA was organizing requisite defense tools. However, since ISA was also responsible for the department's aid program, economic and budgetary considerations inevitably colored their decisions.

All in all, 1962 was a boom time for counterinsurgency intellectuals in Washington. Not only had they sparked the President's interest, but on Vietnam, they found an unlikely ally in Secretary McNamara. He embraced the opportunity to test new tools and techniques for fighting limited wars in the developing world not least because they seemed to provide an economical alternative to conventional deployments. On the one hand, the counterinsurgency experts were concerned about the militarization of field operations. On the other, McNamara was concerned about the ballooning costs of Vietnam operations. Both sets of concerns coalesced in the spring of 1962 and were addressed in the CPSVN that promised to refocus and reduce the US mission in Vietnam.

McNamara's calendar provides insight into the people who may have influenced his understanding of counterinsurgency theory. At the start of April 1962, he met with Robert Thompson twice – one meeting lasted five hours and another for three hours, an unusually long time for someone who customarily scheduled, at most, forty minutes for his meetings.[46] Thompson, a British counterinsurgency expert with experience suppressing the Malayan insurgency, advised the US government on its policies in Vietnam through the British Advisory Mission in Vietnam (BRIAM). He became increasingly prominent as he bypassed US officials in the field and consulted closely with both the Task Force on Vietnam and with Robert McNamara directly. McNamara described Thompson as "somewhat of a legend,"[47] while the British Ambassador to Washington David Ormsby-Gore, who was also an old friend of Kennedy's, noted "how much weight the President attached to Mr. Thompson's views upon the situation in Viet Nam."[48]

In the spring of 1962, as Hilsman presented his "Strategic Concept," Thompson produced his own "Delta Pacification Plan." In it, he stressed the need to have "largely civilian rather than military" advisors at the local level and a greater focus on development.[49] For Hilsman, the plans were explicitly designed to short-circuit what he saw as the militarization of the administration's Vietnam policy. For much of 1962, the administration refined its counterinsurgency strategies, and in July 1962, McNamara began setting an end date for winding down the Defense Department's presence in Vietnam altogether.

As Hilsman noted in a footnote to his plan for South Vietnam, which went through a number of versions between January and March 1962, "The basic approach followed in this plan was developed by Mr. R.G.K. Thompson." The *Pentagon Papers* go further and describe his report as "an unabashed restatement of most of Thompson's major points toward which President Kennedy had, not incidentally, already expressed a favorable disposition."[50] The Foreign Office came to a similar conclusion, noting first that Hilsman's "basic concept owes a great deal to Thompson, with whom he had a long talk while in Saigon" and, second, that the reason McNamara did not much care for Hilsman was that he was "not the most modest of men and is inclined to overrate his own abilities."[51]

However, McNamara paid attention to Thompson as well as to Bernard Fall, another source of inspiration for Hilsman and one of the few people McNamara acknowledged had "educated" him on Vietnam. According to McNamara, Fall was "the best" journalist in South Vietnam.[52] In an anonymous article published in March 1962 that Hilsman widely circulated in the State and Defense Departments, Fall complained that the "United States seeks to win the struggle by mechanical means (helicopters and weed killers) forgetting all over again that a revolutionary war can be won only if the little people in the villages and the hills can be persuaded that they have a stake in fighting on our side."[53]

At their core, Thompson's "Delta Pacification Plan" and Hilsman's "Strategic Concept" made similar recommendations although they diverged on emphasis: Hilsman focused relatively more on civic action and security, while Thompson emphasized strengthening political and administrative structures.[54] Still, they found common ground in the recommendation that South Vietnamese forces, and their American assistants, should focus on guerrilla rather than conventional tactics and push the strategic hamlets program.

In March 1962, with great fanfare, Diem launched Operation Sunrise with the strategic hamlets program at its core. As the "cornerstone" of the counterinsurgency strategy in Vietnam, the strategic hamlets program was designed to produce secure villages where peasants would be separated from the Vietcong by applying the "oil spot" theory of expanding security on the basis of military operations designed to "clear and hold."[55] The gist of "clear and hold" was that military forces should secure an area and extend the "safe" area outward rather than the alternative "search and destroy," which relied on targeted and temporary military engagements.[56] In practice, the strategic hamlets program became a loosely defined rubric where many different agencies dumped their programs.

Both Hilsman and Thompson foresaw some of the main problems that arose when theories are translated into practice. First and foremost, they complained about the lack of civilian-military coordination in Vietnam, a prerequisite for a successful counterinsurgency strategy.[57] Second, Hilsman argued that American military culture was incompatible with the program in Vietnam, and the military's role should therefore be reduced. "MAAG's Jungle Jim and military forces tend to follow tactics more appropriate to conventional, World War II situations than to guerrilla warfare," he wrote.[58] He later explained, "My major policy was to get MACV out of business, that Americans couldn't do anything but advise Diem. This is what it finally came down to."[59]

By the summer of 1962, the administration's counterinsurgency strategies seemed on track in Vietnam, and Michael Forrestal from the NSC staff wrote to Kennedy, "While we cannot yet sit back in the confidence that the job is well in hand, nevertheless it does appear that we have finally developed a series of techniques which, if properly applied, do seem to produce results."[60] However, by December, after a flurry of official visits to Vietnam, Forrestal and Hilsman expressed concern over confusion in the field. In their trip report, they asked, "Is there a plan? This answer is no. There are five or six plans many of which are competing. There is consequently great confusion."[61] As a result, at his American advisors' behest, by the end of the year, Diem consolidated existing plans into a National Campaign Plan (NCP) that matched the CPSVN timetable.

Overall, as the administration moved into 1963, the signs were not good. The new year began with a humiliating defeat for the South Vietnamese forces in Ap Bac. Questions were raised about field reporting, about the ability of the South Vietnamese to fight despite all the assistance they had received and also about the team assembled on the field. Despite these concerns, McNamara instructed the JCS to accelerate the CPSVN timetable for the handover of responsibilities to the South Vietnamese. In the spring of 1963, things got worse as the Catholic Diem regime began a violent crackdown against the Buddhist community, provoking nationwide unrest as well as an angry backlash in the United States. Congressional figures began to describe the country as a "quasi-fascist" state as the Diem regime remained entirely unresponsive to the Kennedy administration's requests for political reform.[62] One of the earliest emblematic images of the Vietnam conflict emerged at this time: the "Buddhist crisis" was seared into the collective consciousness of Americans when a monk set himself on fire in a sign of protest. In May 1962, against this backdrop of increasing tension, McNamara requested and received his second draft of the CPSVN, which proposed an even shorter time frame for withdrawal.

Instead of throwing McNamara's plans off-course, the events in South Vietnam seemed to strengthen his determination to continue to centralize programs and authority under the Defense Department and to move forward with the CPSVN. By July 1963, MACV either ran or coordinated virtually all the programs in South Vietnam. In addition, McNamara moved even more aggressively to make clear that the end goals were to help the South Vietnamese fight *their* war and to insist that it was an insurgency rather than a full-scale conventional war. The overarching objective of each version of the CPSVN and the public announcement in October 1963 was to "prepare the Vietnamese to assume full responsibility by December 1965" with a "withdrawal of all US special assistance units and personnel by that date."[63]

What exactly the South Vietnamese took "full responsibility" for evolved. Earlier drafts recognized a limited external threat in addition to an insurgency; later drafts identified the threat of an insurgency alone. Defining the conflict only as an insurgency had implications for troop planning of US and South Vietnamese forces. As long as the conflict in Vietnam was defined as a conventional engagement where the United States had a major responsibility, engagement was inherently open-ended and produced risks of escalation as battlefield failures led to continued demands for ever-growing force deployments. By setting out clear parameters in October 1963 that the peak of US strength had now been met,[64] the CPSVN sought both to put a break on the escalatory momentum and to halt continued requests for troop strength increases in Vietnam.

Ultimately, Hilsman's greatest ally, whether by design or chance, was McNamara. Whether or not McNamara had concluded that US military culture was "incompatible" with the situation in Vietnam, as Hilsman had done, is not clear. What is clear is that he was concerned with the military's unwillingness to break out of traditional frameworks, that on Vietnam, as in other areas of defense policy, he felt a large doctrinal gap between civilian and military advisors, and as a result, he became increasingly involved in dictating strategy, an area that was traditionally reserved for military commanders.

For instance, in January 1962, as if to confirm Hilsman's fears, the Chiefs reported to the President that "any war in the Southeast Asia mainland will be a peninsula and island-type of campaign – a mode of warfare in which all the elements of the Armed Forces of the United States have gained a wealth of experience and in which we have excelled both in World War II and in Korea."[65] Again, in March 1962, LeMay disregarded McNamara's instructions to focus on clear-and-hold operations and strategic hamlets, dismissing them as "too defensive" and requesting instead that the Air Force be granted fighter jets.[66]

Similarly, in November 1962, US Army Chief of Staff Earle "Bus" Wheeler made a speech in which he noted: "It is fashionable in some quarters to say the problems in Southeast Asia are primarily political or economic, rather than military. I do not agree. The essence of the problem in Vietnam is military."[67] This could not have been more at odds with the official administration policy and, as a result, spurred a flurry of angry memos among Kennedy's advisors, with Hilsman leading the charge.[68] Wheeler was evidently slapped on the wrist for his speech because within months, on a visit to Vietnam, he made a completely different statement and emphasized that "military actions would not be enough to win the war" and the centrality of the strategic hamlets program to this end.[69]

Faced with the Chiefs' "blinkered pursuit of conventional objectives,"[70] McNamara regularly reminded them and Admiral Felt that they were dealing with subversion and not the conventional military threats that they felt prepared to handle.[71] This frustrating back-and-forth troubled Kennedy, who "privately complained that everybody . . . seemed to be forgetting that our role in Vietnam should be political rather than military."[72] Moreover, although the CPSVN specifically indicated that operations should focus on "clear and hold," the services dragged their feet. Hilsman or one of his colleagues at INR angrily annotated one memo from CINCPAC in February 1963 with the following comment: "The number of clear and hold operations for 1962 would not exceed (and probably less than) 15, while the number of search and release operations for last year would probably exceed 100!!"[73]

Aside from these conceptual differences, McNamara was also concerned that bureaucratic divisions along service and civilian-military lines were hampering the administration's strategy in Vietnam. As Thompson and Hilsman observed, the success of the strategy depended on successful inter-agency cooperation. In May 1962, one report from the field read: "we have too many cooks busy spoiling the broth – there are military agencies: Army, Air Force and Navy as well as State Department and other civilian groups all in the area: USIA, CIA, [US]AID, etc. There is no unified command and no comprehensive planning."[74] In his October 1963 report, McNamara concluded that MACV's principal objective of producing a better-coordinated policy on the ground was not succeeding. Early hopes about the "unparalleled opportunities" to create a template of "functioning inter-agency and international effort" in Vietnam that could "serve as guidance in other free world struggles"[75] floundered on the fact that not even Ambassador Lodge and General Harkins, who had been good friends back in Massachusetts, could successfully cooperate. By November 1963, a White House meeting concluded that "there is no country team in Vietnam at the present time in any real sense."[76]

Service rivalries also began to emerge. In particular, there were complaints that MACV was Army-dominated, mirroring charges in Washington that the administration's new defense policies favored the Army over the other services. McNamara himself conceded that while the "primary responsibility in these areas lies with the Army," it was important to expose other services, and especially the Marines and Air Force, to the experience as well.[77] Nevertheless, by the end of 1963, of the

16,000 troops on the field, 10,100 were Army troops; and of the five general officers in key positions, only one was from the Air Force.[78] Army officials were also prone to making "derogatory comments" about Air Force overtures to become involved in counterinsurgency, a field they felt "had always been primarily Army."[79]

To some extent, the Army's experience in counterinsurgency was irrelevant to service Chiefs who believed that a conventional war was around the corner. In the spring of 1962, even General Taylor joined the chorus of military advisors who believed that the "point could quickly come when the VC would come out to fight something resembling a conventional war."[80] Furthermore, in a critical report, the Army itself admitted, "We seem to be still trying to counter insurgency with tools and methods applicable to a conventional war," though it noted, "The Army is nonetheless considerably ahead of the Air Force. They insist on applying the wrong tools in the wrong way."[81]

Inter-service rivalries also loomed large on the use of Vietnam as a testing ground for counterinsurgency. In keeping with his interest in counterinsurgency, Kennedy viewed Vietnam as an ideal "training laboratory"[82] and urged the services to "expose [their] most promising officers to the experience of service there." He "directed that the Services make [Vietnam] a laboratory both for training our people, and for learning the things that we need to know to successfully compete" in what he saw as the "future of war."[83] Rotations in Vietnam became prerequisites for Army promotions and were especially important for the Special Forces. Vietnam taught them to work in fully unconventional "wars of national liberation" contexts, precisely the kind of situation Kennedy wanted them prepared for.[84] The chairman of the Joint Chiefs of Staff chimed in and noted the importance of using "Vietnam in particular, and Southeast Asia in general, as a 'laboratory' for the improvement of US counterinsurgency and remote area conflict capability," something he felt was "very much in the national interest."[85]

In April 1961, in order to "test new techniques," the administration had set up a Combat Development Test Center (CDTC) in South Vietnam as part of a program called Project Agile run out of the Defense Department's Advanced Research Projects Agency (ARPA). By January 1962, the center also reported to the newly created Special Group (CI), and although the center combined military and civilian experts, it reported to the Secretary of Defense and to MACV on its military activities. The center oversaw the testing of a range of more or less controversial tools that included using dogs and high-powered voice amplifiers in the strategic hamlets as well as the more contentious use of herbicides.[86] By September 1962, the Army set up its own test unit center, and three months later, the Air Force did the same.[87]

As a result, by the end of 1962, both CINCPAC and the JCS were expressing concern "about the proliferation of such activities." Not only were the services competing over programs; they also seemed to be bypassing CINCPAC's authority. In keeping with Eisenhower's reforms to command structures, MACV was meant to coordinate operations in Vietnam and report to CINCPAC, which, in turn, reported to the Secretary of Defense. The services, which were no longer meant to have operational responsibility, seemed to be reasserting themselves through the back door under the rubric of "testing." This was the subplot, so to speak, when CINCPAC voiced "concerned about the nature of the tests" that the Army was conducting and expressed "desires to keep tight control and monitory R&D activities in South Vietnam."[88] Ultimately, Admiral Felt and the JCS concluded that testing was spiraling out of control and detracting from the main objective. He recommended that it should therefore be scaled back.[89] By October 1963, experimentation was either reduced or transferred to Thailand and, according to the CPSVN, was being phased out altogether.[90]

Similarly, the CPSVN process addressed concerns over the proliferation of militias and paramilitary forces in South Vietnam. By 1962, MACV oversaw Civil Guard (CG) and Self-Defense Corps (SDC) as well as the hamlet militia, which were charged with more traditional security concerns in the villages as an adjunct to the South Vietnamese Army forces (ARVN). In addition, under the Civilian Irregular Defense Group (CIDG) program, Special Forces under CIA command oversaw an even greater number of forces, many of which played on the country's ethnic and religious divisions. For instance, the Trailwatchers, a force that operated along the Laos and Cambodia borders, drew primarily from the Montagnard minority, while other forces played on Catholic allegiances, including the so-called Catholic Youth and Fighting Fathers forces.

William Colby, the CIA Station Chief who oversaw many of these forces, complained that they lacked order, control and coherence and were wasteful.[91] The CIA could not afford the costs associated with the "rapidly expanding operations."[92] Moreover, the Army began to express anger that its Special Forces, "probably the most mature and best-trained in the Army [were] employed in providing basic training to Vietnamese recruits" and that they were still operating under CIA command while the

Army was running its own parallel programs in Vietnam.[93] For all these reasons, Colby welcomed the decision in July 1962, as part of the CPSVN process, to centralize paramilitary forces under MACV command as part of Operation Switchback and to wind down their numbers in subsequent years. Bringing the Special Forces and their programs within the remit of MACV served, first, to centralize disparate operations around the country in way that promised greater operational coherence and coordination and, second, to secure their long-term financing.

Later versions of the CPSVN also wound down the use of air power on the battlefield, a victory for the counterinsurgency experts over their military counterparts and indeed over its champion McNamara. The gap between the Chiefs and counterinsurgency experts was perhaps at its widest over the use of air power and especially defoliants in Vietnam. McNamara's position in this debate is instructive and illustrates how he did not fit along binary notions of hawks and doves. Although he argued for winding down the US presence in Vietnam, on the one hand, he was enthusiastic about the use of new technology there. He took this position not least because it promised to be relatively cheap and because the South Vietnamese could be trained relatively quickly to use it themselves. He was less attuned to humanitarian concerns over the use of herbicides. When he did push to draw back the program, it was part of a general winding down of the US presence and a tightening of operations in Vietnam.

McNamara had been an early proponent of using air power in Vietnam when the program began in earnest after the Taylor–Rostow report was submitted. One official history has suggested that his enthusiasm for its use derived from the fact that he "could quantify results."[94] Michael Forrestal at the NSC, who opposed the program, wrote, "The main train of thinking was that you cannot say no to your military advisors all the time and, with this I agree."[95] But McNamara had not had many qualms refusing his military advisors' input in the past. Instead, he wanted to prove that the Defense Department could make a valuable contribution to the new models of war fighting. Hilsman explained that to understand the bombing program "it is probably necessary to understand the peculiar stake of the Air Force as an organization," namely that it needed to prove its relevance for counterinsurgency.[96] However, this was true of the Defense Department as a whole: in the aftermath of the Ap Bac battle, Wheeler was dispatched to Vietnam specifically to try to identify how to "use air power in counterinsurgency operations."[97]

While the use of air power in Vietnam was divisive, the defoliation program was particularly so. In the spring of 1962, the administration felt compelled to issue press guidelines to the field about the "much publicized" use of herbicides. Harriman, his friend John Kenneth Galbraith, Hilsman and Forrestal were especially angry about the program as was USIA Director Edward Murrow, who warned that the administration would "pay dearly for [it] in terms of Asian opinion."[98] Confronted with Harkins and Felt's suggestion in December of 1962 to create open-fire zones along the Cambodian border, Harriman "question[ed] the use of airpower in counterinsurgency," complaining that "we must never forget that this is a political war" and reminding his colleagues that "French experience suggests, in fact, that air interdiction is not a useful concept in this kind of warfare."[99] The MAAG also warned that "the indiscriminate use of firepower, regardless of caliber, type or means of delivery cannot be condoned in counterinsurgency operations," that it "only serve[d] to push people into Viet Cong arms."[100]

Aside from its public relations aspects, the program's detractors questioned its military use. Reports from the field that circulated around Washington indicated that the program had achieved only limited success. One Army report bluntly noted that the "defoliation program is a failure. That's the official view now."[101] Chairman of the Joint Chiefs of Staff Lemnitzer remarked that results were "not impressive,"[102] while Harold Brown, McNamara's director of Defense Research and Engineering (DDR&E) who managed Project Agile, wrote that reports about the success of these programs were "overoptimistic."[103] Yet the program continued to be met with "the strong approval of Secretary McNamara, General Taylor" and "the field," which was primarily CINCPAC.[104] Well after he had received reports questioning the value of air operations, McNamara was still telling Kennedy that they were producing "excellent results" and recommending that he give Harkins "free reign."[105]

By November 1962, despite continued requests to continue if not expand the program from MACV, CINCPAC and McNamara, the detractors had convinced President Kennedy to cut back the program and ensure that it be "reoriented upon the original concept as soon as possible." Kennedy also required that each operation receive prior White House rather than OSD approval and that it demonstrate its "operational value."[106]

By the spring of 1963, McNamara had changed his position and was on board. As the CPSVN planning went ahead, the air units were the first to be withdrawn. The initial 1,000-man withdrawal increment included mostly air units, including a C-123 spray detachment and armed helicopters.[107] The President's instructions might have influenced McNamara's change of heart, but Thompson's trajectory on the issue of air power was also revelatory and helps to explain McNamara's about-face.

In April 1962, going against many field reports, Thompson remained generally favorable to the program. He argued that the "use of air in the form of helicopters, C-123 and attack planes" was "remarkably effective," while his only reservation over crop destruction was that "foreigners should not be actively involved." At the same time, he sounded a note of a caution and explained that "many so-called Viet Cong are not fighting for Communism" but instead nationalism that could be reinforced should they see "foreigners killing Vietnamese." In large part, the issue was a public relations one for Thompson, part of the "psychological and information activities" that he advocated and which recommended that foreigners should not be "at the sharp end" but instead should focus on "doctors, USOM [United States Operations Mission] people or civic action people who are handing out services or goods [who] cause no problem."[108]

However, a year later, Thompson had turned sharply on the issue and on a visit to Washington warned President Kennedy against relying on defoliants and air power more broadly. Now he "doubted that the effort involved in defoliation was worthwhile" because of the "automatic aversion of the Asians to the use of unknown chemicals." On air power, he said that, in the long term the "war would be won by brains and feet" rather than helicopters and that he was now "dead against" bombing "as this would leave an indissoluble legacy of bitterness."[109]

Looking back on the spring of 1962, as the contours of US policy for South Vietnam were defined under McNamara's leadership, Thompson's influence on the Secretary is remarkable. He informed McNamara's turn against the use of air power and defoliation and educated him on the counterinsurgency strategy that became enshrined in the CPSVN. However, McNamara welcomed Thompson and Hilsman's plans in the spring of 1962 because they dovetailed with his own managerial priorities. Limiting the US role in South Vietnam and moving away from a traditional military deployment was compatible with McNamara's proposed solutions for the administration's wider economic problems. To the counterinsurgency strategists, the CPSVN made sense from a military perspective; to McNamara, they also made sense from an economic and budgetary perspective.

5

When Military Problems Become Economic Problems

As Secretary of Defense, McNamara was concerned in equal parts with organizing defense policy and with economic and budgetary problems. As a result, it was inherent to his position that he would recognize the economic implications of chosen policies for South Vietnam sooner than most. His support for counterinsurgency strategies in the spring of 1962 coincided with important developments on the economic front and, as such, was conditioned as much by economic as military considerations. Internationally, the balance of payments and gold outflow problem became especially acute, and domestically, an activist Senate squeezed the budget that financed operations in Vietnam. Both contributed to a sense of urgency to move on the problems in South Vietnam in a way that would contain the problem and reduce its potential economic impact.

McNamara may have been, as David Halberstam described, the "can-do man in the can-do society in the can-do era,"[1] but by 1962, both he and Kennedy had become more modest. Their bruising experiences with the Bay of Pigs, the Berlin standoff and the Cuban Missile Crisis had had a sobering effect and brought home the United States' vulnerabilities, not least in its economic foundations.[2] By July 1962, at the same time that McNamara initiated his withdrawal plans from Vietnam, the balance of payments situation had reached a particularly alarming stage. As Dillon informed the President, "Whereas in 1961 only about one-third of our over-all deficit was reflected in a gold loss, so far in 1962 almost 60 percent of our deficit has been reflected in gold losses."[3] Moreover, these

developments happened against the backdrop of a weak domestic economic picture. In June 1962, in the second largest financial crash on
record, the US stock market had lost a quarter of its value just as the
economy was beginning to recover from a lingering recession that kept
unemployment figures around the 6 percent mark.

For the Kennedy administration, this looked like a perfect storm. As
David Rockefeller had suggested to the President, the "time honored" and
easy method to get claimants to hold their dollars would have been to
increase interest rates, but this was not possible for an administration that
had pledged to kick-start the economy in the face of a recession.[4] In 1961,
the Treasury introduced a gimmick that reconciled competing interest rate
needs. It was called Operation Twist. As the name suggests, it twisted the
interest rates to keep long-term interest rates low but short-term interest
rates high. On gold, Dillon used his clout as someone "known in Europe"
to create the London Gold Pool at the end of 1961 whereby the United
States, together with seven European countries, agreed to collaborate on a
joint gold pool to prevent prices from going up as they had during the
"gold flutter of 1960." In addition, in July 1963, the administration
passed the Interest Equalization Tax, which essentially taxed US investments in foreign countries. Combined with other "buy American" programs, by 1963 the administration seemed to have created a complete
program to address its economic concerns. However, all of these steps
and the suggestion from Rockefeller and others that the administration
should boost trade could not ultimately compensate for the fact that it
was not trade but defense installations abroad that drove the balance of
payments deficit.

John Kenneth Galbraith's letters to Kennedy shed light onto the type of
considerations that informed McNamara's proposed solutions and his
decision to focus on troop withdrawals, including in Vietnam. In April
1962, McNamara met with Galbraith for three hours. They knew each
other well: they had met while McNamara was teaching at Harvard
University and had collaborated on a book on corporate structures when
McNamara was at the Ford Motor Company. (The only longer meeting
during this period was with Robert Thompson.[5])

After his meeting with McNamara, Galbraith wrote to President
Kennedy that they were in "basic agreement" over Vietnam. Galbraith
and his friend Harriman were part of a vocal minority of civilian advisors
who argued that the United States was entering into a continuum of
external aggression in Vietnam that was doomed to fail.[6] Although
McNamara shied away from making this kind of sweeping geopolitical

judgment, he knew and respected Galbraith's judgment and would have agreed with another letter where Galbraith warned:

Our present deployment is based on tradition, accident, the mystique of conventional force, and the recurrent feeling that, in the absence of any other feasible lines of action, the movement of troops might help. (I hasten to allow for rational factors as well.) On the whole dollars have not entered the calculation at least until lately. It is much better that they enter as a consideration now than on some subsequent day when we run out. At least why not have a high-powered team draw up a deployment strategy designed to minimize the dollar outlays. The logistical framework and small forces would remain forward. Behind our dollar account would be the troops (and their families) with great emphasis on mobility and air-lift. We might, as compared for example with the sterile commitment in Korea, find it a lot better.

In the same letter, Galbraith attacked the aid program to Formosa and Korea and wondered how "economical" these were and whether the United States was funding "excessively expensive military establishments."[7] Returning to the dollar and gold outflow problem, he cautioned, "We should remind ourselves that our commitments here were established when dollars were plentiful. A dollar shortage would have been good for [Eisenhower's Secretary of State] Mr. [John Foster] Dulles."[8]

Faced with a "dollar shortage," or at least a perceived one, Kennedy did what Galbraith suggested and on June 22, 1962, created a "high-powered team," the Cabinet Committee on Balance of Payments with Dillon as its chairman and McNamara as the driving bureaucratic force behind it. Not only were these two men among the most "high-powered" in the administration, they were also members of the Cabinet who interacted with Kennedy socially and were friends whom he trusted.

Within a month and with his habitual application, McNamara suggested a list of steps to reduce the Defense Department's impact on the balance of payments. These included encouraging the sale of US military equipment primarily to Europeans, coordinating in-country programs with USAID, and working toward removing any redundancies or inefficiencies in the field especially by urging regional countries (such as Japan) to shoulder a greater burden of the costs. In Vietnam, his recommendations coincided with Operation Switchback and the Defense Department's absorption of many of USAID's programs as well as the first draft of the CPSVN.

McNamara's reassessment of troop deployments ran in parallel to the CPSVN and accelerated at the same time as did the CPSVN. In July 1962, McNamara instructed the Joint Chiefs of Staff to produce a five-year deployment plan, an audit of sorts of existing bases abroad "with a view to eliminating all non-essential units," and asked that "this plan should be developed by country, by service, by unit, and fiscal year."[9] This came five days after he had asked for a first draft for the CPSVN. Later, in March 1963, Kennedy asked his advisors to "bring our accounts into balance in a shorter period of time" and that all USAID and Defense programs abroad should be examined on an urgent basis.[10] By April 1963, McNamara asked the JCS to further shorten the CPSVN's phaseout timeline while he also produced a new report for the Cabinet Committee where he described measures aimed out "thinning out our deployments."[11]

In Vietnam as elsewhere, McNamara rationalized many of the troop withdrawals using Galbraith's exact logic, namely that the Defense Department's heavy investments in air- and sealift had removed the need for massive forward positioning of troops. As he explained to Kennedy: "I do not believe the proposed force redeployments will weaken significantly our ability to respond to Communist aggression. The increase in the procurement of Army equipment, airlift aircraft, and the increase in the ferry range of such aircraft have greatly increased our ability to deploy both air and ground forces from the US to theaters of operation within a period of strategic warning."[12]

As part of his reforms at the Defense Department, McNamara had stepped up investments in strategic lift capabilities and initiated a series of exercises culminating in the Big Lift exercise in the fall of 1963, whose purpose was "to test our system" but also to "demonstrate dramatically our redeployment capabilities to our Allies and to the Soviets."[13] In other words, the exercises were designed to reassure allies that technological advances, which would allow for the rapid deployment of troops in the event of a crisis, could offset prospective troop withdrawals. As a result, by the end of 1963, following the logic of cost cutting, the Comptroller projected a worldwide troop reduction of 15 percent over two calendar years.[14]

As Francis Gavin has shown, in Europe the underlying rationale for troop withdrawals was essentially one of fairness: that Europeans should shoulder a greater share of the burden for their own security especially given the new, stated defense policy of flexible response. Kennedy was particularly harsh with European allies. In notes from a December 1961 meeting with the JCS in Palm Beach, Kennedy predicted that the administration would "face the question in 1963" but maintained that he "always felt we could force the Europeans to do more by pulling some of our forces out."[15] In the absence of real movement on that front, Kennedy returned to his criticism of European countries in 1963. In Hilsman's notes of a private meeting, Kennedy complained, "We have to make

Europe pick up their burden. Ridiculous that they are not doing their part. We have pursued a very generous policy in the past. We have to get tougher about this. We must keep our economic house in order."[16]

On the other hand, European states – especially Western Germany and France – also had significant leverage over the United States as they were major holders of dollar reserves.[17] Throughout 1962, going hand in hand with negotiations on troop withdrawals, McNamara accelerated a program of military equipment sales to European countries designed to "offset" the balance of payments deficit.[18] He launched a "buy American" program, reducing local purchases at the defense installations abroad, and he repatriated dependents or support staff in many of the bloated defense installations. These programs were especially successful in Germany and Italy: by 1963, the cost of the US presence in these countries had almost entirely been offset.[19]

In Asia, the dynamic was different. Here, in the preceding decade "Mr. Dulles" had fixed the United States to a number of expensive and "sterile commitments," which Dillon and McNamara argued were more expensive than needed. Therefore, McNamara's priority was to unstick open-ended and growing commitments and to favor instead a greater burden-sharing arrangement that presaged what would become the Nixon Doctrine in the 1970s.[20] Galbraith and McNamara were concerned with the impact of European military alliances on the balance of payments, but their criticisms were particularly scathing in Asia.

For both Galbraith and McNamara, the commitment to Korea was the most outdated and disproportionately expensive. Whereas by 1963 Japan had transitioned to an economic state where the administration could reasonably conclude that it "must depend more on its own self-defense capabilities in the future,"[21] Korea appeared to be stuck in a position of dependence. By June 1963, McNamara wrote to Kennedy: "I believe we should prepare plans for a time-phased reduction of US Army forces in the ROK [Republic of Korea] from 52,400 to about 17,000 by the end of CY65 and a reduction in ROK ground forces from 536,00 to 450,000 by the end of CY67. If this reduction were accomplished, the MAP [Military Assistance Plan] for Korea could be reduced from the $200 million level programmed for FY64 to an annual level of no more than $150 million by FY68."[22] He noted that that with a programmed increase in airlift capability of 300 percent, troops could be redeployed quickly from the West Coast. Moreover, he justified a reduction of the military presence "in view of the Sino-Soviet split and the resulting picture of somewhat deteriorating Chinese Communist capabilities," presumably a euphemistic reference to Mao's Great Leap Forward's devastating effects on China's economy and society.[23]

However, whether in Europe or Asia, the State Department and Joint Chiefs of Staff stymied McNamara's troop withdrawal efforts. They argued that these were too politically explosive and that they potentially undermined the credibility of US commitments around the world. Even McNamara's more modest suggestion to remove dependents from overseas bases riled the Chiefs, who "consider[ed] this entirely unacceptable" and worried that it would strike a "mortal blow to recruiting and would be viewed as the last unbearable step in the subordination of military to civilian needs, with predictable consequences in Congressional outrage."[24]

Paul Nitze, the Secretary of the Navy, who had played a key part in the buildup in Korea as head of the Policy Planning Staff in the State Department from 1950 to 1953, argued that troop withdrawals were "simply impossible," especially in the Far East and Germany.[25] In part, his concern stemmed from a fear that troop reductions "would make it necessary for us to commit ourselves to an immediate nuclear response in the event of any serious threat in Korea and probably elsewhere in the Far East."[26] In other words, echoing Rusk's arguments against troop withdrawals in Europe, a confrontation could quickly become a nuclear exchange in the absence of another credible deterrent.

Meanwhile, George Ball, the Undersecretary of State for Economic Affairs, angrily wrote to his predecessor Dillon that publicly announcing redeployments for balance of payments reasons would be seen "as a sign of weakness" and warned of "grave dangers" in these "matters of life or death." More pointedly, he reminded Dillon that it would be "particularly unbecoming for the Kennedy administration to announce that it was adjusting its defense arrangement for balance of payments reasons, since the President played a leading role in '58 in chastising the Eisenhower administration for – as he put it – placing 'fiscal security ahead of national security.'"[27]

On October 3, 1963, the same day that the administration announced its phaseout plan from Vietnam, Rusk expressed his concerns about troop withdrawals to President Kennedy in dramatic terms. While he accepted that some withdrawals would be necessary, he argued that McNamara's plans for Korea and Japan as well as Europe would create "immense political problems which no amount of effectively devised and assiduously implemented diplomacy and public relations will be able to contravene." He ended ominously: "I would be derelict in my responsibility to you if I did not advise you that, in my considered judgment, the implementation of the DOD proposals . . . would be the gravest sort of mistake, fraught with adverse political and psychological consequences, perhaps out of all proportion to the intrinsic military significance but, nevertheless, carrying a real danger of jeopardizing our entire national security posture."[28]

Rusk's "firm[ness] in his unwillingness to accept any major force reductions"[29] had some impact: it stalled withdrawals from Korea and spurred European allies' efforts at offsetting US expenditures.[30] Also, in keeping with the State Department's objections, McNamara conceded that it was "entirely acceptable" to him that withdrawals, when they happened, should "not be presented as a 'package' implying US withdrawal from its commitment to maintain the integrity and freedom of the Free World" and that they should be done in a discrete fashion in order to give countries "no basis for believing that the program is forced upon us by our balance of payments position."[31] In November 1963, he instructed the JCS that while the plan was still to cut overseas deployments by 15 percent in the next two years, "wherever possible action of low visibility should be taken without public announcement."[32]

The OSD's planned troop withdrawals played an important part in the timing and scope of the withdrawal plans for Vietnam. In July 1963, as McNamara reviewed the "concerted effort during the past two years to reduce the net adverse balance of the Department of Defense transactions entering the international balance of payments," he could proudly point to impressive achievements and statistics, for instance, that "gross expenditures overseas less receipts, was reduced by approximately $850 million – from 2,334 million to 1,477." However, he also acknowledged that "political constraints" got in the way of even greater "successes."[33] One of the main producers of those constraints, George Ball, later reflected on McNamara's efforts: "Bob was prepared to distort any kind of policy in order to achieve some temporary alleviation to the balance of payments, which again to my mind was a function of his preoccupation with quantification."[34]

With the bureaucracy firmly against him, McNamara considered that the troop deployments in Europe and Korea had effectively become "fixed costs" for the time being and turned to controlling those, like Vietnam, that could still be considered "variable costs." Balance of payments issues were on McNamara's mind both before and after his key trip to Vietnam in October 1963. During the October 1963 NSC meetings, when National Security Advisor McGeorge Bundy asked McNamara "what

[was] the point" of announcing a phaseout, McNamara responded, "We need a way to get out of Vietnam. This is a way of doing it. And to leave forces there when they're not needed, I think is wasteful and complicates both their problems and ours."[35] For McNamara, the "waste" and "complications" related, in the short term, primarily to the beleaguered Military Assistance Program that financed Vietnam operations, and more broadly to the balance of payments deficit.

The day before McNamara left for Vietnam in September 1963, during a White House meeting on the balance of payments, he agreed that the DOD would develop "specific, detailed country proposals for reductions," the timing and tactics of which would be coordinated with State.[36] Although these reductions were primarily aimed at Europe, it is difficult to imagine that McNamara would not have applied the same cost-cutting logic to Vietnam on the eve of his departure especially since he had always applied broader fiscal considerations to US policy in Vietnam. Ultimately, troop withdrawals in Vietnam and elsewhere reflected McNamara's sentiment that the OSD "should ruthlessly eliminate all activities, the cost of which is not commensurate with their contribution to our national defense."[37]

In addition, troop withdrawals from Vietnam specifically chimed with a more economical strategy aimed at getting allies to assume a greater share of the responsibilities for their defense, or in his words, a strategy that recognized that the "proper support of indigenous forces on the scene would give a greater return to collective defense than additional US military forces."[38] McNamara supported a strategy of counterinsurgency and self-help because it promised an economically sustainable model for US leadership at a time when its responsibilities around the world were proliferating.

Ultimately, the administration's defense policy reflected its economic priorities and constraints. In Vietnam specifically, the chosen strategy reflected a sense of modesty born of a confrontation with new threats and challenges. Strategies that hinged on counterinsurgency were de facto cheaper as they did not rely on the same amount of logistical support as conventional deployments and because they presupposed self-help on the part of the countries battling the insurgency.

As a result, McNamara led efforts in the administration to redefine the problem in Vietnam in a way that could ensure a more limited commitment: as long as it was an internal, insurgency problem, it would not require the type of support and long-term commitment that he had inherited at the Defense Department for Korea. As Gilpatric remembered, while counterinsurgency was not necessarily McNamara's "dish of tea,"[39] he welcomed its economic implications as a more sustainable model for US leadership internationally and for the Defense Department specifically. It leveraged the department's new investments, notably in air- and sealift capabilities and in the Special Forces, without demanding the type of permanent stations abroad that drove the balance of payments deficit.

As he did with the Korea commitment, McNamara argued that new air and sealift capabilities removed the need for massive pre-positioning of troops in Vietnam. Following Alain Enthoven's advice, which was subsequently confirmed in a RAND report,[40] he held discussions to concentrate the Army's forces in "hubs" in Thailand and in the Philippines from which, if necessary, the United States could intervene in the case of outright aggression, in other words a conventional invasion of North Vietnamese forces.[41] The forces need not be in Vietnam; they could intervene from these "hubs."

In November 1961, at precisely the same time as he was receiving the Taylor–Rostow mission's recommendations to introduce ground troops into Vietnam, President Kennedy took up another, more modest theme in both his public and private pronouncements. In a speech delivered on November 16 at the centennial celebration of the University of Washington, Kennedy said, "We must face the fact, that the United States is neither omnipotent nor omniscient – that we are only 6 per cent of the world's population – that we cannot impose our will upon the other 94 per cent of mankind – that we cannot right every wrong or reverse each adversity – and that therefore there cannot be an American solution to every problem." He warned against those who "urge upon us what I regard to be the pathway to war ... If their view had prevailed, we would be at war today, and in more places than one." Also, he refused the polarizing tendency whereby "each side sees only 'hard' and 'soft' nations, hard and soft policies, hard and soft men. Neither side admits its path will lead to disaster – but neither can tell us how or where to draw the line once we descend the slippery slopes of either appeasement or intervention."[42]

While it is plausible that Kennedy's speech spoke to other issues or situations than the one in Vietnam, Arthur Schlesinger used the speech to subsequently explain that "he thought, and often said, that we were 'overcommitted' in Southeast Asia" and that he was "quite prepared to cut losses and never felt that he had to prove his manhood by irrational bellicosity."[43] Crucially, it was the views of advisors such as Sorensen

that prevailed on Vietnam strategy. On November 24, 1961, just a week
after the speech was delivered, Sorensen quoted directly from the University of Washington speech to make his case for Vietnam and against
Taylor's recommendations. He wrote to Kennedy: "this battle must be
won at the village level; and thus only the Vietnamese can defeat the VC,
we cannot do it for them. Troops of a different country, color and culture
are not as suitable and effective." As for the US role, "we can supply the
weapons, training and financing – no more should be needed" and, in a
line straight from the speech, he warned that "we are not omnipotent or
omniscient" and there "cannot be an American solution to every world
problem."[44]

Throughout his time in office, from the inaugural address onward,
Kennedy returned to the idea that the United States, like all countries,
faced constraints on what it could hope to achieve. In an interview in
December 1962, in which he assessed his first two years in office, Kennedy
described what he had learned about power and responsibility. He
remarked: "In the first place, I think the problems are more difficult than
I imagined they were. Secondly, there is a limitation upon the ability of the
United States to solve these problems ... There are greater limitations on
our ability to bring about a favorable result than I had imagined there
would be. And I think that's probably true of anyone who becomes
President."[45]

Although Sorensen and other colleagues may have perceived the problems in Vietnam as fundamentally military or political problems, in
reality, they were inextricably linked to economic realities. As the Defense
Department's Comptroller Hitch had written, "All military problems are,
in one of their aspects, economic problems in the efficient allocation and
use of resources."[46] When McNamara referred to "waste" in Vietnam or
when Galbraith spoke about the French precedent, they viewed the problem through their own economic lens.

In Galbraith's letter to Kennedy after meeting and being in "basic
agreement" with McNamara in April 1962, he wrote: "There is a conse-
quent danger we shall replace the French as the colonial force in the area
and bleed as the French did ... We should measurably reduce our
commitment ... [and] resist all steps which commit American troops to
combat action and impress upon all concerned the importance of keeping
American forces out of actual combat commitment ... Americans in their
various roles should be as invisible as the situation permits."[47] His
reflections speak to military strategy and specifically to preventing mili-
tarizing the US commitment, but what Galbraith, an economist, meant

when he wrote "bleed as the French" could presumably just as well have been an economic point.

As men like Galbraith and especially Dillon recalled, economic realities and decisions in the Treasury compelled the French withdrawal (and resulting American involvement) from Indochina in the 1950s. Echoing Hitch's remarks, Pierre Mendès-France, who as Prime Minister of France oversaw the country's withdrawal from Indochina, remarked, "Every problem eventually becomes a financial problem. Such was the situation in Indochina: it got off on the wrong foot politically, militarily and morally but its problems became especially acute on a budgetary level."[48] In the period of 1945–1954 when France eventually abandoned its colonial ambitions in Indochina, the war swallowed up over 10 percent of all state expenditures, and Mendès-France explicitly presented withdrawal as a way of getting French finances in order.[49]

Moreover, successive French governments had sought cost-cutting measures in Indochina by introducing very similar steps to those McNamara now encouraged. These included attempts to internationalize the war, using Special Forces–type units to train ethnic and religious minorities, and pursuing a policy of "self-help." The policy had a precursor in the French policy of *jaunissment*, or "yellowing," which shifted fighting responsibilities to local and regional troops. Moreover, France built up and trained national armies in each of the countries of Indochina as an alternative to deploying troops from continental France.[50]

Similarly, a decade later, for the United States, disengagement from Vietnam was part of a general trend that encouraged self-help in countries. In many ways, this policy of self-help, or relying on local forces, presaged the Nixon Doctrine's flagship program, Vietnamization. During the Kennedy administration, a policy of self-help in the developing world was a way of reconciling the existing economic constraints with the administration's interest in guerrilla warfare and wars of national liberation. The policy recalled Kennedy's inaugural address where he indicated that the administration would prioritize aid programs designed to help "people in the huts and villages of half the globe ... help them help themselves." Also, as McNamara explained while preparing his first budget, "The main responsibility against subversion and guerrilla warfare must rest on indigenous populations and forces, but given the great likelihood and seriousness of this threat, we must be prepared to make a substantial contribution in the form of forces trained in this type of warfare."[51]

A report on the administration's military assistance program explained how training geared toward self-help could fulfill a force multiplying function. It read, "Through military assistance, we have sought to strengthen the will and capacity of recipient countries to resist Communist aggression. We have pursued this objective largely by developing local forces for self-defense. And, by linking many of these forces in a system of regional alliances with US participation or pledged support, we have attempted to augment strength through joint defense activities." For guerrilla wars, the report further described that "A strong case can be made that internal security programs are cheaper and more effective where major a guerrilla threat does not already exist."[52]

In theory, the idea that local forces could be tied into regional networks was promising; in practice, it had limited success. Nevertheless, it formed the bedrock of the administration's policy for Southeast Asia. In a letter to Diem in October 1962, Kennedy wrote: "As Viet-Nam gains its victory over adversity and aggression, it will be in a position increasingly to devote its energies to achieving closer cooperation among the community of free Southeast Asian states. Each of these nations has its unique character and philosophy. In common they are confronted not only by grasping Communism but also by the chance to develop together. By sharing the development of their individual capacities they can multiply their mutual strength. The task is as difficult as it is necessary."[53]

While placing the onus on local and smaller forces made sense from a strategic point of view for an administration that was interested in counterinsurgency, it also made economic sense. McNamara defended the military assistance program in Vietnam using cost-efficiency logic. He explained, "One of the main conclusions we draw ... is that proper support of indigenous forces on the scene would give a greater return to collective defense than additional US military forces."[54] Moreover, the administration justified a training program geared toward policing-type operations, rather than military ones, specifically with the issue of costs in mind. Conventional military deployments necessarily came with an "extensive staff and logistic support":[55] in Vietnam, in later years, only about 35 percent of the forces in the field were involved in actual combat.[56]

Ultimately, the strain from the balance of payments deficit prompted a shift toward a policy of self-help, while the counterinsurgency thinking provided its strategic rationale. In a classified oral history, McNamara described the CPSVN as specifically falling within this understanding of guerrilla war. In his words:

I believed that to the extent that we could train those forces, we should do so, and having done it, we should get out ... I believed we should not introduce our military forces in support of the South Vietnamese, even if they were going to be "defeated." Consistent with that belief, some time in the latter part of 1963, following my return from a trip to South Vietnam, I recommended to President Kennedy that we announce a plan to begin the removal of our training forces ... I believed that we had done all the training we could, and whether the South Vietnamese were qualified or not to turn back the North Vietnamese, I was certain that if they weren't, it wasn't for lack of our training. More training wouldn't strengthen them; therefore we should get out. The President agreed.[57]

McNamara's explanation for the CPSVN in the remarkably candid interview was also prominent in his and Taylor's October 1963 report. One of its conclusions read that the advisory effort "cannot assure ultimate success"; this was a "Vietnamese war" which could "be run solely by the Vietnamese."[58]

McNamara also took up this theme in the ensuing NSC meetings. Historians have largely assumed that McNamara was hedging, that his plans were contingent on conditions on the field remaining constant. However, when colleagues remarked that "the difficulty is, this whole thing can be upset by a little greater effort by the North Vietnamese," McNamara was clear. He replied, "Not on the withdrawal of US forces. There's no reason to leave the L-19 squadron." Earlier in the meeting, he had used the L-19 reconnaissance missions to "illustrate the point" that training was all the United States should do: "But it's very simple to train the Vietnamese to fly the L-19s," he explained. "Now why should we leave our L-19 squadron there? At the present time, we've set up a training program to give them seven weeks of language training, four months of flying school, three weeks of transition training with L-19s and they can go out and do the L-19 work."[59]

In order to justify a policy of training, and training alone, the administration had to define the war as "their war" and had to downgrade the relative importance of Vietnam to the struggle against international communism. By 1962, both Harriman and McNamara led the administration-wide effort to redefine the situation in Vietnam along these lines.[60] McNamara's assistant for public affairs, Sylvester, reminded returning officers that in their speaking engagements they should insist that the "US is not fighting this war – it is their war."[61] Harriman repeated this advice to CINCPAC the following month. He insisted that it could not be "overstressed" in the "conduct and utterances in public and private of all US personnel" that the war was "Viet-Nam's war with the Viet-Cong" and that "the responsibility remains with the GVN [government of South Vietnam]."[62]

That ceiling on US responsibility to Vietnam also became prominent in the administration's communications with Diem. In a July 1962 letter, Kennedy reminded Diem that "the struggle is Vietnamese at its center, not American,"[63] an idea that was repeated in a subsequent draft letter in September 1963.[64] In its final form, the September 1963 letter left out a key phrase "this is a Vietnamese conflict and all the United States can do is help." McNamara communicated this in person to Diem during his trip.[65]

In addition, McNamara's strategy required defining the problem as internal to South Vietnam as opposed to external (i.e. North Vietnamese aggression), which would imply a host of international obligations under the 1954 Geneva Accords and the United Nations Charter. In the fall of 1961, as part of efforts to encourage the introduction of ground troops, the State Department had commissioned the so-called Jorden Report, which described the situation in Vietnam as one of aggression from the North. As Rostow explained, "The object of all this, as I have indicated, would be to seize the international community of this problem, develop our case, and lay the basis for the actions that we ourselves may have to take."[66]

By contrast, from 1962 onward, both in private and in public, McNamara described the situation in South Vietnam as mostly "indigenous."[67] A pattern developed whereby McNamara suppressed the international dimensions of the conflict in order to define the conflict as an internal one. In so doing, he could also reduce the conflict in South Vietnam to a manageable, and managerial, problem. In a March 1962 press conference, he tellingly spoke about being "very much encouraged" by the South Vietnamese government's improvements to its "own forces" and described the conflict as a "classic guerrilla fight," not an external threat but rather a "threat to their internal stability."[68] In January 1963, before Congress, he reiterated that the program in Vietnam was one of "training only" and that the country faced "no direct aggression."[69] In June 1963, he explained, "The emphasis is on internal guerrilla warfare and subversion in Vietnam."[70]

McNamara's conclusions were at odds with those of many in the bureaucracy including the State Department and NSC staff but not with another important ally, Senator Michael Mansfield. Mansfield, the Irish-American Senate Majority Leader and former professor of Far Eastern history, published a scathing report following his visit to Vietnam in

February 1962.[71] Like Kennedy during his Senate years, Mansfield had been an early supporter of Diem but now grew weary of the leader's abilities. He warned Kennedy that "it seems to me most essential that we make crystal clear to the Vietnamese government and to our own people that while we will go to great lengths to help, the primary responsibility rests with the Vietnamese ... It is their country, their future which is most at stake, not ours. To ignore that reality will not only be immensely costly in terms of American lives and resources ... The great increase in American military commitment this year has tended to point us in that general direction and we may well begin to slide rapidly toward it if any of the present remedies begin to falter in practice."[72] Echoing McNamara's concerns, Mansfield warned about the slippery slope toward an open-ended commitment if the ends and means of US involvement in South Vietnam were not clearly delineated.

Mansfield added, "we must reassess our interests, using the words 'vital' or 'essential' with the greatest realism and restraint."[73] For the administration, downgrading the relative importance of Vietnam or distinguishing between what Senator Mansfield called "marginal" and "essential" interests was more difficult to do publicly at a time when the domino theory still held sway.[74] Kennedy's interview with CBS in the fall of 1963, which many have treated as evidence that he would not withdraw, in fact included a very ambiguous statement. On the one hand, he insisted that "In the final analysis it is the people and the government [of South Vietnam] who have to win or lose this struggle. All we can do is help." On the other hand, he also said that he did not agree with those "who say we should withdraw," characterizing this as a "great mistake."[75]

McNamara's statements were much less ambivalent. During appropriations hearings in the Senate when Vietnam was discussed, he shrewdly quoted Mansfield's report at length back to him, reciting that US interests were "best serviced by a policy which helps to bring about internal peace in Vietnam but maintains, scrupulously, our advisory capacity." He noted that "This is exactly our objective."[76] Indeed, the administration's objective, just as Mansfield had suggested, had shifted from protecting the South Vietnamese at all costs to leaving the "primary responsibility ... with the South Vietnamese."[77] By co-opting congressional language, he effectively protected the administration.[78]

Implicit in this redefinition was the view that Vietnam was not of paramount importance to the United States. McNamara's edits to the October 1963 report are telling in this regard.[79] In addition to insisting that the end date of 1965 remain in the report – implying that these were the President's instructions[80] – one key line was edited three times: "the security of South Vietnam remains *important* to US security" (emphasis added). William Bundy, the principal drafter, had initially described South Vietnam's security as "vital"; another advisor had crossed this out to read "crucial," but McNamara, just as Mansfield had cautioned, insisted on the rather more ambiguous "important."[81]

Limiting the commitment in Vietnam promised some relief on the balance of payments front. A successful model for combating the insurgency in Vietnam that relied on "self-help" capabilities might be more expensive in terms of aid and training in the short term, but in the longer term would provide a more economically viable strategy for dealing with conflicts in the developing world. Restricting the commitment in South Vietnam also provided some relief from a congressional onslaught against the administration's military assistance program, especially in Asia. Congressional pressures had the dual effect of spurring the OSD to press MACV and the Chiefs for accelerated CPSVN plans and, in the second instance, to seek alternative funding sources for operations in Vietnam. The latter would have fateful consequences in the transition into the Johnson administration.

A policy of phasing out, as envisaged in the CPSVN, could reduce the more immediate pressures on the MAP, which financed the bulk of operations in Vietnam. By early 1963, the Senate Foreign Relations Committee (SFRC), which appropriated that part of the defense budget, began attacking the program and threatened to apply a "meat ax" to it.[82] McNamara's budgetary responsibilities over the MAP shaped the lessons that he drew from the Korean commitment. That experience provided the lens through which he perceived the growing commitment in Vietnam. When he tried to reduce troops or aid to the Republic of Korea because of balance of payments concerns, Secretary Rusk argued that any troop withdrawals would need to be offset by additional aid "without which the Korean economy could not survive."[83] In effect, the immovable commitment to Korea weighed down the MAP. Ultimately, it was ISA, the office that was created to oversee the MAP, that also oversaw the CPSVN plans. Budgetary concerns as much as realities on the ground drove the pressures it applied on military planners to accelerate the CPSVN between the spring of 1962 and the fall of 1963.

Operation Switchback was also at its core a funding story. As earlier chapters described, many in the administration were concerned about CIA operations in Vietnam, including the Special Forces' programs with local militias. On one level, the concerns were about bringing order and control: Gilpatric, who oversaw the Task Force on Vietnam until 1962, recalled that the CIA "was really operating as a quasi-military organization" without proper oversight.[84] The CIA representative echoed this sentiment, explaining that "in principle I am in favor of getting CIA out of this business as much as possible" but that the problems in the past were "largely [about] funding procedures."[85] On another level, therefore, the problems were about funding: the Defense Department had ready access to a greater pool of funds.

The CPSVN detailed the rationale behind transferring the irregular forces to the Defense Department: "To the extent that it is possible to do so, the functions now performed by irregular forces should be assumed by regularly constituted military forces which are appropriately responsive to normal channels of command and which are provided US advice and US assistance through normal MAP channels."[86] Transferring CIA programs to the Defense Department was part of a general process, with CPSVN at its core, designed to streamline and "normalize" both budgetary and organizational procedures in Vietnam in order to eventually phase them out. In practice, the Defense Department had been financing most of the paramilitary programs from the start but only indirectly, by providing a budget line item that ambiguously indicated that the funds were for joint CIA programs and later just "Operation Switchback" programs. The Department of the Army had paid the Special Forces' salary and equipment costs; the MAP covered training costs.[87]

Despite the advantages of providing order and clearer budgetary processes, many of Kennedy's advisors recognized that there were trade-offs to Defense Department control even from a cost-limitation perspective. The CIA station and State Department officials in Washington, and at times General Harkins himself, were concerned that integrating the paramilitary forces into the DOD would make the programs "overly formalized" and thus more expensive and that they would extend the "stay of US advisers and trainers in Viet-Nam."[88] However, even if the DOD was more cumbersome and could end up increasing the costs of these programs, the CIA could not afford them anymore.[89]

The CIA's concerns echoed similar complaints from the USOM office, the USAID program in Vietnam that also financed "information campaigns" and other programs within the strategic hamlets. Although USAID expressed unease with the militarization of programs in Vietnam, they also felt "no issue be made of [it] now because of much more pressing and immediate problems which require resolution."[90] These "more pressing problems" were the broader attack on USAID and DOD's offer to take over budgetary authority for USAID programs that had a military application.[91] In the end, both agencies could not afford a large-scale counterinsurgency program even if this program was supposed to have a civilian rather than military focus.

At the same time, while the Defense Department's budget was more open-ended than those of USAID or the CIA, it was also constrained, not least by its relative transparency. As Gilpatric's successor on the Vietnam Working Group, Chalmers Wood, concluded, "CIA does not have the personnel to carry on this rapidly expanding operation," but DOD "regulations hamper its flexibility in using funds to carry on this unorthodox work."[92] As a result, the CIA retained only the most limited number of "non-Switchback" forces, forces it could financially sustain for the long term and which the Defense Department could not absorb for political reasons, primarily because they involved operations outside South Vietnam's legal borders.

While funding from the Department of Defense seemed relatively more secure, by 1963 it too came under pressure. The pressure increased in the spring when planning began for FY64 and when a number of trends converged to make Vietnam operations especially vulnerable. First, the administration's competing aims of getting the tax cut while maintaining a degree of fiscal balance produced inevitable strains on the budget. In May, McNamara told Kennedy that he "fear[ed] next year, a campaign year," a "wide deficit" was "likely a problem" and that the defense budget could rise by $1 billion "with no increase in programs."[93] The USAID mission in Vietnam also felt the pinch and worried that "questions and concerns are probably going to be worse this year because of the proposed tax cut and a very large deficit has been budgeted for."[94]

The second and more important trend was what Kennedy called "the worst attack on foreign aid that we have seen since the beginning of the Marshall Plan," which had direct implications for Vietnam.[95] During the Kennedy administration, Vietnam operations were largely financed through the MAP. The program had its origins in World War II but was formalized in the Foreign Assistance Act of 1961, which consolidated existing government aid programs. In particular, it set up the USAID program for purely economic programs and created the MAP for defense-related programs.

Unlike the other OSD programs that were confirmed through the SASC, the SFRC appropriated the MAP. The latter included liberal senators, its chairman William J. Fulbright, Mansfield, and Wayne Morse, who were the most virulent critics of US operations in Asia and in Vietnam especially. For instance, after one hearing, McNamara noted that Fulbright was "very critical of the massive aid programs to Vietnam, Taiwan and Korea": Fulbright complained that the United States had "not accomplished a thing in Korea with all of our aid," suggesting "that if we gave the 500 million-odd program for Korea and spread it around Africa, Latin America, India and Egypt, it would do much more good."[96] Similarly, as part of his report to the President, Mansfield had written that he found it "Most disturbing ... that Viet Nam now appears to be only at the beginning of a beginning in coping with its grave inner problems. All the current difficulties existed in 1955, along with hope and energy to meet them. But it is seven years later and $2 billion of United States aid later."[97]

The senators were also concerned with the size of the defense budget. Morse, for instance, used the hearings to argue for cutting back the defense budget at a minimum by 15 percent.[98] McNamara played on Morse's criticism, suggesting in his hearings that if it was "essential for some reason to cut the total defense budget, it should cut those portions other than the military assistance portion because the military assistance program is the tightest portion of the entire budget," although the SFRC had no appropriative authority over the rest of his budget.[99] Even if, for the most part, the senators were favorable to the administration's aid program, with the power of the purse on their side, they used the MAP hearings as an opportunity to voice their criticism of what they saw as the overbearing role of the Defense Department in US foreign policy and sought to curtail the administration's programs in countries such as Vietnam.

Furthermore, the senators used balance of payments concerns to justify cutting back the MAP program. In response, McNamara and the chairmen of the Joint Chiefs of Staff Lyman Lemnitzer and later Taylor insisted that the MAP was a cost-effective program and that while "military efforts" abroad did contribute to the deficit, the MAP "per se does not contribute to our adverse balance of payments" but instead could have a favorable impact on the balance through military equipment sales.[100]

Speaking to Morse's criticism, McNamara insisted, "dollar for dollar, these programs [for countries on the periphery] contribute more to the security of the free world than corresponding expenditures in our defense appropriations."[101]

The issue of reducing the MAP program came to a head in 1963 with the publication in March of a report by the Committee to Strengthen the Security of the Free World (most commonly referred to as the "Clay Committee"). In December 1962, hoping to achieve bipartisan support for the MAP program and thus to meet the SFRC's objections, Kennedy charged the former Military Governor of West Germany and a prominent "Eisenhower Republican," General Lucius Clay, with reviewing the administration's foreign aid strategy.

The committee was asked to investigate the administration's repeated arguments that aid produced a sound investment for US security, or as its mission statement read, "to determine whether [the military and economic assistance programs] were contributing the optimum security of the United States and the economic and political stability of the free world."[102] Although Kennedy recognized that the committee was heavily weighted with Republicans, he hoped that this might help him attract bipartisan support and that it "would somehow get respectable people who would bring pressure to bear on Congress and middle of the road people to do what his experts told him really ought to be done, but which the country didn't seem ready to do."[103]

Instead of producing a policy that helped the administration, the Clay Committee's "miserable document," as one official described it,[104] called for major reform of aid and especially of the MAP where it suggested a "substantial tightening up and sharpened objectives in terms of our national interests." Although the report echoed McNamara's statements that aid provided a sound investment in the United States and its allies' security, it was nevertheless scathing in its assessment of the program and echoed many of the SFRC's criticisms, some of which were especially relevant for Vietnam.

While the Clay Committee welcomed the reforms to the aid program, it also argued that, contrary to McNamara's suggestions, the aid program *was* contributing to the balance of payments crisis, which, it warned, undermined the United States' "role of political, economic and financial leadership in the free world." Moreover, its criticisms of recipient countries were biting. For instance, it cautioned that "many of the countries which have received our aid have not fully performed their part of the assistance bargain," namely by showing "an internal expression of will and discipline." Echoing McNamara's qualms on Vietnam, it also complained that aid programs were particularly weak in countries plagued "by the absence of trained manpower and adequate local institutions."[105]

Crucially, in keeping with its recommendation for "tightening up" the MAP program, the report called for a budget ceiling of $1 billion by no later than FY68.[106] Despite Kennedy's frustration with the public impact of the Clay Committee's report, Dillon also suggested this $1 billion mark as early as February 1962, almost a year before, and the administration was already working toward it. To Rusk, Dillon had written, "I also told the President my view which I mentioned in our meeting last week that the overall balance of payments impact of foreign aid operations including our contribution to the Inter-American Bank, the International Development Association, as well as USAID and military assistance expenditures should not exceed a billion dollars annually as compared to last year's level of about a billion and two hundred million."[107]

Still, the Clay Committee added pressure and urgency to cost-cutting efforts as the SFRC, as well as McNamara, picked up on its suggested deadline to reach the $1 billion threshold by FY68. FY68 also became the cut-off date for the final CPSVN phaseout.[108] The link between the withdrawal plans and the MAP became so clear that MACV submitted a revised version of the CPSVN to CINPCAC in January 1963 with an introduction that advised: "In view of the close relationship between the plan and the Military Assistance Plan, they should not continue to be treated as separate entities."[109]

McNamara explicitly used the SFRC's pressures to accelerate the CPSVN process. Whereas in September 1962, MACV had suggested that "previous MAP ceilings don't apply," by December 1962, planning was being made with "funding limitations" in mind.[110] Also, whereas some training functions had been initially scheduled to continue until 1971, by May 1963, CINCPAC recognized that all programs, including training programs, should be accelerated to end by 1968. In his hearings before the SFRC, McNamara proudly explained the steps his office had taken to implement Clay's recommendations especially on Vietnam. He told the senators, "As a matter of fact, Admiral Felt came in the day before yesterday from the Pacific and brought with him new estimates of the requirements for South Vietnam . . . I told [him] I doubted very much that funds would be available to support a program that large and urged him to reconsider, which he agreed to."[111]

For both McNamara and the SFRC senators, their experience with the Korean commitment colored their concerns about the MAP program for

Vietnam, namely that the United States was stuck with an expensive and open-ended commitment in Korea. Moreover, whereas the MAP program was designed as a cost-efficient tool to deal with situations around the world, expensive commitments in Asia dominated its balance sheet.

The commitment in Korea and its impact on McNamara's motivation for the CPSVN was obvious. In a recording of a private conversation with Kennedy in May 1963, McNamara explained the CPSVN as follows:

> I calculate that we can get it under control, it may take two years, three years possibly but we should now be looking at a time when we'll have a normal military program there. Instead they're proposing a fantastic military assistance program . . . And if you're looking toward a normal relationship so we don't build up another Korea. When I look at what's happened in Korea and the way the US aid is, and how difficult it's going to be to scale that aid down, we certainly don't want another Korea developing in South Vietnam and we're well on our way to doing that.[112]

McNamara had applied his five-year budget planning to the MAP and found that Vietnam would have a "fantastic" effect on the overall budget if current growth trends were maintained.[113] His calculations in preparation for the Senate hearing on the MAP program showed that the Vietnam program was getting very close to equaling Korea's share of the MAP program.

In addition, it was William Bundy at ISA who wrote much of the October 1963 Taylor–McNamara report and who was responsible for overseeing the Vietnam program's implications for MAP and for coordinating policy with USAID.[114] In the preceding months, together with the Deputy Director for Military Assistance William Leffingwell, Bundy sent McNamara a number of reports describing the impact of the "Southeast Asia emergency" on total MAP costs. According to their forecasts, these would rise to $965 million out of a total program budget of $2.5 billion in FY62 and $875 million out of $2.2 billion in FY64.[115] By FY63, the Far East (which also included Korea and Taiwan) accounted for over 44 percent of the total MAP program.[116] As a result, a joint State-Defense study recommended that programs be geared toward "self-help";[117] nowhere was this trend clearer than the October 1963 recommendations for Vietnam.[118]

In endorsing the Clay Committee's recommendations as both "desirable and feasible," the SFRC reminded the administration that each MAP should be "temporary and extraordinary" and should be terminated as soon as possible or when the "recipient country develops the economic capacity to sustain its own defense."[119] In other words, all MAP programs must have a cut-off date. Thereafter, financial support for operations should come from the recipient country or from elsewhere in government. McNamara argued that the Vietnam costs were "temporary" by putting them in a long-term context, noting that they had reached a "peak and [would] start to level off."[120]

According to the CPSVN planning, there would be a Defense Department–financed surge in funding from 1963 to 1965 and then as US forces withdrew by FY67, the South Vietnamese government would fund its military; the USAID station (through USOM) and the CIA would take over funding for the much-reduced number of paramilitary forces until they gradually merged into the National Police Force.[121] The process effectively reduced the conflict in Vietnam to an internal security problem. Moreover, to preempt any delays from the services, by September 1963 the OSD indicated that further funding for Vietnam operations would come from "non-MAP sources," namely the services budgets themselves, for instance, in the handover of materiel that was already in the country.[122]

The configuration of South Vietnamese forces also evolved to reflect these budgetary concerns and the focus on counterinsurgency efforts in Vietnam. As General Harkins explained to his Vietnamese counterparts, the tendency among the Chiefs to build up military establishments that mirrored their own in partner countries was "extremely expensive in both funds and troop support," whereas advisory missions on the lower end of the security spectrum could be more affordable and thus sustainable.[123] A few months earlier, McNamara had rejected the January 1963 draft of the CPSVN on the basis that it was "too large for the GVN to support."[124]

As a result, whereas in earlier drafts the South Vietnamese manning levels for each of the services were roughly equal, by the last version in November 1963 planned troop strengths for a South Vietnamese Navy especially but also Air Force had been drastically cut with a greater onus placed on the Army and the paramilitary forces associated with the strategic hamlet program. In absolute terms, the overall manning levels for all forces, including most paramilitary groups, were more than halved.

The reduction in forces reflected South Vietnam's dual problems of funding and recruitment: as the December 1962 draft of the CPSVN explained, the South Vietnamese government did not necessarily have the ability to "recruit officers and technical staff without damaging the economy."[125] Both MACV and the OSD were concerned about the absence of officers trained to take on more skill-intensive roles envisaged under earlier plans. As a result, the plans were designed to redefine the problem in Vietnam as one of fighting an insurgency and policing. This was relatively cheaper, easier to train for and required smaller force levels.

As for transferring the costs to the South Vietnamese government in the long term, it was not clear that it could finance the various units as the phaseout took hold especially in the face of MAP cuts.[126] The director of USOM in Vietnam commented on an earlier version of the CPSVN that "the force levels being contemplated after 1966, when the insurgency will have supposedly been contained, will result in either an intolerable deficit or an impractically high aid level."[127]

Another report concluded gloomily: "Vietnam is essentially in the same position as Korea, in that the country is not presently viable and that the US aid program essentially makes up the current account deficit through grants."[128] The embassy in Saigon raised similar concerns, noting that it was "hardly surprising that the GVN is overwhelmed with its budgetary problem" considering that "about 18% of GNP" for 1962 was allocated for "security." "In the US," the telegram read, "This would be comparable to about $100 billion for defense, or approximately double our present budget."[129]

McNamara's experience and frustrations with untangling the "sterile commitment" in Korea explain his impatience with rolling back the United States' commitment to Vietnam before it became what the Foreign Office called a "normality" which would make it "more difficult for the Vietnamese ... to achieve true independence."[130] This is what McNamara meant when he told the NSC that "To leave forces there when they're not needed, I think is wasteful and complicates both their problems and ours."[131] It would "complicate" Vietnamese self-reliance and would "waste" finite MAP resources.

In the short term, as the Clay Committee first recommended, the OSD looked into transferring some of Vietnam's costs to the services.[132] In moves that mirrored McNamara's later manipulations of the defense budget during the war, he sought ways to transfer costs or hide their full effect. For instance, in May 1963, he asked that military planners "turn over material in place at no cost to the country MAP program,"[133] in effect burying materiel costs in the services' budgets. McNamara also recommended that ISA explore transferring all the costs of Vietnam operations to the services' budget as he anticipated substantial cuts in FY64.[134] He suggested that this would have a "highly desirable tactical effect" as it could help reduce overall MAP to the $800 million mark (under Clay's recommended $1 billion) by FY65.[135]

William Bundy tentatively reached out to Senator Richard Russell to see whether he would support such a move but preempted any criticism by saying that this would be an "exception to the general rule."[136] He wrote to the Chairman of the SASC,

The fundamental reason for these changes is our belief that military assistance is an essential element of our total national defense effort and should be considered as a part of the budget of the Department of Defense itself ... We believe on balance that it would be sound to transfer this funding responsibility to the DOD budget. A secondary factor is that this would give General Harkins and the field command somewhat greater administrative ease in calling the items they believe are required to produce success.[137]

However, the temporary expedient of shifting the costs for Vietnam onto the services had far-reaching consequences. By removing the MAP program for Vietnam away from SFRC oversight, McNamara also lost much of the rationale for cutting back costs on operations in Vietnam in the short term. In the long term, he also de facto removed one of the biggest sources of pushback on US operations in the country. Moreover, as George Ball suggested, by moving the MAP program in Vietnam away from a coordinated platform with State, it also opened the door for the program in Vietnam to increasingly ignore the USAID program and instead follow military imperatives.

The paradox of the Kennedy's administration's predilection for fighting "new" wars, namely counterinsurgencies that relied heavily on "self-help" models, was that they were designed to be cheaper and thus economically more sustainable in light of the United States' growing list of commitments and the resultant balance of payments deficit. However, since they relied on MAP funding as well, they also drew on a much tighter budget line, one where an activist SFRC was determined to cut back commitments altogether. The SFRC's activism eventually pushed McNamara and the OSD to seek continued funding for Vietnam elsewhere, namely in the military budget, and in so doing inadvertently produced pressures to militarize operations in Vietnam. Just as the OSD taking on a leading role in Vietnam under Operation Switchback swamped out the USAID program, the act of putting the financing for the Vietnam program increasingly under the services' budget raised their role in policy formulation.

Moreover, the budgetary battles over Vietnam operations in this period highlight a key impediment to the Kennedy administration's attempts to intervene in lower-level conflicts. In addition to providing operational coherence, only the Defense Department could provide budgetary reliability. Bundy's letter to Russell explicitly played on the SASC preference for strengthening the military's freedom and their definition of "success." Much as the administration toyed with alternatives to traditional military force, it remained a basic tension in the US government that these alternatives were much harder to deploy in a situation of budgetary stress. Both the SFRC and the SASC were responsible for that state of affairs.

McNamara was a mathematical man, more concerned with budgetary issues than with geopolitics. He was never really concerned with designing strategy for Vietnam but the counterinsurgency strategies fit neatly with his cost-cutting agenda. His reforms at the OSD, especially the PPBS, were about control and about bridging ambitions and strategy laid out in the White House or the State Department with existing limitations of which economic limitations were at the forefront. His particular mindset and his distinct definition of his "job" as Secretary of Defense explain why he led the withdrawal plans from Vietnam under the Kennedy administration as aggressively as he did.

Although it was Kennedy and his counterinsurgency advisors who provided the overall strategy for Vietnam, McNamara welcomed its corollaries. Specifically, that the strategy would significantly reduce the military role of the United States in Vietnam (i.e. the costs for the DOD) at a time when the Senate was squeezing the relevant budgetary allocation, the MAP. In so doing, it could forestall "another Korea" which for McNamara was a budgetary nightmare: a situation that required significant financial outlays and from which it was almost impossible to extricate his department. As McNamara saw it, the United States' responsibilities in places such as Korea were undermining the United States economically. Understanding the importance of these economic issues is central to understanding the credibility of the withdrawal plans.

McNamara's evaluation of the budgetary impact of Vietnam drove his support from the CPSVN from July 1962 onward and his insistence that the administration publicize the plans in October 1963. The public relations aspects of the October 1963 announcements, specifically the initial 1,000-man troop withdrawal scheduled for the end of the year, were important: they addressed congressional pressures on the MAP and sent a message to the Vietnamese that they should take greater responsibility for the war. However, other long-term concerns drove the larger issue of withdrawal and the CPSVN. In particular, the CPSVN reflected

Kennedy's counterinsurgency advisors' pessimistic reading of the unfolding situation in Vietnam and their concerns that US involvement had become overmilitarized. In the fall of 1963, despite his own negative assessment of the prospects for the South Vietnamese to sustain the program he had laid out for them, McNamara pressed on to set it in stone and create a bureaucratic momentum that, he hoped, would make his withdrawal plan irreversible.

6

The Fall of 1963

Historians are divided as to why McNamara set in motion withdrawal plans in July 1962. On the one hand, there are those who argue that McNamara, and perhaps Kennedy as well, believed the war would effectively end by 1965 – that the insurgency could be reduced to "low-level banditry" by that time.[1] On the other, there are those who argue that Kennedy presciently understood that the United States was on a losing path in Vietnam. In fact, neither is correct. Newly available documents show that, in private, McNamara was not optimistic about US prospects in Vietnam but neither was he convinced that all intervention was doomed to failure. Instead, he saw Vietnam as a test case for a new kind of intervention that could be financially sustainable.

During the October 3 NSC meeting, Kennedy specifically pushed McNamara on his conclusion that combat operations would end by 1965. He asked his Secretary whether the withdrawal plans were based on "an assumption that it's going well" and whether this could make the administration look foolish if things turned sour. McNamara explained his two "major premises" for announcing the phaseout date: first, he believed that the "military campaign" would be "complete" by the end of 1965 and "secondly, if it extends beyond that period, we believe we can train them to take over the essential functions and withdraw the bulk of our forces." When McGeorge Bundy asked him "what's the point of doing that?" McNamara responded, "We need a way to get out of Vietnam. This is a way of doing it."[2]

However, the report's nominal co-author Maxwell Taylor was more troubled about the 1965 end date: unlike McNamara, he explained, "I think it is a major question" but reassured the President that the officers he had spoken to largely felt it "would be ample time" to "reduce this insurgency to a little more than sporadic itching." Immediately after their exchange, McNamara again insisted on the date and explained, "I think Mr. President, we must have a means of disengaging from this area. We must show our country what that means. The only slightest difference between Max and me in this entire report is this one estimate ... I'm not entirely sure of that. But I am sure that if we don't meet those dates in the sense of ending the major military campaigns, we nonetheless can withdraw the bulk of our US forces according to the schedule we've laid, worked out, because we train the Vietnamese to do the job." For McNamara, withdrawal was not pegged to victory; instead, he was most focused on "a way to get out." For him, having forces on the ground was complicated for the Vietnamese and wasteful for the United States. When Kennedy agreed on the date, he might have been hedging: "Let's say it anyway. Then in '65 if it doesn't work out we get a new date," he told his colleagues. McNamara was far less flexible (see Figure 6.1).[3]

The *Pentagon Papers* observe that "optimism dominated official thinking" in the 1962–1963 period.[4] While this might have been true of the administration and McNamara's public pronouncements, the reality behind closed doors was more complex. In the months leading up to the July 1962 Honolulu conference, Hilsman complained that a "wave of discouragement" had hit the Pentagon, a phenomenon he found "surprising since the evidence points in quite the other direction."[5] If anything, a consensus emerged in this period that the situation in Vietnam might be approaching a stalemate; Ambassador Lodge, General Taylor, the CIA as well as USOM in Vietnam, among others, all shared the view at different moments. In the fall of 1962, the Task Force on Southeast Asia had described the situation as "basically a stand-off with no clear prospect of victory for either side," while Taylor, in assessing the difference between his visits in October 1961 and 1962, said that whereas before the "Viet Cong [had been] winning the war," by 1962, "no one clearly has the initiative."[6]

Moreover, both McNamara's October trip report and the November 1963 CPSVN focused on the danger that the programs in Vietnam had become "over-extended" or confused and that the administration needed to move to a "consolidation" phase. In addition, the trip report and the Special Group (CI) concluded that the civic action and civil programs as well as the strategic hamlets, which were all at the core of the counterinsurgency program, were "lagging."[7] To a large extent, the narrative about McNamara's optimism on Vietnam relies on his public pronouncements, which remained positive. At the end of the October NSC meetings,

FIGURE 6.1 President Kennedy with Secretary of Defense McNamara and Chairman of the Joint Chiefs of Staff General Maxwell D. Taylor on their return from Vietnam, October 2, 1963. Later in the day, the administration announced its intention to withdraw from the country by 1965.
(Abbie Rowe, White House Photograph Collection, JFKL.)

the press announcement read: "Secretary McNamara and General Taylor reported their judgment that the major part of the US military task can be completed by the end of 1965."[8]

However, as McNamara's remarks during the October meetings suggest, as far as he and his planners were concerned, withdrawal could happen because the Vietnamese would be trained do the job not because there would be peace by 1965. As his trip report explained, "The US advisory effort, however, cannot assure ultimate success. This is a Vietnamese war and the country and the war must in the end, be run solely by the Vietnamese. It will impair their independence and the development of their initiative if we leave our advisers in place beyond the time they are really needed."[9]

Although McNamara's most optimistic advisors (notably General Paul D. Harkins and Thompson) first suggested the 1965 end date, only Harkins seemed to believe that there would be peace by then, having perhaps convinced his mentor Taylor as well. There is no doubt that Harkins' reporting was unequivocally optimistic.[10] In July 1962, he told McNamara that it would take a year to train the Vietnamese;[11] a few months later he predicted "all our programs will come to fruition by the end of 1962."[12] July 1962 was a key date because it was at this time, during the Honolulu conference, that McNamara asked the JCS to begin the handover of military responsibilities to their South Vietnamese counterparts. This timing explains why many have assumed that McNamara began to plan for withdrawal on the basis of Harkins' reporting and resulting "euphoria and optimism."[13]

However, the administration did not especially value Harkins and his staff. Harkins, a man appointed largely because he was Taylor's protégé and longtime friend, had to regularly defend his staff against OSD charges that they were incompetent. He experienced a fall from grace that became particularly acute after the defeat at Ap Bac in January 1963.[14] By the October 1963 NSC meetings, when Taylor cited Harkins' comments, McNamara dismissed them with a brief and cutting quip, "He's not a strong officer."[15] McNamara's colleagues shared his impatience with Harkins. This included the President (who, according to Forrestal, "wanted to get rid of him"[16]), Senator Mansfield (because he was "too optimistic"[17]) and McGeorge Bundy (who later described Harkins as a "dope"[18]). In later years, McNamara was more diplomatic and explained that Harkins "looked and spoke exactly as a general should" but, more bitingly, that although he was "a protégé of the scholarly Max Taylor, he lacked his mentor's intellectual caliber."[19] McNamara's Deputy Gilpatric, less diplomatically remembered that his boss was "just not impressed either by Harkins' record or by the personal attributes of the man when he saw him."[20]

As of 1962, McNamara became increasingly doubtful about field reports, notably from Harkins, and had begun reaching outside traditional channels to cross-check information. This led him to conclude that the United States could not win *militarily* in the traditional sense. His trip to Vietnam in the fall of 1963 confirmed this view. As a result, he put in motion a plan to demilitarize US involvement to meet the new objective of helping the South Vietnamese help themselves. He felt that this could be accomplished within Harkins' timeline. To a large extent, in keeping with Thompson's advice, a public display of optimism was a strategy for McNamara. Projecting optimism was a way of keeping the CPSVN on track "according to the schedule [he had] laid out."[21]

In fact, Thompson's optimistic views and trajectory offer a key to understanding McNamara's. Whereas Harkins' view of victory was predicated on a training mission and on the military aspects of the war, Thompson's was political and focused on training lower-level forces and the construction of strategic hamlets.[22] As such, the decreased military presence envisaged in the withdrawal plans had less impact on his long-range plans. In addition, in his discussions with McNamara, Thompson, unlike Harkins, clearly felt that optimism was a calculated posture to avoid US domestic audiences from turning against the war and to keep the South Vietnamese motivated and confident that they were on the "winning side."

Thompson's trajectory during the July 1962–October 1963 period is informative. In the spring of 1962, Thompson reached the peak of his optimism, prompting McNamara to urge his military commanders to accelerate the withdrawal plans. Using a well-worn phrase, Thompson noted that the "tide has turned"[23] and at a meeting at Fort Bragg, confidently announced that "we definitely are winning."[24] But by the fall of 1963, a shift had occurred. Thompson produced a report that described the current path as a "collision course" and warned of a "grave risk that the only choice before us will be of losing either with or without Diem."[25] In a meeting with Lodge in September 1963, he argued that the United States should stick to Diem even though the Buddhist crisis had derailed progress (contrary to what American military advisors were saying).[26] At the same time, he reassured his American colleagues that, "If everything was to go 50% according to plan, then I would say that there could be a decisive military improvement in twelve months and certainly within two years."[27] This was exactly the time frame that McNamara imposed for the withdrawal plans.

Much of Thompson and McNamara's optimism was calculated to influence events both on the ground and in Washington. Although Thompson was not officially in Vietnam during the McNamara–Taylor visit, McNamara's notes made on the first day bear Thompson's hallmark, in particular, one remarkable phrase: "People want to be on winning side – if word gets around that we have doubts, are cutting aid, or likely to pull out, it will reduce the will of the people in the hamlets to resist."[28] These are almost exactly the same words Thompson penned in a May 1963 letter to the British High Commissioner in New Zealand about the situation in Vietnam where he wrote, "The key to the present situation is confidence. The peasants are not going to stick their necks out unless they think they will be on the winning side. Naturally therefore I have to be optimistic if I am to influence events. You must play as if you are going to win."[29]

Herein lays the key to understanding Thompson's and McNamara's optimism: they did not necessarily believe that everything was going to plan; they were looking for a way to galvanize the troops, both at home and in the field. The idea that optimism was a means to an end was a recurring theme in Thompson's correspondence: he had previously noted that the momentum of the 1962 victories had "inspired confidence in the successful outcome of the war"[30] and that confidence "would be self-generating."[31] Considering the McNamara–Taylor report observed a "general atmosphere of watch-and-wait,"[32] McNamara made a calculated choice to be optimistic because it kept his plan on track. Without an energized South Vietnamese partner and with a Congress threatening to cut off aid, a long-drawn-out program of handing over responsibilities could not happen.

Furthermore, McNamara's tendency to consistently second-guess military advice is hardly compatible with the notion that he was uncritically accepting of Harkins' input. In an oral history, McNamara, using an analogy of factory workers at Ford, commented on "the foolhardiness of combining the intelligence function with the operating function . . . that intelligence estimates that came from the unit that was associated with operations were tainted . . . by the biases that we all have in evaluating our own operations."[33] That critical reading of intelligence estimates influenced the way McNamara received Harkins' reports and subsequently informed the Taylor–McNamara report's conclusions. Going against Harkins' assessment, the report pointed to the continuing issue of poor intelligence,[34] to the fact that the Vietcong effort had "not yet been seriously reduced in the aggregate" and commented that people were unanimous that the strategic hamlet programs was "overextended in the Delta."[35]

McNamara's notes from this trip are also instructive:[36] during a visit to a Special Forces detachment, which was at the vanguard of counterinsurgency, he concluded that "there has been progress in the Delta during the past year (have strategic hamlets, etc.) but not working as much as they claim and their plan for the future is weak." In another area, he described "clearly a miserably planned hamlet program."[37] He met with Professor Patrick J. Honey, a scholar of Vietnamese culture and history, who recognized that they were "in theory great" but "in practice: not." In the Delta, US advisors told him that "in some hamlets [there were] 20–30% VC sympathizers" and that there had been "little or no progress in winning over the people." Within days, Vice President Tho confirmed this alarming assessment, writing that there were "not more than 20 or 30 properly defended hamlets."[38] McNamara's trip file also contained a USOM "informal appreciation" of the strategic hamlets which called it an "idealistic program" that had failed primarily for the reasons that had troubled Thompson, namely a "lack of provincial capability"; it also highlighted the Delta as an area where "communists still control most of the people."[39]

In addition, the trip's purpose was also to ascertain whether or not the Buddhist crisis had affected military progress. Although the people he met with were nearly unanimous in their appraisal that it had not, he wrote that "sympathy for the VC will build up because the devil you don't know is better than the one you do." All in all, these are not the notes of an optimistic man on the cusp of victory.

Several of McNamara's colleagues recall a decisive shift in the fall of 1963. General Krulak, who sat on the Special Group (CI) as the JCS representative and who joined McNamara on his October 1963 trip to Vietnam, expressed his "admiration" for McNamara "because he saw the truth more quickly than most, and he saw through the phoniness of what he was told when he went to Vietnam be it by the Vietnamese, or our own people." Krulak recalled that Kennedy had received "clear indications" from McNamara that the counterinsurgency operations were "not going well" and were "not implemented earnestly and this would morph into a conventional war," something Kennedy explicitly sought to avoid.[40] Forrestal and Hilsman also recall a change in September 1963, a point where McNamara realized that "he had been badly misinformed by Harkins."[41]

Ultimately, the idea that McNamara was optimistic that "victory" would be achieved by 1965 is not borne out either in his September trip notes or in his statements at the ensuing NSC meetings. Although he accepted his military advisors' timeline, he did not accept their positive assessments. He nevertheless continued to make optimistic statements "to influence events" on the ground. The South Vietnamese needed to believe they were "on the winning side" if they were to take over responsibilities in earnest; and in Washington congressional leaders needed to believe it too if he was to avoid cuts to his long-term plans for Vietnam.

The press release after the October 1963 NSC meetings that announced the administration's plans to phase out from Vietnam was not evidence of McNamara's undue optimism. Instead, the statement was first and foremost a maneuver aimed at, among others, members of the administration who could put obstacles in the CPSVN's way.

The administration resisted making a press announcement until October 1963 because publicizing the withdrawal plans committed it to a timetable and a narrative of a war in a deescalating phase. In fact, even though NSAM 263, the summative document of the NSC meetings, instructed that "no formal announcement" should be made about the withdrawal plans, within hours Press Secretary Salinger and Secretary McNamara organized a press conference.[42] As expected, when it came, the announcement produced front-page news: the *Baltimore Sun*'s cover, for instance, was splashed with the headline "McNamara and Taylor Feel US Can Withdraw Most of Troops from Vietnam by End of 1965."[43] The *New York Times* cover featured a photo of President Kennedy listening intently to Taylor and McNamara, with the headline "Vietnam Victory by the End of '65 Envisaged by U.S."[44]

Just as McNamara had insisted on having the 1965 end date included in his trip report, he also insisted on making a public announcement because he knew that it would attract media attention. The announcement fulfilled a number of his short- and long-term objectives. In the short term, the administration hoped to goad the Diem regime into implementing much-needed and long-awaited political reforms that would "win the hearts and minds" of the South Vietnamese as a prerequisite for defeating the Vietcong insurgency.[45] Crucially for McNamara, it also prepared him to counter the criticisms of Senators Fulbright and Mansfield before going to Capitol Hill for yet another MAP hearing the following week.

However, the more important objective for McNamara was a bureaucratic one: that is, to peg the whole, fractured administration to his chosen policy and to create considerable momentum against further escalation. A telling exchange during the October NSC meetings between Kennedy and Salinger speaks to this objective most clearly. When the latter indicated that "the significance of this is that this is a government-wide statement of policy which has the approval of every ...," Kennedy cut him off to add, "And more than that. It's not only that statement ... to obey ... but also the report, the essence of the report, was endorsed by all."[46]

The press release actually contained two distinct announcements: a token, thousand-man withdrawal by the end of 1963 and a gradual phaseout of remaining military personnel by 1965. The thousand-man withdrawal was arguably a public relations exercise aimed primarily at appeasing the SFRC, whereas the overall phaseout was, as the *Pentagon*

Papers has described it, a "political-managerial"[47] move that reflected McNamara's style and priorities.

In tracing it back to its first expression, the token thousand-man withdrawal was clearly always considered separate from the overall withdrawal plans. The idea of announcing a "token withdrawal" originated in discussions with Robert Thompson and the Foreign Office in April 1962 when Thompson suggested that it could be made "when it appear [ed] reasonably certain that the tide had turned in Vietnam."[48] He argued that it was true in July 1962 and by October 1962 suggested that the token withdrawal should take place within approximately a year's time (i.e. in October 1963) and that it should be "well thought out and well-timed, so that it achieved the maximum effect without taking any of the pressure off here."[49] This suggests that the token withdrawal was, first, a public relations move (it should be "well-timed") and, second, distinct from the overall strategy (it should not "tak[e] any pressure off here"). It, therefore, provided a public backdrop against which the administration could present the withdrawal plans but did not affect the content of these plans.[50]

At the same time, the administration had to balance the different audiences in South Vietnam and in Washington. Earlier in the summer, it seemed that announcing a withdrawal achieved the administration's objectives in both settings. In a private conversation, McNamara explained to President Kennedy that "we ought to think about the possibility of pulling 1,000 men by the end of the year," that this was good "for domestic political purposes and also because of the psychological effect it would have on South Vietnam."[51] In keeping with this, MACV and CINCPAC proposed bringing the troops "home by xmas for compassionate and publicity reasons" and envisaged "statements of mutual gratitude" as well as grand ceremonies.[52]

However, after McNamara's trip when he had observed "hedging" and uncertainty on the South Vietnamese part, the decision was made to treat the withdrawal quietly and justify it on the basis that the function was either completed or the South Vietnamese could complete the job themselves.[53] President Kennedy now instructed Lodge that removing the "1,000 US advisors by December of this year should not be raised formally with Diem. Instead the action should be carried out routinely as part of our general posture of withdrawing people when they are no longer needed."[54]

For McNamara, the Senate was the more important audience. During the October meetings, Kennedy specifically asked McNamara about the "advantage" of announcing the thousand-man withdrawal. McNamara responded,

The advantage of taking them out is that we can say to the Congress and the people that we do have a plan for reducing the exposure of US combat personnel to the guerrilla actions in South Vietnam, actions that the people of South Vietnam should gradually develop a capability to suppress themselves. And I think this will be of great value to us in meeting the very strong views of Fulbright and others that we're bogged down in Asia and we'll be there for decades.

Kennedy agreed with McNamara and suggested that any public statement should be "run by" these congressmen.[55] Both Kennedy and McNamara were concerned about losing key allies of the administration's aid program.

For Taylor, the other author of the October 1963 report, the key audience was Diem. Before leaving for Vietnam, he had "thought it would be useful to work out a time schedule within which we expect to get this job done and to say plainly to Diem that we are not going to be able to stay beyond such and such time with such and such forces, and the war must be won in this time period." The minutes of the meeting read: "The President did not say 'yes' or 'no' to this proposal."[56] Unlike McNamara, Taylor went along with a public announcement of the policy to disengage because he hoped to influence the uncooperative regime in Saigon.

Although Robert Kennedy had first suggested that the threat of withdrawal could be used as a pressure tactic,[57] by the time of the October 1963 NSC meetings Taylor alone was pushing the idea. For Taylor, the 1965 deadline was basically arbitrary and primarily a threat designed to get Diem in line in the face of growing pressure within the administration for a coup.[58] McNamara's approach was almost exactly opposite. He lamented the lack of influence, and although the terms of reference of his trip to Vietnam had included finding ways "of influencing Diem," his notes reveal his frustration. In them, he complained, for instance, about "how little leverage we have" on the "completely unsuccessful government in Saigon."[59]

In addition, although McNamara saw the value of "creating uncertainty" in Diem,[60] he was also skeptical that such a strategy could be effective.[61] Both before and after the Taylor–McNamara trip, "pressure programs" were met with skepticism. President Kennedy "did not think that [they were] likely to be effective,"[62] while the Working Group on South Vietnam and the CIA warned that any threat even to "employ its ultimate sanction (pulling out of South Vietnam) would almost certainly be regarded as hollow by the [Government of South Vietnam]."[63]

Ultimately, the Taylor–McNamara report itself presented this strategy not as an optimal policy but as a desperate effort. It noted that they could "increase [the regime's] obduracy," but "unless such pressures [were] exerted, they [were] almost certain to continue past patterns of behavior."[64] Also, the "Selective Pressures" that it did suggest included everything but military cuts, which it deemed especially unfeasible and counterproductive. Notably, it excluded the CPSVN.[65] "In sum," the report read, "The effect of pressures that can be carried out without detriment to the war effort is probably limited with respect to the possibility of Diem making necessary changes."[66] For McNamara, a pressure program, if it achieved anything, was designed to keep the CPSVN on track. A responsive government in South Vietnam would increase the likelihood that a self-sustaining program would be in place by 1965 when the US military withdrew.

The decision to announce the withdrawal plans on October 3, 1963, was also a bureaucratic move. While drafting the Taylor–McNamara report, Chester Cooper, William Bundy and Taylor each questioned the advisability of recommending a 1965 end date. However, McNamara insisted he was "just following orders" and that the date must stay in the report.[67] He also overrode Kennedy's reservations about committing the administration to a set date. After getting the military on board (they drafted the CPSVN), this was a way of getting the whole national security bureaucracy on board as well. By getting all the key actors involved in Vietnam policy to publicly commit to a policy of deescalation and getting Taylor, in particular, to co-own the prediction that most military operations would end by 1965, McNamara effectively neutralized bureaucratic politics.

The end point for the withdrawal plans and in the announcement was not "victory" in a traditional or unambiguous sense. Instead, as laid out in the CPSVN and in NSAM 263, it was "until the insurgency has been suppressed *or* until the national security forces of the Government of South Viet-Nam are capable of suppressing it."[68] Semantics are important here: it was not *and* but *or*. In time, the second alternative took precedence: the South Vietnamese were to fight the war themselves.

Clearly, the nuances of the policy had filtered through the administration effectively since Forrestal detailed the standing policy to Bundy a month later as follows: "The President made the point, as I remember, that our only interest was to help South Viet Nam defend itself against subversive aggression from the North ... More recently we have added a gloss to this formula and implied (in the NSC statement of last month) that we would also withdraw the bulk of our personnel as soon as the South Vietnamese were able to cope for themselves. Secretary McNamara and General Taylor estimated that this might occur in 1965."[69] The policy also filtered to the field with Lodge reiterating to his South Vietnamese counterparts that "Americans are here to help Vietnam stand on its own feet, after which we would go home."[70] Not everyone in the administration necessarily believed that this was the final objective or outcome, but by October 1963 the administration's stated policy and the basis for military planning was that the United States was in the process of disengaging from Vietnam and transferring responsibility to the South Vietnamese.

In a revealing passage in *In Retrospect*, McNamara went into some detail about the divisions in the administration that culminated in the October meeting. Since his written notes for the first draft were relatively blunter, they are used instead. In them, he described three "factions":

Group one believed the Training Mission had been successful and should be withdrawn. Group two believed the Mission hadn't succeeded but had been in place sufficient time to demonstrate success wasn't possible. Group three believed that additional US support, either through a Training Mission or through training supplanted by US combat forces, would be required and was justified.

As he explained, while all these "factions" agreed on the end point, they did not necessarily agree on the way to get there or how close the administration was to meeting its objective. However, a public commitment to his policy and his end date forced their hand and produced administration-wide unity.[71] Indeed, as a State Department cable explained, "We have been making serious effort in conjunction with McNamara–Taylor mission to achieve actual and visible unity within USG [United States government]."[72]

Although McNamara also described the meetings as "heated" and "controversial," in fact this was not entirely correct. His report was sufficiently ambiguous that most participants were convinced that their objectives were being met. Taylor could feel that the pressures on Diem had been raised. Hilsman, who often clashed with McNamara and was prone to making snide remarks about him, was so satisfied with McNamara's position at the October 2, 1963, meeting that he sent him a laudatory letter that read: "I want to express my admiration for a perceptive job performed under the most difficult circumstances imaginable. I think you have brought some badly needed order to both Saigon and Washington, for which I am personally grateful."[73]

Ultimately, the October announcements served a number of important, short-term objectives for McNamara. First, he could "meet" the views of critical congressmen as he prepared to testify before them. Second, by announcing the process of withdrawal but then treating actual withdrawals in a "low-key" way, the administration could try to create uncertainty in the Diem regime without giving the Vietnamese the impression that the United States was "abandoning" them. Last, it consolidated the OSD's policy of phasing out in Vietnam and thus created a bureaucratic momentum in that direction. The latter was not, as Forrestal had suggested, primarily externally oriented "gloss"[74] but an important internal, bureaucratic maneuver.

In an oral history that he gave many years later, McNamara reflected on bureaucratic politics in a way that seems particularly on point for his October decisions. He explained, "I would point out that there is an important distinction between decisions that are a function of bureaucratic politics or decisions that are dominated by bureaucratic politics on the one hand, and, on the other, the implementation of decisions taken in the national interest – implementation which must take account of bureaucratic politics, and in a very real sense neutralize bureaucratic politics."[75]

In October 1963, McNamara hoped that a public announcement might set the policy "in concrete,"[76] but he could not have predicted the events that followed and which threw it off course. His report had sounded a note of caution that events could still create setbacks. Above all the possibility of an "unanticipated coup d'état or death of Diem" loomed. Far from being "unanticipated," McNamara's trip notes showed deep discontent and uncertainty over Diem's future and over whether the war was winnable with him.

McNamara opposed a coup against Diem, although not vehemently, primarily because it introduced uncertainty into his plans. Even before his trip, he was unconvinced that those who favored a coup within the administration, including Hilsman, Harriman, Forrestal and Lodge, knew "how we make this thing work."[77] In February 1962, Diem had survived a first coup attempt when a pair of disgruntled Air Force pilots had bombed his presidential palace. Ever since, rumors of an imminent coup and back channel contacts, notably through the CIA operative Lucien Conein, with would-be replacements to Diem had continued. These continued when McNamara arrived in Saigon. McNamara's notes of his meeting with Professor Honey in Saigon echo his risk aversion despite his frustrations with Diem. They read: "dangerous to make a change ... can we win with this regime, he believes we can't; then what is going to replace it – this is extremely risky."[78]

McNamara never questioned the morality of the administration's involvement in a coup to depose Diem. His only concern was minimizing risk and uncertainty, especially since he saw "no valid alternative." He presciently warned that "A military junta of the Vietnamese generals now planning a coup is not capable of running the Vietnamese government for very long."[79] On October 5, when Conein made a further contact with the plotters, McNamara was more aggressive. In addition to recommending that Conein should come home, he added, "to continue this kind of activity just strikes me as absurd," describing the efforts as "disgraceful."[80]

Ultimately, as McNamara explained to the SFRC, Diem was a prime case of "better the devil you know" and he sought to avoid any distractions or disruptions to his planning process. As a result, after the October meetings, Kennedy belatedly informed Ambassador Lodge to put a stop to communication with would-be coup plotters in Saigon.

However, by the end of November, both Presidents Diem and Kennedy were dead and, with them, McNamara's best-laid plans for Vietnam and for the Defense Department. The ambiguity of the October decisions and announcements was enough to get a very disparate group of advisors to agree to the policy as well as to eventually overturn it. In the end, Kennedy's policy might have been doomed to failure: counterinsurgency strategy with a much-reduced US presence might not have been enough to stave off the insurgency and the Kennedy administration might have been compelled to intervene under domestic pressure or out of a moral impulse that its involvement in the coup against Diem had now inextricably tied the United States to South Vietnam's fate. Moreover, the administration never really solved an underlying dilemma in the counterinsurgency strategies, namely whether security or political issues should take precedence.[81]

McNamara entered the Johnson administration as a, if not *the*, leading player on Vietnam policy. His proximity to the President and his ability to bring order to the administration's most complicated problems had thrust him into that role. However, McNamara's reforms and understanding of civil-military relations were such that he did not design strategy but instead aligned the Defense Department's resources and capabilities with the President's chosen policies. As it happened, the Kennedy's chosen policy was to use Vietnam as a test case for his interest in counterinsurgency, to provide a case study for the "wars of national liberation" that loomed across the developing world.

Although McNamara sat at the helm of the United States' military organization, he did not necessarily favor military solutions to the problems in Vietnam; on the contrary. Instead, the administration moved to a strategy geared toward "self-help," as spelled out in Kennedy's inaugural address, and toward disengagement from Vietnam in part to preempt the trends toward militarization that troubled Kennedy's civilian advisors in 1962. McNamara chose withdrawal not out of optimism but because it was most the coherent and efficient option available to him to meet the views of advisors such as Hilsman and Thompson. Moreover, as a Secretary who spent much of his time concerned with the United States' fiscal constraints and economic concerns, the option to withdraw promised to solve his immediate budgetary problems and, in the longer term, to produce a solution to the balance of payments that had so preoccupied the now slain President. In the transition, much of this would change. The new President was less interested in counterinsurgency and, as a fervent New Dealer and savvy congressional operator, less bothered by his predecessor's economic worries.

7

McNamara's Transition into the Johnson Administration

President Johnson understood the Vietnam policy that he had inherited from Kennedy, and the presidential tapes make clear that McNamara had informed him of the rationale behind the policy of phasing out the US presence in Vietnam. When the administration strayed from that policy, key advisors including Roger Hilsman loudly remonstrated and finally, like most of the counterinsurgency experts from the Kennedy administration, left. During his first meeting on Vietnam on November 24, 1963, the new President framed the issue in far starker and more traditionally military terms than Kennedy had been inclined to do. Moreover, Johnson publicly committed the United States to the survival of South Vietnam, something his predecessor had been more equivocal and ambivalent about. As a result, Johnson's senior advisors began to redefine the problems in Vietnam in ways that were more amenable to an overt US role. They emphasized Hanoi's actions and external factors instead of weakness in the South. As early as February 1964, divisions began appearing between those who favored a decisive military response and those, like McNamara, who saw military options at best as a deterrent action, a form of political communication, rather than a means to victory on the battlefield.

In the early months of the transition, Johnson virtually dictated many of McNamara's early memoranda to him. The Secretary thereafter learned to intuit what his boss wanted to hear. McNamara's March 1964 report, which marked a turning point in the escalatory momentum toward a military solution to the situation in Vietnam, reflected Johnson's stated preferences. Above all, in an election year, Johnson sought – and received – policies that were "disavowable," measures that would do "something" with little or no domestic political cost. Johnson's bullish, if not bullying, personality and search for a consensus also influenced McNamara's disinclination to do more than imply reservations about the administration's policy. It spurred him to gloss over divisions among advisors to produce documents that were designed to represent an administration-wide, if tenuous, consensus.

Within the narrow purview of his role as he defined it, the Secretary of Defense gave the President and Secretary of State the tools that he thought would most economically and effectively meet their objectives. In so doing, he set up the dynamic that would persist throughout the war. He would barter with the Chiefs to incrementally approve their plans for military escalation while he waited, in vain, for the State Department to take the lead in establishing the basis for a political solution.

Moreover, Johnson influenced the underlying economic rationale that had underpinned the CPSVN. Within days of becoming President, responding to changed economic conditions and to his own philosophical bent, Johnson made it clear to his advisors that he was less concerned about the balance of payments than Kennedy had been and more committed to Keynesian economics. Johnson's main focus was on domestic issues and his ambition to surpass Roosevelt's achievements under the New Deal. Many of Kennedy's advisors, who had complained that he was overly concerned with the gold outflow and insufficiently Keynesian, applauded Johnson as he launched the Great Society programs. Faced with new domestic commitments that stretched the administration's resources, McNamara started down a slippery slope of manipulating budgetary figures to underplay the costs of the conflict in Vietnam.

As well, Johnson refashioned decision-making processes to avoid messy and open policy debates, which influenced the quality of advice he received.[1] Just as Kennedy had dismantled the formal NSC structures that had informed the Eisenhower administration's policies, Johnson reorganized the flow of advice and information to better reflect his personality. Borrowing from a system that he had used as Senate Majority Leader, he convened weekly Tuesday lunches where key decisions were made with just his three principal advisors.[2] He also relied on a different and narrowing set of advisors to inform his Vietnam policy. As the war escalated, he became more inclined to receive the views of the Joint Chiefs of Staff, of external advisors who did not have the full body of intelligence available and of Secretary of State Rusk. Key counterinsurgency experts that he disliked, most notably Roger Hilsman, were pushed aside.

If on the surface and in public, McNamara became responsible for the war, behind the scenes his role was remarkably consistent across the two administrations: he did not articulate strategy per se; he implemented policy and acted as a bridge between the strategy and ambitions determined by the White House and State Department and existing capabilities and constraints. With a new President who wanted to do "something" militarily, on the one hand, and existing constraints, on the other, he presented military options that provided alternatives to traditional military deployments. The constraints that most troubled McNamara were, as always, economic and budgetary ones. More surprisingly, given that he became the face of the administration's "credibility gap," McNamara felt the administration should rally public support for the expanding commitment in Vietnam. In spite of his private reservations, McNamara produced the key documents that made escalation in Vietnam more likely and slid into the role of scapegoat for a policy that he, sooner than most, considered flawed.

The traditional view of McNamara's role in the Johnson administration, and specifically his contribution to the administration's decisions to escalate in the period between 1964 and 1965, relies on a particular interpretation of his position in the Kennedy administration and on a tendency to minimize the importance of the CPSVN plans. The withdrawal plans are usually described as secret, tentative or the product of Kennedy's vision alone; a mere blip in the otherwise inevitable upward trajectory of US involvement in Vietnam.[3] However, this view conveniently ignores the complicating fact that McNamara led Kennedy's withdrawal plans and that they were publicized, budgeted for and set within an intellectual framework, a strategy of sorts, even if that strategy was doomed to fail as the situation in Vietnam came undone.

McNamara himself appeared to confirm the orthodox interpretation of his role in escalating the war in Vietnam in his memoirs, *In Retrospect*. However, in earlier drafts, McNamara explained that publicly announcing a timetable for disengagement from Vietnam in October 1963 had been controversial and added that, "I recognized the possibility that the decision could be overturned. I urged that the decision be publicly announced, thereby setting it in concrete."[4] This goes against the grain of those who say that Johnson "consciously continued his predecessor's Vietnam policy ... to demonstrate his resolve by standing firm in Vietnam"[5] or that "Johnson never heard of the secret plans for getting out."[6] In his first drafts, McNamara emphasized that Kennedy believed that a successful intervention in Vietnam relied on having a strong South

Vietnamese political base and, in the absence of a reliable partner, moved toward a policy of withdrawal. McNamara identified several occasions during the Johnson administration – particularly, November 1964 and most of 1965 – when withdrawal could have been considered on the same premise.

The end point for US involvement as laid out in final draft of the CPSVN, in NSAM 263 and in the press statement that emerged from the October 1963 NSC meetings would come when "the insurgency has been suppressed *or* until the national security forces of the Government of South Viet-Nam are capable of suppressing it."[7] Johnson knew that the objective was *or*, not *and*. He also knew that McNamara had led efforts to make the second objective the preeminent one, that is, that he supported a movement toward self-help and felt that this was ultimately a war that only the South Vietnamese themselves could win.

One presidential recording of a conversation between Johnson and McNamara on February 25, 1964, shows that McNamara had communicated the standing policy on Vietnam to Johnson in detail. In the exchange, which is worth quoting at length, Johnson, like a good student, reiterated "what [McNamara] said to [him]" and revealed his particular lens and points of view. On the policy of self-help, Johnson explained:

And it's their war, it's their men, and we're willing to train them, and we have found that, over a period of time that we kept the Communists from spreading like we did in Greece and Turkey with the Truman Doctrine ... We've done it there by advising; we haven't done it by going off dropping bombs, we haven't done it by going out and sending men to fight and we have no such commitment there. But we do have a commitment to help the Vietnamese defend themselves. And we're there for training and that's what we've done.

Later in the conversation, he added, "All right then the next question comes is how in the hell does McNamara think, when he's losing a war, that he can pull men out of there. Well McNamara's not fighting a war, he's training men to fight a war and when he gets them through High School, they will have graduated from High School ... And if he trains them to fight and they won't fight, he can't do anything about it." Johnson understood that Kennedy and McNamara's policy was one of training and training alone.[8]

In public and before Congress, McNamara continued to defend the validity of his policy, arguing that it was still on track. He explained, "I don't believe we should leave our men there to substitute for Vietnamese men who are qualified to carry out the task, and this is really the heart of the proposal. I think it was a sound proposal then and I think so now."[9] At about the same time, other key advisors, including Sorensen and Hilsman, reminded Johnson about both the limited character of the US commitment to South Vietnam and, for Hilsman's part, the counter-insurgency aspects of the strategy there. In January 1964, for instance, Sorensen suggested that "you can continue to emphasize that the South Vietnamese have the primary responsibility for winning the war – so that if during the next four months the new government fails to take the necessary political, economic, social and military actions, it will be their choice and not our betrayal or weakness that loses the area."[10] Hilsman complained that the administration was straying from the strategic concept for South Vietnam because he believed that "if we can ever manage to have it implemented fully and with vigor, the result will be a victory."[11]

Even if Johnson recognized that he was changing Kennedy's policy, he was also responding to changed circumstances on the ground. The United States' government's complicity in the assassinations of Diem and his brother Ngo Dinh Nhu had created additional responsibilities. The period that followed Diem's assassination produced a heightened sense that South Vietnam was on the verge of collapse and that projects, notably the strategic hamlets program, were falling short of their aims. For its part, Hanoi stepped up its activities in the South and dispatched combat troops in a bid to achieve a quick victory before the United States could enter the war in earnest.[12]

Crucially, as McNamara had feared in the summer and fall of 1963, the coup leaders had not "made this thing work" and instead almost immediately descended into acrimonious divisions.[13] The gamble had not paid off and all of the problems that had undermined existing programs in South Vietnam throughout 1962 and 1963 – the country's shaky economic viability, leadership, military focus and coherence as well as its "will to win" – worsened. Despite McNamara's early reservations about the coup, which he shared with others, notably William Colby at the CIA, they expressed little bitterness. Instead, describing a professional ethic he shared with McNamara, Colby later wrote, "The basic discipline of the career officer, civilian or military, moved me to accept as mistaken even what appeared to be wrong; my attention was directed to the problems ahead that needed to be solved rather than to recriminations about the past."[14]

The situation in Vietnam would have unsettled any administration's plans to disengage. In December 1963, following his first trip back to

Vietnam after the assassinations of Presidents Diem and Kennedy, McNamara found the situation "very disturbing" and warned that "current trends, unless reversed in the next 2–3 months, will lead to neutralization at best and more likely a Communist-controlled state."[15] In a tense meeting in Saigon, he berated the coup leaders for their inability to govern and implement realistic programs. In his private notes from the trip, he worried that the "greatest weakness is an indecisive, drifting government," while "a second major weakness is a country team which lacks leadership, is poorly informed and is not working to a common plan."[16]

At about the same time, DCI McCone, who traveled to Vietnam with McNamara, wrote, "It is abundantly clear that statistics received over the past year or more from the GVN officers and reported by the US mission on which we gauged the trend of the war were grossly in error." About the Delta region that had disturbed McNamara only two months earlier, McCone wrote, "Conditions in the delta and in the areas immediately north of Saigon are more serious now than expected and were probably never as good as reported."[17]

While they may have been heightened in the aftermath of Diem's assassination, concerns about Vietnamese leadership, the lack of cooperation in the US country team, the overextension of the strategic hamlet program or even poor intelligence were not new. During the October 1963 NSC meetings, President Kennedy's "only reservation" with announcing the planned phaseout in Vietnam was that "if the war doesn't continue to go well, it will look like we were overly optimistic."[18] McNamara responded to Kennedy's reservation by saying that although he was "not entirely sure" that the insurgency could be brought under control by 1965, the withdrawal could nevertheless go ahead by that date since it depended only on the South Vietnamese completing a predetermined training program.[19]

Two aspects of the NSC October 1963 meetings could have kept the CPSVN on track regardless of the situation on the ground. First, that the objective continued to be to help the South Vietnamese fight the insurgency themselves and, as a corollary to this, that the US government resisted taking on a greater role in fighting the insurgency despite repeated recommendations in Washington and from the field missions to do so. One field report in October 1963 had warned, "The current war in Vietnam is too important a business to leave to the Vietnamese politicians particularly in view of the fact that it is being waged at the expense of the US taxpayer."[20] In spite of an expanded assistance mission, the administration had defined the conflict in South Vietnam in terms that would limit the United States' commitment. As Kennedy had indicated, "In the final analysis it is the people and the government [of South Vietnam] who have to win or lose this struggle."[21]

Second, the NSC October 1963 meetings and the subsequent press statement had been designed to create bureaucratic momentum behind a policy of disengagement with the hope that it would prove irreversible. At the time, while McNamara accepted that "there may be shades of difference," President Kennedy reasoned, "I think it ties it all down," or, as McGeorge Bundy explained: "by God we hang everybody in every department on to it." McNamara was adamant about and succeeded in having a press statement out in order to "peg" everyone behind a policy of disengagement.[22]

As McNamara scribbled in his first notes for *In Retrospect*: "[Kennedy] was willing to supply limited support – in the form of logistics and US military trainers and advisors to help the Vietnamese help themselves with the clear objective of withdrawing that support after it had been long enough to help the Vietnamese develop a capability to help themselves if they were capable of doing so. By July–October 1963, he and I agreed that time had come."[23] As the preceding chapter explained, the October 1963 announcement of a phased withdrawal was not premised on an optimistic reading of the situation in Vietnam. Rather, it hinged on other variables including the Kennedy administration's interest in counterinsurgency. McNamara's suggestion in the final draft of *In Retrospect* that it was only in December 1963 that he realized that "earlier reports of military progress had been inflated" was, at best, disingenuous.

It was not until January 1964, when it became clear that Johnson was uninterested in the CPSVN, that McNamara began advancing the argument that his plans had always been conditional on the situation in South Vietnam. His statements to various audiences at that time, including the House Armed Services Committee: (HASC), provide putative evidence that as far as McNamara was concerned the CPSVN had always been contingent on progress in the field, progress that he had believed was forthcoming in the fall of 1963.[24] However, until that point, McNamara was largely, and at times deliberately, myopic to negative reports coming from the field. Instead, managerial priorities and realities in Washington conditioned the timetable and content of the CPSVN. By rewriting the history of the CPSVN, McNamara was also disguising the change in policy that was happening during the transition.

The decision to expand US involvement in South Vietnam as the situation there deteriorated was also, to some extent, a product of bureaucratic machinery rather than an individual's decision. Yet, as one scholar has written, "The dominant variable of any advisory system is the personality of the President."[25] Given McNamara's strict conceptions of loyalty, the President was in fact "the" determining variable in understanding his shift. And while it may be unfair to characterize Johnson's approach to Vietnam as less sophisticated than Kennedy's, this was precisely McNamara's assessment. He explained that Johnson had removed key qualifiers to the US commitment to South Vietnam, notably a strong political base and the ability of the South Vietnamese to win the war themselves. He added, "In that sense, I think his view was what I termed more simplist [*sic*]. I don't like the term but, for the minute, it conveys my thought."[26]

President Johnson's rather more "simplist" understanding of Vietnam shaped the terms of the debate and the scope of the recommendations that McNamara presented to him. In one telling exchange with McNamara on March 2, 1964, Johnson instructed McNamara: "I want you to dictate to me a memorandum of a couple of pages, uh four letter words and short sentences and several paragraphs so I can read it and study it and commit to memory … the Vietnam picture if you had to put in 600 words or maybe a thousand words if you have to go that long. But just like you'd talk."[27] These types of exchanges add credence to the view that Johnson lacked the nuance of his predecessor on foreign policy issues, "which left him vulnerable to clichés and stereotypes about world affairs."[28]

The presidential recordings of conversations between President Johnson and McNamara also often reveal a hierarchical relationship confirming Yarmolinsky's view that if McNamara's relationship with Kennedy had been one of "real mutual trust and affection," Johnson "was his boss, and he was Johnson's most useful servant."[29] Whereas McNamara often interrupted Kennedy and at times dominated their conversations, Johnson lectured and dictated, instructing McNamara that "I'll tell you what I'd say about it." In exchanges that sometimes appeared excessive, Johnson complimented McNamara, calling him "McCan-do-man" or his "executive VP," somebody he valued because "I need to issue instructions and see that they're carried out."[30] McNamara's old colleagues and friends, particularly Robert Kennedy, became "outraged by McNamara's servility" and the "humiliations" he endured "out of deference to Johnson or his office."[31] Ultimately, McNamara's relationship to Johnson reflected his ambivalent depiction of Johnson as someone who was "by turns open and devious, loving and mean, compassionate and tough, gentle and cruel ... a towering, powerful, paradoxical figure."[32] Their relationship also explains McNamara's role during the transition.

Despite his flattering remarks, Johnson allowed and even encouraged McNamara to become the public face of escalation in Vietnam. In the key period of the spring of 1964, Senator Morse first designated the war in Vietnam as "McNamara's war," a moniker President Johnson reveled in. The presidential recordings are replete with references to Johnson's amusement with the notion: he laughed that it was unfair that it was "only McNamara's war"[33] or described the situation as "your war in Vietnam."[34] For his part, McNamara slavishly took responsibility for the complicated situation because it would "take a lot of heat off of you Mr. President."[35] When, in September 1964, press reports first started pointing the finger at Johnson for the administration's policy in Vietnam, he teased McNamara that it "looks to me that [Texas Governor] John Connally, the two of you got together and transferred it from McNamara's war to Johnson's war," that he had "never heard a word about Johnson's war until the two of you got together," and mused that "I kind of enjoyed [Senator Barry] Goldwater's talk about McNamara's war."[36] Ultimately, just as Kennedy had made McNamara the public face of the withdrawal plans and charged him with the organization of a policy for Vietnam, Johnson ensured that McNamara was also identified with the decision to escalate.

However, the impetus for escalation had come from Johnson, not McNamara. Johnson had defined the parameters of the discussion on Vietnam with his almost immediate commitment to "win" in Vietnam.[37] McNamara wrote that "President Johnson made clear to Lodge on November 24 [1963] that he wanted to win the war, and that, at least in the short run, he wanted priority given to military operations over 'so-called' social reforms. He felt the United States had spent too much time and energy trying to shape other countries in its own image. Win the war! That was his message."[38] Although in an interview with CBS in the wake of that meeting, Ambassador Lodge stated that "policy [was] unchanged and that "it was not a decision-making type meeting," Johnson's "message" influenced the shape of policy in the ensuing months.[39]

Within weeks, Johnson wrote to General Taylor that "The more I look at it, the more it is clear to me that South Vietnam is our most critical *military* area right now" (emphasis added).[40] In turn, this fed into the kind of advice he demanded from McNamara. During McNamara's first trip back to Vietnam in December 1963, his team's terms of reference as he communicated them to Ambassador Lodge were to plan for "varying levels of pressure all designed to make clear to the North Vietnamese that the US will not accept a communist victory in South Vietnam and that we will escalate the conflict to whatever level is required to ensure defeat."[41] With Mansfield and others floating the idea that negotiated neutralism might be an avenue the administration should explore for South Vietnam, Rusk felt it necessary to reassure the South Vietnamese with an "authoritative statement of American war aims and policy on neutralization."[42] That policy was established before McNamara had left Washington. As Forrestal wrote to Lodge, the primary reason that "McNamara is coming out" was to send a signal "that we are against neutralism and want to win the war."[43]

In the same February 25, 1964, tape where Johnson spelled out the Kennedy/McNamara policy, he also revealed his distinctive perspective and biases. For instance, he told McNamara, "We have a commitment to Vietnamese freedom. Now, we could pull out of there, the dominos would fall, that part of the world would go Communist." This was a stronger commitment than McNamara had allowed in his October 1963 report.[44] It was also the only exchange where Johnson directly addressed the withdrawal plans. The remarks challenge the idea that he chose to continue Kennedy's policy in Vietnam. He said: "I always thought it was foolish to make any statements about withdrawing. I thought it was bad psychologically. But you and the President thought otherwise and I just sat silent."[45]

During his "silent" years as Vice President, and on the rare occasions when he had been consulted, Johnson had encouraged "tougher" responses. During his trip to South Vietnam in May 1961, he promised that the United States would stand "shoulder to shoulder" with South Vietnam and, in a seemingly unprompted way, asked Diem if he needed US or SEATO intervention.[46] In his trip report, he reiterated the domino theory and argued that "The failure to act vigorously to stop the killing now in Viet Nam may well be paid for later with the lives of Americans all over Asia."[47] Even while he recognized the dangers of finding the United States embroiled in a "jungle war," he argued for a substantial increase in economic aid and a more active military role. He ended his report to the President ominously: "There is a chance for success in Viet Nam but there is not a moment to lose. We need to move along the above lines and we need to begin now, today, to move."[48] Kennedy and McNamara largely ignored the Vice President's warnings and recommendations.

Now that Johnson was President, however, McNamara could not ignore him, and on paper, McNamara became a leading force behind the decisions to favor military tools in Vietnam. At the same time that McNamara was insisting on the limited character of the US commitment to Vietnam, his memoranda encouraged aggressive policies that represented a clear break with the policies he had supported until then. As early as December 1963, armed with his negative appraisal of the situation in Vietnam, McNamara recommended that the administration should be "preparing for more forceful moves."[49] By March 1964, in his first joint trip back to South Vietnam with Maxwell Taylor, his already pessimistic appraisal of the situation darkened further and he came out even more strongly in favor of the very same military response that he had resisted during the Kennedy administration.

McNamara's March trip report was riddled with contradictions and reflected long-standing bureaucratic conflicts. McNamara wrote that the policy of phased withdrawal and of considering the conflict as one for which "the South Vietnamese must win and take ultimate responsibility" was "still sound." At the same time, he inferred that this was no longer a substitute for victory in the traditional sense. Now he wrote, "The US at all levels must continue to make emphatically clear that we are prepared to furnish assistance and support for as long as it takes to bring the insurgency under control."[50] The report's suggested policy directions were equally contradictory. On the one hand, it stated the "so-called 'oil spot' theory is excellent" and reiterated the key role for counterinsurgency programs. On the other, it recommended preparing for graduated "air pressure" over North Vietnam.[51] Until this point, the counterinsurgency strategy had been designed as a substitute to conventional force and precluded a bombing program. Even if the report made due reference to neutralization and withdrawal, it also quickly rejected them as viable policy options.

Ambassador Ormsby-Gore's notes from a dinner with McNamara the night before he departed on this March trip suggest that even if McNamara was publicly expanding the commitment to South Vietnam and proposing policy options that would extend "American military commitments," in private, he still held on to a policy he later ascribed to Kennedy, namely that there would be no point in expanding the US commitment to South Vietnam without a viable political base in the country. The Ambassador found McNamara "more despondent about the situation there than I have ever seen him" and very concerned about South Vietnam's new leadership's ability to "restore morale and achieve growing popular support." Later, he wrote: "He was not in a belligerent mood and although he has spoken to me previously about examining the possibilities of hurting the North Vietnamese, I gained the strong impression that unless he came back feeling that there was a reasonable chance of pulling the situation round in South Vietnam, there would be no value in risking a further extension of American military commitments in the area such as would result from trying to carry the conflict over the border into the North."[52]

Instead, McNamara's trip and report were stage-managed with a view to placating emerging divisions in the administration and on the home front in an election year. Just days before the trip, Johnson basically dictated what would eventually became the report's policy suggestions: "I'd like you to say that there are several courses that could be followed." These were: sending in troops, neutralization that would result in "Commies ... swallow[ing] up South Vietnam," pulling out which would result in dominos falling throughout the region or continuing training.[53] In other words, the crucial March 1964 report was not so much a reflection of McNamara's views as it was what Johnson said he'd "like [McNamara] to say."

William Bundy, who replaced Hilsman as Assistant Secretary of State for Far Eastern Affairs, wrote most of the March report as well as McNamara's subsequent speech in Washington before the latter had even left for Saigon. The State Department was on the ascendancy on Vietnam in these early months. William Sullivan headed a State-led working group that had supplanted the Special Group (CI) in overseeing activities in Vietnam. The State Department took a more traditional approach to the problems in Vietnam and moved away from counterinsurgency theories. In particular, from December 1963, the department sought to resuscitate the Jorden report that McNamara had previously suppressed and Rostow had championed, which argued that the problems in Vietnam were a result of external aggression from the North rather than a product of failures in the South.[54]

While it was true that Hanoi had accelerated infiltration and stepped up its activities in the wake of the Diem coup, this changed focus also reflected a willingness in the State Department to prepare for actions against the North. By February, both Rostow and William Bundy thought the trip team should "make an effort to produce a lucid assessment of the relative role of external intrusion" and that "the answer may lie in hoarding certain firm, relatively recent evidence."[55] Sensing the public

FIGURE 7.1 A page from John T. McNaughton's scrapbooks. Left: Secretary of Defense McNamara arrives in Saigon and walks with newly minted Prime Minister General Khanh to his right and Ambassador Henry Cabot Lodge to his left. His Assistant for International Security Affairs McNaughton is in the background, flanked by General William Westmoreland to his left and General Paul Harkins to his right, March 8, 1964. Right: McNaughton at a reception at the US Embassy in Saigon, undated (March 1964). The trip was largely a public relations exercise; the trip report was written before they left.
(John T. McNaughton scrapbooks, John T. McNaughton family collection.)

relations opportunity, Johnson suggested McNamara himself "carry off the plane a recoilless rifle as evidence of North Vietnamese support."[56]

McNamara's March trip was a public relations exercise (see Figure 7.1). The uptick of terrorist activities in South Vietnam, including the bombing of a movie theater in Saigon in February, had created pressures for the administration to do more, at least to protect its own citizens. However, given the electoral calendar, Johnson wanted to delay actions that might be too visible or contentious. In December 1963, McNamara had considered "disavowable actions." A month later, the President approved sabotage actions against the North known as OPLAN 34A that were only nominally under South Vietnamese control. By

March, McNamara lifted his resistance to the introduction of jets to
Vietnam under the Air Force's Farmgate operations: officially, they were
introduced for "logistical reasons"; unofficially, they were deployed to
prepare strikes on the North "contrary to policy that US was to train
VNAF [Vietnamese Air Force]."[57] In his notes from the March trip,
McNamara looked for "plausibly deniable" actions that might "make
plain US can bring military pressures to bear on North Vietnam without
being overt."[58] His new Assistant Secretary for International Security
Affairs, John T. McNaughton, cautioned that "there is no magic formula" before they left for Vietnam.[59] Yet this was exactly what the
administration sought: a policy that would shift the situation on the
ground without attracting attention outside Vietnam.

The administration also wanted a policy that could give the impression
that civilians and the military were united. McNamara's instructions to
the trip team speak to his efforts at forcing a consensus. He indicated that
they would not prepare a final written report, but that, instead, he would
report orally to the President. He asked them to minimize contact with the
press and not to send interim reports back to their own departments.[60]
Where divisions existed, McNamara overruled them. In January and
February, the Joint Chiefs of Staff had suggested the administration move
toward victory by removing "self-imposed restrictions," but McNamara
capitalized on divisions in their midst. Where the Army agreed with
McNamara that the problems in Vietnam inherently lay in the South,
the Air Force suggested an aggressive push on the North. McNamara
distilled the Chiefs' contradictory views under his recommended
"actions." Before he left, he proudly told Johnson, "Divide and conquer
is a pretty good rule in this situation. And to be quite frank, I've tried to
do that in the last few weeks and it's coming along quite well."[61]

Crucially, McNamara had to reconcile the momentum toward escalation with continued insistence that withdrawal was still on the cards as
the South Vietnamese were trained. Robert Thompson counseled that
while the prospects for winning were "gloomy," the situation was "not
yet desperate" if the administration refocused on pacification without a
too strong US presence. He now cautioned against mentioning withdrawal and suggested the administration might put a positive spin by
saying it would stay "as long as it may be necessary."[62] Accordingly,
McNaughton edited Bundy's passage of the trip report to add that assistance would be provided "regardless of how long it takes" and that
"previous judgments that the major part of the US job could be completed
by the end of 1965 should now be soft pedaled and placed on the basis

that no such date can now be set realistically until we see how the conflict works out."[63] Still, within ten days of submitting the report, planning for the withdrawal of US forces from Vietnam was formally, though not publicly, terminated.[64] When the 1,000-man withdrawal did go ahead, it was done on the basis of "efficiencies" rather than as part of a larger program of phasing out.

Ultimately, the mood that Ormsby-Gore had observed on the eve of the trip was likely less a reflection of McNamara's concerns about what he might find in South Vietnam and more about the momentum he could see was gathering in Washington around the option of using military force and against his plans for phased withdrawal.[65] This is not to say that Johnson did not share McNamara's concerns about the policies on offer. In a private conversation with Richard Russell on the eve of McNamara's departure, Johnson worried about the options available to him and the lingering feeling that he was boxed in, not "know[ing] any way to get out."[66] Nevertheless, he encouraged McNamara to come back with recommendations that increased US involvement in South Vietnam.

Ever the political animal, Johnson was especially concerned about the domestic reaction to the growing commitment in Vietnam. The timing of the trip and McNamara's subsequent speech in Washington coincided with increasing murmurs in the SFRC and in editorial pages about the situation in South Vietnam and President de Gaulle's renewed push for neutralization of the entire Indochinese peninsula. In January 1964, an exchange of letters between Senator Mansfield and Johnson spurred a discussion within the administration about the limits of the United States' commitment to Vietnam. Using the same arguments McNamara had made in the preceding months, Mansfield addressed the danger of "another China in Vietnam" and noted, "Neither do we want another Korea. It would seem that a key (but often overlooked) factor in both situations was a tendency to bite off more than we can chew. We tended to talk ourselves out on a limb with overstatements of our purpose and commitment." He ended with a warning to the President that "there ought to less official talk of our responsibility in Vietnam and more emphasis on the responsibilities of the Vietnamese themselves."[67] In the days before the trip, in front of the SFRC, both Rusk and McNamara had to rebut liberal senators' contention that the situation was hopeless, that it was essentially a civil war as the influential columnist Walter Lippmann had written and to justify why the administration was not pursuing the neutralization route.[68] "The basic purpose of the speech," Sullivan explained, "is to obtain broad support and particularly to state objectives which will be endorsed by the Mansfields and the Lippmanns. More pointedly, it is intended to separate the Mansfields from the Morses."[69]

Thus, ten days after his return from Vietnam, in the speech that William Bundy had also written for him on the back of the trip report, McNamara publicly defended a shift toward a more open-ended commitment to counter growing criticism in the United States. His speech continued to make reference to Vietnam as a "test case" for counterinsurgency even while it now put more onus on the external dimensions of the conflict.[70] Whereas the October 1963 announcement promised a commitment until "the insurgency has been suppressed or until the national security forces of the Government of South Viet-Nam are capable of suppressing it," he now publicly pledged a US commitment for "as long as it takes," as Robert Thompson had suggested.[71] The speech, and the trip report, were pieces of a delicate balancing act aimed at convincing disparate critics that the administration was not planning a major escalation, that the fundamental policy was continuing but instead, as Johnson explained to McNamara, "going to do more of the same, except we're going to firm it up and strengthen it."[72]

The March 1964 shift represented the particular flavor of an administration with Lyndon Johnson at its helm. Just as the October 1963 policy and the CPSVN flowed from a policy framework set out by President Kennedy, McNamara's increasingly hawkish recommendations in early months of 1964 flowed from President Johnson. In addition, Johnson's reorganization of national security decision-making had an indirect influence on policy outcomes: it elevated Rusk on Vietnam policy. The idea that Johnson continued Kennedy's policy has also relied on stressing the continuity of personnel. The reality is that key advisors were quickly sidelined, including Robert Kennedy, who had led the Special Group (CI), and Averell Harriman, who was made roving Ambassador for African Affairs. Other advisors, such as Sorensen, Forrestal and Hilsman, who had signaled early on to Johnson that the administration was not keeping to the Kennedy administration's policy, were also set aside.

Rusk, instead of more junior counterinsurgency experts such as Hilsman, now had greater clout. In the October 1963 NSC meetings, when the Kennedy administration committed itself publicly to a policy of disengagement, Hilsman and Harriman, not Rusk, had represented the State Department. Rusk was in Europe at a NATO summit at the time. Not only was he absent from the key NSC meetings, he was brought up to speed on the policy only *after* the public announcement had been made. Since the strategy that underpinned McNamara's withdrawal plans stemmed from advisors like Hilsman rather than Rusk, their subsequent removal from decision-making on Vietnam was also significant.

Sorensen, who had alerted Johnson to the limits of Kennedy's commitment and who had suggested ways of disengaging from Vietnam in a way that would not endanger US credibility, was the first to go. Kennedy's assassination had particularly affected him. In January, he indicated that he "didn't want to come back" to the White House, which he described as a "very sad place."[73] In private, he spoke harshly about Johnson: "to me he personified the kind of hyperbole and hypocrisy that defined the worst aspects of politics in my eyes."[74] These comments suggest that his reasons for leaving hinged on his personal dislike of Johnson.[75]

Forrestal was also sidelined and eventually left. In the early days of the transition, Forrestal had gone along with the administration's moves. At McGeorge Bundy's request, he produced an economic and political program to match McNamara's planning for graduated escalation. However, he was ambivalent about the administration's proclivity to define the conflict in increasingly conventional military terms. By the spring of 1964, he broke with McGeorge Bundy and wrote, "What we are dealing with is social revolution by illegal means, infected by the cancer of Communism." He also went back on his suggestion that physical security achieved through military means was a prerequisite for the other social and economic programs. He now said: "I believed this, too, until after the third or fourth trip to Vietnam. But the problems are not separable. The Viet Cong know this. It is why they are winning. To the extent we manage our economic assistance, our military action, and our political advice so as to perpetuate a social and economic structure which gave rise to the very problem we are fighting, we will fail to solve the problem." Ultimately, by January 1965, he too left the administration, disillusioned and depressed.[76]

As for Hilsman, under the new administration he reaped the consequences of his antagonistic relationship with both the military and his boss, Rusk, whom he had continuously circumvented in the past. Although as a fellow Texan, Hilsman felt that he and President Johnson "should have gotten along," he became isolated in the new administration.[77] Rusk later said, "I fired him because he talked too much at Georgetown cocktail parties."[78] Taylor explained that Hilsman was dismissed because he had antagonized military advisors by second-guessing their recommendations – "it just shows what happens when you put a West Pointer in the State Department" – and because he "drove McNamara mad."[79] In an effort to avoid a noisy departure, he was offered the

Ambassadorship in the Philippines where he had spent a part of his childhood. He chose instead to resign.[80] Despite the administration's attempts to contain the news of his resignation, it made the front page of the *New York Times* of February 25, 1964, where he insisted, "I am not quarreling with policy" and praised Johnson for his "vigor and sureness."[81]

Not one to keep his opinions to himself, however, Hilsman protested loudly within corridors of power that the administration was not continuing Kennedy's policy and he continued to voice this opinion after he left government. In a document entitled "Last Will and Testament: South Viet-Nam and Southeast Asia," which he sent to Rusk on March 10, 1964, Hilsman reacted to the administration's gradual move away from the counterinsurgency strategy he had helped to design. He reminded his former boss that the strategy rested on the "Strategic Concept for South Vietnam," though he did not mention that the "Strategic Concept" was his work. He described the strategy as still "basically sound" even while he acknowledged its failings on the field. He also responded to the administration's choice to consider more traditional, military tools and wrote: "In sum, I think we can win in Viet-Nam with a number of provisos. The first is that we do not over-militarize the war – that we concentrate not on killing the Vietcong and the conventional means of warfare, but on an effective program for extending the areas of security gradually, systematically and thoroughly. This will require better team work in Saigon than we have had in the past and considerably more emphasis on clear and hold operations and on policy work than we ourselves have given to the Vietnamese."[82]

By May 1964, after a final meeting with McNamara, Robert Thompson too was forced to acknowledge that the new administration was no longer listening to him and that "his usefulness had come to an end." The British advisory mission closed at the end of 1964 by which time Thompson had concluded that the war was no longer winnable and the administration should move to negotiations.[83] In a scathing analysis of the Johnson administration, he explained how, in the early months of 1964, in part because the new President relied "too much" on military advisors and "tradition" rather than advisors like him, the "original position, in which the United States was merely helping the South Vietnamese to win its own war, was gradually changed, to one in which it had to interfere in South Vietnam."[84]

Ultimately, all the key individuals who questioned the administration's decisions on Vietnam or provided the intellectual rationale for a counterinsurgency strategy were pushed out. McNamara, who could have kept their voices alive within national security decision-making, chose to be loyal to the President. Many months later, in March 1965, after the start of Operation Rolling Thunder, McNamara reassured Johnson that the administration was in general agreement and that leaks to the press were less likely now. He noted, "There's been more unity both beneath and above surface on Vietnam in the last few months than at any time in the last several years. And more unity in the upper levels than you did, let's say in the Hilsman/CIA/Defense Department wrangle."[85]

Personnel changes in Washington shifted the focus away from counterinsurgency in Vietnam, as did practical realities about the South Vietnamese and US mission's inability to execute and implement existing plans. Coups in Vietnam succeeded themselves and each fresh government promised a new pacification plan. But political instability and corruption undermined each attempt. The US mission, which splintered along bureaucratic lines, was also incapable of coordinating different civilian and military programs. In the military field, where many irregular forces had already been subsumed under military command, the "conventionalization" of forces began in earnest. One Special Forces history explained how "very few hamlet militia were trained after November 1963, almost none after April 1964."[86]

The administration's move toward a more open-ended commitment to Vietnam in 1964 had important repercussions on the economic issues that had underpinned the CPSVN. The counterinsurgency strategy had dovetailed with McNamara's efforts to tackle the balance of payments deficit, while the CPSVN addressed the SFRC's attack on the MAP as well as the Kennedy administration's general tendency toward fiscal restraint. By contrast, Johnson embraced Keynesian economics and was willing to run large deficits. Even so, while the administration moved to a more "forceful" program in Vietnam that no longer fell within the limited purview of a traditional military assistance program, Johnson encouraged McNamara to cut costs and especially to undervalue costs for Vietnam lest they scuttle his domestic ambitions by provoking a congressional debate over his ambition to have both "guns and butter."[87] Given his bridging role at the OSD, McNamara early on recognized the tensions inherent in the White House's competing ambitions.

Even as he integrated the notion that South Vietnam's problems were externally driven in his reports and pubic pronouncements, McNamara was reluctant to call the situation in Vietnam a "war." By keeping the Defense Department's peacetime accounting, it was relatively easier for him to underestimate the true costs of the war. In the first months of the administration, Johnson instructed McNamara to underestimate his annual budget requests for the Department and for Vietnam specifically. McNamara submitted the budget to Congress in the fall knowing full well that he would submit a supplementary request in the spring. He suggested this delaying technique to President Johnson but as early as December 1963 expressed concern that it might "screw up the integrity of the budgeting process here."[88]

McNamara's willingness to loosen his control of the budget is explicable when set against the backdrop of the administration's broader economic policies. Unlike Kennedy, who erred on the side of fiscal conservatism and, in so doing, angered his liberal economic advisors, Johnson was applauded for his willingness to embrace Keynesianism. He proceeded with Kennedy's planned tax cut even as he significantly increased federal spending on social programs as part of his Great Society. To Walter Heller, he explained that he was a "Roosevelt New Dealer" and "to tell you the truth, John F. Kennedy was a little too conservative to suit my taste."[89] While Kennedy had ruled out the possibility of expanding spending on the back of the balance of payments deficit and faced greater resistance from the business community as well as Congress, these constraints bothered Johnson much less.[90]

Paradoxically, President Johnson seemed to reassure the business community and, as some of the offset programs with European allies and a "buy American" program within the Defense Department began to take effect, the balance of payments crisis seemed to have subsided by 1964. Also, as Secretary Dillon, who stayed on for the first year of the Johnson administration, recalled, "Now Mr. Johnson had plenty of other things to do and he didn't have this sort of interest. He knew it was important. He supported our effort in helping international monetary cooperation – and later on I think he developed a real interest in it when he had more time. But that came, I guess, after I'd left."[91]

Dillon, who had benefited from an unusually close relationship with President Kennedy and encouraged him to err on the side of fiscal prudence, saw his influence wane in the transition and recalled a President who "wasn't interested in what was going on" on the economic front.[92] In December 1963, he tried in vain to attract the new President's attention to defense outlays overseas and was irritated when Johnson went further than his predecessor in promising to keep six divisions in Europe "so long as they are needed," adding "and under present circumstances there is no doubt that they will continue to be needed." He warned the President that the Republicans could use the need to reduce overseas deployments, not least for balance of payments reasons, as a campaign issue and that it was time for substantial troop reductions especially in Europe.[93]

Johnson promised Senator Harry Byrd, the Senate Finance Committee's Chairman, a reduction in federal expenditures to below the $100 billion mark in exchange for the passage of the Kennedy tax cut.[94] Although this reduction had largely been agreed on between Dillon and President Kennedy, it allowed Johnson to "appear even more conservative in cutting expenditures than maybe he really was."[95] In order to keep expenditures down while moving ahead with the costly Great Society programs, Johnson had to cut back elsewhere, notably on the defense budget. Although the PPBS program was explicitly designed not to have budgetary ceilings de facto, McNamara reintroduced them to fit Johnson's guidelines. As he explained to Johnson in a private discussion about the FY64 budget, the JCS wouldn't "know that I set the dollar limit first."[96]

Kennedy's liberal critics praised the "spectacular savings" made to the defense budget and what they saw as the reallocation of funds to welfare spending. They also applauded Johnson's "great skill in dealing with Congress"[97] even while some mournfully noted that, on the domestic front, "President Kennedy apparently had to die to create a sympathetic atmosphere to his program."[98] At the Defense Department, the published numbers were impressive. McNamara cut the defense budget by almost $2.5 billion in FY64 and a further $1.2 billion in both FY65 and FY66. He achieved these cuts by moving ahead with his base closure and cost reduction programs, both initiated under the Kennedy administration, but more problematically by delaying procurement decisions.[99] For a time, McNamara's efforts kept Vietnam off the radar and avoided a congressional debate on the administration's broader economic policies.

As Kennedy's counterinsurgency and fiscally conservative advisors' influence waned in the Johnson administration, the rationale for the CPSVN fell apart. Instead, by May 1964, when McNamara returned again to Vietnam, he had to contend with obvious failures in the field and particularly with the growing pressure to do "something" to stop the situation in South Vietnam from unraveling (see Figure 7.2). McNamara blamed Lodge for many of the program's failures. In his memoirs, he described Lodge as "aristocratic and patrician to the point of arrogance."[100] In private, he thought Lodge lazy, as the Ambassador was known to disdain administrative tasks and run "a pretty relaxed daily regime."[101] He scarcely respected the rest of the country team. He

FIGURE 7.2 A page from John T. McNaughton's scrapbooks. Secretary of Defense McNamara arrives again in Saigon. He walks with Ambassador Lodge, General Harkins (who was about to retire), General Khanh and McNaughton behind him, May 12, 1964.
(OSD Photograph, John T. McNaughton scrapbooks, John T. McNaughton family collection.)

described Joseph Brent, the head of the USOM, as "washed up"; Ogden Williams, who headed the rural affairs program, as "not filled with a sense of urgency"; and concluded that there was "no effective direction of the counterinsurgency program in the country team."[102]

In lieu of the existing policy, a bureaucratic consensus around bombing North Vietnam emerged. Ambassador Lodge joined the chorus of advisors who argued that a bombing program could bolster existing programs in the South, that it could create breathing room for the South while forcing the North to negotiate or reduce infiltration. McNamara's May trip was thus designed to study when and whether to start bombing and how it could complement activities in the South. Where previous South Vietnamese leaders had resisted such a bombing program, the new Prime Minister Nguyen Khanh, with some nudging from Lodge, now described it as "desirable." McNamara agreed to study the bombing program even if the presidential recordings, even more than the written record, reveal that he questioned its effectiveness and bemoaned Wheeler's emphasis on "planes." He explained to Johnson: "And the planes, Max Taylor agrees, are not the answer to the problem. Whether we should have more planes is another question but it's not going to make any difference in the short-term, that's for certain."[103]

Still, with an election nearing, Johnson needed political protection against Lodge and the Chiefs. McNamara returned from his May trip to a letter from Representative Carl Vinson, the Chairman of the HASC, who drew attention to an article in *US News & World* by one of his constituents, an Air Force widow who, in contrast to liberal critics, decried the "incompetence, cowardice... among many of the public officials directing war operations."[104] With his strong foreign policy credentials and centrist views on social issues, Lodge was a potential political threat to Johnson, who might add to the chorus about civilian timidity in Vietnam. In March, while McNamara was in Vietnam, Lodge had won the Republican primary election in New Hampshire although he was not officially campaigning as he was precluded from doing so as a civil servant.[105] Fearing public criticism on Vietnam policy, Johnson asked McNamara to "build up a record" of support for Lodge. In a press conference, the President had underhandedly commented that "he makes recommendations from time to time. We act promptly on those recommendations."[106] For his part, McNamara quoted Lodge's memos in his testimony to the SFRC.[107]

The Chiefs were equally troublesome for Johnson. In April, Johnson warned McNamara, "Well let's give [Wheeler] more of something. Because I'm going to have a heart attack if you don't give him more of something."[108] Thus, when McNamara arrived in Vietnam in May, he told MACV that the main priority was winning the war and that they would have everything they needed to achieve that objective. In May 1961 and again in May 1964, for Johnson, traditional military means could achieve a "winning" formula, something neither McNamara nor even Maxwell Taylor recommended.[109] Even though he described the Chiefs as "fools,"[110] in April 1964, Johnson asked McNamara if he had "anybody [who] has a military mind that can give us a military plan for winning that war." This represented a break in policy on Vietnam because until this point the Chiefs had very little say in designing policy.[111] A recording on April 30, 1964, is particularly revealing in this regard. Johnson indicated that "What I want is somebody that can lay up some plans to trap these guys and whoop hell out of them, kill some of

them, that's what I want to do," to which McNamara responded, "I'll try
to bring something back that'll meet that objective."[112]

By the spring of 1964, Johnson appeared to fall into the trap Galbraith
had warned of in the spring of 1962, namely "the mystique of conventional force, and the recurrent feeling that, in the absence of any other
feasible lines of action, the movement of troops might help."[113] Despite
lacking an overarching strategy, McNamara's May 1964 report and the
NSC discussion that followed set the administration on a path to conventional war against North Vietnam. In reference to the overall objective to
"win," McNamara's trip report warned that "We are continuing to lose.
Nothing we are now doing will win."[114] However, in the NSC discussions, it was McCone ("we should go in hard and not limit our actions to
pinpricks") and McGeorge Bundy who argued most vehemently for
planning a bombing program against the North.[115] In the next days,
Bundy reiterated his conviction that military planning should move forward within a "larger framework – the US national interest and the future
of Southeast Asia – that I hope we will all be thinking as the discussion
goes on."[116]

However, Galbraith's concern about traditional deployments of
troops was also an economic one. In the key May 1964 discussions,
McNamara argued that any planning for a bombing program should
also involve an information program for the public and Congress, who
would ultimately have to fund expanded operations. Rusk argued that
doing so could put the President in a "precarious position."[117] Again
in June 1964, McNamara suggested to Johnson that "many of us
agree" that "if we're going to go up the escalating chain, then we're
going to have to educate the people Mr. President and we haven't done
so yet." Johnson refused, remarking, "They're going to be calling you a
warmonger."[118]

Nevertheless, at Johnson's request to have "a military mind" give "a
military plan for winning the war," McNamara led a meeting in Honolulu in June 1964 with CINCPAC and MACV commanders where the full
range of military plans and contingencies was considered. These included
the use of tactical nuclear weapons, the deployment of ground troops and
the first version of a JCS list of 94 targets that would become a major
bone of contention between civilians and the military. On the basis of that
list, McNamara began planning for a graduated escalation bombing
program.[119] Economists such as Thomas Schelling, who was an old friend
of McNaughton's dating back from their work on the European Payments Union and then at Harvard University, provided the intellectual

rationale for a progressively escalating bombing campaign. In theory, bombing would signal to North Vietnam that the United States was serious about preserving an independent South Vietnam and thus induce them to reduce their infiltration and opt for negotiated settlement. Crucially, it promised maximum civilian control and the greatest economy of effort each step of the way, precluding the need for the deployment of ground troops.

The notion of tying air strikes to a political settlement had gained traction since McNamara's last two trips to Vietnam. The idea, at first, was to send messages to Hanoi through the nominally independent commission in charge of overseeing the Geneva Accords in Indochina, which included representatives from Canada, Poland and India. In December 1963, McNamara's notes of a meeting with Harkins and Lodge included the following comment: "associate the plan with the warning to the NVN [North Vietnamese] thru the Pole (stop or we will hurt you)," and in March 1964, McNamara's questions included "if the escalation track is chosen, could we start with recon over North Vietnam Laos [and] move to negotiation in an international body at every step."[120] In May, Lodge, who had been pessimistic about the prospects for negotiation, had come around to the idea that "strikes against the North coupled with the Canadian gambit" might be the key to success.[121] As a result, about two weeks after McNamara met with his military advisors in Honolulu, the Canadian ICC Commissioner, Blair Seaborn, went to Hanoi to convey the message that "the US public and official patience with North Vietnamese aggression is growing extremely thin."[122]

For McNamara, therefore, military planning was aimed at inducing political not military or battlefield outcomes. Military advisors were not, therefore, relevant to decision-making. President Johnson and McNamara's differing views about the proper role of military authorities was particularly evident where staffing in South Vietnam was concerned. In June 1964, when General William Westmoreland replaced Harkins, discussions turned to replacing Ambassador Lodge as well. President Johnson favored Taylor, suggesting that "Taylor can give us the cover we need with country, conservatives and Congress." McNamara tried repeatedly to stall Taylor's selection by suggesting George Ball as his "first choice." He also proposed Gilpatric, McGeorge Bundy and even himself. Echoing complaints that had followed the creation of MACV in the spring of 1962, McNamara worried that Taylor's selection would spark criticism that the administration was "putting [Vietnam policy] in the hands of the military" and that there were inherent "problems with a military man." Rather than respond to the substance of McNamara's criticism, Johnson curtly dismissed it, saying, "Well that's what it is."[123]

Johnson was ultimately more interested in political cover than in making any substantive decisions about Vietnam. Events worked in his favor. In June, the Republican party confirmed the arch-conservative Cold Warrior Barry Goldwater as its presidential candidate. Casting the Republican senator as a dangerous extremist, Johnson sought to mollify both sides of the aisle. He thus delayed key decisions and moved to a holding pattern that would demonstrate toughness and moderation in equal measure. In August, a series of naval incidents in the Bay of Tonkin provided just the opportunity to get bipartisan support behind his ambiguous policies. On August 2, North Vietnamese vessels attacked the destroyer USS *Maddox*. Taylor argued for a strong response. None came as McNamara cautioned that the event was not significant militarily, that "Taylor [was] over-reacting" and that it was not clear that the attacks had been intentional.[124] Moreover, on August 3, he told the President that the actions had likely been a defensive response to US and South Vietnamese recent covert operations in the area, the "plausibly deniable" actions the administration had stepped up in the preceding months.[125]

However, the following day, the *Maddox* and another destroyer, the *Turner Joy*, reported further attacks. Almost immediately, the OSD began receiving reports that "freak weather events" and "overeager sonarmen" might have produced false reports.[126] In an NSC meeting on August 4, some advisors worried that the administration might be accused of "fabricating the incident." McCone unambiguously stated that North Vietnamese actions had been defensive. Unmoved, Rusk concluded: "An immediate and direct reaction by us is necessary. The unprovoked attack on the high seas is an act of war for all practical purposes. We have been trying to get a signal to Hanoi and Peking. Our response to this attack may be that signal."[127] Ultimately, before the waters of the Gulf of Tonkin had settled, the State Department prepared a draft congressional resolution and presidential speech, which argued that the administration should receive bipartisan support for retaliatory and "defensive" actions. McNamara and Rusk led a flurry of congressional outreach efforts to convince both sides that the actions envisaged would meet their preferences. To conservative senators, McNamara shared intelligence that the North Vietnamese were likely responding to recent attacks and insisted the military would have all they needed; to liberal senators, he insisted on the limited character of the response. Tracing a moderate path, Johnson explained to the American people that he had been compelled to respond, that his actions demonstrated "firmness" and were "limited and fitting" as he launched Operation Pierce Arrow, the retaliatory air attacks over North Vietnam.[128]

By August 10, Johnson signed the Tonkin Gulf resolution into law. Only Senators Morse and Ernest Gruening dissented. Congress, the resolution read, "approves and supports the determination of the President, as Commander in Chief, to take all necessary measures to repel any armed attack against the forces of the United States and to prevent further aggression."[129] The resolution gave the President free reign in Vietnam. It was a political masterstroke, a "tribute to the Secretaries of State and Defense" as Johnson put it. By lunchtime on August 10, Johnson concluded that it was now time for the administration to take the initiative in Vietnam and "asked for prompt study and recommendations as to ways this might be done with maximum results and minimum danger."[130]

The August incidents and the ensuing resolution produced several important outcomes for the Johnson administration and thus for McNamara. First, it provided Johnson with official bipartisan support around one of his most politically troublesome foreign affairs problems, enough to carry him through the election. However, in conducting air strikes over North Vietnam, the administration inadvertently opened floodgates. The pressures to continue bombing and to escalate further in Vietnam with every fresh incident grew steadily. With less congressional pushback, the administration spent the rest of the year planning for the military escalation that would come in 1965.

In November, William Bundy headed a new interdepartmental committee that, together with McNaughton, spelled out options for Vietnam that would essentially frame the debate for the next year. Option A involved "present policies indefinitely" with no US-led negotiation track. Option B, the "fast squeeze," added "fairly rapid" military moves in support "of our present objective of getting Hanoi completely out of South VN [Viet Nam] and an independent and secure South VN reestablished." Option C, the final "progressive squeeze and talk," promised a "steady deliberative approach" of "graduated military moves" with negotiations in mind; but, rather ominously, these "would have to be played largely by ear."[131] Only the recently promoted Chairman of the JCS Wheeler defended Option B to McNamara. Option C, in all its vagueness, therefore became the reasonable policy.[132]

The administration prepared to escalate despite widespread misgivings. McNamara noted, "Dean [Rusk] believes the harder we try and fail the worse we are hurt."[133] McNaughton, despite similar concerns that he shared privately with Forrestal, who was preparing to leave, questioned the shift toward a deepening commitment in Vietnam when there were "clear indications of the inability of the South Vietnamese to defend themselves."[134] Still, a policy of self-help was no longer viable and decisions loomed. While McNaughton, and indeed Senator Russell, argued that Khanh's lack of cooperation and South Vietnamese weakness might provide a front for withdrawal, the option was widely rejected. Although they began to consider options for the deployment of ground troops, neither McNamara nor Taylor believed they were a good idea. Where before Westmoreland and others had argued that a stable government in South Vietnam was a precondition for initiating a more sustained bombing campaign, that it would divert resources and attention from the more pressing problems on the pacification front, both McNamara and Taylor now felt that military actions might offer a "glimmer of light" to the South.[135]

Instead, as would become even more pronounced in 1965, bombing promised a controllable and economical alternative to the deployment of troops, a more palatable route than the other options presented and a policy where a consensus could hold. Although McNamara did not envisage going after the JCS's full ninety-four targets, he nonetheless cultivated ambiguity to keep them in line. As he conferred with them about further retaliatory moves, he wrote to the President that they "consider this first step towards attack on the 94 target list; if no action, most chiefs feel should withdraw from South Vietnam."[136] The President's response was appropriately vague: "say to chiefs we are reaching a point where our policy may have to harden – don't want to start something we can't finish, and in agreement there must be retaliatory actions that are swift."[137] On the civilian side, others worried about the efficacy of the bombing: "the problem is the need to convince military leaders (and not only on the GVN side) that gimmickry and technology are not decisive. For example, air power can be most helpful if properly used but can also be counter-productive," one member of the Vietnam Working Group complained.[138] Whatever consensus existed, therefore, was forced and relied on ambiguity. It failed to clarify objectives and left basic questions over strategy unanswered.

The transition to the Johnson administration marked a change for McNamara. The new Commander-in-Chief had little interest for counterinsurgency and preferred options that conveyed toughness. He felt less constrained by some of the economic issues that had weighed on Kennedy. He therefore was more open to considering traditional military tools. By 1965, all the advisors that had advanced the underlying rationale for pacification programs in Vietnam had left. For all intents and purposes, counterinsurgency ideas would not resurge for another two years. At the same time, with each successive coup in South Vietnam, the situation worsened, and with it, the policy of self-help became increasingly tenuous. The planning for withdrawal was swiftly dropped, but McNamara continued to maintain the veneer of a US commitment that was limited to assistance long after he and his colleagues had concluded that South Vietnam would collapse without direct US involvement. In just a few months, McNamara canceled the plans that he had carefully developed between July 1962 and the fall of 1963. He did so because of his definition of his job: he saw himself less as a strategist and more as a resource allocator, someone who could align plans and resources to a strategy set out by the State Department and the President. When the "strategy" changed, so too did planning in the OSD.

More than anything, 1964 was a year where the Johnson administration sought to delay difficult political and military decisions. In an election year, the onus was on identifying military actions in Vietnam that were deniable or covert and that would avoid domestic reactions. Johnson was most interested in placating sources of dissent, be it Lodge, the Chiefs, liberal critics from his own party or fiscal conservatives from both sides of the aisle. As a result, McNamara was sent on successive trips to Vietnam for public relations purposes and to do as he had in the fall of 1963, namely enforce a consensus and thus minimize politically damaging discord. The Tonkin Gulf incidents occurred at a time when the administration had already decided to do "something" militarily. The resulting congressional resolution gave the administration the breathing space to consider military options more freely. By 1965, Johnson had decided to act militarily but he now delayed economic decisions. It was Johnson's failure to contend with economic factors that would strain McNamara's relationship with the President to breaking point.

8

Decisions, Indecisions, Visions and Revisions

By 1965, the administration was primed to make military moves in Vietnam. Johnson's landslide electoral victory in his own right had strengthened his place as Commander-in-Chief, and the Tonkin Gulf resolution, as McNamara observed, gave him "a blank check authorization for further action."[1] In relatively quick order, between January and July 1965, troop numbers increased, and their mission changed. At the start of the year, 23,300 "advisors" were present in Vietnam. A month later, the graduated bombing campaign Operation Rolling Thunder began with a first deployment of Marines just a few weeks later. By April, troops – no longer advisors – numbered over 60,000. The first combat unit, the 173rd Airborne Brigade, arrived in May. And in June and July, McNamara increased the troop ceiling to 120,000 then 175,000 men. The year ended with more than 184,000 US troops in Vietnam and plans for a troop increase to 400,000 in the following year and a further 200,000 the year after that.

Each of these increases reflected unsatisfying compromises and a built-in momentum of military escalation. Johnson chose escalation in Vietnam but ignored the domestic and economic implications of those decisions. For a time, McNamara thought he could plan for escalation without damaging his own ambitions in the defense department or the US economy. By July, he felt otherwise. As the troop numbers and US responsibilities in South Vietnam expanded, McNamara argued for calling up the reserves and for a budgetary realignment. His advice went unheeded and the first rupture in his relationship to the President emerged. Furthermore, McNamara supported incremental increases in troops and air sorties even though he had little faith in their chances of military success because he believed that negotiations would be forthcoming and that the war would therefore be short. The illusion of civilian control gave way to the reality that war has a momentum of its own. The notion that the war would be short-lived gave way to the reality that the administration had no realistic outcome in mind and no appetite for political dialogue with the North. By the fall, McNamara considered leaving.

The documentary record largely validates Johnson's prediction that McNamara would be judged as a "warmonger," the architect of the decisions to escalate in 1965. However, as his colleagues at the OSD cautioned, McNamara's written record is problematic and, in some ways, misleading. Daniel Ellsberg, who rejoined the Department of Defense in 1964 as McNaughton's special assistant, explained that memoranda in the OSD were written and marked as "drafts" on the understanding that "other people could see them; that they could be leaked," that they were primarily designed to provide "talking points" even if the drafter thought it was "terrible idea."[2] McNamara countered Johnson's accusation that his colleagues at the OSD were leaking information by boasting that virtually everyone in his department was "in the dark" over decisions in Vietnam.[3] The written record, therefore, is incomplete by design. Unbeknownst to McNamara, McNaughton, who as the war escalated became his point man on Vietnam and one of his few confidants, kept secret diaries. Together with the recordings of Johnson's phone conversations with McNamara, the diaries provide a glimpse into McNamara's private thoughts at this key juncture in the Vietnam War and in his career as Secretary of Defense.

As he saw it, McNamara's job was to loyally defend the administration's policy and precluded a role in articulating strategy. PPBS, DPMs and all his innovations at the OSD were explicitly designed to plan for force requirements in support of a strategy articulated in the White House or the State Department. From a bureaucratic perspective, if strategy is the broader articulation of the objectives to be achieved by the application of military force, a theory on the use of those forces, according to McNamara's view of the bureaucratic process, should have come from the State Department and White House. His role as Secretary of Defense was to think about tactics, namely translating strategy into a series of military exchanges in the cheapest possible way and in a way that guaranteed maximum civilian control. As he explained in an oral history for the OSD, the Secretary of Defense's role was only to "comment on the military implications."[4] This definition of his job underpinned each of his recommendations in 1965.

FIGURE 8.1 President Lyndon B. Johnson (left) and Secretary of Defense
McNamara (right) drive at the LBJ ranch, December 22, 1964.
(Yoichi Okamoto, White House Photo Office, LBJL.)

McNamara and all of President Johnson's senior advisors understood
that 1965 would be a time for decision (see Figure 8.1). In January 1965,
McNamara and McGeorge Bundy wrote to President Johnson that defeat
in Vietnam was inevitable unless the United States used military power
"decisively" or "deploy all our resources along the track of negotiation."[5]
However, using the same economic rationale that had underpinned the
CPSVN, McNamara resisted deploying ground troops: it would be difficult to fund through the MAP and it would put new strains on the balance
of payments at a time when the situation was improving. Even while he
supported acting "decisively," McNamara pushed back on the JCS and
McGeorge Bundy's suggestion for "larger US forces" because of what he
called their "general heaviness."[6]

In spite of McNamara and others' recommendations, Johnson avoided
grappling with the economic consequences of his decisions on Vietnam.
He avoided trade-offs that might have prevented the inflation and international monetary crisis that Vietnam caused. Just as counterinsurgency
advisors who influenced strategy departed in 1964, so too did key
advisors on the economic front, chiefly Treasury Secretary Dillon, who,
in March 1965, submitted his resignation. From the outset, Dillon had

been unimpressed with the new Commander-in-Chief's command of economic issues. Dillon warned that cooperation from allies and the private sector on sustaining the dollar's role under Bretton-Woods system required assurances that the administration would not export inflation and thus would keep an eye on spending and on its balance of payments. Unlike Kennedy, Johnson often refused to return Dillon's phone calls as colleagues warned that the President was "usurping" the Treasury Secretary's role.[7]

In February, economic and military issues were heightened and intertwined. In the span of just a few days, the course of the US war in Vietnam changed as did the tenor of transatlantic cooperation on international monetary issues. On February 1, Johnson referred to the prospect of devaluation during an impromptu exchange with the press. Seething from previous experiences where he had noted the President's "confusion" on economic matters, Dillon reprimanded White House staff that "talk makes everything worse" and offered to provide Johnson's assistant Bill Moyers "a paper which I published last spring which reflects my detailed thoughts."[8] When the President's off-the-cuff statement appeared in the *Wall Street Journal* on February 4, Dillon wrote to the newly appointed Chairman of the Council of Economic Advisers that a "change in the price of gold" was not "acceptable or proper."[9] On the very same day, de Gaulle convened a press conference where he attacked the role of the dollar in the Bretton-Woods system and suggested a return to the gold standard. France's previous cooperation on international monetary issues came to an end and Dillon's departure exacerbated the feeling in Europe and elsewhere that the Johnson administration would not exercise fiscal restraint.

Nevertheless, in response to de Gaulle's presentation, McNamara and Johnson went on the offensive to prove that the administration was, in fact, still dealing with the balance of payments deficit. In a statement to Congress, Johnson unequivocally rejected devaluation and, with transatlantic cooperation now in doubt, proposed new measures to curtail private capital flows. He rebuffed de Gaulle and said, "Those who fear the dollar are needlessly afraid. Those who hope for its weakness, hope in vain."[10] On a parallel track, McNamara spoke to a group of bankers and business representatives at the White House. Using data from his recent annual report on the balance of payments, he projected a reduction of defense expenditures that impacted the international balance of payments from their peak of $2.8 billion in 1961 to a projected $1.25 billion in 1967. He explained that efforts from preceding years were beginning to "take shape," including the Defense Department's use of local forces and "thinning out" of overseas deployments.[11]

In Vietnam, however, the scene was set for an increased deployment and the implementation of military plans that had been designed in 1964. On February 7, the US base of Camp Holloway in Pleiku was attacked. McGeorge Bundy, who was in Vietnam, encouraged Johnson to move forward on more aggressive measures. Over the next week, with fresh Viet Cong attacks in South Vietnam and after a first series of US reprisal air attacks, Johnson approved Operation Rolling Thunder. Where previous bombing raids were designed to retaliate, now their purpose was to punish and bring "sufficient pressure to bear on the DRV to persuade it to stop its intervention in the South."[12] During a series of NSC meetings, McNamara supported this sustained bombing campaign. Wheeler remarked, "The secretary of defense is sounding like General LeMay. All he needs is a cigar."[13] The administration also finally released the Jorden Report and began planning for the deployment of the 9th Marine Expeditionary Brigade, which had been activated in the aftermath of the Tonkin events. Ostensibly deployed to carry out "active defense" of the US base in Da Nang, the Marines landed in March. In a moment of great symbolism, the President canceled a planned meeting on the balance of payments to make room for an NSC meeting on Vietnam.[14]

Johnson's military and civilian advisors never agreed on the bombing program's central objectives. In South Vietnam, they included lifting morale, curtailing infiltration and supporting the ground campaign. Where North Vietnam was concerned, they were designed to "communicate" and induce the North's representatives to come to the negotiating table. In Washington, they were intended to do "something" that played to US technological advantages and minimized both the chances of domestic upheaval and the prospect of a military confrontation with the Soviet Union or China. In April, DCI McCone resigned in anger after unsuccessfully lobbying for a more aggressive bombing campaign even as he was censoring CIA reports that McNamara also read and which questioned the effectiveness of any bombing program.[15] For the Joint Chiefs, a bombing campaign was a step in the right direction. John McConnell succeeded LeMay as Air Force Chief of Staff. Like the other Chiefs who were all gradually replaced under McNamara, McConnell lacked the military clout of his predecessor and was more willing to get behind Wheeler's efforts at glossing over disagreements and discomfort in the services to produce common JCS positions that fit within the civilian advisors' parameters.[16] The Chiefs therefore supported the administration's bombing campaign despite their discomfort and reservations over its military value.

McNamara's support of the bombing program fit with his own priorities and philosophy at the Department of Defense. It promised a creative and civilian-controlled substitute for the introduction of ground troops. With pressure building to do "something," Taylor and McNamara questioned the suitability of "white-faced soldiers" as they both tried to preempt deployments of ground troops. McNamara never believed that bombing alone would end the war nor that it would do very much to solve the central problem of guerrillas in the South. For him, Operation Rolling Thunder was not designed to produce military outcomes but to "signal political resolve" to the North and thus encourage a political settlement. McNamara also believed the bombing program would limit the budgetary impact and domestic repercussions of escalation. Bombing, instead of MAP-dependent programs, would obviate the need for the type of expensive and "heavy" defense installations that had weighed down the balance of payments. Crucially, bombing would draw more readily on the armed services' budget and, in so doing, hide the financial costs of escalation.

However, as the administration increasingly drew on the services' budgets, the SASC rather than the SFRC took on a greater role in overseeing policy. A major constraint on funding for Vietnam was thus removed. Chairman of the SASC Russell was determined that the services have all the resources that they needed despite his misgivings about the Vietnam commitment. As presaged in Vinson's exchange with McNamara in 1964, the SASC's charge that McNamara was shortchanging the services tilted the balance of power toward the Chiefs and increased pressure on civilian decision-makers to give them more of "something." On March 1, 1965, just under a year after planning for withdrawal had been suspended and, with it, pressures to decrease funds allocated to Vietnam, McNamara wrote to the Chiefs: "Occasionally, instances come to my attention indicating that some in the Department feel restraint imposed by limitations of funds. I want it clearly understood that there is an unlimited appropriation available for financing aid to Vietnam. Under no circumstance is lack of money to stand in the way of aid to that nation."[17]

Despite McNamara's promises of "an unlimited appropriation," the SASC understood that McNamara's budget was undervalued and that it relied on problematic assumptions. In his testimony to the SASC, McNamara admitted that he used "somewhat arbitrary assumptions regarding the duration of the conflict in Southeast Asia," namely that the war would end, as if by magic, by June 30 of each given fiscal year.[18] He then submitted supplemental requests to make up the difference. Ironically, one of McNamara's greatest contributions to the defense budgeting process was to *extend* time horizons to better capture the full costs of defense programs and operations. In Vietnam, he did the opposite. He then used his authority as Secretary of Defense to create new channels for additional funds, including submitting supplemental requests to Congress and creating an "Emergency Fund, SEA," which was specifically earmarked for the services' production and construction needs. The first supplemental request specifically for Vietnam passed in May 1965 for $13.1 billion, most of which McNamara had known he would need when he first presented the FY65 budget in December 1963, while his request for the Emergency Fund, SEA, was submitted in August 1965.[19]

In a further manipulation of the budgetary process, McNamara drew on the services' operating budgets and existing resources. He avoided stockpiling equipment as had been done during the Korean War and instead relied on existing services' stocks. He calculated ammunition costs based on past usage even as operations increased and were projected to increase further. Using this technique to provide support to forces in the field drew the costs of operations in Vietnam from the services' normal operating budgets.[20] McNamara's creative accounting eventually became a focal point for congressional anger over the administration's policies in Vietnam because it had blurred the costs of operations in Vietnam.

Moreover, as the Vietnam War escalated, McNamara accelerated cost-saving measures elsewhere. This kept the overall defense budget down and allowed the administration to continue to preserve a pretense of fiscal responsibility. He accelerated the base closure program at home and abroad and instituted new programs aimed at greater cost-effectiveness within the Department of Defense. Crucially, as part of a broader program aimed at either delaying and canceling expensive new programs and procurement decisions for the FY66 budget, McNamara explicitly embraced a nuclear posture based on MAD in March 1965. The idea that existing stocks of nuclear weapons were sufficient to prevent a nuclear confrontation preempted a growing chorus for an anti-ballistic missile (ABM) program, which McNamara believed was "massive, costly" and likely ineffective.[21]

For a time, McNamara's accounting gimmicks and cost-saving measures largely avoided a politically charged debate about the potential inflationary effects of spending on Vietnam. In June 1965, the Great

Society legislation passed, as did a further tax cut. But McNamara's creative bookkeeping was inevitably a short-term solution. It could be sustained only if the war was brought to a swift end or if the budget was adapted to the reality that the United States was in fact fighting a "war" in Vietnam.

During the first months of 1965, McNamara believed a bombing program would be relatively inexpensive and induce a political solution to the problems in Vietnam and thereby prevent the introduction of ground troops. Although the first deployment of Marines had landed in Da Nang on March 8, in a conversation on March 30, McNamara warned the President against the recommendations coming from the Chiefs to send additional forces for purposes other than defense. He explained that Taylor believed that ground troops would have "great difficulty" in a "counterinsurgency role" and concluded that "Our troops, while admirably trained, are poorly trained as counter-guerrilla."[22] He also warned that the Viet Cong and North Vietnamese forces could match increases in South Vietnamese and US forces. In spite of this, the administration planned for additional troops in more offensive roles. Johnson remarked: "I don't think anything will be as bad as losing and I don't see any way of winning but I would sure want to feel that every person who had an idea, that his suggestion was fully explored."[23] Unfortunately, alternative plans that were politically palatable to Johnson and militarily feasible did not emerge.

Instead, various advisors and agencies played down the risks behind the introduction of ground troops. They argued that the United States could play to its distinct advantages and thus avoid a similar experience to the French. The Air Force thought that existing airlift capabilities could vastly increase mobility and thus change the traditional ratios of forces needed to defeat an insurgency. Later, Lodge, too, who would return to Vietnam in the summer of 1965, was optimistic about the United States' naval power: "We don't need to fight on the roads," he explained, "We have the sea." Lodge "visualized our meeting Viet Cong on our own terms," and added, "We don't need to spend all our time in the jungles."[24] The problem, as McGeorge Bundy warned, was quite simple: "I see no reason to suppose that the Viet Cong will accommodate us by fighting the kind of war we desire."[25]

In March, McNamara and his colleagues at the OSD became increasingly uncomfortable with the shifting sands on Vietnam. McNaughton was sent to Vietnam to study the JCS recommendations to deploy three divisions and step up air raids to deal with a "bad and deteriorating" situation. McNaughton returned from Vietnam with an updated version of his three options. To McNamara, he wrote that policy was "drifting" and warned about the lack of clear objectives and tendency within the US government to discount options "between 'victory' and 'defeat.'" He candidly spelled out the objectives of the US presence in Vietnam, which he quantified as 70% "to avoid a humiliating US defeat," 20% to prevent Chinese domination of the country and region and only 10% to guarantee "a better, freer way of life" in South Vietnam. He added that they also included "to emerge from the crisis without unacceptable taint from the method used" and "not – to 'help a friend.'" He laid out the central paradox of growing US involvement in Vietnam: on the one hand, the "main aim" was strengthening South Vietnam; on the other, planned efforts would "probably fail to prevent collapse." The key objective, therefore, if the United States could not effectively organize a viable pacification program, was to negotiate a way out and ensure that if and when South Vietnam did collapse, the United States emerge as a "good doctor," its international credibility as unharmed as possible.[26]

Within a month, however, McNamara himself went to Vietnam and Honolulu and returned supporting the deployment of 82,000 troops, suggesting they would "be effective against the Viet Cong and would release ARVN forces for more distant operations."[27] This number was less than the JCS recommended and more than Taylor wanted. It flew in the face of his own trip notes where he and many of the advisors worried about the dangers inherent to introducing US troops, the continuing poor standards in ARVN forces and the South Vietnamese government's inability to date to "consolidate its political bases in the countryside." He projected that troop numbers would go up to 270,972 in a second phase with the United States adopting increasingly offensive roles.

McNamara also supported expanding the bombing program, although its value was in doubt. His military advisors had indicated that it had had little effect on infiltration and the State Department concluded that "over-eagerness" for negotiations would be "counter-productive and self-defeating." For McNamara, the bombing program was meant to reduce infiltration and spur negotiations, yet McNamara was now defending bombing to "convince Hanoi authorities that they cannot win," and added that "It is the creation of this frame of mind which will finally end infiltration."[28] He presented some of his concerns and doubts to Johnson and warned that bombing "cannot be expected to do the job alone" and that it would not constitute a strategy for "victory." Nevertheless, he defended the program on "psychological" and "physical" grounds.[29]

Although the theory of graduated pressure was aimed at encouraging negotiations, Johnson had no appetite for them. In April and May, he rejected British and UN attempts at mediation and only grudgingly accepted McNamara's suggestion to pursue a bombing pause in May with a view to kick-start negotiations. Johnson was uncomfortable with the bombing pause because he did not believe North Vietnam was prepared to negotiate in good faith. The fact that Robert Kennedy had privately lobbied for the pause did not help and Johnson disdainfully referred to it as "Bobby Kennedy's pause." The pause lasted less than a week and bore no results. The President felt vindicated and told McNamara, "I would say to Mansfield, Kennedy, Fulbright that we notified the other people – and for six days we have held off bombing. Nothing happened. We had no illusions that anything would happen. But we were willing to be surprised ... No one has even thanked us for the pause."[30]

Similarly, a brief renewed interest in pacification in the spring and summer of 1965 was political cover for the administration's escalation against growing domestic criticism from the left, including from "Mansfield, Kennedy and Fulbright." In April, Johnson spoke of a Tennessee Valley Authority–type of economic development program for Southeast Asia and sparked a renewed interest in economic and social development programs in Washington. In the weeks before Johnson's speech, McNamara had responded to SFRC criticism of the US posture in Vietnam. To Senator Morse, one of the two holdouts from the Tonkin Gulf Resolution and an increasingly vocal critic of Vietnam, McNamara defended the MAP program role in guaranteeing a "minimum risk of United States involvement in local wars along the far-flung frontier of freedom."[31] Lodge returned to Vietnam in August 1965 together with Edward Lansdale with a mandate to refocus attention on pacification. While McNamara and McNaughton continued to argue that the solution to the problems in Vietnam were rooted inside South Vietnam, for the administration, pacification efforts never amounted to much more than public relations.

The way Johnson framed discussion in March and April 1965 explains the break between McNaughton and McNamara's private doubts and their public support of escalation. First, Johnson had grown increasingly frustrated with his advisors and policies in Vietnam, which seemed either politically impractical or doomed to fail. He chastised McNamara, Rusk and the Joint Chiefs and said that he was "tired of taking the blame."[32] McNamara stepped in because, as he told Rusk, "someone has to make a decision."[33] Second, Johnson influenced the administration's decision to downplay changes in policy. McNamara understood that the program he was proposing marked a qualitative and quantitative shift. He recommended that the administration reach out to congressional leaders about the changed mission. Johnson overruled him to avoid a public debate.[34]

The origins of McNamara's eventual disillusionment with the war were rooted in the early months of 1965 and became more acute in the follow-up decisions of July. Insofar as McNamara viewed the role of Secretary of Defense as a resource allocation function, he was concerned with the looming gap between the administration's growing commitment in Vietnam and in its inability to rally the domestic resources to sustain the expansion. His falling-out with the administration also hinged on what he considered to be a lack of an overarching strategy with a clear end point that would justify escalating costs within the DOD. In March 1965, while Johnson praised the "psychological impact" of sending the Marines rather than the "Sunday school stuff" that had preceded it, McNamara complained that the administration needed a clearer plan and should "be less rigid about talks." He used similar language to McNaughton's and told Johnson, "My sense is that we're drifting from day to day and we ought to have inside government what we're going to say tomorrow and then next week."[35] Although he complained about the lack of strategy, he did not step in to fill the void.

When bombing failed to achieve a quick political solution, McNamara hoped a more significant escalation might. In a later oral history interview, McNamara remarked that one key lesson that he had learned from the Bay of Pigs disaster was that the United States should "not move militarily except with massive force in relation to the requirement; and then that massive force [should be] controlled with utmost care and restraint."[36] This seems to have been his position in June and July when Westmoreland requested additional troops. McNaughton and McNamara prepared a series of draft reports that culminated in Johnson's July 28 press conference announcement that ground troops in Vietnam would increase to 125,000 men. Some months later, McNaughton wrote in his diaries: "Bob was a 'B' man (fight hard and bargain *out*); I said I was a 'C' man because our chemists won't permit 'B' ('C' is to withdraw, seeking the best possible cover for it)." He added that Rusk was an 'A' man: "make the enemy back down."[37]

In his first draft report in June, McNamara argued that the United States should either escalate decisively or get out. If it chose to escalate, he recommended increasing troops to 200,000, mobilizing the reserves and expanding the air campaign, including mining North Vietnamese harbors while intensifying diplomatic efforts. The United States would henceforth take over lead responsibility for fighting the war in the South and the North and, the logic went, force Hanoi to the negotiating table or at least encourage a more favorable settlement.[38] Reaction to the report was immediate, none more so than from McGeorge Bundy, who described it as "rash to the point of folly." Bundy echoed earlier comments that both McNamara and McNaughton had made when he challenged the assumptions underlying McNamara's recommendations: troop increases "untested in the kind of war projected," increased bombing "when the value of air action we have taken is sharply disputed" and a naval quarantine "when nearly everyone agrees the real question is not in Hanoi, but in South Vietnam."[39]

Bundy's comments beg the question: by taking a more aggressive stand, had McNamara suddenly overcome all his doubts or did he instead feel compelled to don more hawkish views within the administration to force the notion of incremental increases to a logical conclusion? That McNamara would reject all his previous concerns to support the introduction of large-scale ground troops, an option he had consistently resisted up to this point, is improbable. That he would suddenly share Westmoreland's views was similarly doubtful.

Instead, as escalation loomed, the OSD took a more active role in overseeing operations in the field. McNaughton, with Wheeler's special assistant Andrew Goodpaster, had started to study existing estimates of what the United States might have to do to win in Vietnam. Another McNamara confidant, Deputy Secretary of Defense Cyrus Vance, had set up a number of working groups on Vietnam. Crucially, Alain Enthoven at the Office of Systems Analysis became involved on Vietnam for the first time. Enthoven later explained that the idea behind his work was that by systematically analyzing data, the OSD could "forestall the over-Americanization of the war, the pervasive optimism of official estimates on how well we were doing and the twisted priorities that developed in the expenditure of billions of dollars."[40] McNamara and Enthoven would later become infamous for their reliance on metrics to assess operations in Vietnam. At the time, however, the Secretary of Defense was reacting to the paucity of reliable estimates from the field. Westmoreland often relied on anecdotal evidence and "instinctive" recommendations and projections. This frustrated McNamara as progress failed to materialize.[41]

By better quantifying the costs of the troop deployments, McNamara could also force the civilians involved in decisions to consider their economic implications and to confront the in-built momentum of troop

FIGURE 8.2 Secretary of Defense McNamara (left), John T. McNaughton (middle) and General Westmoreland (right) listen to a briefing in Saigon, Vietnam, July 1965.
(OSD Photograph, John T. McNaughton family collection.)

increases. Each incremental troop introduction created fresh needs for more troops. General Krulak, who had been reassigned to oversee the logistics of the Marines in the Pacific, had reacted angrily to Westmoreland's increases in Navy deployments in March 1965. He argued that their deployment to Phu Bai airbase had more to do with the Army's investment in a communications facility in the area, a central component of Westmoreland's request for additional troops, than it did with military practicalities. In his words, "dollar economics wagged the tail of the military deployment."[42] As troops were deployed, and new programs set up, their security and logistical needs expanded as well, rapidly ballooning the numbers and costs of US personnel in the country.

For the OSD, the key difference between McNamara's first draft and Johnson's announcement was on the issue of aligning resources to new commitments. With Enthoven and Vance, McNamara agreed that the planned escalation would have to include a publicity campaign and "felt that we should make it clear to the public that American troops were already in combat."[43] Instead, Johnson said the United States was fighting a "different kind of war."[44] The OSD advisors also recommended calling up the reserves and national guard, extending tours of existing troops, increasing draft calls and submitting a substantial budgetary supplement to Congress. McNamara reached out to John C. Stennis, the Chairman of the Defense Subcommittee in the Appropriations Committee, to prepare him for the eventuality.[45] In private, the OSD advisors felt that a tax increase would now become inevitable, and Vance referred to the 1961 Berlin Crisis when Kennedy had considered a temporary tax to offset potential inflationary pressures of increased defense spending.[46] These measures were never taken.

McNamara later suggested that the only time he openly disagreed with Johnson was on these key budgetary decisions made in July. He could not argue otherwise: where previous disagreements were smoothed over in private, in this instance, the President quite publicly overruled him. On July 15, McNamara had been sent on another performative trip to Vietnam to rubber-stamp the decision to escalate (see Figure 8.2). In Saigon, he heard from Vance that Johnson had decided not to ask for supplementary funds, and although Johnson initially accepted a reserve call-up, he reneged on this too within a few days. Johnson publicly talked of being at war but refused to put the domestic economy on a war footing for political reasons. In the absence of congressional support, the President did not seek a tax increase. He worried that the upcoming Medicare bill and Voting Rights Act would be compromised if a "war psychosis" took hold.[47] Bundy and Rusk likewise worried that such moves would "elicit drama" at home and abroad and argued that the administration should downplay the change in policy.[48] As a result, Johnson recommended that McNamara use his transfer authority – in other words, drawing from resources elsewhere in the defense budget – and seek supplemental funding only in January after the administration's domestic legislative agenda had passed.[49]

The final July report and ensuing decisions represented an uncomfortable blend of policies that were aimed at producing a compromise and consensus, but which satisfied no one. They did not go as far as Westmoreland's initial recommendations and went too far for its critics. Although McNamara wrote that the war was entering a conventional phase where the United States could "seek out the Viet Cong in large scale units," to the Joint Chiefs, he drew on CIA reports to argue that this was "highly improbable." Wheeler argued for more offensive actions while he

admitted that the "lack of tactical intelligence" might impede their effectiveness.[50] As he was wont to do, Johnson relied on advisors who did not
have access to the full body of intelligence on Vietnam to validate his
decisions. He convened the "Wise Men," a group of prominent figures
that included John McCloy, Dean Acheson and Robert Lovett, who
encouraged him to act decisively in Vietnam.[51] McNamara grew increasingly irritated with Johnson's reliance on external advisors like the "Wise
Men" who often encouraged the President to disregard the OSD's
concerns.

The problem was also that alternatives were not presented to a
President who wanted to act militarily in Vietnam but also wanted to
avoid international or domestic consequences. Arguably, no policy that
could satisfy Johnson's competing objectives existed. The JCS took a full
month to submit their "Concept for Vietnam." It dismissed the theories of
graduated pressure and argued instead for a far more aggressive use of
military force. Similarly, George Ball, who argued that the administration
should be prepared to let South Vietnam collapse, "had [his] day in
court" but was outnumbered in an administration who feared the international repercussions of withdrawal from Vietnam. Johnson refuted
Ball's argument that the South Vietnamese could not win, and he jokingly
remarked, "But I believe that these people are trying to fight. They're like
Republicans who try to stay in power, but don't stay there long."[52] The
concluding section of McNamara's report offered just a hint of optimism
about the path ahead: "The overall evaluation is that the course of action
recommended in this memorandum – if the military and political moves
are properly integrated and executed with continuing vigor and visible
determination – stands a good chance of achieving an acceptable outcome
within a reasonable time in Vietnam."

The ambiguous idea of an "outcome" was itself a product of a compromise and reflected an unsatisfactory consensus about objectives in
Vietnam. McNamara and McNaughton's first drafts had talked of a
"settlement" because military escalation was geared toward political
negotiations. They also introduced the idea of an extended bombing
pause to that effect. Lodge had suggested using the term "outcome"
instead because he did not believe a political settlement was likely: "perhaps a conference between North and South Vietnam could produce
something at the right time," he thought, "when our side is strong
enough, but that is doubtful too."[53] Similarly, Lodge's Deputy U. Alexis
Johnson commented that the administration should "say nothing further
with respect to negotiations" and opposed the idea of a pause.[54]

McNamara sought a political settlement because he had little faith in South Vietnam's ability to fight the war itself. The central dilemma of how the United States could "win" with a collapsible ally in the South was left in limbo during the July decisions. In the early months of 1965, McNamara supported the idea that the United States should wait until South Vietnam stabilized before escalating. By July, his public position had become aligned with that of the JCS, namely that escalation might provide the breathing room for South Vietnam to strengthen. In private, however, McNaughton and McNamara supported the idea of a coalition government with a Communist role in the South on the assumption that the existing South Vietnamese government would never be strong enough to survive alone.

However, McNamara merely implied this position in his statements at NSC meetings. He rejected the country team's "more optimistic" assessment of what he termed the "non-government" in South Vietnam. Lodge argued that the United States should act "regardless of the Government" as the United States could not "count on stability in South Vietnam."[55] Although the country team noted some improvement under Prime Minister Nguyen Cao Ky and President Nguyen Van Thieu, McNamara estimated that they would not last the year. By early August, he made a remarkable admission: "no country in history has been victorious in battle when its central government has been weak and unstable."[56]

McNamara had become the public face of an escalation that made no sense. If a military victory was impossible and if South Vietnam would not, as he believed, become viable in the foreseeable future, then a political settlement, however tenuous, was the only feasible outcome. The State Department had no appetite for negotiations, yet escalation went ahead all the same. As Secretary of Defense, McNamara understood that the United States could not escalate significantly, as it was doing, without committing resources to that end. But no publicity campaign, no reserve call-up and no tax increase occurred. Within months, even Johnson's liberal Council of Economic Advisers worried that the administration could not push through with the Great Society programs, the war in Vietnam and keep inflation down without a tax increase.[57] McNamara understood all these things in July and yet still went on record supporting the United States taking a leading role in Vietnam. In the months that followed, it would put him at loggerheads with Johnson and precipitate his decision to leave government.

During the July decisions on Vietnam, McNamara began to discreetly prepare for a life after the DOD. When he had accepted the position of

Secretary of Defense, he had asked for the "closest possible, personal working relationship with the President and ... [his] full backing and support so long as he is carrying out the policies of the President."[58] Had he concluded that this condition was no longer being met and that his usefulness to the President had come to an end? Was he angry about becoming a figurehead for an escalation that he did not want? Was he anxious that the piecemeal fashion in which Johnson accepted his recommendations would undermine his record of success at the DOD? The record is not clear. One of Johnson's "Wise Men," John McCloy, offered him the Ford Foundation presidency. He noted, "I told him I had given the matter of my future a little thought but I showed a conditional interest."[59] The job offers accelerated in the fall of 1965, including the presidency of US Steel, which sent his old mentor Tex Thornton to lobby on their behalf. The presidency of the Rockefeller and especially the Ford Foundation attracted him most. He eventually demurred: "when the Vietnam thing got so serious he had to withdraw himself from consideration."[60]

McNamara was torn between his private views about the weaknesses of the administration's policy and his conception of loyalty to the Commander-in-Chief and of the role as Secretary of Defense. Given his privileged vantage point, he understood that if the war continued, its economic costs could not be hidden indefinitely and could scuttle his objectives at the Defense Department. He had taken an oath of office where he had sworn to protect the Constitution, which included a duty to tell the truth to the Congress. And yet he could not get past his loyalty to the office of the President. As he explained in an interview given after he was fired, "Around Washington, there is this concept of higher loyalty. I think it's a heretical concept, this idea that there's a duty to serve the nation above the duty to serve the President, and that you're justified in doing so. It will destroy democracy if it's followed. You have to subordinate a part of yourself, a part of your views."[61]

Ultimately, McNamara committed no "heresy" and remained out of loyalty to the President, but he did this at a personal and professional cost. On November 2, 1965, Norman Morrison, a Quaker anti-war activist, self-immolated outside McNamara's office window. Morrison's wife released a statement, which McNamara later quoted in *In Retrospect* that read: "He felt that all citizens must speak their convictions about our country's actions." Unlike Morrison, McNamara failed to do this at time when his convictions had real import. He had allowed escalation in

Vietnam to go forward under false pretenses and in an economically unsustainable fashion. He had put loyalty to the President over his better judgment. On a personal level, in his memoirs he reflected on the tragedy of Morrison's death and his reflexive tendency to "bottle[e] up [his] emotions": "at moments like this I often turned inward instead."[62] He turned inward in many ways, both emotionally and professionally. From July onward, he fell into a pattern where he held back "in deciding how hard to push" with Johnson, putting his "feel for his relations and effectiveness with the President" above his professional obligation to present the White House with the truth.[63]

As the year went on, his influence on the President waned and his position became increasingly tenuous. Between July and December, continued military difficulties created additional pressures to further expand the US commitment in Vietnam. The disastrous battle of the Ia Drang Valley in November 1965, the first major engagement between US and North Vietnamese forces, created a fresh demand for more troops. Returning from another trip to Vietnam, McNamara recommended troop increases to about 400,000 in 1966 and to 600,000 in 1967. At the same time, McNamara told Johnson: "I am more and more convinced that we ought to think of some action other than military action as the only program there. I think if we do that by itself, it's suicide. I think pushing out 300,000, 400,000 Americans out there without being able to guarantee what it will do is a terrible risk and a terrible cost."[64]

As troop numbers and air sorties increased into the fall of 1965 with little success, McNamara and colleagues around him returned to the ideas of the Kennedy administration and its focus on counterinsurgency. In September 1965, Hilsman, who was now a professor at Columbia University, criticized the administration and declared that the decision to bomb North Vietnam was "tragic." On Johnson's instructions, McGeorge Bundy "read the riot act" to Hilsman and "arranged to have the same tune played at him hard by people he respects, beginning with Averell Harriman and Adam Yarmolinsky."[65] Yarmolinsky, who was now McNaughton's deputy, continued to correspond with Hilsman. In November 1965, Hilsman sent him an article by Bernard Fall that was highly critical of the bombing program and its "confidence in total material superiority," arguing that the administration was inextricably tying its credibility to a doomed and "fundamentally weak" South Vietnamese government, noting that the "bomber can't do anything about that."[66] In June 1965, Fall had received several visits from American policy-makers, including

Army Chief Johnson and Paul Kattenburg. The latter had secretly met with Fall in his home and transmitted Fall's critical views to the Vietnam Working Group.[67] At the time, Fall was largely ignored.

By contrast, in November, even while Yarmolinsky patronized Hilsman's "academic uneasiness in an uneasy world," he nonetheless forwarded both Hilsman's letter and the Fall article to McNamara and John McNaughton, adding, "I think this is probably worth your reading in its entirety, and perhaps assigning for analysis."[68] Two months later, McNamara referred to this article in an exchange with McNaughton. In his diary, McNaughton noted: "He referred also to an article which said that you can't lick guerrilla wars without a political base and you can't lose them if you have such a base ... The implication was that Thailand would resist guerrilla efforts even if SVN [South Vietnam] went down the drain. Also, the point was made that a great power can absorb *political* defeats, but not *military* ones – and that our great mistake was to let a likely political defeat get turned into a likely military defeat."[69]

As military reports looked increasingly unfavorable, McNamara renewed his pressure for negotiations and for a bombing pause. In mid-November, *Look* magazine published an Eric Sevareid interview with US Ambassador to the United Nations Adlai Stevenson before the latter's death in July. In it, Stevenson accused the administration of shutting the door on UN Secretary General U Thant's mediation efforts.[70] In private, Johnson dismissed Stevenson as an "amateur" and as having a "martyr complex." Nevertheless, McNamara used the opportunity to encourage Johnson to look for political openings and to implement a longer bombing pause. He presented the President with his assessment that the chances of military success were now even or "1 in 3." He told the President, "We may not find a military solution. We need to explore other means."[71] McNaughton's diaries recorded a revealing exchange with U. Alexis Johnson. He wrote, "He (and State) think the future holds more than the present, and therefore had to be dragged into the present Pause. I (and DOD) think the future holds less than the present, that things are getting worse, that we have to pour more in to stand still – so strong diplomatic initiatives (and a compromise) are called for now."[72]

Johnson resisted the pause, as did many of his civilian and military advisors: "Don't we know a pause will fail?" he asked his Secretary of Defense and presented the JCS view that a pause would undo existing military progress.[73] McNamara pushed back, dismissing the Chiefs' arguments as "baloney," and agreed with Johnson that they could use concerns over the budget and inflation to force the Chiefs to demur.[74] In early December, ignoring Johnson's pressures, the Chairman of the Federal Reserve William McChesney Martin increased interest rates, in large part because of his concerns over escalation in Vietnam and its inflationary effects.[75] McNamara drew on this embarrassing development for his own purposes.

The impact of McNamara's intervention was effective, if short-lived. When Johnson's skeptical advisors pushed for an early resumption of bombing, McNamara interrupted his vacation to visit the President at his Texas ranch to convince him otherwise.[76] McGeorge Bundy explained that the President "acquiesced" to McNamara's request after Taylor also "[came] around" to the idea and notably after Johnson received the results of a Harris poll, whose question he had personally written, indicating support for the pause.[77] Nevertheless, using his personal access to the President, McNamara overrode widespread resistance to the pause from advisors as disparate as Rusk, William Bundy, Thompson and Clark Clifford, the Chairman of the President's Intelligence Advisory Board, who would eventually succeed McNamara. Using similar language to Johnson, Clifford felt that the administration had "talked enough about peace" and that a pause would therefore be a sign of weakness.

In an underhanded critique of their existing intelligence, McNamara also preempted the Chiefs' anger by asking them, "If at any time you believe the pause is seriously penalizing our operations in the South, please submit to me immediately the evidence backing up your belief."[78] The pause produced a flurry of diplomatic activity. Johnson "talked directly with [Ambassador to the UN Arthur] Goldberg and Harriman," who, if only for symbolic reasons, was appointed as "someone moving throughout the world trying for peace."[79] Whether or not McNamara played on the fact that he had recently considered leaving, he nevertheless and finally used his influence on the President to force a political opening.

On January 29, the pause ended in failure. Only two weeks earlier, McNamara had shared his view that "the Pause is paying off very well," but Johnson and most of his advisors disagreed.[80] Rusk shared Johnson's view that the pause had been a mistake and produced no diplomatic breakthrough as McNamara had predicted: "The enormous efforts made in the last 34 days," Rusk concluded, "have produced nothing."[81] To add to McNamara's humiliation, Johnson reconvened the "Wise Men" who encouraged him to extend the bombing campaign to include targets McNamara had heretofore resisted: the only "worthy" targets, they suggested, were the petroleum, oil and lubricant (POL) industrial targets in the Haiphong and Hanoi areas.[82]

In his diaries, McNaughton noted the following exchange: "Bob mentioned that 'for your information, the bombing resumes tomorrow noon.' I asked what the theory is. He said 'First, to give the right signal to the North [we have not weakened]; second, to give the right signal to the South; third to increase the cost of infiltration [more North Vietnamese devoted to repair]; fourth, to keep pressure on the North to settle; and fifth, to give us a chip for the bargaining table.'"[83] He might have added a sixth, unstated objective, which was to rebuke McNamara. Johnson grew increasingly frustrated with McNamara's "softness" on Vietnam and suspicious of his friendship with Robert Kennedy.[84] McNamara had ultimately staked his personal relationship with Johnson on the bombing pause, and when it failed to produce clear successes, Johnson blamed him first.

The United States' involvement in Vietnam changed substantially from January to December 1965. So too did McNamara as a person and as a Secretary of Defense. At the start of the year, with McGeorge Bundy, he had written to the President that "our obligations to you simply do not permit us to administer our present directives in silence and let you think we see really hope in them."[85] As the year went on, he allowed Johnson's political calculations to distort his recommendations and learned to calibrate his views to the President's biases. In his diary, McNaughton noted an exchange with Ray Cline, a colleague at the CIA, where "he referred to the last days of Stalin (per Khrushchev), when no one could tell his woes to anyone for fear he would be turned, and done, in. I mentioned that we even have a minor degree of the same problem in Washington!"[86] McNamara was, in effect, silenced. He had become the public face of a US military commitment to Vietnam that he questioned. He provided the rationale for Operation Rolling Thunder, which he initially welcomed, and for the deployment of troops that soon followed, which he did not.

More important, with his accounting gimmicks, he had allowed the administration to sidestep an informed debate on the extension of its commitment to Vietnam. McNamara understood that the 1965 decisions marked a turning point where the nature of US involvement in Vietnam changed. He knew also that the war could not be sustained without either rallying domestic support and resources or providing a clearer end point. Neither was forthcoming and yet he stayed. The most probable reason for this was rooted in his view that no one better than he could resist the pressures to escalate further and in the threat that, as a result, China would enter the war. Above all, he stayed out of his loyalty to the presidency.

McNamara's mistakes in Vietnam were not that he was the preeminent "hawk," the key advisor pressuring President Johnson to escalate in Vietnam with air power and troops, but that he defined his job and loyalty in a way that was too constraining. As the official OSD history explains, "McNamara had promised an efficient and affordable defense. Vietnam ruined those goals."[87] Given this and the fact that he had been quicker than most to assess the economic costs and strategic weaknesses underpinning Johnson's chosen policy for Vietnam, he should have spoken out for his own office as well as for the administration, if not for his country.

9

McNamara in Crisis, 1966–1968

It's a story of a king who is building a palace, a huge extensive edifice, and he subsequently realizes that he can't complete it within his lifetime and he is distraught. He instructs his carpenters to imprint on every stone and beam, "After me cometh a builder; tell him, I too, am known."

Robert S. McNamara, April 29, 1994[1]

With the failure of the bombing pause, McNamara's influence on Vietnam decision-making decreased. He remained Secretary of Defense until February 1968 but spent much of the intervening period drifting further apart from President Johnson, who began to overrule him. After a fresh round of personnel changes, including McGeorge Bundy's departure to take the job McNamara had wanted as president of the Ford Foundation, McNamara became isolated in an administration that continued to favor "hard" options on Vietnam despite questionable results. As it did, McNamara's achievements at the Defense Department began to unravel.

The year 1966 was one of interlocking personal, economic, military and political crises (see Figure 9.1). The consequences of escalation in Vietnam ricocheted onto the domestic and global economy. In March, funding for Vietnam was removed entirely from MAP channels and came under the SASC. The SFRC and SASC both attacked the Secretary for his lack of candor and for the consequences of the administration's political and economic obfuscations. Stung by congressional criticism and the label of "McNamara's war," he informed the Democratic backlash to the President through Robert Kennedy and set out to restore his reputation and protect his legacy at the Defense Department. His friendship with

FIGURE 9.1 From left to right, General Westmoreland, Secretary of State Rusk and Secretary of Defense McNamara attend Honolulu Conference on the Vietnam War, February 2, 1966.
(Yoichi Okamoto, White House Photo Office, LBJL.)

Robert Kennedy exacerbated his disenchantment with the war and strained his loyalty to Johnson to the breaking point. Like many Kennedy holdovers, he drew explicit and unfavorable comparisons between the two Presidents that he had served.

In Vietnam, despite a burst of diplomatic activity in the spring of 1966, the prospect of a negotiated settlement in Vietnam all but ended. Instead, escalation continued with no clear objective in sight. With nothing left to lose, McNamara belatedly stepped out of his self-imposed restrictions and began to question the administration's strategy openly. He returned to the ideas that he had defended in the Kennedy administration and, in 1967, bypassed the State Department and effectively stepped in to run a peace overture himself.

The end of the bombing pause coincided with developments that set the tone for the rest of the year. Within the administration, McNamara and other "Kennedy men" became increasingly critical of civilian leaders in the White House and State Department. Many, including Cyrus Vance, McGeorge Bundy and George Ball, left. McGeorge Bundy's departure was a "tragedy" for McNaughton and McNamara, who "didn't see how

things could work at all well" when Rostow replaced Bundy in a downgraded National Security Advisor role.[2] McNamara's private conversations with McNaughton about Rostow's promotion were unflattering to
the President and to his new advisor. About Johnson, he remarked that
"he wants a paper shuffler. He says he has enough trouble arriving at
decisions when he gets advice from two people; three people is too
many." About Rostow, he observed that he "is full of ideas; the trouble
is – so many of them are wrong."[3] Harriman was even harsher and
described Rostow as "a menace because of his bent toward escalation."[4]
Harriman also criticized William Bundy, whom he said was "just not up
to the job," adding, "State is terribly weak at the top,"[5] an assessment
that he shared with Michael Forrestal, who felt "all the [State] bureaus
have fallen into the hands of people without imagination," and that "Bill
Bundy was the worst of them all."[6]

Like many holdovers from the Kennedy administration, McNamara
began to draw direct parallels with John F. Kennedy's policies for Vietnam in a way that challenged Johnson's contention that he had merely
carried through commitments that he had inherited from his predecessor.
This was potentially politically explosive for Johnson, who once
recounted that "the thing I feared from the first day of my presidency"
was that Robert Kennedy would "reclaim the throne in memory of his
brother."[7]

In February 1966, McNamara reflected on "the Kennedy policy" for
Vietnam and how it differed from Johnson's. McNaughton's diary reads,
"McNamara this morning, while talking with Cy[rus Vance] and me, said
that 'there is not a piece of paper – no record – showing when we changed
from an advisory effort to a combat role in Vietnam. I am prepared to say
that the United States should not, in the case of covert insurgencies, do
more than provide advice and material help to a country. That we should
either go to the source of the trouble, like bombing North Vietnam or take
it to an international tribunal. He said that that *was* the Kennedy policy'"
(emphasis in original).[8] McNamara considered the Johnson administration's inability to produce a strategy that relied on the purposeful application of military force or alternatives to military force, and maintained
that "What we need is a theory that will limit our role"; that bombing
had relied on a gamble that "we could pull it off" rather than a strategy
per se.[9]

A "theory" to limit the US role in Vietnam gained urgency as congressional anger about the war mounted. The SFRC spearheaded the Democratic backlash against the Vietnam War when in February, Senator

Fulbright launched televised hearings that condemned the administration and McNamara's conduct of the war specifically. At the same time, however, it continued to weaken the MAP program, which might have supported alternatives to traditional military tools. By March 1966, to bring the MAP under the $1 billion mark as he had promised to do in 1963, and with Fulbright's support, McNamara formally transferred Vietnam costs into the DOD budget, leaving only minor internal security programs in the USAID budget. McNamara criticized the Fulbright committee for gutting the MAP while the defense budget received funds the administration did not request nor need and explained that the military budget "makes no sense without military assistance."[10]

On February 19, in reaction to Rusk's testimony in front of the Fulbright hearings, Robert Kennedy issued a statement where he questioned the direction of Vietnam policy and suggested a coalition government in the South. Kennedy's comments in February 1966 had a direct connection to McNamara's growing frustrations. To the press, McNamara rather implausibly said, "I talked to Bobby Kennedy briefly on another matter Friday afternoon, and he indicated that he was going to make a statement, but we didn't go into the detail of it."[11] On the contrary, the sheer volume of meetings they shared in 1965, which accelerated in the spring of 1966, suggests otherwise. McNamara spoke to Kennedy at least five times in the days before his statement and again two days later.[12] Moreover, in an oral history interview, Senator Edward "Ted" Kennedy remembered how his brother and McNamara's meetings "were never really reported," that McNamara would "always go over [to Hickory Hill] for a couple of hours" and that "McNamara was beginning to have very serious second thoughts, but was unwilling or unable – or both – to be able to change it. I think talking to McNamara deepened Bobby's concern."[13] By February, McNamara, who was unable or unwilling to change the course of the war from inside the administration, contributed to shifting the debate *outside* the administration.

Johnson criticized "Fulbright, Bobby Kennedy, Teddy Kennedy, Morse" and reminded McNamara that their failure to "cohese" had meant that they "didn't get anything through in the 1961–64 period."[14] Johnson questioned Fulbright's motives and cruelly attacked the senator as menopausal and "off his rocker."[15] He questioned the patriotism of SFRC critics instead of engaging with the content of their disagreements.[16] By contrast, McNamara and his colleagues at ISA were sympathetic to Fulbright's criticism even if they blamed him for having inadvertently created budgetary pressures toward militarization. After one particularly heated exchange, McNaughton noted in his diary: "My guilty feeling went with our pretention that the answers are simple – as if Fulbright had *nothing* to his arguments. It's the difference between the pose of a leader and the ruminations of an intellectual."[17]

For its part, the SASC condemned McNamara for short-changing service needs for operations in Vietnam. He dismissed their accusations as "ridiculous" and quoted his field commanders' satisfaction with the support they were receiving. He proudly explained that the Vietnam buildup had occurred without the type of domestic upheaval that the Korean War had caused and added that "we seem to take a masochistic pleasure in flailing ourselves with imaginary weakness."[18]

Congressional anger also grew over McNamara's failure to disclose the true costs of escalation in 1965. On Johnson's request and against his better judgment, McNamara had delayed asking for the full costs of the 1965 escalation until he presented his budget statement in January and submitted a supplemental budget request for Vietnam. Despite claims that the United States could afford both guns and butter without inflationary pressures, the cost of the Vietnam War had doubled from earlier projections and set off inflation. McNamara had favored a graduated bombing program, in part, because it appeared to be the most economical option. The truth was that the cost of operations had become "unbelievably expensive" especially as airplane losses went up. In April alone, forty-four airplanes were lost over Vietnam. McNamara therefore concluded that the numbers predicted for the FY67 were also significantly under-valued and that he would need an additional $14 billion above his budget request if the buildup continued at its present rate and if the war did not end by June, as his budget had assumed.[19]

Chairman of the Federal Reserve Martin had increased interest rates in December over inflationary fears when he understood the true extent of McNamara's manipulations. As they became clearer to others, fears mounted and the stock market plunged. Johnson's more liberal advisors, including the Chairman of the Council of Economic Advisers Gardner Ackley and Bureau of Budget Director Charles Schulze, now joined Martin and urged the President to pass a tax increase. A temporary excise tax was enacted in March.[20]

However, in a midterm election year, Johnson wanted to avoid both a debate about the budget and a broader tax increase. He preferred to focus on more favorable economic indicators, including low unemployment and GDP growth. These were more favorable to a Democratic adminis-tration that had pushed through a tax break promising that it would jump-start the economy. He criticized liberals as "not prudent folk" and reacted angrily to Ackley and Martin's "talk" during an election year, saying they "must not admit it, not even feel it in [their] own minds," hoping that "if I could keep [the budget] low, I could get my Great Society authorized." McNamara agreed to delay a tax increase if the situation became "clearer" in the second half of the year but warned that the OSD should nevertheless be more transparent with Johnson's economic advisors so they could provide the President with well-informed advice.[21]

By April, as the budgetary numbers exploded with no end in sight and with domestic pressure building, McNamara became desperate. In private, "in an unguarded moment" he told McNaughton, "I want to give the order to our troops to get out of there so bad that I can hardly stand it."[22] With a new Buddhist crisis in South Vietnam in the spring of 1966, the country descended into "semi-anarchy," leading many advisors to conclude that "the Vietnamese whose total incapacity to behave themselves should amount to at least a minimum justification for our dumping them."[23] When US forces were caught in the crossfires of South Vietnamese violence, Galbraith, Harriman and Kaysen each proposed a version of McNaughton's suggestion to McNamara that "all-out internecine strike in VN would provide us as good an excuse as we could find to disengage."[24] "The problem, of course," as McNaughton wrote in his diary, was "how."

When the South Vietnamese government promised elections within five months as a way of resolving the crisis, McNamara sensed an opportunity. As Robert Kennedy had done in his February statement, he recommended that the South Vietnamese try for a coalition government with the Viet Cong.[25] To the SFRC, he laid the political groundwork for the gambit and explained, "It is our goal to allow those people to choose the form of political institutions under which they prefer to live. I suppose you could conceive of them choosing some form other than a democratic form. If they did, we would adhere to that choice."[26] Crucially, he understood that the Viet Cong "might or might not take over"; the implication, as McNaughton observed, "is that we'll then let South Vietnam's chips falls where they may."[27]

The underlying issue, however, was that the administration had no shared understanding of what US objectives in Vietnam were. By the spring of 1966, McNamara was less concerned about the international consequences of Vietnam and had effectively concluded that the United States was "on a losing wicket in Vietnam."[28] His objective, therefore, joined McNaughton's of withdrawing while minimizing the international and domestic fallout. A coalition government and a negotiated settlement by the end of the year met his objectives and could be financed without additional budgetary upheaval. However, both he and McNaughton observed that "Rusk kept the US eye on the VC total capitulation!"[29] They concluded that the administration "must crack through the obstacles to re-examining our objectives (which Bob said neither Rusk nor the President is ready for). Otherwise, none of the sensible actions get taken."[30] Strategy and the meaningful application of military force was impossible without clearer and agreed-on objectives.

Against this backdrop, Ball and McNaughton prepared a report suggesting a fresh set of options for the United States' efforts in Vietnam. These options included: more of the same, pushing the South Vietnamese toward a settlement or "grab (or create) an excuse to exit." McNaughton annotated the implied objectives for McNamara. For example, next to a sharp escalation or the present program, he wrote "victory?"; next to freezing the program, he wrote "compromise?"; and next to his favored policy of disengagement, he wrote "loss-minimization."[31]

As McNamara's appraisal of what might constitute realistic objectives in Vietnam shifted, so too did the urgency to adjust military tools accordingly. He described bombing as a "side show of minor military importance," whose only value was in encouraging a settlement and whose outcome was unlikely to "cause North Vietnam to fold."[32] His view that the bombing program was largely unsuccessful was confirmed in a series of reports in March and April. McNamara had commissioned an independent study of the air war. It agreed with the CIA that bombing had not appreciably affected the North's ability to fight the war in the South nor had it attained any of its other, ancillary objectives.[33] Unlike McNamara, however, the JCS, with a strong advocate in Rostow, encouraged Johnson to move forward on striking industrial targets in the Hanoi–Haiphong area, including bombing POL storage areas and mining Haiphong harbor.[34]

In response, the OSD resuscitated an old idea about building a barrier aimed at curtailing infiltration into South Vietnam. McNamara and his colleagues were of two minds on the project. On the one hand, it appealed to McNamara's interest in projects that relied on "imaginative use of technology," which might obviate the need for further bombing and thus reduce casualties.[35] McNaughton described one especially lively discussion on the subject where "Before long [McNamara] was bouncing around the room, looking at maps of [Southeast Asia] and of Europe (to compare the Iron Curtain). He said, 'Give me $2 billion and I'll build a barrier no one can get through.'"[36] On the other hand, JCS and OSD experts largely rejected the barrier as both impracticable and cost-prohibitive. McNamara and his colleagues at the OSD welcomed the program in the spring of 1966 "because the military reject it with enthusiasm and because it would introduce another variable (presumably debate-provoking)."[37] In other words, in bringing up the barrier again, McNamara hoped to force a discussion about the efficacy of bombing in light of its now obvious economic and human costs.

While McNamara's friends recognized that he did not "urge his private views on the President with the force that he does with his old friends of the Kennedy years,"[38] he nevertheless came out much more forcefully than he had hitherto dared in support of negotiations and against the bombing program. This was a significant break for a Secretary of Defense who had scrupulously resisted interfering in what he saw as the State Department's domain. From January to June, several "promising"[39] peace overtures emerged, including a mission led by Chester Ronning, a retired Canadian diplomat, that coincided with the debates over bombing POL targets. Rusk dismissed Ronning's mission: "quite frankly," he told the Embassy in South Vietnam, "I attach no importance to this trip and expect nothing of it."[40] By contrast, McNamara urged to the President to hold off on military moves and wait.[41]

Ultimately, the diplomatic avenues came to naught and, with them, so too did McNamara's attempts to prevent further expansion of the bombing program. By June, he fell in line, and in what McNaughton described as a "staged NSC meeting" where the "President obviously had arrived at his decision earlier,"[42] he acquiesced to bombing the POL targets and blandly observed that "no senior military leader recommends anything other than proceeding with this program."[43] In a private conversation with Johnson, however, he reiterated his reservations: "it just scares me to see what we're doing there ... going after a bunch of half-starved beggars ... the great dangers and it's not a certainty, but it's a danger we need to look at is that they can keep that up almost indefinitely."[44]

Despite his unsuccessful attempts at holding the line in the spring of 1966, McNamara and his colleagues drew lessons from their failures that would inform the future course of diplomacy in Vietnam. First, for them, the lack of coordination between political and military moves had scuttled even modest openings. Although McNamara micro-managed the selection of bombing targets, commanders in the field often determined the timing of the raids, which had on occasion coincided with diplomatic moves.[45] Hanoi overestimated the United States government's ability to coordinate its military and political tracks and therefore saw the attacks as gestures of bad faith. Second, intransigence on both sides was a problem.[46] McNaughton observed that "it could be that adversaries might miss opportunities to settle because they insist on moving their settlement terms up and down as the tides of conflict flow better or worse."[47]

While McNamara could do little about North Vietnamese inflexibility, his colleagues urged him to push through on the US side. Johnson's presumptive "ambassador for peace"[48] Harriman encouraged McNamara to get "involved in the political aspects of Vietnam" and argued that this would not pervert his conception of State and Defense roles since "military action was in part political."[49] Harriman was even more candid with McNaughton, whom he had mentored when they had worked together on the Marshall Plan. In July, just as a new Italian-Polish led effort code-named "Marigold" was gathering steam, Harriman pulled McNaughton aside and told him, "If you and Bob don't do it, it won't be done ... State is making no initiatives on the diplomatic side."[50] By September, Harriman was "exercised about our apparent inability to get negotiations started" and described Rusk as "a cork in the bottle."[51] The view that Rusk was unwilling to compromise enough for a political settlement and instead viewed the problems in Vietnam "in highly moralistic terms" was widely shared among skeptical advisors.[52]

As McNamara became embattled and isolated both within the administration and outside, he sensed his days at the Pentagon were numbered. He therefore moved to restore his public image and protect his legacy at the Defense Department. Since the fall of 1965, McNamara had had regular meetings with the journalist Stewart Alsop in view of producing a profile of the Secretary. The article was finally published in May 1966 and read like an obituary. "McNamara seems likely to go down in history as one of the very greatest public servants this country has produced," Alsop wrote. The article began with what McNamara later concluded was his greatest achievement, namely his role in changing the US nuclear posture to reflect that it was "impossible to win an all-out nuclear exchange." Alsop implied that McNamara had wanted to leave for some time and felt that five years, in other words, January 1966, was the "outside limit a Secretary of Defense could usefully serve." McNamara confessed that "I've failed" on Vietnam but defended the value of civilian control and his focus on "rationality" despite the fact that "war is an emotional and irrational affair." To Alsop, he explained that "reason" had "shield[ed] him from the terrible pressures to which a Secretary of Defense is subjected – the pressures which killed James Forrestal."

Alsop tried to humanize McNamara and wrote of his different "sides": he "sound[ed] like a sort of mechanical oracle" and talked of emotion "as on old-fashioned preacher might talk about sin, as the source of all errors," but "beneath the coolly assured surface" was a "McNamara who shows himself very rarely – an emotional McNamara." Behind the descriptions about the "gay and charming guest, who has been known to dance a mean Frug" resided the main point of the article, which was to convey that the personal attacks that impugned his character had affected McNamara. It described that he teared up when he felt his honesty was questioned. The article accepted, as McNamara did, that the concentration of power and discipline he had enforced at the OSD may have grated others but explained that it took "simple courage" to make these decisions in the first place.

Alsop and others acted as mouthpieces for McNamara's attempts at rehabilitation. To his credit, Johnson also countered Fulbright's caricatured image of McNamara as a number-crunching, unfeeling architect of the war. He recounted a conversation with Fulbright to McNamara explaining that if he had any reservations, "they were because you were not combatative enough, that you had too much of the professor approach, were too much like him – both of you these goddamn crazy scholars, going around here with a pencil in your ear and want to try to dream out something when you sometimes have to stand up ... Your friend Rusk is more of a militarist than McNamara. He just couldn't conceive of it."[53] To others, Johnson similarly said, "They had pictured McNamara as being a big, fat President of Ford. And he's not."[54] McNamara's notes from his MAP hearings took a similarly defensive line; he scribbled: "I majored in Philosophy not Statistics or Military Science."[55]

McNamara continued this public relations offensive in a series of speeches that coincided with Alsop's article, first at his daughter's commencement ceremony at Chatham College and then before the American Society of News Editors in Montreal. In the latter, he built on his notes from the SFRC hearings and attacked the "tendency to think of our security problem as being exclusively a military problem – and to think of the military problem as being exclusively a weapons-system or hardware problem." He directly challenged the premise for US involvement in Vietnam, suggesting that communism was not a monolithic threat on the world stage and often merely appended itself to conflicts that were rooted in poverty. He added his own view on what the United States *should* have done in Vietnam, without saying so directly: "Experience confirms what human nature suggests: that in most instances of internal violence the local people themselves are best able to deal directly with the situation within the framework of their own traditions."[56]

He ended the speech on a measured note; the man who had been the spokesperson for "rationality" in government policy now reflected on "Man." He asked, "Is he a rational animal?" Answering his own question, McNamara concluded, "All the evidence of history suggests that Man is indeed a rational animal but with a near infinite capacity for folly. His history seems largely a halting, but persistent, effort to raise his reason above his animality. He draws blueprints for utopia. But never quite gets it built. In the end he plugs away obstinately with the only building material really ever at hand: his own part-comic, part-tragic, part-cussed, but part-glorious nature."[57] After more than five years "plugging away" in office, McNamara may have been reflecting on his failed "blueprints."

A measure of just how far apart McNamara's and Johnson's views on Vietnam had become was illustrated just the day before McNamara made his speech in Montreal. Johnson delivered a speech in Chicago in sharp contrast to McNamara. He noted the lessons from World War II were that "the road to peace is not the road of concession and retreat," that in Vietnam as elsewhere, "The failure to meet aggression means war, not peace." He complained about "Nervous Nellies" who could become "frustrated and bothered and break ranks under the strain, and some will turn on their leaders, and on their country, and our own fighting men." He ended with a line that could not have differed more from McNamara's view: "The men who fight for us out there tonight in Vietnam – they are trying to find a way to peace. But they know – and I don't understand why we don't all recognize that we can't get peace just for wishing for it. We must get on with the job until these men come marching home."[58]

A few months later, in a closed meeting with faculty members at Harvard University, McNamara explained the rationale behind his Montreal speech: "I got so goddam frustrated that I had to have some release ... Montreal was an immature act. My responsibility is not to build my image but to manage a department. In those terms, Montreal was a luxury. You don't inspire men to obey commands by casting doubt on a central doctrine of their reason for being; that is, that security equals military power." When he was asked about the role the speech may have had in changing the terms of the debate on Vietnam within the

FIGURE 9.2 New York Senator Robert F. Kennedy (left) and Secretary of Defense McNamara (right), November 5, 1964. Their friendship would create tensions between McNamara and President Johnson.
(OSD photograph collection: OSD Historical Office.)

administration, McNamara made a telling remark: "That's not really my problem. What I have to worry about is keeping the lid on Vietnam and in that battle, Montreal cost me plenty. I'm not sorry that I made it."[59]

The Montreal speech fueled Johnson's suspicions that Robert Kennedy was behind his Secretary's newfound softness (see Figure 9.2). In particular, McNamara had suggested a universal service program in the United States as a way of renewing a sense of national purpose and addressing the unequal burdens of the draft. This was a quintessentially "Kennedy" idea; Robert Kennedy had considered a domestic peace corps program during his brother's administration. In the months before McNamara's speech, the issue of reforming the draft had gained a prominent advocate in Senator Edward Kennedy as it had become clear that poorer African Americans were disproportionately dying in Vietnam.[60] Edward Kennedy later confirmed that his brother Robert had spurred his interest: "I remember walking into Bobby's house, probably '65, '66, and he mentioned the draft and who was fighting the war," he remembered. "It was all the poor and the blacks ... He said, I can't take that on. I had an interest in that, so I started offering these amendments."[61]

While many observers celebrated the "real McNamara"[62] for standing up in Montreal, his political counterparts were more circumspect. British Ambassador to Washington Sir Patrick Dean reported back to London that "there is also probably some intention on McNamara's part to improve his personal image ... by refuting the idea that he is a militarist by temperament," adding that "he is known to be sensitive to the popular description of the Vietnamese operation as 'McNamara's War.'"[63] Closer to home, Townsend Hoopes, who would soon replace McNaughton at ISA, applauded the "agile, almost discrete declaration of independence from the rigidity and growing irrationality of official policy on fundamental issues."[64] Hoopes and the British Embassy assessed that the speeches also represented a revealing break for McNamara, where he stepped away from technical speeches on defense issues to question existing policies for Vietnam and the Cold War. Ambassador Dean observed that it was the "first time so far as I know that the Secretary of Defense has made a major public statement of this sort directed more to a review of foreign policy than to strategy or military questions proper."[65]

As the year progressed, McNamara turned away from "military questions proper" and became involved in the diplomatic and political aspects of the war, as Harriman and others had suggested he should. As the midterm elections neared, congressional criticism from the SFRC quieted and Johnson tried to dampen remaining criticisms from the military and from those who argued that the administration did not have a credible negotiating position. McNamara was instrumental in each of these efforts, although he privately felt "the President should change both his Secretaries of State and Defense" after the election.[66]

In October, he was sent back to Vietnam for the first time in more than a year to nominally consider a fresh request for more troops. Admiral Sharp had requested a troop increase to 570,000 by the end of 1967, a higher number than McNamara had projected in 1965. A month before midterm elections, Johnson wanted McNamara to silence military advisors who increasingly criticized civilians for their timidity and parsimony. Republicans, including Richard Nixon, began to use these views in their political campaigning. In Vietnam, Westmoreland reassured McNamara that "not a single operation" was hampered "in any way by logistical problems," and the "only service" where he saw problems was the Air Force, which expressed "frustrations over 'restrictions' and failure to accomplish what they thought they could."[67]

On his return, McNamara spoke glowingly of operations in Vietnam. Behind the scenes, however, he and McNaughton prepared a scathing report for the President and claimed that there had been no progress since 1961. The pacification programs that McNamara had encouraged had, if anything, "gone backward" and the stalemate that he had found in the fall of 1965 was still there but "at a much higher level of conflict." The bombing program was no more successful. He concluded that the administration should therefore stabilize military operations and redouble its efforts on pacification, focus on clear and hold strategies and, crucially, build up the South Vietnamese capabilities to wage the war themselves while pressuring them into negotiations, however unpromising those negotiations may be.[68] The United States needed a way out of Vietnam. McNamara thus began a slow arc back to his objectives and policies of 1963.

Also in October, Johnson convened a meeting in Manila with allies fighting in South Vietnam to assess the situation there and provide a public plan for peace. Soviet Foreign Minister Andrei Gromyko had suggested that the United States provide a firmer timetable for its promise that it would withdraw troops as and when North Vietnam did.[69] With this in mind, Johnson dictated much of what would become the "Manila communiqué." The "most interesting place," McNaughton observed, was the fifth clause, which stated: "The people of South Vietnam will ask their allies to remove their forces and evacuate their installations as the military and subversive forces of North Vietnam are withdrawn, infiltration ceases, and the level of violence *thus* subsides."[70] McNaughton resisted the final clause, which initially read "and the level of violence subsides," because he and others did not want to "commit the United States to settling *internal* South Vietnamese squabbles" (emphasis in original). To assuage OSD concerns, the word "thus" was introduced.[71] The official position, therefore, became that South Vietnam's internal problems would be theirs alone and that the United States would disengage if North Vietnam promised to do the same.

By 1967, McNamara expressed "surprise that he is still Sec Def" (see Figure 9.3).[72] Although he continued to consider job offers, he felt an obligation to stay as long as the war went on and as long as he continued to believe that he could hold back more dramatic military choices. Johnson hoped to keep him on until the 1968 election but began to "express doubts ... about his loyalty and stability."[73] Above all, he grew increasingly suspicious of McNamara's friendship with "Bobby," which suggests that he kept him within the administration because he was too much of a political liability outside it. McNaughton concluded that his

FIGURE 9.3 Secretary of State Rusk (left), President Johnson (middle) and Secretary of Defense McNamara (right) attend a meeting on Vietnam, January 20, 1967. By 1967, McNamara expressed surprise that he was still at the Pentagon and was frustrated by the State Department and White House's inflexibility on the subject of negotiations.
(Yoichi Okamoto, White House Photo Office, LBJL.)

boss was a lame duck, that he had suffered a "diminution of power, of influence," and that "under Kennedy and in the early Johnson days, I sensed a semi-conspiratorial relationship with McNamara – in which things were accomplished despite bureaucratic hurdles ... Now I sense that the President is on the 'hard' side of Bob – e.g., on Vietnam, in Europe, regarding Anti-Ballistic missiles, etc."[74]

Throughout 1966 and increasingly throughout 1967, Johnson began to overrule McNamara's judgement. In Vietnam, on several occasions, he reinstated air targets that the JCS had recommended but which McNamara had rejected.[75] In August, the semblance of civil-military harmony gave way to bitter exchanges when Senator Stennis convened hearings that were officially meant to assess the conduct of the air war over Vietnam but unofficially to "get McNamara."[76] The Secretary scoffed at the Chiefs and, somewhat ironically given his positions in the past, told Stennis that the United States could not "win the war on the cheap by bombing."[77]

As McNamara's relationship with the Chiefs deteriorated, Johnson tried to improve civil-military relations. He included Wheeler in his Tuesday lunches and encouraged the Chiefs to report directly to him.[78] Similarly, McNamara had resisted an ABM program and ran a personal channel with the Soviet embassy to that end.[79] He had told McNaughton that "there are few things that I fight hard with the President, but this will be one of them."[80] In September 1967, Johnson countermanded him and approved a "light" version of the ABM. Johnson's overtures to the Chiefs undermined one of McNamara's most important achievements at the OSD, that is, that the direct reporting lines that had existed between the President and the Chiefs had been broken and that civilians at the OSD had been given a mediating role.

Johnson also stymied McNamara's long-standing efforts at redeploying troops in Europe and Asia. These had gone ahead on a small scale, if surreptitiously, as troops and equipment were redeployed to Vietnam and not returned.[81] However, in 1966, McNamara had resumed more robust planning for troop reductions for balance of payments reasons. With France's withdrawal from NATO's integrated military command, Germany also began backing away from its offset agreements and Britain cut its conventional forces in the face of its own economic problems. At home, Senator Mansfield pushed for a reduction in US forces in Europe. ISA wholeheartedly supported Mansfield's efforts, if not publicly, as a way of pushing through its plans to "dual-base" forces, namely repatriating forces to the United States and using investments in mobility to redeploy those forces as needed. In response, European Allies in NATO finally accepted a defense posture based on flexible response but only then "to lock [US] conventional forces in Europe."[82] John McCloy was appointed as the administration's envoy to Europe to deal with the thorny issue of troop realignments. With Johnson's support, he joined State and the JCS in resisting the OSD's efforts.

As his professional achievements fell apart, so too did McNamara himself. By 1967, he was a broken man. He commissioned a study, which became known as the *Pentagon Papers*, with the express aim of identifying the mistakes that had led to the Vietnam War and to prevent a similar catastrophe from occurring again. In relatively quick succession, he lost his three of his closest advisors, the few he could count on as confidants: Yarmolinsky, whose relationship to Johnson had soured, left, as did Vance. In July, McNaughton was killed in an airplane accident. Closer to home, his relationship with his son broke down over the war and his beloved wife Margaret developed ulcers, which her friends referred to as

"Bob's ulcer."[83] The "emotional McNamara" described in Alsop's article became more and more visible. Despite his attempts at public redemption, McNamara was attacked wherever he went. Angry students encircled him at Harvard University, which dampened his hopes of returning there.[84] In March 1967, he was attacked on the ski slopes of Zermatt in Switzerland, and in September, for the second time, an anti-war protestor tried to set his home in Aspen on fire.[85]

McNamara experienced a moral crisis over Vietnam decisions. Whereas in Montreal and elsewhere in 1966, he had merely intimated his discomfort about them, in 1967, they exploded into the open. In February, he condemned the bombing program in a meeting where his colleagues described a "distraught and tense McNamara, eyes tearing and voice faltering."[86] In August, during one of Johnson's Tuesday lunches, McNamara denounced the JCS's recommendation to bomb densely populated areas around Hanoi and said "he was not worried about the heat [he would get from Congress over bombing limitations] as long as he knew what we were doing is right."[87] Although in the early years of the Vietnam commitment, McNamara had extended tours of duty as a resource allocation measure, without considering the human impact on the men he was deploying, and had recommended a sustained bombing campaign with minimal concern for the resulting casualties, this all began to change. To make the human costs of decisions explicit to others, he asked the JCS to provide estimates of civilian and US forces casualty figures with their recommendations.

One of McNamara's favorite poems was T. S. Elliot's "Four Quartets," and he quoted one passage regularly, including during an appearance on *Meet the Press* in February 1968, on the day he left the Pentagon, in the preface of his memoirs and at the end of the documentary *The Fog of War*. It reads, "We shall not cease from exploration / And the end of all our exploring / Will be to arrive where we started / And know the place for the first time." In his last months at the Pentagon, the policies he suggested for Vietnam did just that: at the end of his "exploring," he returned to where he had started and presented very similar policies to the ones he had in 1963.

In May, McNamara and McNaughton put pen to paper and in a DPM argued that the war was unwinnable and was "acquiring a momentum of its own that must be stopped."[88] The immediate impetus for McNamara's DPM was Westmoreland's latest request for an additional 200,000 troops and "an extension of the war into the VC/NVA sanctuaries (Laos, Cambodia, and possibly North Vietnam), mining of North Vietnamese ports and a solid commitment in manpower and resources to a military victory."[89] It coincided with a separate JCS posture statement, which indicated that drawdowns in forces abroad to meet Vietnam requirements had resulted in their inability to effectively meet contingencies that might arise elsewhere in the world.[90]

McNamara described the ensuing debate as a "'65 type watershed":[91] Westmoreland's request necessarily required a reserve call-up and "would not win the Vietnam War, but only submerge it in a larger one."[92] Going against Rostow's and the Chiefs' resistance, McNamara suggested that the United States reassess its objectives in South Vietnam. He presented the same arguments that McNaughton had made since 1965 and wrote that the administration should begin to reduce the importance of South Vietnam in its public pronouncements and accept a role for the Viet Cong in the South. While the debate in Washington raged, McNamara helped to establish the Civil Operations and Rural Development Support (CORDS) program, the first fully integrated pacification program under Westmoreland's command. As he had in 1963, he understood that other agencies were less capable of coordinating complex and expensive operations. McNamara's implied objective in May 1967 was therefore to plan for withdrawal and refocus efforts back to the village level in South Vietnam and away from the "big war" of attrition.

Officially, McNamara went back and forth on bombing throughout this debate. In reality, he informed Robert Kennedy's statement on March 2, the first since February 1966, which called for a unilateral bombing halt and an offer to begin negotiations "within a week."[93] A month earlier, McNaughton had observed that McNamara "would have been willing to do so" as well.[94] In public, for a time, the Secretary of Defense supported Johnson's decision to expand the targets under Operation Rolling Thunder. By May, though, he called for restrictions on bombing of areas south of the 20th parallel and, in September, joined Kennedy's position and encouraged Johnson to unilaterally and indefinitely stop the bombing program.[95] In a gesture of good will and with an eye to Robert Kennedy, Johnson suggested that he would call off bombing and meet "tomorrow" if "productive discussions" were possible and if North Vietnam "would not take advantage of the bombing cessation or limitation."[96] McNamara called for a cessation without conditions.

His position shifted because of enduring doubts about bombing but also because he had taken a lead role in the so-called Pennsylvania Initiative. Although Rusk and Johnson had never had great confidence in this latest effort at a political settlement, McNamara described it as the "most interesting" negotiation "we have ever had" and, as Harriman had suggested to him, stepped into a role that should have been the State Department's.[97] The mission was run through Harvard Professor Henry Kissinger and two French emissaries, Herbert Marcovitch and Raymond Aubrac, an old friend of Ho Chi Minh's.[98] In September, however, Kissinger had conveyed Marcovitch's anger that "every time I brought a message we bombed the center of a North Vietnamese city. If this happened one more time, he was no longer prepared to serve as channel."[99] Marcovitch's complaint represented exactly the type of misalignment of political and military tools that had bothered OSD officials the year before. McNamara was therefore eager to learn from past mistakes and thought a bombing cessation would put the ball firmly in North Vietnam's court.

When the Pennsylvania Initiative collapsed in mid-October, McNamara "precipitated the last act" of his tenure as Secretary of Defense.[100] In his March statement, Kennedy had reiterated his support for a coalition government in the South and suggested the progressive withdrawal of US forces from there under international auspices. During a Tuesday lunch on October 31 and the next day in writing, McNamara made the same suggestion and in great detail. He spelled out the human costs of likely escalations over the next fifteen months: some "10,900 to 15,000 dead," 30,000 to 45,000 "requiring hospitalization" and further destruction in the South. He questioned whether pacification could "accelerate considerably" but noted with annoyance that none of the JCS's recommendations focused on the South. In lieu of the policies currently under consideration, he recommended a program that would stabilize US forces and progressively hand over the fighting to the Vietnamese. It bore a striking resemblance to the same policies that he had advocated for in October 1963 only "at a much higher level of conflict."

Still, McNamara's reflexive tendency to self-censor out of loyalty to the President endured (see Figure 9.4). He placed a cover note on the memo in which he told the President, "Because these may be incompatible with your own [views], I have not shown the paper to Dean Rusk, Walt Rostow or Bus Wheeler."[101] On the very same day, Johnson asked McNamara to brief the "Wise Men" about the bombing program without disclosing his own views or the memo he had just submitted. In contrast to McNamara, they concluded that bombing continued to be a useful negotiating chip.[102] About the meeting, McNamara later noted that "no President should bring into important discussions of events outsiders who really have no full understanding" of the problems.[103]

FIGURE 9.4 President Johnson (left) and Secretary McNamara (right) in a Cabinet meeting on the Vietnam War, February 7, 1968. McNamara was days away from leaving the Pentagon to become president of the World Bank. (Yoichi Okamoto, White House Photo Office, LBJL.)

In later years, McNamara recalled that he "never heard" from Johnson about his November 1 memo. Instead, on November 29, Johnson released a statement announcing McNamara's departure from the Pentagon to become the new president of the World Bank. He explained that the Secretary had agreed to stay at the Pentagon "so long as the President considered it necessary" and that it was now time for a "fresh person," that he "could not justify asking Secretary McNamara indefinitely to continue the enormous burdens of his position." He pointedly added, "the course of our participation to the war in Vietnam is firmly set."[104] In his own statement and meetings with the press, McNamara alluded to the fact that he had considered leaving "in the past two years" and that he had not planned on staying at the Pentagon as long as he had, but that "I have done so because of my feeling of obligation to the President and the nation."[105]

However, much as McNamara later prevaricated on the subject, he was fired. Moreover, the World Bank was not an anodyne choice. As an international civil servant, McNamara was forbidden from taking part in domestic politics. Johnson thus neutralized a possible political threat.

What most concerned Johnson was not just that his Secretary was finding it more and more difficult to support administration policies – that was not new – but instead that his collusion with Robert Kennedy was becoming obvious. In the days before the President's announcement, McNamara had had an unusual amount of contact with both Robert Kennedy and Adam Yarmolinsky, who was now working behind the scenes to promote a Kennedy challenge to Johnson.[106]

At his departure ceremony, Johnson awarded McNamara the Medal of Freedom and predicted that a revolution would come to the World Bank under McNamara's guidance, the same revolution that he had effected at the Department of Defense. In comments that harkened back to McNamara's Montreal speech, he said McNamara's work would now concern "the most important war of all" as he would "attack the root causes of violence and turmoil – poverty, disease, ignorance and hopelessness."[107] In a room filled with Cabinet members as well as Robert and Edward Kennedy, McNamara choked up, "I became so emotional, I could not respond," he recalled.[108] Coughing nervously and holding back tears, he said, "Mr. President, I cannot find the words to express what lies in my heart today. And I think I better respond on another occasion."[109]

Conclusion

One of the last events that McNamara oversaw as Secretary of Defense was the Tet Offensive, which began in January 1968. In a bid to achieve a quick battlefield victory, North Vietnamese forces staged simultaneous attacks in South Vietnam where they hoped to generate a popular uprising. None was forthcoming. Although the Tet Offensive was a military success for the United States and its ally in the South, playing as it did to their strengths, it was nevertheless a political disaster. The administration's lack of candor undermined public faith in the US government's ability to tell the truth. Images of the attacks on the US Embassy in Saigon undermined both General Westmoreland's and the US government officials' statements that the campaign had demonstrated the success of existing programs in Vietnam.

In the wake of the first attacks, Westmoreland cabled back to Washington, "We are now in a new ball game where we face a determined, highly disciplined enemy, fully mobilized to achieve a quick victory," and requested an additional 200,000 troops to "seize the opportunity to crush him."[1] It was left to McNamara's successor Clark Clifford to engage in the latest administration debate over troop increases. McNamara warned him to do "whatever we can to prevent the financial requirements" of the latest increase "from ruining us" in the domestic and international economic spheres.[2]

In July 1965, McNamara had supported troop increases on the condition that the necessary economic and political resources were enlisted. Johnson chose, however, to deploy troops but delay the costs of escalation. By 1968, this was no longer possible. Tet provoked a political crisis because the administration had not "educated the people" as it had gone "up the escalating chain," as McNamara had recommended.[3] It also marked an economic fork in the road. McNamara had hidden the financial costs of escalation by drawing down troops and resources around the world and, in so doing, depleting the military's so-called strategic reserve. By 1968, any further troop deployment in Vietnam necessarily entailed rebuilding the reserve and thus required significant defense outlays.[4]

With Tet, also, the consequences of McNamara's creative accounting became apparent. McNamara was correct in his private assessment that "there is no piece of paper – no record – showing when we changed from an advisory effort to a combat role in Vietnam."[5] The administration, and McNamara himself, had blurred that line deliberately. From a budgetary perspective, the United States never actually went to war under McNamara. It was not until 1968 that the OSD dropped its budgetary assumption that the war would end by June and instead accepted that the war could go on indefinitely. Congress was finally provided with the full anticipated costs of operations in Vietnam.[6]

Early on, McNamara had resisted troop deployments in Vietnam over concerns about the balance of payments deficit and the international confidence that was required to protect the dollar's role in the international monetary system. Predictably, Tet produced jitters on the gold market. As Enthoven wrote to Clifford, "The extent of such speculation is influenced by many factors other than the size of the US deficit [including] unsettling events such as the onset of the Vietnam War, the extent to which US officials lose their confidence in the public."[7] Rusk and Rostow now also accepted that further troop deployments would have economic repercussions. Rostow worried that the crisis "could set in motion a financial and trade crisis which would undo much that we have achieved in these fields in the past twenty years and endanger the prosperity and security of the Western world."[8] By March, the London gold pool, a major component of transatlantic cooperation on international monetary issues, closed. Ultimately, economic events were as important as military considerations in determining the consequences of Tet. Economic factors, in fact, conditioned Johnson's announcement that he would not deploy additional troops but instead move to a bombing halt with a view to a negotiated settlement.[9] In other words, in the aftermath of Tet, Johnson came around to a very similar view to the one that McNamara had presented to him in 1965.

This book provides an important corrective on the mistakes typically ascribed to McNamara for his role during the Vietnam War, chiefly, his putative naive optimism about the situation in Vietnam and his blind hawkishness. In his diary, McNaughton recorded: "McNamara, the day before we left for Greece, remarked to Tim Hoopes and me that 'we've made mistakes in Vietnam ... I've made mistakes. But the mistakes I made are not the ones they say I made.' I said, 'I know.' The fact is that he believes we never should have gotten into the combat role out there."[10] The new evidence presented here supports McNamara's conclusion and suggests that he had often been prescient about problems with the US involvement in the war, including the economic costs of a growing commitment to Vietnam, the inherent weakness of the South Vietnamese ally and eventually, the failure of the Johnson administration to produce a clear and viable strategy.

Drawing for the first time on the full body of primary evidence, this book reinterprets McNamara's role in a war so closely associated to his name. By extending the research on Vietnam to bring together other bodies of literature, for instance, economic or bureaucratic histories, another interpretation of McNamara is possible. Moreover, new sources, in particular transcripts of the Kennedy and Johnson tapes, McNamara's handwritten notes during his trips and hearings, his calendar, Yarmolinsky's papers and McNaughton's diaries shed a different light on his interaction with colleagues and provide invaluable evidence that the gap between McNamara's public and private persona was wider than was heretofore known. The written record looks very different when it is juxtaposed against these other sources.[11] McNaughton's diaries, for example, show just how substantial the difference between McNamara's written statements and his private thoughts were; the presidential recordings shed light on how much, or little, of McNamara's written recommendations were actually representative of his own views; and the economic papers often explain the timing of key decisions.

By looking at McNamara's decisions for Vietnam from the bureaucratic vantage point of the OSD, new findings emerge about his "mistakes" and new counterfactual questions add to the more commonly asked, "What would JFK have done?" They include: could the counterinsurgency strategy in Vietnam have worked if it had been scrupulously applied into the Johnson administration? Could a less militant SFRC have permitted a viable MAP-led program in South Vietnam? Could a stronger and more creative State Department have prevented the seemingly inexorable process toward a military solution in South Vietnam? What would have happened if Johnson had been less a New Dealer and more a fiscal conservative as his predecessor had been? Would an alternative view of civil-military relations have produced better outcomes? And, finally, would a less loyal Secretary of Defense, on balance, have been better for the country?

WHAT WOULD JFK HAVE DONE?

One of the more remarkable outcomes of researching this period has been to become aware of how men who were otherwise rational, controlled, even cold, could also be so personally and emotionally attached to the Presidents they served. This was particularly true with Kennedy. Elspeth Rostow, who undertook many of the oral history interviews for the John F. Kennedy Presidential Library, placed a cover letter on her interview transcript with General Taylor, which read:

During the space of four days I watched two men talk for the record about Jack Kennedy but in both cases the record will be incomplete. One was Maxwell Taylor, the other was Joseph Alsop. Neither could explain why the President means so much to him, neither had known the depth of his affection until November 22. Alsop, after finishing the tape, said: "I had no idea that I loved him. I don't go in for loving men. But nothing in my life has moved me as it did – not even the death of my father. And everyone has said the same. Ros Gilpatric – now Ros doesn't go in for men, don't you know – Ros said he's never got over it. And Bob McNamara said the same thing. And Mac Bundy. As if he were the one thing they most valued and could never replace." Joe was walked around the room as he talked, the parrots were squawking, and he took off his glasses angrily to wipe his eyes. It was different at Ft. Myers. The General was talking about the 22nd of November in his usual efficient, precise way. The tape was on. Suddenly he stopped, sitting very stiffly in his chair and looking out at the flagpole in front of the house. He was crying too much to continue. There is a pause on the tape, and then we go on.[12]

Rostow's notes provide insight into the depth of affection and loyalty these men showed President Kennedy both during his time in office and after his assassination. Personal relationships mattered in the Kennedy administration and shaped the substance of policy. At the same time, the trauma of the assassination no doubt contributed to many of these advisors' arguments in later years that Kennedy was determined to withdraw from Vietnam on the eve of his death. His loss was not just a personal tragedy but also a national tragedy, whose ripple effects flowed all the way to Vietnam.

This book does not necessarily exclude their arguments; they are perfectly compatible. The book does, however, offer another, less glamorous story. It contends that the story of how the CPSVN was agreed on and eventually dropped, and how the escalation of US involvement in

Vietnam occurred, is also a bureaucratic one. In practice, policy on Vietnam was a product of compromise and adaptations to what was organizationally and financially possible in Washington and Saigon. In that bureaucratic story, McNamara was the leading advocate for withdrawal whenever that option was on the table; he was its main architect and driving force.

WHAT IF MCNAMARA HAD INHERITED ANOTHER MODEL FOR CIVIL-MILITARY RELATIONS?

As he told the Harvard faculty in the wake of his Montreal speech, for McNamara, his job was to keep the lid on Vietnam and manage a department; it was not to cast doubt on existing doctrines. As soon as he began to concern himself with Vietnam in the spring of 1962, McNamara tried to keep a lid on economic costs and on pressures to escalate as he balanced civilian and military priorities and concerns. In this respect, he was following the philosophy of civil-military relations behind the Defense Reorganization Act to the letter. As the act envisaged, his role was not to comment on strategy but to organize "effective, efficient and economical" military resources in the service of civilian objectives and strategy. He organized the services in "unified direction under civilian control of the Secretary of Defense."[13]

The process of setting strategy was a one-way street. Civilian advisors were responsible for articulating a strategy, and relevant military advisors translated it into an operational strategy. The Secretary of Defense's role was to ensure that the two matched, that force structures and budgets were suitably aligned. To begin to comment on strategy would introduce a feedback loop where the parochial priorities of the services could distort strategy. In so doing, it would undermine McNamara's central achievements at implementing civilian control.

This was not to say that McNamara did not favor one strategy over another. To a large extent, civilian priorities conditioned his enthusiasm for counterinsurgency in the Kennedy years and for the bombing program in the Johnson administration. Both promised the economical and civilian-controlled application of force. Like the barrier concept, they were also designed to avoid expensive troop deployments. The central point of defense economics, as McNamara's "whiz kids" developed it, was that existing economic conditions determined the breadth of commitments any administration could take on and the resources they could responsibly allocate to those ends.

McNamara understood the economic costs inherent to an expanding commitment in Vietnam. In many ways, the CPSVN and the bombing program were perfect platforms for McNamara to display his achievements at the Defense Department. They showed his ability to bring the Chiefs into line with a new and civilian-led strategy. The CPSVN also addressed Kennedy's economic priorities while providing an economically promising model for intervening in the wars of national liberation in which the President had taken an interest. Furthermore, it showcased how his new investments at the Defense Department, notably in air- and sealift capabilities, could serve those objectives. Even when the CPSVN process stopped, for reasons that had more to do with Johnson's economic and political preferences than with the situation on the ground per se, McNamara foresaw the domestic and economic implications of the chosen policy.

In assessing McNamara's contributions to the problems of Vietnam, a central question emerges: what was the alternative model of civil-military relations given the history of the OSD up to this point? Was it to allow the armed services a greater voice in setting strategy at the outset? As H. R. McMaster has persuasively argued, the Chiefs may not have been capable of doing so. When they made recommendations that diverged from McNamara's framework, they often failed to factor in the economic consequences of the military actions proposed and the Cold War context, in which the United States' international image also mattered. Alternatively, was it for the Defense Department to take on a greater role in diplomatic aspects of the conflict, since McNamara was inclined to be "less rigid" about negotiating? The evolution of the OSD and the underlying progression of civil-military relations until the 1960s made both options problematic.

WHAT IF THE STATE DEPARTMENT HAD BEEN STRONGER?

By understanding how McNamara conceived of the OSD in relation to the making of strategy, the responsibility for choosing the right or wrong strategy shifts away from the Defense Department and toward the State Department and White House. Historians have not been kind to Dean Rusk and this book will not soften assessments of his contributions on Vietnam, although it does raise the question of whether escalation in Vietnam might have been different if there had been a stronger, better-run State Department (see Figure C.1).

FIGURE C.1 Secretary of Defense McNamara (left) in conversation with Secretary of State Dean Rusk, July 25, 1965. Despite their differences on policy matters, McNamara had great affection for his colleague.
(Yoichi Okamoto, White House Photo Office, LBJL.)

Hindsight has not necessarily colored the criticisms that historians have leveled at Rusk; they already existed at the time. Advisors at the State Department and beyond, not least McNamara himself, were regularly frustrated with him then and even more so in later years. Despite his personal affection for Rusk, one commentator correctly assessed Montreal's speech as an expression of McNamara's "dissatisfaction with the unimaginative and inflexible policies in the State Department."[14] As early as 1961, Rusk's Ambassador to Vietnam, Nolting, rather undiplomatically wrote to his boss: "vigor in the Department of Defense in this situation needs to be matched by equal vigor in the non-military aspects if the proper proportions are to be maintained in our total effort there."[15] A year later, CINCPAC observed, "State waffles and evades."[16]

Rusk has served as a useful foil to historians who have tried to add nuance to their assessments of other advisors in the Kennedy and Johnson administrations. As an "unyielding, unquestioning rock of containment certitude" with a quiet demeanor, he stands in contrast to his colleagues with their private conflicts and public charisma.[17] There was some truth also to Rusk's observation that McNamara would inevitably "end up looking like a dove" because his role was "to present the arguments for limiting military force," whereas Rusk's was to defend South Vietnam "in the face of those who would call the whole thing off."[18] As a result, Rusk can easily be caricatured.

Nevertheless, Rusk's mistakes were real and multiple, and trickled down throughout the Johnson administration when his role became central to articulating a strategy for Vietnam and to opening avenues for a political settlement. In producing post-mortem assessments of the failures in Vietnam, many key advisors pointed the finger at bureaucratic forces and specifically at Rusk's weakness in representing a civilian view. Hilsman, for instance, explained that the responsibility of the White House and especially the State Department was to "leverage political aspects," something they did not do.[19] Paradoxically, because McNamara was so efficient as a manager, and despite his personal reluctance to define problems as primarily military, he made it easier for the President to do just that. He became a victim of his own success.

In part, as Yarmolinsky noted, State did not "leverage political aspects" as much as it could have because, contrary to Huntington's concerns in *The Soldier and the State*, civilians had "allow[ed] themselves to become militarized."[20] President Johnson's suggestion that McNamara should "lay up the plans to whoop the hell" out of adversaries in South Vietnam speaks to this. Similarly, in later years, McNamara was frustrated at Rusk's intransigence and his espousal of the "victory ethos" of the military. To McNaughton, he explained that he "agreed with me that our increased deployments each time were hoped (by him and me) to provide strength from which a *compromise* could be struck; each time Rusk kept the US eye on the VC total capitulation!"[21] The failure of negotiations was not Rusk's alone but he consistently downplayed the value of existing peace overtures. In turn, without political channels, McNamara's attempt at "communication" through bombing made no sense.

COULD THE COUNTERINSURGENCY STRATEGY UNDER THE KENNEDY ADMINISTRATION HAVE WORKED?

Under the Kennedy administration, the hurdles to properly organize for counterinsurgency were also rooted in weaknesses at the State Department. The Kennedy administration made some leeway in terms of organizing for counterinsurgency in new, more civilized ways, for instance, through the Special Group (CI). However, Hilsman and his colleagues always worried about the ability of the US government and its fragmented agencies to work together coherently in the field. In November 1963, as the CPSVN took hold in Vietnam, Hilsman worried that "once the MACV/CINCPAC/JCS channel was set up, it would inevitably become formal, requiring JCS action and Special Group action for every move, thus getting us into a somewhat rigid position that would make timing to fit the political situation difficult."[22] Although the CPSVN brought order and a degree of secured funding for Hilsman's preferred program, it also removed the flexibility and informality that his program required operationally.

In the early years of US involvement in Vietnam, decision-makers quarreled and struggled to find the right balance of responsibility across the different government agencies. When the Defense Department took over the CIA and USAID's programs under Operation Switchback in 1962, field officers complained but were silenced as their bosses weighed up the budgetary advantages. Later, Yarmolinsky, writing to William Kaufmann, a former colleague, explained: "I agree that we have come to understand that the threat of sub-limited war requires more than just a military response but I question whether we are 'learning to orchestrate all the instruments.' Aren't we rather still in the stage of having learned that they need to be orchestrated, but are still having a good deal of difficulty even getting them to harmonize – and too often the violins end up several bars after the drums and cymbals?"[23] In each instance, bureaucrats did not want to shake the boat too aggressively and held on to the hope that existing bureaucratic arrangements, even if they were less than ideal, might work.

When the counterinsurgency program was gradually dropped in the transition to the Johnson administration, Kennedy's erstwhile counterinsurgency advisors in the NSC and State Department complained. They were impotent before a President and Secretary of State uninterested in their ideas and alarmed at the chaotic situation in South Vietnam. While McNamara could ignore or suppress negative reports from the field in the lead-up to the October 1963 NSC meetings, it became much more difficult to do so in the aftermath of the Diem assassination with stepped-up infiltration from the North and chronic political instability in the South. This raises another question, namely could the counterinsurgency strategy have worked with changed circumstances on the ground?

COULD DIFFERENT FUNDING ARRANGEMENTS
IN WASHINGTON HAVE PRODUCED
DIFFERENT OUTCOMES?

The imbalance in the State-Defense relationship was not just the product of personalities and of each Secretary's abilities and weaknesses. It was also a funding story that to some extent was beyond the control of both. Military solutions were more readily available and funded. Because military approaches were easier to fund and the Defense Department was better configured to organize complex operations, they produced what Yarmolinsky called "centrifugal tendencies." Ultimately, as operations in Vietnam became more extensive and, therefore, expensive, the more likely it became that responsibility for them would be shifted to the Defense Department. Moreover, with a MAP and USAID program under continuous attack, the budget naturally shifted to the services. This bureaucratic dimension was at the heart of McNamara's comments in Montreal (see Figure C.2).

As Yarmolinsky added, faced with "built-in deadlines" that are inherent to crises, Presidents, he argued, turned to "what they can do best," which, in the US system, was invariably military solutions. With Johnson particularly, military options promised a degree of short-term success to a politician who wanted "something," that is, quick-fix solutions that were easily deployable. As an agency that was set up to prepare for contingencies and to deal with "large organizational problems," the Defense Department, Yarmolinsky argued, "out-perform[ed] State" each time.[24] McNamara took over the problems in Vietnam in 1962 because his department could more easily absorb the costs involved and because he and his staff promised to bring order where other agencies, especially the State Department, had failed. As escalation occurred, he could draw on a "strategic reserve" surreptitiously, whereas civilian agencies had no reserve resources to speak of.

Both Hilsman and Yarmolinsky suggested that the underlying problem in the US government and in Vietnam specifically was that resources were consistently siphoned to the Defense Department rather than to State in the first place, because it was "harder to galvanize people" around the State Department, which lacked "the constituency or natural allies in industry or Congress," both of which the Pentagon had.[25] For Yarmolinsky, flexible response had actually made the problem worse. Rather than "demilitarizing the process," McNamara's reforms had "only prun[ed] the branches of the military tree. It continued to flourish,

FIGURE C.2 A page from John T. McNaughton's scrapbooks: McNaughton (left)
and Secretary of Defense McNamara (right) attend SFRC hearings where they
defended the value of the Military Assistance Program, April 20, 1966.
McNamara would build on this testimony during his Montreal speech the
following month.
(OSD Photograph, John T. McNaughton family collection.)

stunting the growth of the civilian organisms that grew in its shadow."[26]
Flexible response had made the Department of Defense even more ubiquitous because it made it nominally applicable to an even greater range
of contingencies. The services first became involved in Vietnam precisely
because they were encouraged to use it as a laboratory for their new
responsibilities under flexible response.

Yarmolinsky wrote that "So long as the present military means are
available, situations like Vietnam are going to recur": without a more
wholesale reform of the policy process, military solutions would always
be favored. Only "political leadership that exercises superhuman qualities" could prevent it.[27] Paradoxically, by investing and producing a
well-run Defense Department, the United States had reduced its flexibility
in its interactions with the world.

Moreover, it is a bitter irony that the same senators who expressed concern about the growing commitment in Vietnam as early as 1962 and worried that it was becoming overmilitarized hastened the process along. The advocate senators in the SFRC, including Fulbright and Mansfield, inadvertently reduced their leverage over the administration's Vietnam policy by attacking the MAP program. Even while Russell and his colleagues on the SASC might have expressed reservations over the commitment in Vietnam as well, they were more concerned with ensuring that the services had all the resources they asked for. In so doing, they shifted the balance toward military options.

WHAT IF JOHNSON HAD BEEN LESS OF A NEW DEALER?

This book raises another counterfactual. Given the different economic sensibilities of Presidents Kennedy and Johnson, would the war in Vietnam have happened if Johnson was less of New Dealer? Gaddis and others have presented Kennedy as a spendthrift Keynesian. This book suggests otherwise. Instead, by looking at the early decisions on Vietnam from the vantage point of the OSD, an altogether different interpretation emerges. As Secretary of Defense, McNamara was uniquely positioned to see how economic constraints weighed on strategic choices. Contrary to Gaddis' contention, Kennedy was troubled by what he perceived as the United States' economic weaknesses. His and McNamara's decisions in Vietnam into 1963 were a product of a feeling not of omnipotence but rather of vulnerability. In this, he was very different from his successor, who disapproved of Kennedy's fiscal conservatism.

McNamara and Dillon's efforts, most notably on the balance of payments during the Kennedy administration, challenge the idea that the administration saw itself as being at the apex of US power and militancy. It disputes the argument that under Kennedy "optimistic America answered the summons of the trumpet and went to war in Vietnam"[28] and a related point: that McNamara advocated or even favored military solutions for Vietnam. The Kennedy administration chose a limited strategy that was contingent on self-help for Vietnam in part because of what Kennedy perceived as "limitations on the ability of the United States" to "bring about a favorable result" there.[29]

By the spring of 1962, international crises in Laos, Berlin and Cuba had humbled the Kennedy administration. However, in many respects, its more modest approach to South Vietnam predated these crises and reaffirmed the central idea of Kennedy's inaugural address, which was less a "clarion call" for US militancy and more a call for people in the United States and abroad to become agents in their own future or, in the words of the address, "to help them help themselves."[30]

Refocusing US foreign policy on the notion of self-help gained added urgency in 1962 when a jump in the balance of payments deficit and the gold outflow occurred. Just as Eisenhower had before him, Kennedy worried that an unstable economic base and international monetary system could undermine every aspect of the US power.[31] Together with Dillon, McNamara led efforts to redress the deficit. McNamara played a leading part on the balance of payments because the Defense Department's overseas operations largely drove the deficit and because his cost-saving reputation, the quality that distinguished him above all else, was at stake. As a result, the CPSVN timetable directly matched the timing and pace of McNamara's efforts to address the balance of payments outflow.

With Kennedy's assassination, many things changed. This included a change in advisors on Vietnam, to the clear detriment of key players on counterinsurgency, including Hilsman and Robert Kennedy. Johnson's preference for military solutions also changed the general tenor on Vietnam, as did his search for consensus among his advisors. One of the most decisive changes, however, derived from his different appreciation of economic problems. With less restraint on the economic front and more fiscally conservative advisors such as Dillon sidelined, the pressures to reduce commitments in Vietnam and elsewhere diminished at a key juncture in the escalation of the US involvement.

From 1965 onward, McNamara and others raised economic concerns with Johnson and worried that escalation in Vietnam, if it was not matched with either a tax increase or tighter domestic spending, might produce inflationary pressures. The President's commitment to the Great Society and to surpassing Roosevelt's achievements under the New Deal trumped their judgments. He tried to bully and censor officials, such as Federal Reserve Chairman Martin, who confronted him with the economic implications of his decisions for Vietnam. He feared a congressional debate over his decision for Vietnam because, above all, he wanted to protect his Great Society programs. If Johnson had been a little more fiscally conservative, he might have been more willing to critically question the value of the US commitment in South Vietnam.

WHAT IF MCNAMARA HAD DEFINED "LOYALTY" DIFFERENTLY?

This brings us to McNamara himself, the man behind the office. Speaking of his boss and friend, Yarmolinsky commented, "My own view ... is that if McNamara is remembered at all by history, he will not be remembered as a manager, he will not be remembered as the 'architect of Vietnam' although he may be remembered unhappily that way ... But I think he'll be remembered as the person who was, really, the first and most effective educator of the American people on the true nature of military weapons."[32] Ensuring that legacy or "building his image" as he said to the Harvard faculty might have been an objective of his speech in Montreal and other efforts in the spring of 1966, but it could not ultimately remove the overbearing shadow of Vietnam.

In Stewart Alsop's article, McNamara had said, "My mistakes have been mistakes of omission, not commission."[33] Responding to the article, McNaughton "told him that one of his greatest 'errors of omission' (about which he had told Stewart Alsop) was in continuing to recommend force deployments *in order to give us bargaining leverage* when the government was not *taking* any bargaining steps" (emphasis in original).[34] A less charitable way of paraphrasing McNaughton's comment is that McNamara recommended troop deployments without any faith in their ability to achieve anything at all. By 1968, some 20,000 US servicemen had died in Vietnam and many more South and North Vietnamese, and 1968 would become the deadliest year yet.[35] McNamara's role in that was no small omission.

McNamara's loyalty to the President, which served his bureaucratic ends well, became troublesome when he became the public face of a program that he understood was fundamentally flawed. Because of his loyalty to the President, he "omitted" to express his doubts and legitimate questions even while he oversaw ever-increasing troop deployments and casualties. Crucially, it led him to "omit" information to the Congress, whose important constitutional responsibility it was to oversee the multifaceted implications of the growing commitment in Vietnam. When the administration decided to deploy Marines to Da Nang, Johnson initially suggested that McNamara might announce that they were a "security group" or something equally innocuous. McNamara resisted, by saying that the administration would be "accused of falsifying the story."[36] His comment suggests that he understood that the ambiguity that Johnson cultivated was tantamount to a lie, yet he continued to play a central role in obscuring the reality of the administration's decisions for Vietnam.

This raises an additional counterfactual, namely could the war in Vietnam have gone differently if McNamara had not been so loyal and instead voiced and acted on his concerns? Although McNamara considered leaving the Johnson administration as early as the fall of 1965, he nevertheless stayed on until February 1968. When he did break ranks with the administration, he replaced his loyalty to Johnson with renewed loyalty to the Kennedys. His disenchantment with the war was, in fact, intimately connected to Robert Kennedy's ascendancy as a political threat to Johnson.

The idea that McNamara was uninformed or did not seek advice beyond traditional military channels was not borne out in the research leading to this book. Quite the contrary. In addition to his long exchanges with John Kenneth Galbraith and Robert Thompson, which began in 1962, in the fall of 1963, he spoke to Patrick Honey, who convinced McNamara to oppose the coup against Diem, not because of any moral concerns but because the alternative leaders could not sustain the program he had laid out for South Vietnam. In this assessment, Honey and McNamara were spot-on. In later years, McNamara drew on Bernard Fall, who was critical of the bombing program and its "confidence in total material superiority," and warned the Johnson administration that it was tying its credibility to a doomed and "fundamentally weak" South Vietnamese partner.[37]

Although McNamara knowingly accepted the label that Vietnam was "McNamara's war," behind the scenes the situation at the OSD was more complex. Some of the most virulent complaints emerged at ISA even if they rarely went beyond its walls.[38] In some respects, ISA was the logical place for dissent as it bridged the capabilities of the Defense Department and the strategy, or lack thereof, of civilians at the State Department. Ultimately, it was at ISA under McNamara that the policy of Vietnamization emerged, a policy that eventually provided the basis for US disengagement from Vietnam. Paul Warnke at ISA, who played a leading part in designing Vietnamization, stayed on to serve both of McNamara's successors, Clark Clifford and President Richard Nixon's Secretary of Defense, Melvin Laird.

Ultimately, McNamara emerges from this history as a man who was concurrently both a hawk and a dove and who was also more reflective than conventional interpretations allow. While the OSD's "checks and balances" characteristics, especially insofar as they led to McNamara's support for withdrawal in the early years and for pacification efforts throughout the war, could qualify McNamara as a "dove" on Vietnam, his unrepentant defense of the use of technology throughout the war was "hawkish." From the outset, McNamara encouraged defoliation programs and applied similar statistical models to the bombing campaign in Vietnam to those he had used during World War II. If by April 1966, he had decidedly turned against the war, he nevertheless defended the idea of building a barrier between North and South Vietnam. Put together, his policies on Vietnam do not fit into a hawk/dove dichotomy.

McNaughton's diaries and the telephone recordings in particular do not support the notion that McNamara believed the idea that Fall criticized, namely that military tools could achieve what were ultimately political objectives in South Vietnam. In a recently declassified oral history, McNamara made a remarkable admission for someone who, on the written record, planned for increased levels of military force: "I don't think I ever believed that a military victory, in the normal sense of the words, was achievable."[39] The preceding chapters tend to confirm his observation.

However, McNamara continued to muffle his and his colleague's dissent in order to fulfill his professional obligations to the President as he narrowly defined them. McNaughton observed, "So much in government depends upon subordinates taking hints and carrying out the mood of the President ... Bob (and I) is much less effective if the President is really trusting the Chiefs, for example. Such a shift in outlook makes quite a difference in the 'power' one (ISA) has – whether he is listened to, gets his way, etc. We'll see how things go."[40] Both Kennedy and Johnson commanded loyalty; Johnson also demanded it. When he sensed McNamara's growing discomfort with policies, he blamed him for leaks and for "disloyalty in the highest ranks [with] various Cabinet members spreading anti-administration information around town."[41] As McNaughton correctly observed, as soon as McNamara stopped presenting the views he knew the President wanted to hear, he would be removed.

Understanding McNamara's strict codes of loyalty is fundamentally important to grasp how someone who tried to keep the United States out of Vietnam could also be held responsible for the war. In many respects, he was the perfect fall guy, someone who held his reservations and concerns quiet notwithstanding his comments in Montreal. McNamara commanded the same loyalty from his colleagues as he showed to the Presidents he served. Some went on to dedicate books to him. Their treatment of Ellsberg when he betrayed their loyalty codes and leaked the *Pentagon Papers* – crossing the street to avoid him, treating him as an outcast – derived from their sense that he had breached their codes of loyalty.

However, every quality, in excess, can become a tragic flaw. In November 1966, McNamara was invited to a dinner at Robert Kennedy's home for the Russian poet Yevgeny Yevtushenko, whom he had cited before his October 1963 trip to Vietnam. After a frank exchange where the poet accused the Secretary of being a "crocodile of war" and McNamara shared his own frustrations with his inability to end the war promptly,[42] the poet left, saying, "They say you are a beast. But I think you are a man."[43] McNamara's most important mistakes on Vietnam were situated in his human flaws. His sense that it was "heretic" to speak out when he understood the futility of continued troop deployments, or when he understood the potentially catastrophic impact of Vietnam on the domestic and international economic situation, is a terrible mark on his legacy.

Appendix: Cast of Characters

Acheson, Dean	Secretary of State, 1948–1953; member of the "Wise Men" during the Johnson administration.
Ackley, Hugh Gardner	Chairman of the Council of Economic Advisers, 1964–1968.
Alsop, Joseph (Joe)	Prominent journalist and syndicated columnist; personal friend of President Kennedy's; brother of Stewart.
Alsop, Stewart	Prominent journalist and political analyst; brother of Joe.
Aubrac, Raymond	French resistance hero; friend of Ho Chi Minh's.
Ball, George	Undersecretary of State for Economic and Agricultural Affairs, 1961–1966.
Bell, David E.	Director of the Bureau of Budget, 1961–1962; first director of USAID, 1962–1966.
Bradley, Omar N.	US Army General, field commander in North Africa and Europe during World War II; US Army Chief of Staff, 1948–1949; first formal Chairman of the Joint Chiefs of Staff, 1949–1953.
Brent, Joseph	Director, United States Operations Mission (USOM), 1962–1964.
Bundy, McGeorge	National Security Advisor, 1961–1966; President of the Ford Foundation, 1966–1979; brother of William P. Bundy.
Bundy, William P.	Deputy (1961–1963) then Assistant Secretary of Defense for International Security Affairs, 1963–1964; Assistant Secretary of State, East Asian and Pacific Affairs, 1964–1969; brother of McGeorge Bundy.

Burke, Arleigh A.	Chief of Naval Operations, 1955–1961.
Byrd, Harry F.	US Senator (Democrat) from Virginia, 1933–1965; Chairman, Senate Finance Committee, 1955–1965.
Clay, Lucius D.	US Army General, deputy to General Eisenhower, 1945; Commander in Chief US Forces in Europe and Governor of American Zone, Germany, 1947–1949; Chairman of Committee to Strengthen the Security of the Free World ("Clay Committee"), 1962–1963.
Clifford, Clark	Chairman of the President's Intelligence Advisory Board, 1938–1968; Secretary of Defense, 1968–1969.
Colby, William E.	OSS in World War II; Deputy (1959–1960) then Chief of CIA Station, Saigon, 1960–1962; Deputy (1962) then Chief of CIA Far East Division, 1962–1967; director of CORDS, Vietnam, 1968–1971; director of CIA, 1973–1976.
Conein, Lucien "Lou"	OSS in World War II; CIA operative in South Vietnam, 1963–1968.
Connally, John B.	Secretary of the Navy, 1961; Governor of Texas, 1963–1969.
Cronkite, Walter	Broadcast journalist; anchorman of CBS Evening News, 1962–1981.
De Gaulle, Charles	French General, leader of the Free French, 1940–1944; post-war head of the Provisional Government of the French Republic, 1944–1946; Prime Minister of France, 1958–1959; President of France, 1959–1969.
Dean, Sir Patrick Henry	British diplomat; Ambassador to the United States, 1965–1969.
Diem, Ngo Dinh	First President of South Vietnam, 1955–1963.
Dillon, C. Douglas	Patrician and financier; US Ambassador to France, 1953–1957; Undersecretary of State for Economic Affairs, 1957–1961; Secretary of the Treasury, 1961–1965.
Dulles, John Foster	Secretary of State, 1953–1959.
Eisenhower, Dwight D.	US Army General, Supreme Allied Commander of the Allied Forces in Europe, 1943–1945; Governor of the American Zone, Germany, 1945; US Army Chief of Staff, 1945–1948; President of Columbia University, 1948–1953; first temporary Chairman of the Joint Chiefs of Staff, 1949; first Supreme Commander of NATO (SACEUR), 1951–1952, US President, 1953–1961.
Ellsberg, Daniel	PhD candidate at Harvard University and RAND strategic analyst, consultant on nuclear issues to OSD, 1959–1964; Special Assistant at ISA, 1964–1965; State Department advisor on

	pacification in Vietnam, 1965–1967; RAND analyst during which time he worked on the *Pentagon Papers*, 1967–1971, before eventually leaking them to the *New York Times* in 1971.
Enthoven, Alain C.	Economist at RAND, 1956–1960; Deputy Comptroller and Assistant Secretary of Defense for Systems Analysis, 1961–1965; Assistant Secretary of Defense for Systems Analysis, 1965–1969.
Fall, Bernard B.	War correspondent and historian; expert on Indochina.
Fay, Paul B.	Old Navy friend of President Kennedy's, Undersecretary (1961–1965) and Secretary of the Navy, 1963.
Felt, Harry D.	US Navy Admiral, Commander in Chief of Pacific Command (CINCPAC), 1958–1964.
Forrestal, James V.	Secretary of the Navy, 1944–1947; first Secretary of Defense, 1957–1949; father of Michael Forrestal.
Forrestal, Michael V.	Staff member on NSC, 1962–1967; son of James Forrestal, unofficially adopted by Averell Harriman.
Fulbright, J. William	US Senator (Democrat) from Arkansas, 1945–1975; Chairman, Senate Foreign Relations Committee, 1959–1974.
Galbraith, John K.	Harvard economist; US Ambassador to India, 1961–1963.
Gates, Thomas S.	Undersecretary (1953–1957) then Secretary of the Navy, 1957–1959; Deputy (1959) then seventh Secretary of Defense, 1959–1961.
Gilpatric, Roswell	Undersecretary of the Air Force, 1951–1953; member of Symington Committee, 1960; Deputy Secretary of Defense, 1961–1964.
Goldberg, Arthur	Associate Justice of the Supreme Court, 1962–1965; US Ambassador to the United Nations, 1965–1968.
Goldwater, Barry M.	US Senator (Republican) from Arizona, 1953–1965 and 1965–1987; Republican presidential nominee, 1964; member of Senate Armed Services Committee, later its Chairman, 1985–1987.
Goodpaster, Andrew J.	US Army General, director of the Joint Staff, JCS, 1966–1967; Deputy Commander of Military Assistance Command, Vietnam (MACV), 1968–1969.
Gromyko, Andrei	Soviet politician; Minister of Foreign Affairs, 1957–1985; Chairman of the Presidium, 1985–1988.
Gruening, Ernest H.	US Senator (Democrat) from Alaska, 1959–1969.
Halberstam, David	Journalist; *New York Times* correspondent to Vietnam, 1962–1964; former academic tutee of McGeorge Bundy at Harvard.
Harkins, Paul D.	US Army General, Commander of MACV, 1962–1964.

Harriman, W. Averell	US diplomat and politician; US Ambassador-at-large, 1961; representative to International Conference on Laos, 1961–1962; Assistant Secretary of State, Far Eastern Affairs, 1961–1963; Undersecretary of State, Political Affairs with responsibility for Africa, 1963–1965; US Ambassador-at-large, 1965–1969.
Harris, Seymour E.	Economic advisor to President Kennedy, 1960; senior consultant to the Secretary of the Treasury, 1961–1968.
Heller, Walter W.	Keynesian economist; Chairman of the Council of Economic Advisers, 1961–1964.
Hilsman, Roger	OSS in World War II; director of INR, State Department, 1961–1963; Assistant Secretary of State, Far Eastern Affairs, 1963–1964; professor at Columbia University, 1964–1990.
Hitch, Charles J.	"Father" of defense economics, head of Economics Division at RAND, 1948–1961, Assistant Secretary of Defense (Comptroller), 1961–1965. Co-author, with Roland N. McKean, of *The Economics of Defense in the Nuclear Age*, the "bible of defense economics."
Honey, Patrick J.	Lecturer, School of Oriental and African Studies (SOAS) (1949–1965); Visiting Professor, Cornell University (1964) and Reader, University College London (1965–1985) specializing on Vietnam.
Hoopes, Townsend W.	Deputy Assistant (1964–1965) then Principal Deputy Secretary of Defense at ISA, 1965–1967.
Johnson, Louis A.	Assistant Secretary of War, 1937–1940; second Secretary of Defense, 1949–1950.
Johnson, Lyndon B.	US Representative from Texas (Democrat), 1947–1949; US Senator, 1949–1961; Senate Majority Leader, 1955–1961; Vice President, 1961–1963; President of the United States, 1963–1969.
Johnson, U. Alexis	Deputy Undersecretary of State for Political Affairs, 1961–1964; Deputy Ambassador to South Vietnam, 1964–1965; Deputy Undersecretary of State for Political Affairs, 1965–1966.
Kaufmann, William W.	Nuclear strategist; researcher at RAND, 1956–1961; advisor to Defense Department (1961–1981), Professor at MIT, 1961–1984.
Kaysen, Carl	Deputy National Security Advisor, 1961–1963; Professor at Harvard University, 1964–1966.
Kennedy, Edward "Ted" M.	US Senator (Democrat) for Massachusetts, 1962–2009; brother of John F. and Robert F. Kennedy.

Kennedy, John F.   US Senator (Democrat) from Massachusetts, 1947–1953; President of the United States, 1961–1963.

Kennedy, Robert F.   Attorney General, 1961–1964; Chair of the Special Group (CI), 1962–1963; US Senator (Democrat) from New York, 1965–1968; brother of John F. Kennedy.

Khanh, Nguyen   South Vietnamese Army officer; Prime Minister of South Vietnam, 1964.

Khrushchev, Nikita S.   Leader of the Soviet Union, 1953–1964.

Kissinger, Henry   Harvard political scientist; National Security Advisor, 1969–1975; Secretary of State, 1973–1977.

Komer, Robert W.   CIA analyst then Director of Intelligence, 1957–1961; staff member, NSC, 1961–1965; interim National Security Advisor, 1966–1967; head of CORDS, 1967–1968.

Krulak, Victor H.   US Marine Corps General; representative for the JCS to Special Group (CI), 1962–1964.

Ky, Nguyen Cao   Prime Minister of South Vietnam, 1965–1967; Vice President of South Vietnam, 1967–1971.

Lansdale, Edward G.   OSS in World War II; advisor to Ngo Dinh Diem, 1953–1957; Deputy Assistant to Secretary of Defense of Special Operations, 1957–1963; advisor on pacification efforts in Vietnam, 1965–1968.

LeMay, Curtis E.   US Air Force General; Commander 8th Air Force, England, 1941–1943; head of Strategic Air Command, 1948–1957; Air Force Chief of Staff, 1961–1965.

Leffingwell, William M.   Deputy Director for Military Assistance at ISA, 1961–1965.

Lemnitzer, Lyman L.   US Army General; Army Chief of Staff, 1957–1960; Chairman of the JCS, 1960–1962; Supreme Allied Commander at NATO (SACEUR), 1963–1969.

Lippmann, Walter   US reporter; influential syndicated columnist.

Lodge, Henry Cabot Jr.   US Senator (Republican) from Massachusetts, 1937–1944; US Ambassador to the United Nations, 1953–1960; vice presidential candidate, 1960; US Ambassador to South Vietnam, 1963–1964 and 1965–1967.

Lovett, Robert A.   Assistant Secretary of War for Air, 1941–1945; Undersecretary of State, 1947–1949; Deputy (1950–1951) then fourth Secretary of Defense, 1951–1953; offered but declined Defense and Treasury Secretaryships by President Kennedy.

MacArthur, Douglas. US Army General; Supreme Allied Commander for
Allied Powers in Japan, 1945–1951; Commander of
UN Forces in Korea, 1950–1951, until public falling
out over strategy with President Truman.

Mansfield, Michael J. US Senator (Democrat) from Montana, 1953–1977;
Senate Majority Leader, 1961–1977; member, Senate
Foreign Relations Committee.

Marcovitch, Herbert Head of the Institut Pasteur in Paris.

Marshall, George C. US Army General; Army Chief of Staff, 1939–1945;
Secretary of State, 1947–1949; third Secretary of
Defense, 1950–1951.

Martin, William Chairman of the Federal Reserve, 1951–1970.
McChesney

McCloy, John J. President of the World Bank, 1947–1949; Assistant
Secretary of War, 1942–1945; US Commissioner for
Occupied Germany, 1949–1952; member of the
"Wise Men" committee.

McCone, John A. Director of the CIA, 1961–1965.

McConnell, John P. US Air Force General; Chief of Staff of the Air Force,
1965–1969.

McElroy, Neil H. President of Procter & Gamble, 1948–1957; sixth
Secretary of Defense, 1957–1959.

McGarr, Lionel C. Lt. General of US Army; Commander of Military
Assistance Advisory Group (MAAG), Vietnam,
1960–1962.

McKean, Roland N. Research economist at RAND, 1951–1963; co-creator
of PPBS and co-author, with Charles J. Hitch, of *The
Economics of Defense in the Nuclear Age*, the "bible
of defense economics."

McNamara, Robert S. President, Ford Motor Company, 1960; eighth
Secretary of Defense, 1961–1968.

McNaughton, John T. Professor of law at Harvard Law School, 1953–1961;
Deputy Assistant Secretary for Arms Control,
1961–1962; General Counsel of the Department of
Defense, 1962–1964; Assistant Secretary of Defense
at ISA, 1964–1967.

Mendès-France, Pierre Prime Minister of France, 1954–1955.

Morrison, Norman Quaker peace activist who self-immolated outside
Robert McNamara's office in 1965.

Morse, Wayne L. US Senator (Republican, Independent and, from 1955,
Democrat) from Oregon, 1945–1969; member,
Senate Foreign Relations Committee, later vocal and
early opponent of war in Vietnam.

Nes, David G. US career diplomat; Deputy Chief of Mission to South
Vietnam, 1964.

Neustadt, Richard E.	Political scientist, advisor to Kennedy administration transition team, 1960–1961 and informally thereafter.
Nhu, Ngo Dinh	Brother and advisor to President Diem, husband of "Madame Nhu"; head of South Vietnam's Special Forces and secret police, 1955–1963.
Nitze, Paul H.	Director of Policy Planning at the State Department, 1950–1953 where he was the principal author of NSC 68; Assistant Secretary of Defense at ISA, 1961–1963; Secretary of the Navy, 1963–1967.
Nixon, Richard M.	Vice President of the United States, 1953–1961; President of the United States, 1969–1974.
Nolting, Frederick	US Ambassador to South Vietnam, 1961–1963.
Ormsby-Gore, David	Long-time friend of President Kennedy; British Ambassador to the United States, 1961–1965.
Phillips, Rufus	CIA officer in Laos and Vietnam, 1954–1962; Assistant Director for Rural Affairs, USOM Saigon, 1962–1964; consultant to USAID and State Departments on Vietnam, 1965–1968.
Quarles, Donald A.	Assistant Secretary of Defense for Research and Engineering, 1953–1955; Secretary of the Air Force, 1955–1957; Deputy Secretary of Defense, 1957–1959.
Richardson, John H.	CIA Station Chief Saigon, 1962–1963.
Rockefeller, David	US banker at Chase National Bank (later renamed Chase Manhattan Bank after a merger he helped to oversee); expert in international banking.
Rockefeller, Nelson	Governor of New York, 1959–1973; Chair of President Eisenhower's Advisory Committee on Government Organization (1952).
Ronning, Chester A.	Canadian diplomat.
Roosevelt, Franklin D.	President of the United States, 1933–1945.
Rostow, Walt W.	Economist and modernization theorist; OSS in World War II; Deputy National Security Advisor, 1961; Chairman of the Policy Planning Council in the State Department, 1961–1966; National Security Advisor, 1966–1969.
Rusk, Dean	Secretary of State, 1961–1969.
Russell, Richard B.	US Senator (Democrat) from Georgia, 1933–1971; Chairman of the Senate Armed Service Committee, 1951–1953 and 1955–1969.
Salinger, Pierre E. G.	White House Press Secretary, 1961–1964.
Schelling, Thomas C.	Harvard economist and expert in game theory.
Schlesinger, Arthur M. Jr.	Historian and special assistant to President Kennedy, 1961–1963.

Schulze, Charles	Assistant (1962–1966) then director of the Bureau of the Budget, 1966–1968.
Seaborn, J. Blair	Canadian diplomat; member of the International Commission for Supervision and Control (Vietnam), 1964–1967.
Sevareid, Eric	US author and CBS journalist, 1939–1977.
Shoup, David M.	General of US Marine Corps; Commandant of the Marine Corps, 1960–1963.
Shriver, Robert Sargent	First director of the Peace Corps, 1961–1966; President Kennedy's brother-in-law.
Sorensen, Theodore C.	Chief legislative aide to Senator Kennedy, 1953–1960; President Kennedy's primary speechwriter, 1961–1963; White House Counsel, 1961–1964.
Stennis, John C.	US Senator (Democrat) from Mississippi, 1947–1989
Stevenson, Adlai	Governor of Illinois, 1949–1953; US Ambassador to the United Nations, 1961–1965.
Symington, William Stuart	Secretary of the Air Force, 1947–1950; US Senator (Democrat) from Missouri, 1953–1976; author of Symington Committee Report, 1960; member of Senate Foreign Relations and Armed Services Committees.
Taylor, Maxwell D.	US Army General; superintendent of West Point Academy, 1945–1949; Author of *The Uncertain Trumpet*, 1960; Army Chief of Staff, 1955–1959; leader of Task Force to investigate failure of the Bay of Pigs invasion, 1961; Military Representative to President Kennedy, 1961–1962; Chairman of the Joint Chiefs of Staff, 1962–1964; US Ambassador to South Vietnam, 1964–1965.
Thant, U.	United Nations Secretary General, 1961–1971.
Thieu, Nguyen Van	President of South Vietnam, 1965–1975.
Thompson, Robert G. K.	British counterinsurgency expert, with experience suppressing Malayan insurgency; head of BRIAM, 1961–1965.
Thornton, Charles Bates "Tex"	Leader of team at Office of Statistical Control in the US Army Air Forces during World War II that included McNamara; later led team to Ford Motor Company.
Truman, Harry S.	President of the United States, 1945–1953.
Vance, Cyrus "Cy" R.	General Counsel of the Department of Defense, 1961–1962; Secretary of the Army, 1962–1964; Deputy Secretary of Defense, 1964–1967.
Vinson, Carl	US Representative (Democrat) from Georgia, 1914–1965; Chairman of the House Armed Services Committee, 1949–1953, 1955–1965.
Warnke, Paul C.	General Counsel of the Department of Defense, 1967; Assistant Secretary of Defense at ISA, 1967–1969.

Westmoreland, William C.	US Army General, Commander of MACV, 1964–1968.
Wheeler, Earle G. "Bus"	US Army General; Army Chief of Staff, 1962–1964; Chairman of JCS, 1964–1970.
Wilson, Charles E.	President of General Motors, 1941–1953; fifth Secretary of Defense, 1953–1957.
Wood, Chalmers	Second Secretary at US Embassy Saigon, 1957–1959; Vietnam desk officer at State Department, 1959–1963.
Yarmolinsky, Adam	Member of Kennedy transition team, 1960–1961; Special Assistant to McNamara, 1961–1964; Deputy Assistant Secretary of Defense at ISA, 1965–1966; Professor Harvard Law School, 1966.

Endnotes

Introduction

1 Quoted in Deborah Shapley, *Promise and Power: The Life and Times of Robert McNamara* (New York: Little Brown, 1993), 265.

2 William P. Bundy Oral History Interview by William W. Moss, April 25, 1972, JFKL, p. 21.

3 "US Policy on Viet-Nam: White House Statement," October 2, 1963. Retrieved online November 2, 2014, *Mt. Holyoke Documents Relating to American Foreign Policy, Vietnam*: https://goo.gl/W4Gwo7.

4 In this respect, it builds especially on Paul Hendrickson, *The Living and the Dead: Robert McNamara and the Five Lives of a Lost War* (New York: Vintage Books, 1996).

5 Andrew Preston, *The War Council: McGeorge Bundy, the NSC, and Vietnam* (Cambridge, MA: Harvard University Press, 2006), 10.

6 Graham T. Allison, and Philip Zelikow, *Essence of Decision: Explaining the Cuban Missile Crisis* (New York: Longman, 1999), 307.

7 Craig, for instance, describes three typical stages of historiography in US foreign policy and on the Kennedy administration: an "orthodox" stage that reflects the "political mood of the day" when a President leaves office and that typically relies by journalistic accounts and memoirs, followed by a "revisionist" stage as new sources appear, concluding in a more nuanced stage with "mature literature" that is "refined by relatively full access to the archival record." Campbell Craig, "Kennedy's International Legacy, Fifty Years On," *International Affairs* 89:6 (2013): 1367. See also Michael J. Hogan and Thomas G. Paterson (eds.), *Explaining the History of American Foreign Relations*, 2nd edn. (Cambridge: Cambridge University Press, 2004) for a comprehensive account of the waves in the historiography of US foreign policy, as historians have transitioned along orthodox-revisionist-post-revisionist lines as well as along methodological choices, from realist historians that focused relatively more on nationalist dimensions of foreign policy toward multiarchival, gender and cultural history. Similar critical historiographical reviews

include Michael J. Hogan and Frank Costigliola, *America in the World: The Historiography of American Foreign Relations since 1941* (Cambridge: Cambridge University Press, 2013); John Lewis Gaddis, "The Emerging Post-Revisionist Synthesis on the Origins of the Cold War," *Diplomatic History* 7 (Summer 1983): 171–190; Thomas W. Zeiler, "The Diplomatic History Bandwagon: A State of the Field," *Journal of American History* 95:4 (March 2009): 1053–1073; Peter Novick, *That Noble Dream: The Objectivity Question and the American Historical Profession* (Cambridge: Cambridge University Press, 1988), part 4. For Vietnam specifically, see John Dumbrell, *Rethinking the Vietnam War* (New York: Palgrave Macmillan, 2012), 5–21; Mark Philip Bradley and Marilyn B. Young, *Making Sense of the Vietnam Wars: Local, National and Transnational Perspectives* (Oxford: Oxford University Press, 2008); Gary R. Hess, "The Unending Debate: Historians and the Vietnam War," *Diplomatic History* 2 (Spring 1994): 239–264.

8 On this type of criticism, see especially H. R. McMaster, *Dereliction of Duty: Lyndon Johnson, Robert McNamara, the Joint Chiefs of Staff, and the Lies That Led to Vietnam* (New York: HarperCollins, 1997); U. S. Grant Sharp, *Strategy for Defeat: Vietnam in Retrospect* (San Rafael, CA: Presidio Press, 1978); William C. Westmoreland, *A Soldier Reports* (New York: Doubleday, 1976); David R. Palmer, *Summons of the Trumpet: US–Vietnam in Perspective* (San Rafael, CA: Presidio Press, 1978); Harry G. Summers, *On Strategy: the Vietnam War in Context* (Honolulu, HI: University Press of the Pacific, 2003); Shelby L. Stanton, *The Rise and Fall of the American Army: US Ground Forces in Vietnam, 1965–1973* (Novato, CA: Presidio Press, 1995); Douglas Kinnard, *The War Managers* (Annapolis, MD: Naval Institute Press, 2007); Gary R. Hess, "The Military Perspective on Strategy in Vietnam," *Diplomatic History* 10:1 (January 1986): 91–106.

9 This was very much Hilsman's line, not least in Roger Hilsman Oral History Interview No. 1, Paige E. Mulhollan, May 15, 1969, LBJL. George Ball recalled McNamara's anger at dissent over the administration's policies, that a memo that he wrote in September 1964 questioning the administration's policy on Vietnam was greeted with hostility: "McNamara, in particular, was absolutely horrified. He treated it like a poisonous snake. The idea that people would put these kinds of things down on paper!" George Ball Oral History Interview No. 1 by Paige E. Mulhollan, July 8, 1971, LBJL.

10 Shapley, *Promise and Power*, dedication.

11 Hendrickson, *The Living and the Dead*, dedication.

12 Phil Rosenzweig, "Robert S. McNamara and the Evolution of Modern Management," *Harvard Business Review* (December 2010): 87–93.

13 R. J. Sutherland, "Cost-Effectiveness and Defense Management; Mr. McNamara's Pentagon" (paper presented at the ORD Informal Paper, Ottawa, 1966); Thomas Norris, "A Giant of Management" (paper presented at the 38th Annual Meeting of the Academy for Management, undated); Henry Brandon, "Kennedy Fights the Generals," *Sunday Times* (May 27, 1962); William W. Kaufmann, *The McNamara Strategy* (New York: Harper & Row, 1964); Theodore H. White, "Revolution in the Pentagon," *Look Magazine* (April 23, 1963).

14 As Andrew Preston has also noted, the "false dichotomy between 'hawks' and 'doves' characteristic of works on US involvement in Vietnam" is unhelpful and does not capture the complexity of advisors. Andrew Preston, "The Soft Hawk's Dilemma in Vietnam: Michael V. Forrestal at the National Security Council, 1962–1964," *International History Review* 25:1 (March 2003): 67.

15 Shapley, *Promise and Power*, 291.

16 Douglas Brinkley, "The Stain of Vietnam: Robert McNamara, Redemption Denied," *Foreign Affairs* 72:3 (July 1993).

17 For histories that deal specifically with the OSD and the armed services in the Vietnam War, see Andrew F. Krepinevich, *The Army and Vietnam* (Baltimore, MD: Johns Hopkins University Press, 1986); Robert Buzzanco, *Masters of War: Military Dissent and Politics in the Vietnam Era* (New York: Cambridge University Press, 1996); McMaster, *Dereliction of Duty*.

18 The "economic context" is understood to mean the prevailing domestic economic conditions that existed during McNamara's tenure at the OSD, rather than the global economic order as understood by more left-wing historians. For this body of literature, see especially Gabriel Kolko, *Vietnam: Anatomy of War, 1940–1975* (London: Allen & Unwin, 1986).

19 The secondary literature on the economic history of the 1960s, and especially Barry Eichengreen's work, has also been useful in challenging the conventional wisdom that balance of payments concerns became salient only later in the 1960s. Ultimately, the economic concerns that Gavin has emphasized for Europe were, in fact, especially significant for Vietnam. Francis J. Gavin, *Gold, Dollars, and Power: The Politics of International Monetary Relations, 1958–1971* (Chapel Hill: University of North Carolina Press, 2004); Barry Eichengreen, "From Benign Neglect to Malignant Preoccupation: US Balance-of-Payments Policy in the 1960s," in George L. Perry and James Tobin, eds., *Economic Events, Ideas, and Policies: The 1960s and After* (Washington, DC: Brookings Institution Press, 2000).

20 In emphasizing the economic dimensions of the Kennedy administration as it pertains to defense, the book connects rather more to earlier histories of that administration. While some see a "hagiography" or "worshipful" approach in the "Camelot School" of books produced by Kennedy's advisors such as Theodore Sorensen or Arthur J. Schlesinger in the years immediately after the assassination, these books are also interesting because they dedicate far more pages to the economic troubles that faced the President than to issues such as Vietnam, which has tended to be the focus of later histories. For instance, while Robert Dallek in a key biography of President Kennedy spends only one chapter on the economic situation of the early 1960s, and intertwines that discussion with domestic issues more broadly, Sorensen dedicated five chapters to the same issues. Robert Dallek, *John F. Kennedy: An Unfinished Life, 1917–1963* (London: Allen Lane, 2003); Arthur M. Schlesinger Jr., *A Thousand Days: John F. Kennedy in the White House* (New York: Greenwich House, 1983); Theodore C. Sorensen, *Kennedy* (New York: Smithmark, 1995).

21 Robert Miller has described this trajectory most vividly in stating that "decisions by Kennedy served to move US policy forward in a straight line from

those taken by the Truman and Eisenhower administrations; they progressively burdened the United States with ever-greater responsibility for the fate of South Vietnam, thereby correspondingly reducing South Vietnam's incentives for shaping its own future itself. Failure became inevitable." Robert H. Miller, "Vietnam: Folly, Quagmire, or Inevitability?," *Studies in Conflict & Terrorism* 15 (April 1992): 114. Similarly, and in less stark terms, the *Pentagon Papers* describe the 1962–1963 period of planning for withdrawal as follows: "In retrospect, this experience falls into place as a more or less isolated episode of secondary importance; eventually abortive, it had little impact on the evolution of the Vietnam War." *Pentagon Papers*, Gravel edn., vol. 2 (Boston: Beacon Press, 1971), chapter 3. Retrieved online December 12, 2014, *Mt. Holyoke Documents*: https://goo.gl/GF23ZC.

22 Senator Mansfield quoted in Kai Bird, *The Color of Truth: McGeorge Bundy and William Bundy: Brothers in Arms* (New York: Simon & Schuster, 1998), 260; Roswell Gilpatric Oral History Interview by Ted Gittinger, November 2, 1982, LBJL; Kenneth P. O'Donnell et al., *Johnny, We Hardly Knew Ye* (Boston: Little, Brown, 1970), 15–18. By contrast, historians such as Frederik Logevall, Lawrence Freedman, Howard Jones, John Newman and, most recently, Marc Selverstone have acknowledged that the withdrawal plans were not a mere cosmetic exercise but reflected real interests within the administration. However, these same historians are divided on their interpretation of the evidence. Logevall and Freedman see Kennedy as "ambivalent" and pragmatic on Vietnam and reject the notion that Kennedy would have continued his plans to disengage from South Vietnam after the situation there collapsed into 1964. By contrast, Howard Jones and John Newman have gone the furthest in arguing that Kennedy's "decision to withdraw was unconditional, for he approved a calendar of events that did not necessitate a victory." Howard Jones, *Death of a Generation: How the Assassinations of Diem and JFK Prolonged the Vietnam War* (Oxford: Oxford University Press, 2003), 377; James K. Galbraith, "Exit Strategy," *Boston Review* (October/November 2003). In a somewhat more conspiracy theorist vein, Newman argues that Kennedy, with complicit support from McNamara, neutralized his more hawkish advisors and was planning to use his military advisors' overly optimistic reporting against them by getting them to publicly commit to an irreversible withdrawal timetable. He calls this a "deception within a deception." John M. Newman, *JFK and Vietnam: Deception, Intrigue, and the Struggle for Power* (New York: Warner Books, 1992), 321–322. Although Newman assigns a greater role to McNamara in leading the withdrawal plans, he, like most historians who have concerned themselves with the withdrawal plans in the Kennedy administration, has focused primarily on President Kennedy himself and his personal qualities or prescience.

23 The chapters ahead build on Selverstone's work but narrow its scope, by focusing almost exclusively on the OSD and civil-military relations. By focusing on McNamara alone, new light is cast on the people and bureaucratic forces that shaped and influenced his positions on Vietnam. Marc J. Selverstone, "It's a Date: Kennedy and the Timetable for a Vietnam Troop Withdrawal," *Diplomatic History* 34:3 (June 2010): 485–495.

24 Brian VanDeMark, *Into the Quagmire: Lyndon Johnson and the Escalation of the Vietnam War* (New York: Oxford University Press, 1995), 7. See also Francis X. Winters, *The Year of the Hare: America in Vietnam, January 25, 1963–February 15, 1964* (Athens: University of Georgia Press, 1997).

25 On this issue, Freedman writes, "1964 was not a good year for doubters, many of which were squeezed out of the lower ranks of the administration." Lawrence Freedman, "Vietnam and the Disillusioned Strategist," *International Affairs* 72:1 (1996): 141.

26 Robert S. McNamara Oral History Interview No. 1 by Walt W. Rostow, August 1, 1975, LBJL.

27 Townsend Hoopes, *The Limits of Intervention: How Vietnam Policy Was Made – and Reversed – During the Johnson Administration* (New York: W. W. Norton, 1973), 240.

28 Hohler, UK Embassy, Saigon to Warmer, FO, July 14, 1961, Reel 8: FO 371/160114, FO Files: The USA, Series Two: Vietnam 1959–1975, National Archives, Kew.

29 Robert S. McNamara Oral History Interview by OSD Historical Office, July 24, 1986, Folder: OSD OH 3, Box I:109, RSM Papers, LoC.

30 Dr. Daniel Ellsberg, phone interview with author, January 10, 2013.

31 Adam Yarmolinsky interview by Brian VanDeMark, April 1, 1995, Folder: Yarmolinsky, 1993, Box II:104, RSM Papers, LoC.

32 Newman, *JFK and Vietnam*.

33 MC LBJ Presidential Recordings: President Johnson and McNamara, January 2, 1964. WH 6401.03, Conversation 1149.

34 Robert S. McNamara OH No. 1. by Walt W. Rostow, January 8, 1975, LBJL.

Chapter 1

1 The average tenure for all of McNamara's successors was 696 days in office. McNamara stayed in office 2,595 days.

2 This framework builds loosely on the political scientist Samuel Huntington's theories. Huntington distinguished three trends. For him, civilian control was consolidated along three lines: strategic planning, combat command and resource allocation. This book fuses the strategic planning and combat command into one: civilian control of strategy in both planning and execution. Samuel P. Huntington, "Defense Organization and Military Strategy," *The Public Interest* 75 (Spring 1984): 22.

3 Adam Yarmolinsky, "Civilian Control: New Perspectives for New Problems," *Indiana Law Journal* 49:4 (Summer 1974): 654–672.

4 Steven Casey, *Selling the Korean War: Propaganda, Politics and Political Opinion in the United States 1950–1953* (New York: Oxford University Press, 2008), 173.

5 Ernest R. May "The US Government, a Legacy of the Cold War," *Diplomatic History* 16:2 (1992): 270. For additional resources on the Defense Department as a militarized outcome of the Cold War, see Carolyn Eisenberg, "The New Cold War," *Diplomatic History* 29:3 (June 2005): 423–427; John L. Gaddis, *Strategies of Containment* (Oxford: Oxford University Press, 2005): 8;

Stephanie C. Young, "Power and the Purse: Defense Budgeting and American Politics, 1947–1972," PhD dissertation, University of California, Berkeley, 2009; Melvyn P. Leffler, *A Preponderance of Power: National Security, the Truman Administration and the Cold War* (Stanford, CA: Stanford University Press, 1992); Saki Dockrill, *Eisenhower's New-Look National Security Strategy, 1952–61* (New York: St. Martin's Press, 1996), chapter 1. In addition, for a discussion on the singular role of the Korean War and NSC 68 in shaping the defense budget and the role of the Defense Department, see Casey, *Selling the Korean War*, chapter 7; Ernest R. May, ed., *American Cold War Strategy: Interpreting NSC 68* (Boston: Bedford/St. Martin's, 1993); Samuel F. Wells Jr., "Sounding the Tocsin: NSC68 and the Soviet Threat," *International Security* 4 (Spring 1979): 116–158; Walter S. Pool, *The JCS and National Policy, 1950–1952* (Washington, DC: Office of Joint History, 1998); Robert Jervis, "The Impact of the Korean War on the Cold War," *Journal of Conflict Resolution* 24:4 (December 1980): 563–592.

6 Samuel P. Huntington, "American Ideals versus American Institutions," *Political Science Quarterly* 97:1 (Spring 1982): 11.

7 At first, as agreed on in January 1942, the organization was called the Organization of the Joint Chiefs of Staff (OJCS). Steven L. Rearden, *The Formative Years: 1947–1950*, vol. 1: *History of the Office of the Secretary of Defense* (Washington, DC: OSD Historical Office, 1984), 17.

8 Ibid., 388.

9 Ibid., 314–316, 391.

10 Daniel Yergin, *Shattered Peace: The Origins of the Cold War and the National Security State* (New York: Penguin Books, 1980), 201. For an account of the unification debate, see Douglas T. Stuart, *Creating the National Security State: A History of the Law That Transformed America* (Princeton, NJ: Princeton University Press, 2008), 74–106.

11 Yergin, *Shattered Peace*, 201–203.

12 Samuel P. Huntington, *The Soldier and the State: The Theory and Politics of Civil–Military Relations* (Cambridge, MA: Harvard University Press, 1957).

13 Samuel P. Huntington and Andrew J. Goodpaster, *Civil-Military Relations* (Washington, DC: American Enterprise Institute for Public Policy Research, 1977), 11.

14 Eliot A. Cohen, *Supreme Command: Soldiers, Statesmen, and Leadership in Wartime* (New York: Anchor Books, 2002), 243.

15 Dale R. Herspring, *The Pentagon and the Presidency: Civil-Military Relations from FDR to George W. Bush* (Lawrence: University of Kansas Press, 2005), 2.

16 Alain Enthoven, McNamara's Assistant Secretary for Systems Analysis, and his colleague Wayne Smith were particularly critical of this axis. They complained that the Senate had "not produce[d] strong budgetary oversight" because it relied on the authority of the military officials rather than evidence per se, asking generals what they wanted and supporting it, without critically assessing needs. Alain C. Enthoven and K. Wayne Smith, *How Much Is Enough? Shaping the Defense Program, 1961–1969* (New York: Harper & Row, 1971), 310.

17 General Maxwell D. Taylor, *The Uncertain Trumpet* (Westport, CT: Greenwood Press, 1974), 20–21, 92–95.

18 Enthoven and Smith, *How Much Is Enough?*, 96.

19 James Roherty provides useful labels to distinguish between two types of Secretaries of Defense among McNamara's predecessors: first, those that were primarily concerned with the managerial aspects of the job, which he called "functionalist," and the policy-makers, which he called "generalist." James Roherty, *Decisions of Robert S. McNamara: A Study of the Role of Secretary of Defense* (Coral Gables, FL: University of Miami Press, 1970), 100.

20 May, "The US Government, a Legacy of the Cold War," 275.

21 See also Keith D. McFarland and David L. Roll, *Louis Johnson and the Arming of America* (Indianapolis: Indiana University Press, 2005); Leffler, *A Preponderance of Power.*

22 May, "The US Government, a Legacy of the Cold War," 271.

23 Gaddis, *Strategies of Containment*, 85–86.

24 Rearden, *The Formative Years: 1947–1950*, ii.

25 Douglas Kinnard, *The Secretary of Defense* (Lexington: University Press of Kentucky, 1980), 2, 204.

26 Rearden, *The Formative Years*, 74.

27 Ibid., 132.

28 Ibid., 140.

29 On this, see, for instance, John W. Spanier, *The Truman–MacArthur Controversy and the Korean War* (Cambridge, MA: Harvard University Press, 1959); Richard H. Rovere and Arthur Schlesinger Jr., *The MacArthur Controversy and American Foreign Policy* (New York: Farrar, Straus & Giroux, 1965).

30 Yergin, *Shattered Peace*, 194.

31 Walter Millis, ed., *The Forrestal Diaries* (New York: Viking, 1951), 300–301. The diaries offer a privileged view into Forrestal's frustrations in his dealings with the President and the services.

32 Rearden, *The Formative Years*, 330–338.

33 Ibid., 336.

34 Yergin, *Shattered Peace*, 207.

35 The quote comes from his Navy physicians' official statement. "Fatigue Blamed for Condition of Forrestal," *St. Petersburg Times* (April 12, 1949): 6. On his growing mental health issues, see Townsend Hoopes and Douglas Brinkley, *Driven Patriot: The Life and Times of James Forrestal* (Annapolis, MD: Naval Institute Press, 1992); James C. Olson, *Stuart Symington: A Life* (Columbia: University of Missouri Press, 2003), 164–175.

36 The last person to see him was his successor, Louis Johnson. Yergin, *Shattered Peace*, 208.

37 Hoopes and Brinkley, *Driven Patriot*, preface.

38 Huntington, "Defense Organization and Military Strategy," 24.

39 MC LBJ Presidential Recordings: President Johnson and McNamara, January 2, 1964, WH 6401.03, Conversation 1149.

40 "Nomination of Robert S, McNamara," 87th Congress (January 17, 1961) (Senate Committee on Armed Services), p. 1. Hearing ID: HRG-1961-SAS-0005, US Congressional Hearings Digital Collection Historical Archives, 1824–2003.

41 McFarland and Roll, *Louis Johnson*, 197–199.
42 Ibid.
43 Ibid., 354.
44 Johnson to Thurman A. Stout, August 30, 1950, Folder: 3, Box 109, Louis A. Johnson Papers, Secretary of Defense, Correspondence, UVAL.
45 "Marshall Urges Enduring Defense," *New York Times* (November 25, 1950): 6.
46 Bart Barnes, "Financier Robert A. Lovett, 90, Former Secretary of Defense, Dies," *Washington Post* (August 5, 1986): D6.
47 Quoted in Gerard Clarfield, *Security with Solvency: Dwight D. Eisenhower and the Shaping of the Military Establishment* (Westport, CT: Praeger, 1999), 95.
48 Ibid.
49 Quoted in Melvyn P. Leffler, "Defense on a Diet: How Budget Crises Have Improved US Strategy," *Foreign Affairs* (November/December 2013). Retrieved online November 2, 2014: http://fam.ag/132TXkn.
50 Ibid.
51 Kinnard, *The Secretary of Defense*, 622.
52 Robert Coughlan, "Top Managers in 'Business Cabinet,'" *Life Magazine* (January 19, 1953): 100. Another press report described a mere "eight millionaires" instead. "Washington Wire," *New Republic* (December 15, 1952).
53 See also Jay M. Parker, *The Colonels' Revolt: Eisenhower, the Army and the Politics of National Security* (Newport, RI: Naval War College, 1994).
54 "Department of Defense Reorganization Act of 1958," August 6, 1958. Retrieved online December 17, 2014, Government Printing Office: http://goo.gl/YvG93U.
55 Ibid.
56 Louis Kraar, "Defense Dynamo: McNamara Centralizes Pentagon Control, Puts Civilians in Command," *Wall Street Journal* (February 19, 1962).
57 For an earlier iteration and the intellectual framework for McNamara's reforms, see Charles J. Hitch and Roland N. McKean, *The Economics of Defense in Nuclear Age* (Santa Monica, CA: RAND, 1960).
58 President Dwight D. Eisenhower "Military-Industrial Complex Speech" (speech, January 17, 1961), Public Papers of the Presidents, Dwight D. Eisenhower, 1960, p. 1035–1040.
59 Ibid.
60 For more recent literature on the missile gap controversy, see Christopher Preble, *John F. Kennedy and the Missile Gap* (DeKalb: Northern Illinois University Press, 2004).
61 Olson, *Stuart Symington: A Life*, 360–362.
62 Thomas Norris, "A Giant of Management" (paper presented at the 38th Annual Meeting of the Academy for Management, undated).
63 W. H. Lawrence, "Symington Panel Urges Revamping of the Pentagon," *New York Times* (December 6, 1960): 1.
64 "Defense Organization," November 17, 1960, Folder: Transition Memoranda, Topic memoranda 1, Box 17, Neustadt Papers, Government Consulting Files, JFKL.

65 Ibid.

66 McMaster, *Dereliction of Duty*, 2.

67 Robert A. Lovett OH No. 1 by Dorothy Foedlick, July 20, 1964, JFKL, p. 10.

68 Kraar, "Defense Dynamo."

69 "President Kennedy's Appointments," American Department FO to Prime Minister, January 26, 1961, PREM 11/4574, National Archives, Kew.

70 David Halberstam, *The Best and the Brightest* (New York: Ballantine Books, 1969), 219.

71 As part of his work for the Ford Foundation's Fund for the Republic, Yarmolinsky had produced a study on individuals that had been unfairly treated under McCarthyism and the federal security program. On a visit to Ann Arbor, McNamara and Yarmolinsky met and discussed Yarmolinsky's report as well as McNamara's work on auto safety. He described McNamara saying: "I think his whole bent is towards service. We are put on the earth to be useful." Adam Yarmolinsky Oral History Interview No. 1 by Daniel Ellsberg, November 11, 1964, JFKL.

72 Halberstam, *The Best and the Brightest*, 228.

73 Robert S. McNamara and Brian VanDeMark, *In Retrospect: The Tragedy and Lessons of Vietnam* (New York: Vintage Books, 1995), 8.

74 Rosenzweig, "Robert S. McNamara and the Evolution of Modern Management," 89; *The Fog of War*, directed by Errol Morris (Sony Pictures Classics, 2004), DVD.

75 McNamara and VanDeMark, *In Retrospect*, 10.

76 Ibid.

77 Ibid., 15.

78 Halberstam, *The Best and the Brightest*, 237.

79 Rosenzweig, "Robert S. McNamara and the Evolution of Modern Management," 87–93.

80 Robert McNamara Oral History Interview by the Secretary of Defense Historical Office, April 23, 1986, Folder: OSD OH 1, Box I:109, RSM Papers, LoC.

81 Ibid.

82 McNamara and VanDeMark, *In Retrospect*, 17.

83 "McNamara Defines His Job," *New York Times* (April 26, 1964).

84 Robert McNamara Oral History Interview by the Secretary of Defense Historical Office, April 23, 1986, Folder: OSD OH 1, Box I:109, RSM Papers, LoC.

85 McNamara to President elect Kennedy, December 12, 1960, Folder: Secretary of Defense letter of acceptance, 1960, Box II:46, RSM Papers, LoC.

86 Chairman Richard Russell, 87th Congress, "Military Construction Authorization FY63" (June 14, 1962) (Senate Committee on Armed Services), p. 14. Hearing ID: HRG-1962-SAS-0053, US Congressional Hearings Digital Collection Historical Archives, 1824–2003.

87 Kraar, "Defense Dynamo."

88 Joshua E. Klimas, "Balancing Consensus, Consent, and Competence: Richard Russell, the Senate Armed Services Committee and Oversight of America's Defense, 1955–1968," PhD dissertation, Ohio State University, 2007.

89 Robert McNamara Oral History Interview by the Secretary of Defense Historical Office, April 23, 1986, Folder: OSD OH 1, Box I:109, RSM Papers, LoC.
90 Kaufmann, *The McNamara Strategy*, 189.
91 Enthoven and Smith, *How Much Is Enough?*.

Chapter 2

1 Robert McNamara Oral History Interview No. 1 by the Secretary of Defense Historical Office, April 23, 1986, Folder: OH 1 for OSD, Box I:109, RSM Papers, LoC.
2 Ibid.
3 Roherty, *Decisions of Robert S. McNamara*, 66.
4 Robert S. McNamara Oral History Interview No. 1 by Walt W. Rostow, January 8, 1975, LBJL.
5 Jeffrey G. Barlow, "President John F. Kennedy and the Joint Chiefs of Staff," PhD dissertation, University of South Carolina, 1981, p. 110.
6 Roswell Gilpatric Oral History Interview No. 1 by Ted Gittinger, November 12, 1982, LBJL.
7 Carl Kaysen Oral History Interview No. 1 by Joseph E. O'Connor, July 11, 1966, JFKL.
8 Robert S. McNamara Oral History Interview No. 1 by the Secretary of Defense Historical Office, April 23, 1986, Folder: OH 1 for OSD, Box I:109, RSM Papers, LoC.
9 Interview between Brian VanDeMark and Adam Yarmolinsky, April 1, 1993, Folder: Yarmolinksy 1993, Box II:104, RSM Papers, LoC.
10 Robert McNamara Oral History Interview No. 1 by the Secretary of Defense Historical Office, April 23, 1986, Folder: OH 1 for OSD, Box I:109, RSM Papers, LoC.
11 "Senate Probes "Muzzling" of Military," *Washington Post* (1961): A4.
12 Later, he was institutionalized after he tried to lead a citizen militia in a standoff over the forced desegregation at the University of Mississippi and then released after it emerged that he was fit to stand trial. He continued to be involved in conspiratorial militant groups throughout the South. Clive Webb, *Rabble Rousers: The American Far Right in the Civil Rights Era* (Athens: University of Georgia Press, 2010), 141–149.
13 "Senator, Pentagon Aide Clash in 'Muzzling' Quiz," *Los Angeles Times* (1962): 3.
14 "Citizens Council Interview, March 1962," MP 1986.01, Citizens' Council Forum Film Collection, Reel 0030, Mississippi Department of Archives and History.
15 McNamara to Taylor, June 11, 1963, Folder: Reading File, June 1963, Box 118, RG200, RSM Records, Reading Files, NARA.
16 Ibid.
17 "Text of the Lovett Statement Defending Civilian Limitations upon the Military," *New York Times* (1962): 19.

18 James Reston, "On Getting Run Over by a Gravy Train," *New York Times* (March 15, 1963).

19 Henry Brandon, "Kennedy Fights the Generals," *Sunday Times* (May 27, 1962); Kraar, "Defense Dynamo."

20 Robert Kennedy's ninth child, born in January 1965, was named Matthew Maxwell Taylor.

21 Maxwell Taylor Oral History Interview by the Secretary of Defense Historical Office, October 18, 1983, Folder: In Retrospect, Background and research materials, misc., Box II:95, RSM Papers, LoC.

22 Jones, *Death of a Generation*, 114.

23 Robert McNamara OH Interview 1 by the Secretary of Defense Historical Office, April 23, 1986, Folder: OH 1 for OSD, Box I:109, RSM Papers, LoC.

24 David Callahan, *Dangerous Capabilities: Paul Nitze and the Cold War* (New York: Edward Burlingame, 1990), 198–199.

25 "Administration Appointments" Ormsby-Gore to FO, May 25, 1962, PREM 11/4574, National Archives, Kew.

26 Robert McNamara Oral History Interview 1 by the Secretary of Defense Historical Office, April 23, 1986, Folder: OH 1 for OSD, Box I:109, RSM Papers, LoC.

27 Robert S. McNamara Oral History Interview by Walt W. Rostow, January 8, 1975, LBJL.

28 Callahan, *Dangerous Capabilities*, 206, 248.

29 "President Kennedy's Appointments" American Department, Foreign Office to PM Macmillan, January 26, 1961, PREM 11/4574, National Archives, Kew.

30 Robert McNamara Oral History Interview 1 by the Secretary of Defense Historical Office, April 23, 1986, Folder: OH 1 for OSD, Box I:109, RSM Papers, LoC.

31 "McNamara Defines His Job," *New York Times* (April 26, 1964).

32 Chester L. Cooper OH Interview by Joseph E. O'Connor, June 9, 1966, JFKL.

33 Schlesinger, *A Thousand Days*, 421.

34 Robert A. Lovett Oral History Interview by Dorothy Foedlick, July 20, 1964, JFKL.

35 Schlesinger, *A Thousand Days*, 407.

36 Hilsman Notes, May 9, 1962, Folder: May 1962, 1–9, Box 8, Newman Papers, Research Materials, JFKL.

37 Ibid.

38 Theodore H. White, "Revolution in the Pentagon," *Look Magazine* (April 23, 1963).

39 Brock Brower, "Robert S. McNamara Interview," *Life Magazine* (May 10, 1968).

40 Caroline Kennedy and Michael Beschloss, *Jacqueline Kennedy: Historic Conversations on Life with John F. Kennedy* (New York: Hyperion Audiobooks, 2011), part 2.

41 Brower, "Robert S. McNamara Interview."

42 Daniel Ellsberg phone interview with author, January 11, 2013.

43 Kaufmann, *The McNamara Strategy*, 189.

44 Bell to McGeorge Bundy and McNamara, January 30, 1961, Folder: Defense budget, Box I:109, RSM Papers, LoC.
45 Alain C. Enthoven, "Tribute to Charles J. Hitch," *OR/MS Today* 22:6 (December 1995).
46 Ibid.
47 Hitch and McKean, *The Economics of Defense.*
48 Enthoven, "Tribute to Charles J. Hitch."
49 Henry Brandon, "Kennedy Fights the Generals," *Sunday Times* (May 27, 1962).
50 Chief of Naval Operations Arleigh Burke's oral history remembers Paul Fay as a "nice guy, very pleasant" but a "dead bee," someone who "needed to be worked around ... He never worked very hard and he never knew what was going on." Arleigh A. Burke Oral History Interview by Joseph E. O'Connor, January 20, 1967, JFKL.
51 Paul Nitze Oral History Interview by Dorothy Fosdick, May 22, 1964, Folder: 6, Box 118, Nitze Papers, LoC.
52 Enthoven, and Smith, *How Much Is Enough?*, 160.
53 "FY1963 Defense Budget Issues," Bell to President Kennedy, November 13, 1961, Folder: Defense Budget, Box I:109, RSM Papers, LoC.
54 Nitze to Norris in preparation for his article "Robert S. McNamara: Pentagon Genius," *Giants in Management*, January 10, 1978, Folder: Articles & Misc. Writings, Box II:89, RSM Papers, LoC.
55 Lawrence S. Kaplan et al., *History of the Office of the Secretary of Defense,* vol. 5: *The McNamara Ascendancy: 1961–1965* (Washington, DC: US Government Printing Office, 2006), chapter 17.
56 Robert S. McNamara Oral History Interview No. 1 by Walt W. Rostow, August 1, 1975, LBJL.
57 James Fallows, Douglas Brinkley and Ralph Williams debate (National Public Radio, January 8, 2003). Retrieved online November 2, 2014: http://goo.gl/i5xlqo.
58 Adam Yarmolinsky, *The Military Establishment: Its Impacts on American Society* (New York: Harper & Row, 1971), 418–419.
59 The CEA included Gardner Ackley, Kermit Gordon, Walter Heller, Joseph Pechman, Paul Samuelson and James Tobin. See Council of Economic Advisers Oral History Interview No. 1 by Joseph Pechman, August 1, 1964, JFKL.
60 Gilpatric to Sorensen, March 11, 1963, Folder: Defense Department, Subject Files 1961–64, Box 31, Sorensen Papers, JFKL.
61 Among the more vocal opponents was Richard M. Nixon: the members of Kennedy's Council of Economic Advisers recalled that the President exclaimed, "God, look at what Nixon is doing to me on this whole question of fiscal responsibility!" Council of Economic Advisers Oral History Interview No. 1 by Joseph Pechman, August 1, 1964, JFKL, p. 217.
62 C. Douglas Dillon Oral History Interview No. 7 by Harvey Brazer, September 22, 1964, JFKL.
63 Jim F. Heath, *John F. Kennedy and the Business Community* (Chicago: University of Chicago Press, 1969), 30.

64 Seymour E. Harris, *Economics and the Kennedy Years and a Look Ahead* (New York: Harper & Row, 1964), 27.

65 See, for instance, Morris J. MacGregor Jr., *Integration of the Armed Forces, 1940–1965* (Washington, DC: Department of the Army, 1985), chapter 20.

66 Council of Economic Advisers Oral History Interview No. 1 by Joseph Pechman, August 1, 1964, JFKL, p 175.

67 Robert Kennedy later named one of his children after Dillon and Averell Harriman: Douglas Harriman Kennedy.

68 C. Douglas Dillon Oral History Interview No. 2 by Dixon Donnelley, November 10, 1964, JFKL, p. 26.

69 Kaysen to McGeorge Bundy, June 4, 1963, Folder: Balance of Payments and Gold General, Box 291a, NSF, Subjects, Balance of Payments, JFKL.

70 Facts about the Budget and Debt, January 1963, Folder: Budget Federal, Box 29, Subject Files 1961–64, Sorensen Papers, JFKL.

71 US Balance of Payments Chart, 1962, Folder: Balance of Payments, 1961–62, Box 29, Subject Files 1961–64, Sorensen Papers, JFKL.

72 Facts about the Budget and Debt, January 1963, Folder: Budget Federal, Box 29, Subject Files 1961–64, Sorensen Papers, JFKL.

Chapter 3

1 Gaddis speaks vividly about this "break" and its political motives: "There was somehow the feeling that the promise – and indeed the legitimacy – of a new generation of national leadership would be called into question if its programs were not made to differ visibly and substantially from what had gone before." Gaddis, *Strategies of Containment*, 197.

2 President John F. Kennedy, "Inaugural Address" (speech, Washington, DC, January 20, 1961). Retrieved online on November 2, 2014, JFKL: http://goo .gl/aAlb5O.

3 Theodore H. White, *The Making of the President 1960* (New York: Atheneum, 1961), 382.

4 Gaddis, *Strategies of Containment*, 203.

5 Ball to Dillon, July 9, 1963, Folder: Balance of Payments and Gold General, Box 291a, NSF, Subjects, Balance of Payments, JFKL.

6 On the relationship between the balance of payments deficit, gold outflow and the Kennedy administration's foreign policy, see especially Gavin, *Gold, Dollars, and Power*, and Francis J. Gavin, "The Gold Battles within the Cold War: American Monetary Policy and the Defense of Europe," *Diplomatic History* 26:1 (2002): 61–94.

7 Scott Farris, *Kennedy and Reagan: Why Their Legacies Endure* (Guilford, CT: Lyons Press, 2013), 221.

8 Kennedy later expanded on this idea in his first state of the union address when he said, "Our role is essential and unavoidable in the construction of a sound and expanding economy for the entire non-communist world, helping other nations build the strength to meet their own problems, to satisfy their own aspirations – to surmount their own dangers." President Kennedy, "Annual Message to the Congress on the State of the Union" (Washington,

DC, January 30, 1961). Retrieved online December 13, 2014, American Presidency Project: http://goo.gl/J8YOFd.

9 President John F. Kennedy, "Inaugural Address" (speech, Washington, DC, January 20, 1961). Retrieved online November 2, 2014, JFKL: http://goo.gl/pXnAx7.

10 Yarmolinsky, "Civilian Control: New Perspectives for New Problems," 663.

11 Eisenhower too had made similar speeches; see, for instance, President Dwight D. Eisenhower, "Atoms for Peace" (speech, United Nations General Assembly, December 8, 1953). Retrieved online November 2, 2014, Atomic Archive: http://goo.gl/14Dji3.

12 President John F. Kennedy, "Address to U.N. General Assembly" (speech, United Nations General Assembly, September 25, 1961), Folder: 48, Box 35, POL, JFKL.

13 The JCS's principal opposition to the Test Ban Treaty, which banned tests in the atmosphere, in the water and in space, was that verification systems were inadequate to ensure the Soviets did not resume testing. In return, they asked for a number of "safeguards," including maintaining the existing program on "standby" should the treaty fall apart. "Statement of the Position of the Joint Chiefs of Staff on the Three-Environment Nuclear Test Ban Treaty," August, 12 1963. Retrieved online November 4, 2014, GWU Online: http://goo.gl/PF8asE.

14 John F. Kennedy, Commencement Address at American University, Washington, DC, June 10, 1963, Folder: 2, Box 45, POF, JFKL.

15 White House Tapes: President Kennedy and Taylor, December 5, 1962. Retrieved online November 2, 2014, MC: http://goo.gl/tTytNy.

16 Alain C. Enthoven, "Reason, Morality and Defense Policy," *America* (April 13, 1963): 494.

17 Adam Yarmolinsky Oral History Interview No. 2 by Daniel Ellsberg, November 28, 1964, JFKL.

18 Robert S. McNamara, "Address at Michigan University" (speech, Ann Arbor, MI, June 18, 1962), PREM 11/3709, National Archives, Kew.

19 Although Kennedy's campaign alleged that Eisenhower had allowed a "missile gap" to widen between the United States and the Soviet Union, soon after coming to office, Gilpatric inadvertently made a public statement to the effect that none existed. The upheaval around his passing comment led to a Defense Department appraisal of relevant capabilities that essentially concluded that there never had been a gap, and in the longer term, led to the creation of a Defense Intelligence Agency that was designed to cross-check and centralize the services' intelligence efforts since the services were the only bodies who believed in a missile gap. "The Missile Gap Controversy," McNamara to President Kennedy, March 3, 1963, Folder: Statement file, Box I:100, RSM Papers, LoC. For his part, according to Maxwell Taylor, Kennedy never believed there had been a missile gap. Maxwell Taylor Oral History Interview No. 1 by Elspeth Rostow, April 12, 1964, JFKL.

20 "Record of a Meeting Held at the White House," April 28, 1962, PREM 11/3648, National Archives, Kew.

21 Adam Yarmolinsky Oral History Interview No. 2 by Daniel Ellsberg, November 28, 1964, JFKL.

22 Ibid.

23 Bird, *The Color of Truth*, 209–210; "SIOP 63 Briefing," Lemnitzer to President Kennedy, September 22, 1962. Retrieved online November 2, 2014, GWU Online: http://goo.gl/c9pGNh.

24 JCS to CINCAL et al., May 9, 1961. Retrieved online November 2, 2014, GWU Online: http://goo.gl/qidJvm.

25 White House Tapes: John F. Kennedy and Taylor, December 5, 1962. Retrieved online November 2, 2014, MC: http://goo.gl/EBDLkd.

26 Kaplan et al., *The McNamara Ascendancy*, 322.

27 Aaron L. Friedberg, *In the Shadow of the Garrison State: America's Anti-Statism and Its Cold War Grand Strategy* (Princeton, NJ: Princeton University Press, 2000), 142.

28 Francis J. Gavin, *Nuclear Statecraft: History and Strategy in America's Atomic Age* (Ithaca, NY: Cornell University Press, 2012), 33.

29 Gaddis, *Strategies of Containment*, 177–178.

30 Taylor, *The Uncertain Trumpet*.

31 C. Douglas Dillon Oral History Interview No. 5 by Harvey Brazer, September 22, 1964, JFKL, p. 93.

32 Radio Free Europe, Background Information USSR (Munich, January 20, 1961). Retrieved online November 2, 2014, Open Society Online Archives: http://goo.gl/yGE1RA.

33 Report of the Military Assistance Steering Group Report, December 12, 1961, Folder: MAP – Six Countries Studies, December 1961–January 1962, Box 9, RG200, RSM Records, Defense Programs and Operations, 1961–67, NARA.

34 Robert S. McNamara, "Address to the Fellows of the American Bar Foundation Dinner" (speech, Chicago, IL, February 17, 1962), p. 1, Reel 12: FO 371/162583. FO: The USA, Series One: USA Politics and Diplomacy, Part I: The John F. Kennedy Years, 1960–1963, National Archives, Kew.

35 "Annual Review 1961" Ormsby-Gore to Home, January 1, 1962, Reel 12: FO 371/162583. FO: The USA, Series One: USA Politics and Diplomacy, Part I: The John F. Kennedy Years, 1960–1963, National Archives, Kew.

36 "Administration Appointments" Ormsby-Gore, UK Embassy, Washington to Foreign Office, December 1, 1961, Reel 12: FO 371/162583, FO: The USA, Series One: USA Politics and Diplomacy, Part I: The John F. Kennedy Years, 1960–1963, National Archives, Kew.

37 Hella Pick, "President's Big Guns Defend Foreign Aid," *The Guardian* (April 9, 1963).

38 "Hearings before the Committee on Foreign Affairs, House of Representative," 88th Congress (April 5, 8, 9 and 10, 1963), Folder: Background and Research Material, Box II:89, RSM Papers, LoC.

39 NSAM No. 124, January 18, 1962, Folder: Special Group (CI) – 4/6/61–6/7/62, Box 319, NSF, M&M Series, JFKL.

40 McGeorge Bundy to President Kennedy, January 2, 1962, Folder: Special Group (CI) – 4/6/61–6/7/62, Box 319, NSF, M&M Series, JFKL.

41 Paul Nitze Oral History Interview by Dorothy Fosdick, July 7, 1964, Folder: 6, Box 118, Nitze Papers, LoC.
42 Roswell Gilpatric Oral History Interview by Dennis J. O'Brien, May 27, 1970, JFKL.
43 Parrott to President Kennedy, March 22, 1962, Folder: Special Group (CI) – 4/6/61–6/7/62, Box 319, NSF, M&M Series, JFKL.
44 Recent scholarship has been critical of Kennedy's policies toward Latin America and of the Special Group's efforts there. Specifically, the criticism is that despite the rhetoric of economic and political progress, efforts in Latin America favored military groups that would continue to be a source of instability in the region, and hold it back economically. Stephen G. Rabe, *Most Dangerous Area in the World: John F. Kennedy Confronts Communist Revolution in Latin America*. (Chapel Hill: University of North Carolina Press, 1999).
45 Komer to Special Group (CI), April 10, 1962, Folder: April 1962 1–9, Box 8, Newman Papers, Research Materials, JFKL.
46 Thomas David Jr. to Attorney General Kennedy, January 7, 1963, Folder: Special Group (CI) – 4/6/61–6/7/62, Box 319, NSF, M&M Series, JFKL.
47 Robert Kennedy to McGeorge Bundy, March 13, 1963, Folder: March 1963 11–15, Box 11, Newman Papers, Research Materials, JFKL.
48 David to Robert Kennedy, January 7, 1963, Folder: Special Group (CI), 7/62–11/63, Box 319, NSF Files, M&M Series, JFKL.
49 Robert Komer would later become rather infamous as director of the Civil Operations and Revolutionary Development Support program (CORDS) in South Vietnam under President Johnson (earning the nickname "Blowtorch Bob") during which time he also oversaw the controversial Phoenix Program. The latter has received renewed attention in the United States as counterinsurgency has regained prominence; see, for instance, Steven J. Weidman, *Resurrecting Phoenix: Lessons in COIN Operations* (Newport, RI: Naval War College, 2006). Retrieved online November 2, 2014: http://goo.gl/pmWom9; John Prados, "Phoenix and the Drones," *Passport* 43:3 (January 2013).
50 Komer to Special Group (CI), April 10, 1962, Folder: April 1962 1–9, Box 8, Newman Papers, Research Materials, JFKL.
51 Komer to McGeorge Bundy, July 23, 1962, Folder: Special Group (CI) Meetings, 6/8/62–11/2/62, Box 319, NSF Files, M&M Series, JFKL.
52 Victor H. Krulak Oral History Interview by William W. Moss, November 19, 1970, JFKL.
53 On this, see also Krepinevich, *The Army and Vietnam*, 259.
54 Christopher K. Ives, *U.S. Special Forces and Counterinsurgency in Vietnam: Military Innovation and Institutional Failure, 1961–1963* (London: Routledge, 2007), 64–72.
55 "Summary of Military CI Progress Including Civic Action since 27 December 1962," JCS to Special Group (CI), June 25, 1963, Folder: June 1963, Box 3, RG59, Records of the Special Group (CI), NARA.
56 Report to the President on FY1962 Budget by Secretary McNamara, February 20, 1961, Folder: FY1962 Budget, Box 10, RG200, RSM Records, Defense Programs and Operations, 1961–67, NARA.

57 Joseph Alsop, "The President's New Design," *The Guardian* (February 5, 1961).
58 President Kennedy to US Army, April 11, 1962. Retrieved online November 2, 2014, JFKL: http://goo.gl/Kggzyz.
59 Robert S. McNamara, "Address to the Fellows of the American Bar Foundation Dinner" (speech, Chicago, IL, February 17, 1962), Reel 12: FO 371/162583. FO: The USA, Series One: USA Politics and Diplomacy, Part I: The John F. Kennedy Years, 1960–1963, National Archives, Kew.
60 Adam Yarmolinsky, "Remarks at the Commencement Exercises" (speech, US Army Special Warfare School, Fort Bragg, NC, July 3, 1963), Folder: Speeches 1963, Box 66, Yarmolinsky Papers, JFKL.
61 Yarmolinsky to Vance, July 13, 1962, Folder: July 1962, Box 11, Yarmolinksy Papers, JFKL.
62 Thomas L. Hughes Interview by Charles Kennedy, July 7, 1999, Frontline Diplomacy. Retrieved online November 2, 2014, Foreign Affairs Oral History Collection of the Association for Diplomatic Studies and Training: http://goo.gl/wLwc6c.
63 Adam Yarmolinsky, "Remarks at the Commencement Exercises" (speech, US Army Special Warfare School, Fort Bragg, NC, July 3, 1963), Folder: Speeches 1963, Box 66, Yarmolinsky Papers, JFKL.
64 For a more detailed study of Special Forces' actions in Vietnam during this time, the CIA has recently declassified a number of reports, including Thomas Ahern Jr., *CIA and Rural Pacification in South Vietnam*. Retrieved online November 2, 2014, CIA Electronic Reading Room: foia.cia.gov; Francis J. Kelly, *Vietnam Studies: U.S. Army Special Forces, 1961–1971* (Washington, DC: Department of the Army CMH Publication 90-24, 1989).
65 Memorandum for the Record, Meeting of the Special Warfare Coordinating Group (Focal Point), May 4, 1962, Folder: May 1962 1–9, Box 8, Newman Papers, Research Materials, JFKL.
66 Council of Economic Advisers Oral History Interview No. 1 by Joseph Pechman, August 1, 1964, JFKL, p. 372.
67 Douglas Dillon Oral History Interview by Paige E. Mulhollan, June 29, 1969, LBJL, p. 165.
68 Eichengreen, "From Benign Neglect."
69 The Council of Economic Advisers recalled that the surge in gold was also connected to polls in October 1960 showing Kennedy in the lead, which had troubled the business community at home and abroad. Council of Economic Advisers Oral History Interview No. 1 by Joseph Pechman, August 1, 1964, JFKL, p. 94.
70 Galbraith to President Kennedy, October 20, 1960. John Kenneth Galbraith, *Letters to Kennedy* (Cambridge, MA: Harvard University Press, 1998), 29.
71 Carl Kaysen Oral History Interview No. 1 By Joseph E. O'Connor, July 11, 1966, JFKL.
72 Paul Nitze Oral History Interview by Dorothy Fosdick, July 11, 1964, JFKL.
73 Gary Richardson, Alejandro Komai and Michael Gou, "Roosevelt's Gold Program," *Federal Reserve History* (2003). Retrieved online November 2, 2014, Federal Reserve History Resources: http://goo.gl/52T8Yo.

74 Message to the Congress on the State of the Union" (speech, Washington, DC, January 30, 1961). Retrieved online November 2, 2014, American Presidency Project: http://goo.gl/2Ft5kX.

75 C. Douglas Dillon OH History Interview No. 1 by Dixon Donnelley, July 30, 1964, JFKL, p. 3.

76 Press Release, February 6, 1961, Folder: Message on the Balance of Payments, Box 535, Galbraith Papers, WH Files, JFKL.

77 Ibid.

78 "The Politics of the Payments Balance," Galbraith to President Kennedy, September 18, 1963, Folder: Balance of Payments [General] 1963, Box 535, Galbraith Papers, WH Files, JFKL.

79 C. Douglas Dillon Oral History Interview No. 8 by Seymour Harris, August 18, 1964, JFKL, p. 155.

80 Harris, *Economics of the Kennedy Years*, 50.

81 David Rockefeller letter to President Kennedy, June 6, 1962, Folder: Balance of Payments, 1961–62, 11/2/61–9/20/62, Box 29, Sorensen Papers, Subject Files 1961–64, JFKL.

82 C. Douglas Dillon Oral History Interview No. 8 by Seymour Harris, August 18, 1964, JFKL, p. 152.

83 Federal Reserve Bank of St. Louis, "The United States Balance of Payments 1946–1960," *Monthly Review* 43:3 (March 1961): 4.

84 Senator John F. Kennedy, "Statement on the Balance of Payments" (speech, Philadelphia, PA, October 31, 1960). Retrieved online January 10, 2014, American Presidency Project: http://goo.gl/FdTRfB.

85 "Guns and Butter," *The Observer*, London (August 25, 1962).

Chapter 4

1 "Developments in Viet-Nam Between General Taylor's Visits: Oct 1961–Oct 1962," Brubeck to McGeorge Bundy, October 8, 1962, Folder: October 1962 1–10, Box 9, Newman Papers, Research Materials, JFKL.

2 Telephone conversation between President Kennedy and McNamara, May 7, 1963, Tape 85, Presidential Recordings, JFKL.

3 Roger Hilsman, *The Politics of Policy Making in Defense and Foreign Affairs* (New York: Harper & Row, 1971), 166–167.

4 Newman, *JFK and Vietnam*, chapter 16.

5 Robert S. McNamara interview by Brian VanDeMark for *In Retrospect*, December 7, 1963, Folder: Interview McNamara, 7/12/93, Box II:100, RSM Papers, LoC.

6 Wood to Hilsman, April 18, 1963, *FRUS, Vietnam January–August 1963*, vol. 3, doc. 97.

7 Secretary's calendar 1963, Folder: Calendar 1963, Box II:67, RSM Papers, LoC.

8 Roswell Gilpatric also led this Task Force, which included Edward Lansdale, the former OSS operative in Vietnam who was also a friend of South Vietnamese President Diem.

9 On Kennedy's rejection of proposals on neutralization, see especially Fredrik Logevall, *Choosing War: The Lost Chance for Peace and the Escalation of War in Vietnam* (Berkeley: University of California Press, 1999), 72.

10 Exchange of letters between Presidents Diem and Kennedy, May 15 and June 9, 1961, Folder: 2 Vietnam Security, 1961, Box 128a, POF, JFKL.

11 Roswell Gilpatric Oral History Interview No. 1 by Dennis J. O'Brien, May 5, 1970, JFKL.

12 Robert McNamara, "Hearings on the Committee on Foreign Affairs, House of Representatives," 87th Congress (1st Session, June 7–8, 1961), Folder: In Retrospect Background and Research Material, Chapter 2, Box II:89, RSM Papers, LoC.

13 For more information on the commitment that the Kennedy administration had inherited, see especially Fredrik Logevall, *Embers of War: The Fall of an Empire and the Making of America's Vietnam* (New York: Random House, 2013), 710.

14 Edward Cuddy, "Vietnam: Mr. Johnson's War – Or Mr. Eisenhower's?," *Review of Politics* 65:4 (September 2003): 355.

15 President's Questions for the Meeting on South Viet Nam, November 11, 1961, Folder: 2 Vietnam Security, 1961, Box 128a, POF, JFKL.

16 Notes on combat troops in Vietnam, Theodore Sorensen, November 3, 1961, Folder: Vietnam 5/9/61–10/1/63, Box 55, Sorensen Papers, Subject Files 1961–64, JFKL.

17 Maxwell Taylor Oral History Interview No. 1 by Elspeth Rostow, April 12, 1964, JFKL; State Department Report to President Kennedy, November 3, 1961, Folder: 2 Vietnam Security, 1961, Box 128a, POF, JFKL.

18 Maxwell Taylor and Walt Rostow Report: Vietnam, Subjects, Summaries and Suggested Courses of Action, Folder: Rostow/Taylor Report, Box 203, NSF, Country Series, Vietnam, JFKL.

19 CINCPAC to Secretary of State, October 25, 1961, Folder: Taylor Trip, Vietnam – 10/12/61–10/19/61, Box 251a, NSF, Regional Security Series, JFKL.

20 Taylor to President Kennedy, November 1, 1961, Folder: Taylor Trip, Vietnam – 10/12/61–10/19/61, Box 251a, NSF, Regional Security Series, JFKL.

21 McGeorge Bundy to Taylor, October 28, 1961, Folder: Taylor Trip, Vietnam – 10/12/61–10/19/61, Box 251a, NSF, Regional Security Series, JFKL.

22 McGeorge Bundy to President Kennedy, November 15, 1961, Folder: Vietnam 5/9/61–10/1/63, Box 55, Sorensen Papers, Subject Files 1961–64, JFKL.

23 U. Alexis Johnson to McGeorge Bundy, November 11, 1961, Folder: 2 Vietnam Security, 1961, Box 128a, POF, JFKL.

24 McNamara to President Kennedy, November 9, 1961, Folder: Background and Research Materials, Chapter 2, Box II:89, RSM Papers, LoC.

25 Notes of a meeting, the White House, November 11, 1961, *FRUS, Vietnam 1961*, vol. 1, doc. 236.

26 Preston, *The War Council*, 96.

27 *Pentagon Papers*, Part IV.B.1, p. 9, 31.

28 Callahan, *Dangerous Capabilities*, 180. Also, many of Kennedy's aides remember that Kennedy would cite General MacArthur's warnings against a

land war in Southeast Asia and that "whenever he'd get this military advice from the Joint Chiefs ... he'd say 'Well, now, you gentlemen, you go back and convince General MacArthur, then I'll be convinced.'" Arthur M. Schlesinger Jr., "What Would He Have Done?," *New York Times* (March 29, 1992). Though he approved a substantial escalation in training and advisors, he never seemed to have detracted from his view that the United States should not apply direct force, that this would "return the situation in Vietnam to that which existed when the French were fighting a colonial war there." Memorandum of Conference with the President, September 11, 1963, Folder: Meetings on Vietnam, 9/11/63–9/12/63, Box 316, NSF, M&M Series, JFKL.

29 Draft Letter from President Kennedy to President Diem, December 1961, Folder: Vietnam, General, 12/11/61–12/13/61, Box 195a, NSF, JFKL.

30 Roswell Gilpatric Oral History Interview by Dennis J. O'Brien, May 5, 1970, JFKL.

31 On Nolting's isolation, see also Frederick Nolting, *From Trust to Tragedy: The Political Memoirs of Frederick Nolting, Kennedy's Ambassador to Diem's Vietnam* (Westport, CT: Praeger, 1988); interview of Frederick Nolting, April 30, 1981. Retrieved online November 2, 2014, Open Vault Archives: http://goo.gl/cHWDLE.

32 Roger Hilsman insisted that the choice was apolitical and that Lodge had been chosen for objective reasons. His Memcon of a conversation with a journalist reads: "As a matter of fact, if you are going to play that game, you would pick a liberal like Chet Bowles. Mr. Hilsman said that Mr. Lodge is bilingual in French; he has been interested in Vietnam. He is a Major General in the Army Reserve. Last year when he took his two weeks' active duty he was in the Pentagon studying Vietnam and the tactics, and was fascinated with the place." (Memorandum of Telecon between Mr. Bob Donovan of Herald Tribune and Mr. Hilsman, June 27, 1963, Folder: Chronological Files 6/63, Box 6, Hilsman Papers, Memoranda of Conversations, JFKL.) Later, Kennedy's friends and advisors David Powers and Kenneth O'Donnell suggested the President was "astonished along with rest of the Boston Irishmen on the White House staff" by Rusk's choice but that he nonetheless approved "because the idea of getting Lodge mixed up in such a hell of a mess as the one in Vietnam was irresistible." Early drafts of *Johnny We Hardly Knew Ye*, Folder: Chapter 1, Box 12, O'Donnell Papers, JFKL.

33 The notes were in respect of a discussion over what to do if the coup against Diem failed. Notes from a Meeting, August 28, 1963, Folder: Vietnam, General, 11/3/63–11/5/63, CIA Reports, Box 201, NSF, Countries Series, Vietnam, JFKL.

34 Schlesinger, *A Thousand Days*, 442.

35 There is some debate about whether Rostow's removal was a demotion, as John Newman suggests, or instead a promotion to something better fitted to his background as an economic historian, as Andrew Preston suggests. Newman, *JFK and Vietnam*, 140–141; Preston, *The War Council*, 62.

36 Schlesinger, *A Thousand Days*, 442–446.

37 Rostow to President Kennedy, December 6, 1961, Folder: Vietnam, General, 12/6/61–12/7/61, Box 195a, NSF, JFKL.

38 "Military Command in South Vietnam," McNamara to President Kennedy, December 22, 1961, Folder: Vietnam, General, 12/19/61–12/23/61, Box 195a, NSF, JFKL.

39 "Trip Report" Weigand and Franks to DFI, April 1962, Folder: April 1962 1–9, Box 8, Newman Papers, Research Materials, JFKL.

40 Hohler, Saigon to Peck, FO, February 15, 1962, Reel 14: FO 371/166700, FO Files: The USA, Series Two: Vietnam 1959–1975, National Archives, Kew.

41 Nolting to Rusk, December 19, 1961, Folder: Vietnam, General, 12/19/61–12/23/61, Box 195a, NSF, JFKL.

42 "Should Police Programs Be Transferred to DOD," Komer to McGeorge Bundy and Taylor, April 18, 1962, Folder: Special Group (CI) – 4/6/61–6/7/62, Box 319, NSF, M&M Series, JFKL.

43 Janow to Phillips, May 15, 1963, Folder: AID CIF, Box 1, RG59 Vietnam Working Group, NARA.

44 JCS to President Kennedy (via Secretary of Defense McNamara), January 27, 1962, Folder: Southeast Asia, General 1/61–12/62, Box 231a, NSF, Regional Security Series, JFKL.

45 Robert S. McNamara, "Address to the Fellows of the American Bar Foundation Dinner" (speech, Chicago, IL, February 17, 1962), Reel 12: FO 371/162583. FO: The USA, Series One: USA Politics and Diplomacy, Part I: The John F. Kennedy Years, 1960–1963, National Archives, Kew.

46 Robert McNamara Calendar, 1962, Folder: Calendar, 1962, Box II:66, RSM Papers, LoC.

47 "American Position on South Viet Nam," UK Embassy, Washington to Foreign Office, April 17, 1962, Reel 17: FO 371/166721, FO: The USA, Series Two: Vietnam 1959–1975, National Archives, Kew.

48 "South Viet Nam" Ormsby-Gore to South East Department, Foreign Office, September 18, 1963, Reel 25: FO 371/170101, FO: The USA, Series Two: Vietnam 1959–1975, National Archives, Kew.

49 Strategic Concept for South Vietnam, Hilsman, February 2, 1962, Folder: Vietnam, Box 3, Hilsman Papers, Memoranda of Conversations, JFKL; "BRIAM Report to the Vietnam Task Force," Thompson, April 14, 1962, Folder: Vietnam, Box 3, Hilsman Papers, Memoranda of Conversations, JFKL.

50 *Pentagon Papers*, Part IV B2, p. 29.

51 "Roger Hilsman," Denson to Seconde, February 9, 1962, Reel 14: FO 371/166700, FO: The USA, Series Two: Vietnam 1959–1975, National Archives, Kew.

52 Transcript NSC meeting, October 3, 1963: Tape 144/A49, Cassette 2/3, Folder: Fog of War, background and research materials, Box II:114, RSM Papers, LoC; Shapley to McNamara, November 12, 1986, Folder: Shapley, Deborah, Promise and Power, Correspondence, Box II:120, RSM Papers, LoC.

53 Z, "The War in Viet-Nam: We Have Not Been Told the Whole Truth," *New Republic* (March 12, 1962).

54 On the differences between Hilsman and Thompson's approach, see especially Peter Busch, *All the Way with JFK?: Britain, the United States and the Vietnam War* (Oxford: Oxford University Press, 2003), 102–107.

55 Honolulu Briefing Book (Part II), November 20, 1963, Folder: Vietnam, Honolulu Briefing Book, 11/20/62, Part II, Box 204, NSF, Countries Series, Vietnam, JFKL.

56 Unfortunately, in a Vietnamese context, the strategic hamlets program bore an uncanny resemblance to Diem's earlier and doomed Agroville Program, which many at the time noted could seem to "peasants as old wine in newly labelled bottles." *Pentagon Papers*, Gravel edn., vol. 2.2.

57 Memorandum for the Record, Hilsman, December 1962, Folder: Vietnam Hilsman Trip, 12/62–1/63, Box 3, Hilsman Papers, Memoranda of Conversations, JFKL.

58 "A Strategic Concept for South Vietnam," Hilsman to Taylor, January 1962, Folder: Vietnam, General, Reports and Memos, 1/62–2/62, Box 195a, NSF, JFKL.

59 Roger Hilsman Oral History Interview No. 2 By Dennis J. O'Brien, August 14, 1970, JFKL.

60 Forrestal to President Kennedy, September 18, 1962, Folder: September 1962: 18–28, Box 8, Newman Papers, Research Materials, JFKL.

61 Memorandum for the Record, Roger Hilsman, December 1962, Folder: Vietnam Hilsman Trip, 12/62–1/63, Box 3, Hilsman Papers, Memoranda of Conversations, JFKL.

62 FO to De Zalueta, September 6, 1963, PREM 11/4759, PM's correspondence, National Archives, Kew.

63 "Comprehensive Plan for South Vietnam," Harkins to MAAG, September 8, 1962, Folder: September 1962 1–4, Box 8, Newman Papers, Research Materials, JFKL.

64 Honolulu Briefing Book (Part II), November 20, 1963, Folder: Vietnam, Honolulu Briefing Book, 11/20/62, Part II, Box 204, NSF, Countries Series, Vietnam, JFKL.

65 JCS to President Kennedy (via Secretary of Defense McNamara), January 27, 1962, Folder: Southeast Asia, General 1/61–12/62, Box 231a, NSF, Regional Security Series, JFKL.

66 Jacob Van Staaveren, *USAF Plans and Policies in South Vietnam: 1961–1963* (Washington, DC: USAF Historical Liaison Office, 1965), 34.

67 General Earl Wheeler, "The Design of Military Power" (speech, Fordham University, NYC, November 7, 1962), Folder: November 1962 1–15, Box 9, Newman Papers, Research Materials, JFKL.

68 "Extracts from General Wheeler's Speech," Hilsman to Harriman and Forrestal, February 2, 1963, Folder: Vietnam 2/1/63–3/21/63, Box 3, Hilsman Papers, Memoranda of Conversations, JFKL.

69 "Viet Nam: Summary for Week Ending January 30," UK Embassy, Saigon to FO, January 20, 1963, Reel 23: FO 371/166763, FO Files: The USA, Series Two: Vietnam 1959–1975, National Archives, Kew.

70 Yarmolinsky, "Civilian Control: New Perspectives for New Problems."

71 Record of a Small Meeting with Secretary McNamara in Admiral Felt's Office, October 8, 1962, Folder: Vietnam, General 1962, Box 519, Harriman Papers, LoC.

72 Early drafts of *Johnny We Hardly Knew Ye*, Folder: Chapter 1, Box 12, O'Donnell Papers, JFKL.

73 CINCPAC to JCS, February 14, 1963, Folder: February 1963 9–20, Box 11, Newman Papers, Research Materials, JFKL.

74 Memorandum for the Record, Meeting of the Special Warfare Coordinating Group (Focal Point), May 4, 1962, Folder: May 1962 1–9, Box 8, Newman Papers, Research Materials, JFKL.

75 Cottrell to US Embassy, Saigon, April 1962, Folder: Vietnam, General, 4/1/62–4/10/62. Box 196, NSF, JFKL.

76 Memorandum for the Record of Discussion at the Daily White House Staff Meeting, Washington, November 22, 1963, 8 a.m, *FRUS, Vietnam August–December 1963*, vol. 4, doc. 322.

77 "Requirements for Advisory Personnel in Vietnam," McNamara to Wheeler, December 21, 1962, Folder: Vietnam, General, 1/6/62–1/12/62, Box 195a, NSF, JFKL.

78 Van Staaveren, *USAF Plans and Policies*, 27, 34.

79 Memorandum for the Record, Meeting of the Special Warfare Coordinating Group (Focal Point), May 4, 1962, Folder: May 1962 1–9, Box 8, Newman Papers, Research Materials, JFKL.

80 Memorandum of a Conference with the President, March 7, 1962, Folder: Conferences with the President, JCS – 10/61–11/62, Box 345, Clifton Series, NSF, JFKL.

81 "ACTIVE Progress of 1 June 1963," Rowny, US Army to Wheeler, July 9, 1963, Folder: July 1963 15–27, Box 13, Newman Papers, Research Materials, JFKL.

82 The JCS produced a report entitled "Southeast Asia as a Training Laboratory" for the Special Group (CI), which specifically described Vietnam as a chance for the military to showcase their participation in counterinsurgency activities. The report suggested that "the services are receiving rich benefit from the experiences of Southeast Asia and are confident that lessons learned in that locale will have applicability in other areas where insurgency may erupt." "Military Training Related to CI Matters," Lemnitzer, JCS to Special Group (CI), January 20, 1962, Folder: Special Group Military Training Report, 1/30/62, Box 319, NSF, M&M Series, JFKL.

83 Memorandum of a Conference with the President, December 4, 1961, Folder: Conferences with the President, JCS, 1/61–2/61, Box 345, NSF, Clifton Series, JFKL.

84 Kelly, *US Army Special Forces*, 10.

85 "Project Agile," Memorandum for the Record, ARPA, August 13, 1961, Box 3, RG59 Records of the Special Group (CI), NARA.

86 Status Report on the Presidential Program for Viet-Nam, July 10, 1961, Folder: Vietnam, General, Presidential Program Status Reports, Box 195a, NSF, JFKL.

87 Van Staaveren, *USAF Plans and Policies*, 63.

88 Review of GVN Situation by JCS, 17–18 December 1962, Honolulu Conference, January 4, 1963, Folder: January 1963 1–4, Box 10, Newman Papers, Research Materials, JFKL.

89 Ibid.
90 Newman, *JFK and Vietnam*, 266–270.
91 Colby to Harriman, February 22, 1963, Folder: Defense Affairs, 1963, Box 1, RG59 Vietnam Working Group, NARA.
92 "Operation Switchback," Wood to U. Alexis Johnson, February 7, 1963, Folder: Defense Affairs, 1963, Box 1, RG59 Vietnam Working Group, NARA.
93 CINFO to MACV, July 9, 1962, Folder: July 1962 6–17, Box 8, Newman Papers, Research Materials, JFKL.
94 Kaplan et al., *The McNamara Ascendancy*, 276.
95 Ibid.
96 Hilsman, *The Politics of Policy Making*, 41–44.
97 Van Staaveren, *USAF Plans and Policies*, 54.
98 "Crop Destruction in Vietnam," Forrestal to President Kennedy, September 28, 1962, Folder: September 1962 18–28, Box 9, Newman Papers, Research Materials, JFKL.
99 "Interdiction," Harriman to Nolting, March 22, 1963, Folder: March 1963 19–21, Box 11, Newman Papers, Research Materials, JFKL.
100 Eggleston, MAAG, August 27, 1962, Part I, Reel I, Westmoreland Papers, RSC.
101 Review of Orientation Tour Report to South Vietnam, March 27, 1962, Folder: March 1962 27–31, Box 8, Newman Papers, Research Materials, JFKL.
102 Lemnitzer to McNamara, March 30, 1962, Folder: March 1962 27–31, Box 8, Newman Papers, Research Materials, JFKL.
103 Harold Brown to McGeorge Bundy, April 11, 1962, Folder: Vietnam, General, 4/1/62–4/10/62, Box 196, NSF, JFKL.
104 Forrestal to McGeorge Bundy, October 4, 1962, Folder: Miscellaneous, Box II:95, RSM Papers, LoC.
105 "Defoliant/Herbicide Program in South Vietnam," McNamara to President Kennedy, November 16, 1962, Folder: November 1962 16–29, Box 10, Newman Papers, Research Materials, JFKL.
106 "Summary of Decisions Taken at 7th SecDef Honolulu Conference," Joint Chiefs of Staff minutes, October 8, 1962, Folder: October 1962 1–10, Box 9, Newman Papers, Research Materials, JFKL; Review of GVN Situation by JCS, 17–18 December 1962, Honolulu Conference, January 4, 1963, Folder: January 1963 3–4, Box 10, Newman Papers, Research Materials, JFKL.
107 "Revised Plan for the Republic of Vietnam," CINCPAC to JCS, May 11, 1963, Folder: May 1963: 10–15, Box 11, Newman Papers, Research Materials, JFKL.
108 Cottrell to Harriman, April 6, 1962, Box 2, RG59 Vietnam Working Group, NARA.
109 "Situation in Viet Nam," Memorandum of a Conversation, between President Kennedy and Ambassador Ormsby-Gore, Robert Thompson, BRIAM, April 4, 1963, Folder: Pol Affairs – RGK Thompson Visit to US – April 1963, Box 2, RG59 Vietnam Working Group, NARA.

Chapter 5

1 Halberstam, *The Best and the Brightest*, 215.

2 President Kennedy's first State of the Union address was almost entirely devoted to the problems confronting the country, and especially its economic woes. John F. Kennedy, "Annual Message to the Congress on the State of the Union" (speech, Washington, DC, January 30, 1961). Retrieved online November 2, 2014, American Presidency Project: http://goo.gl/B8apfO.

3 Memorandum for the President, Cabinet Committee on Balance of Payments, July 27, 1962, Folder: Balance of Payments – Gold 5/5/62–7/31/62, Box 29, Sorensen Papers, Subject Files 1961–64, JFKL.

4 For more information on the domestic economics, especially the Kennedy tax cut and the gold outflow problem, see George L. Perry et al., *Economic Events, Ideas and Policies: The 1960s and After* (Washington, DC: Brookings Institution Press, 2000).

5 Robert McNamara Calendar, Folder: Calendar, 1962, Box II:66, RSM Papers, LoC.

6 Harriman was more ambivalent than Galbraith on Vietnam. While he, like Galbraith, argued "against the value of the introduction of American troops to strengthen morale" because this could produce a "certain adverse political reaction, particularly when a country has just emerged from colonial rule," he did not argue for disengagement either. For instance, in October 1963, in trying to make the case that intervention in South Vietnam was more viable than it had been in Laos, he explained to Arthur Schlesinger, "South Vietnam is quite different [from Laos] as the logistics are in our favor and that country is of enormous political, strategic and economic importance." Harriman to Schlesinger, October 17, 1963, Folder: 2 Vietnam Security, 1961, Box 128a, POF, JFKL.

7 As General Harkins explained to his Vietnamese counterparts as well, the tendency among the Chiefs to build up forces that mirrored their own in partner countries was "extremely expensive in both funds and troop support," whereas advisory missions on the lower end of the security spectrum could be more affordable and thus sustainable. Harkins to Thuan, June 28, 1963, Folder: June 1963: 21–28, Box 12, Newman Papers, Research Materials, JFKL.

8 Galbraith to President Kennedy, May 31, 1962. Galbraith, *Letters to Kennedy*, 48.

9 Memorandum for the President, Cabinet Committee on Balance of Payments, July 27, 1962, Folder: Balance of Payments – Gold 5/5/62–7/31/62, Box 29, Sorensen Papers, Subject Files 1961–64, JFKL.

10 Memorandum for the President, Cabinet Committee on Balance of Payments, March 2, 1963, Folder: Balance of Payment – Gold General: 6/62–3/63, Box 291a, NSF, Subjects – Balance of Payments, JFKL.

11 Minutes of a meeting of the Cabinet Committee on the Balance of Payments, April 18, 1963, Folder: Balance of Payments and Gold Committee Report, Box 291a, NSF, Subjects – Balance of Payments, JFKL.

12 Draft memorandum, McNamara to President Kennedy, September 19, 1963, *FRUS Foreign Economic Policy*, vol. 9, doc. 36.

13 Ibid.
14 Diego Ruiz-Palmer, "Big Lift," *AirFan: Le magazine de l'aéronautique militaire internationale* 419 (October 2013).
15 Handwritten Notes by McNamara, JCS Meeting with President Kennedy in Palm Beach, December 27, 1961, Folder: Palm Beach Notes, Box 28, RG200, RSM Records, Defense Programs and Operation, NARA.
16 Meeting of the NSC meeting with the President, Roger Hilsman minutes, January 22, 1963, Folder: Memoranda of Conversations, Box 6, Hilsman Papers, JFKL.
17 Gavin, "The Gold Battles," 61–94.
18 During the Eisenhower administration, Douglas Dillon had been the principal envoy to Germany to try to negotiate "offset" arrangements. Gavin, *Gold, Dollars, and Power*, 47.
19 McNamara to President Kennedy, July 16, 1963, Folder: Reading File, July 1963, Box 118, RG200, RSM Records, Reading Files, NARA.
20 Victor Cha has shown that it was under the pressure of reduced economic assistance to South Korea and Japan that both countries moved toward a normalization of relations in 1965 and points to the Nixon Doctrine as a culminating point in a long-standing policy in the United States of encouraging the two countries to cooperate in order to allow for the withdrawal of US troops. Victor D. Cha, *Alignment Despite Antagonism: The US–Korea–Japan Security Triangle* (Stanford, CA: Stanford University Press, 1999).
21 McNamara to Armed Services Secretaries, July 16, 1963, Folder: Reading File, July 1963, Box 118, RG200, RSM Records, Reading Files, NARA.
22 CY is calendar year. "Force Reductions in Korea," McNamara to Chairman of the Joint Chiefs of Staff Taylor, November 6, 1963, Folder: Reading File, November 1963, Box 119, RG200, RSM Records, Reading Files, NARA.
23 Ibid.
24 "Status Report on the Department of Defense and the Balance of Payments," Kaysen to McGeorge Bundy, May 20, 1963, Folder: Balance of Payments, Box 291a, NSF, Subjects – Balance of Payments, JFKL.
25 Ibid.
26 Ibid.
27 Ball to Dillon, July 9, 1963, Folder: Balance of Payments and Cabinet Committee, Box 291a, NSF, Subjects – Balance of Payments, JFKL.
28 "Department of Defense Proposals for Further Reductions in Balance of Payments Drain," Rusk to President Kennedy, October 3, 1963, Folder: Balance of Payments, 1963, Box 292, NSF, Subjects – Balance of Payments, JFKL.
29 "Status Report on the Department of Defense and the Balance of Payments," Kaysen to McGeorge Bundy, May 20, 1963, Folder: Balance of Payments, Box 291a, NSF, Subjects – Balance of Payments, JFKL.
30 McNamara to President Kennedy, June 4, 1963, Folder: Reading File, June 1963, Box 118, RG200, RSM Records, Reading Files, NARA; McNamara to Armed Services Secretaries, July 16, 1963, Folder: Reading File, July 1963, Box 118, RG200, RSM Records, Reading Files, NARA.

31 McNamara to President Kennedy, July 16, 1963, Folder: Reading File, July 1963, Box 118, RG200, RSM Records, Reading Files, NARA.

32 McNamara to Armed Services Secretaries, JCS and key agencies, Department of Defense, November 11, 1963, Folder: Reading File, November 1963, Box 119, RG200, RSM Records, Reading Files, NARA.

33 McNamara to President Kennedy, July 16, 1963, Folder: Reading File, July 1963, Box 118, RG200, RSM Records, Reading Files, NARA.

34 George Ball Oral History Interview No. 1 by Paige E. Mulhollan, July 8, 1971, LBJL, p. 2.

35 Transcript, NSC meeting, October 3, 1963: Tape 144/A49, Cassette 2/3, Folder: Fog of War, background and research materials, Box II:114, RSM Papers, LoC.

36 Memorandum for the Record, McGeorge Bundy, September 23, 1963, Folder: Balance of Payments, Box 292, NSF, Subjects – Balance of Payments, JFKL.

37 US Balance of Payments Chart, 1962, Folder: Balance of Payments, 1961–62, Box 29, Subject Files 1961–64, Sorensen Papers, JFKL.

38 Robert McNamara and General Taylor, 87th Congress, "Briefing Presented at the Foreign Assistance Act of 1963" (Senate Committee on Foreign Relation) (1st Session, June 13, 1963). Hearing ID: HRG-1963-FOR-0027, US Congressional Hearings Digital Collection Historical Archives, 1824–2003.

39 Roswell Gilpatric Oral History Interview No. 2 by Dennis J. O'Brien, May 27, 1970, JFKL.

40 RAND Corporation, *Limited War Patterns, Southeast Asia* (Santa Monica, CA: RAND, 1962), Folder: Southeast Asia General, RAND Report, 7/62, Box 231a, NSF, Regional Security Series, JFKL.

41 "Analyses of Division Deployment Times and Associated Costs in SE Asia," Summary Sheet to the Army Chief of Staff, November 1962, Folder: November 1962, Box 9, Newman Papers, Research Materials, JFKL.

42 President John F. Kennedy "Address at the University of Washington 100th Anniversary Program" (Seattle, WA, November 16, 1961). Retrieved online November 2, 2014, JFKL: http://goo.gl/GZbGjJ.

43 Schlesinger to Joseph S. Clark, January 5, 1971. Andrew Schlesinger and Steven Schlesinger, *The Letters of Arthur Schlesinger* (New York: Random House, 2013), 403.

44 Sorensen to President Kennedy, November 24, 1961, Folder: Vietnam November 1961, Box 55, Sorensen Papers, Subject Files 1961–64, JFKL.

45 President John F. Kennedy, "After Two Years: A Conversation with the President," *ARC Identifier 52813, USIA* (1963). Retrieved online November 2, 2014: http://goo.gl/ozT5Au.

46 Hitch and McKean, *The Economics of Defense*, 3.

47 Galbraith to President Kennedy, April 4, 1962, Folder: April 1962 1–9, Box 8, Newman Papers, Research Material, JFKL.

48 In French, "Tout problème n'est pas financier mais le devient un jour. Ainsi de l'affaire d'Indochine: mal engagée politiquement, militairement et moralement, précisait-il, elle tournait plus mal encore sur le plan budgétaire." Hugues Tertrais, *Le piastre et le fusil: le coût de la guerre d'Indochine, 1945–1954* (Paris, FR: IGPDE, 2002), 23.

49 Ibid.

50 Ibid., 119 for detailed statistics.

51 "Report to the President on FY1962 Budget by Secretary McNamara," February 20, 1961, Folder: FY1962 Budget, Box 10, RG200, RSM Records, Defense Programs and Operations, NARA.

52 "Report of the Military Assistance Steering Group Report," December 12, 1961, Folder: MAP – Six Country Studies, Dec 1961–Jan 1962, Box 9, RG200, RSM Records, Defense Programs and Operations, NARA.

53 President Kennedy to President Diem, October 24, 1962, Folder: 10: Vietnam General, 1962, Box 128, POF, JFKL.

54 Robert McNamara and General Taylor, 87th Congress, "Briefing Presented at the Foreign Assistance Act of 1963" (Senate Committee on Foreign Relation) (1st Session, June 13, 1963). Hearing ID: HRG-1963-FOR-0027, US Congressional Hearings Digital Collection Historical Archives, 1824–2003.

55 Interdepartmental Seminar on the Problems of Development and Internal Defense, Fourth Session, February 1963, Folder: Defense Affairs, 1963, Box 1, RG59 Vietnam Working Group, NARA.

56 For a detailed account of historical trends in "tooth-to-tail" ratios, namely the proportion of fighting forces relative to support forces, see John J. McGrath, *The Other End of the Spear: The Tooth-to-Tail Ratio (T3R) in Modern Military Operations* (Fort Leavenwroth, KS: Combat Studies Institute Press, 2007).

57 Robert McNamara Oral History Interview No. 3 by the Secretary of Defense Historical Office, July 24, 1986, Folder: OSD Oral Histories, Box I:109, RSM Papers, LoC.

58 Report of the McNamara–Taylor Mission to South Vietnam, 24 September–1 October 1963, Folder: Vietnam, McNamara–Taylor Report, 10/1/63, Box 4, Hilsman Papers, Memoranda of Conversations, JFKL.

59 Transcript, NSC meeting, October 3, 1963: Tape 144/A49, Cassette 2/3, Folder: Fog of War, background and research materials, Box II:114, RSM Papers, LoC.

60 Both Thompson and Harriman had expressed concern in the spring of 1962 that the United States was "losing sight of this." Thompson had reported back to the Foreign Office that he detected "a tendency amongst Americans to lose sight of the fact that it is Diem's own war" with the concomitant risk that "the game [would] be taken out of the minor league and promoted to the major league." ("Need for a General Review of the Situation with the United States," Warmer, FO, March 19, 1962, FO 371/166702, Reel 14, FO Files, USA: Series Two: Vietnam 1959–1975.) In a memo to McGeorge Bundy, Harriman had suggested adopting the "same posture in Vietnam as did in Greece, i.e. this is not a US war – it will be won or lost by the Vietnamese." (Forrestal to McGeorge Bundy, May 5, 1962, Folder: May 1962 1–9, Box 8, Newman Papers, Research Materials, JFKL.)

61 Sylvester to All Services, March 1962, Folder: Vietnam, General, 3/29/62–3/31/62, Box 196, NSF, JFKL.

62 Harriman to US Embassy, Saigon and CINCPAC, April 4, 1962, Folder: April 1962 1–9, Box 8, Newman Papers, Research Materials, JFKL.

63 Draft Letter from President Kennedy to President Diem, undated, Folder: Vietnam, General, 12/11/61–12/13/61, Box 195a, NSF, JFKL.

64 State to Embassy Saigon, September 24, 1963, *FRUS, Vietnam August–December 1963*, vol. 4, doc. 147.

65 Memorandum of a Conversation, Gia Long Palace, Saigon, September 29, 1963. *FRUS, Vietnam August–December 1963*, vol. 4, doc. 158.

66 "Contingency Planning for Southeast Asia," Memorandum from Rostow to U. Alexis Johnson, September 29, 1961, Folder: Southeast Asia, General, Box 231, NSF, Regional Security Files, JFKL.

67 Telephone conversation between President Kennedy and McNamara, May 7, 1963, Tape 85, Presidential Recordings, JFKL.

68 Press briefing by Secretary McNamara, March 27, 1962, Folder: News Conference and Press Briefings, 1962, Box 182, RG200, RSM Records, Unclassified Records of News Conferences and Public Statements, 1961–67, NARA.

69 Secretary McNamara Statement to Congress on FY1964 Budget, January 21, 1963, Folder: FY1964 Statement to Congress, Box 22, RG200, RSM Records, Defense Programs and Operations, NARA.

70 Robert McNamara and General Taylor, 87th Congress, "Briefing Presented at the Foreign Assistance Act of 1963" (Senate Committee on Foreign Relation) (1st Session, June 13, 1963). Hearing ID: HRG-1963-FOR-0027, US Congressional Hearings Digital Collection Historical Archives, 1824–2003.

71 In their biography of President Kennedy, Kenneth O'Donnell and David Powers claim that Mansfield's criticism made a profound impression on Kennedy, who turned to a policy of disengagement from Vietnam after their meeting. This research has not found any evidence of this claim, although Mansfield's views chimed with others within the administration at that time. Kenneth P. O'Donnell et al., *Johnny, We Hardly Knew Ye*, 16–17.

72 Report by Senate Majority Leader Mansfield to President Kennedy, December 18, 1962, *FRUS, Vietnam 1962*, vol. 2, doc. 330.

73 Ibid.

74 *Pentagon Papers*, Part V.A.1C, p. 26.

75 "Interview with the President, Hyannis Port, Massachusetts on CBS," September 2, 1963, *FRUS, Vietnam August–December 1963*, vol. 4, doc. 50.

76 Robert S. McNamara Hearings before the Subcommittee on Foreign Operations, Committee on Appropriations, House of Representatives, 88th Congress, May 14–15, 1963, p. 92, Folder: In Retrospect Background and Research Material, Chapter 3, Box II:89, RSM Papers, LoC.

77 "Senator Mansfield's Report on Viet Nam" Ormsby-Gore to FO, February 27, 1962, Reel 27: FO 371/170110, FO: The USA. Series Two: Vietnam 1959–1975, National Archives, Kew.

78 This episode is also intriguing because several of Kennedy's advisors have suggested that Mansfield's report had a powerful impact on Kennedy and that it was on the basis of this report that he began the process of phased withdrawal. O'Donnell et al., *Johnny, We Hardly Knew Ye*, 16.

79 Similarly, McNamara made telling edits to a draft speech on Vietnam in December 1962: he removed any indication that the United States was leading the effort in the country, replaced the word Communist "aggression" with

"attacks" and the description of a "Communist directed military threat" with a "drive for domination of the country." Also, contrary to his well-known frustrations, he indicated that the South Vietnamese government "has become more cooperative" rather than "is becoming." Proposed remarks for Secretary McNamara for Mutual Broadcasting System Program Dealing with South VN, December 4, 1962, Folder: News and Press Briefings, 1962, Box 182, RG200, RSM Records, Unclassified Records of News Conferences and Public Statements, 1961–67, NARA.

80 Wiliam P. Bundy Oral History Interview No. 3 by Elspeth Rostow, November 12, 1964, JFKL. Also, Chester Cooper, in his memoirs, writes at length about being "surprised and outraged" at the 1965 end date. He recounts an interaction with William Bundy: "Finally, in utter exasperation Bill said, 'Look, I'm under instructions!' In Washington that closes any argument, unless recourse is taken by tackling the Instructor. Mac called Secretary McNamara, but was unable to persuade him to change his mind. McNamara seemed to have been trapped too; the sentence may have been worked out privately with Kennedy and therefore imbedded in concrete. The words remained and McNamara and the Administration were to pay a heavy price for them. They were not ignored by the waiting press." Chester Cooper, *The Lost Crusade: America in Vietnam* (New York: Dodd, Meade, 1970), 215–216.

81 Report of the McNamara-Taylor Mission to South Vietnam, 24 September–1 October 1963, Folder: Vietnam, McNamara–Taylor Report, 10/1/63, Box 4, Hilsman Papers, Memoranda of Conversations, JFKL.

82 "Statement by Secretary of Defense Robert S. McNamara," 88th Congress 1 (May 15, 1963) (Subcommittee on Foreign Operations Appropriation), p. 93. Hearing ID: HRG-1963-HAP-0043, US Congressional Hearings Digital Collection Historical Archives, 1824–2003.

83 "Department of Defense Proposals for Further Reductions in Balance of Payments Drain," Rusk to President Kennedy, October 3, 1963, Folder: Defense Department, Box 292, NSF, Subjects – Balance of Payments, JFKL.

84 Roswell Gilpatric Oral History Interview No. 2 by Dennis J. O'Brien, May 27, 1970, JFKL.

85 Heavner to Harriman, March 22, 1963, Folder: Defense Affairs, 1963, Box 1, RG59 Vietnam Working Group, NARA.

86 Honolulu Briefing Book (Part II) including Comprehensive Plan – Vietnam, November 20, 1963, Folder: Vietnam, Honolulu Briefing Book, 11/20/62 – Part II, Box 204, NSF, Country Series, JFKL.

87 Lansdale to Gilpatric, November 9, 1961, Folder: Laos, 1961–69 (7), Box 7, NSA, Info C&C, GFL.

88 "Hamlet Militia," Wood to Trueheart, May 22, 1963, Folder: Defense Affairs, 1963, Box 1, RG59 Vietnam Working Group, NARA.

89 On the CIA's early role in South Vietnam, see especially the recently declassified CIA histories. Thomas Ahern Jr., *CIA and the Generals: Covert Support to Military Government in South Vietnam*; Ahern, *CIA and Rural Pacification*; Thomas Ahern Jr., *CIA and the House of Ngo*. Each retrieved online November 2, 2014, CIA Online Library: http://goo.gl/zl1TWn.

90 "Aid Submission, November 18, 1963," Folder: Vietnam, General 11/16/63–11/22/63, State Cables, Box 202, NSF, Country Series, Vietnam, JFKL.

91 Extracts from the Pentagon Papers (Vol. II) on the 6th Honolulu Conference. Folder: Background and Research Material, Chapter 3, Box II:89, RSM Papers, LoC.

92 "Operation Switchback," Wood to U. Alexis Johnson, February 7, 1963, Folder: Defense Affairs, 1963, Box 1, RG59 Vietnam Working Group, NARA.

93 Telephone conversation between President Kennedy and McNamara, May 7, 1963, Tape 85, Presidential Recordings, JFKL.

94 USAM/Viet-Nam Director's Staff Meeting, March 19, 1963, Folder: AID-7 Program Operations, Box 1, RG59 Vietnam Working Group, NARA.

95 President John F. Kennedy (press conference, Washington, DC, November 14, 1963), Box 140, McGeorge Bundy Papers, NYU Research and Reference Files, JFKL.

96 Notes for Senate Foreign Relations Committee Military Assistance Hearings, June 14, 1962, Folder: MAP Hearings, Box 15, RG200, RSM Records, Defense Programs and Operations, NARA.

97 "Senator Mansfield's Report on Viet Nam" Ormsby-Gore to FO, February 27, 1962, Reel 27: FO 371/170110, FO: The USA. Series Two: Vietnam 1959–1975, National Archives, Kew.

98 "Statement by Secretary of Defense Robert S. McNamara," 88th Congress 1 (May 15, 1963) (Subcommittee on Foreign Operations Appropriation). Hearing ID: HRG-1963-HAP-0043, US Congressional Hearings Digital Collection Historical Archives, 1824–2003.

99 Ibid., p. 96.

100 Ibid.

101 This was a direct quote from the Clay Committee's Report. Ibid.

102 "Report to the President of the United States from the Committee to Strengthen the Security of the Free World," March 20, 1963. Folder: National Security S and O, Box 11, Neustadt Papers, JFKL.

103 Paul Samuelson quoted in Council of Economic Advisers Oral History Interview No. 1 by Joseph Pechman, August 1, 1964, JFKL, p. 255; on the bipartisan aspects of the Clay Committee, see also General Lucius D. Clay Oral History Interview by Richard Scammon, July 1, 1964, JFKL.

104 In an indication of how badly this exercise backfired, Kennedy himself apparently said, "That son of a bitch Clay. I should have known better." Carl Kaysen Oral History Interview No. 1 by Joseph E. O'Connor, July 11, 1966, JFKL.

105 "Report to the President of the United States from the Committee to Strengthen the Security of the Free World," March 20, 1963, Folder: National Security S and O, Box 11, Neustadt Papers, JFKL.

106 Ibid.

107 Dillon to Rusk, February 20, 1962, Douglas Dillon Oral History Interview No. 2 by Dixon Donnelley, November 10, 1964, JFKL, p. 149.

108 Although even colleagues at ISA raised questions about this assumption, suggesting, "There is no experience to show that mopping up in a CI

situation is appreciably cheaper than building up. The GVN may have to keep large number of forces in being for 5–10 years." "Proposed FY65–69 MAP Projection for Far East," Rear Admiral Heiz to ISA, December 28, 1962, Folder: December 1962, 7–31, Box 10, Newman Papers, Research Materials, JFKL.

109 *Pentagon Papers*, Vol.IV.B.4.

110 "Comprehensive Plan for South Vietnam," Harkins to MAAG, September 8, 1962, Folder: September 1962 1–14, Box 8, Newman Papers, Research Materials, JFKL.

111 "Statement by Secretary of Defense Robert S. McNamara," 88th Congress 1 (May 15, 1963) (Subcommittee on Foreign Operations Appropriation), p. 83. Hearing ID: HRG-1963-HAP-0043, US Congressional Hearings Digital Collection Historical Archives, 1824–2003.

112 Telephone conversation between President Kennedy and McNamara, May 7, 1963, Tape 85, Presidential Recordings, JFKL.

113 McNamara to William Bundy, September 4, 1963, Folder: Reading File, September 1963, Box 118, RG200, RSM Records, Reading Files, NARA.

114 Record of a Small Meeting with Secretary McNamara in Admiral Felt's Office, October 8, 1962, Folder: Vietnam, General 1962, Box 519, Harriman Papers, LoC.

115 Leffingwell to McNamara, March 8, 1961, Folder: MAP FY1962–1966, Box 14, RG200, RSM Records, Defense Programs and Operations, 1961–67, NARA.

116 Kaplan et al., *The McNamara Ascendancy*, 429–431.

117 Report of the Military Assistance Steering Group Report, December 12, 1961, Folder: MAP – Six Country Studies, December 1961–January 1962, Box 9, RG200, RSM Records, Defense Programs and Operations, NARA.

118 Although McNamara knew the SFRC was highly critical of the dominant role of Asia on the MAP, in his testimony, he put the number even higher: he indicated that 70 percent of the FY64 MAP program went to nine countries in South Asia, the Far East and Near East, and he mentioned Vietnam first among those countries, even if it was not the largest recipient of MAP aid.

119 "Statement by Secretary of Defense Robert S. McNamara," 88th Congress 1 (May 15, 1963) (Subcommittee on Foreign Operations Appropriation). Hearing ID: HRG-1963-HAP-0043, US Congressional Hearings Digital Collection Historical Archives, 1824–2003.

120 "McNamara Says Aid to Saigon Is at Peak and Will Level Off," *New York Times* (1962), Folder: May 1962, 1–9, Box 8, Newman Papers, Research Materials, JFKL.

121 The OSD was clearly impatient with AID by December 1962 and suggested that they too should begin planning for long-term funding arrangements for these forces with the South Vietnamese Ministry of the Interior. "Comprehensive Plan for SVN," Harkins to Felt, December 7, 1962, Folder: December 1962 1–4, Box 10, Newman Papers, Research Materials, JFKL.

122 Information Brief, "Comprehensive Plan for South VN (CPSVN)," August 27, 1963, Folder: August 1963 25–27, Box 13, Newman Papers, Research Materials, JFKL.

123 Harkins to Thuan, June 28, 1963, Folder: June 1963 21–28, Box 12, New-man Papers, Research Materials, JFKL.

124 Information Brief, "Comprehensive Plan for South VN (CPSVN)," August 27, 1963, Folder: August 1963 25–27, Box 13, Newman Papers, Research Materials, JFKL.

125 "Comprehensive Plan for SVN," Harkins to Felt, December 7, 1962, Folder: December 1962 1–4, Box 10, Newman Papers, Research Materials, JFKL.

126 A Federal Reserve Board study commissioned by the State Department in April 1963 questioned the South Vietnamese government's ability to cope with a reduction of US assistance and urged greater "self-help" and "buy American" measures to reduce the balance of payments impact of operations there. It was highly critical of AID and the government of South Vietnam; as a result, the State Department tried to have it reclassified. General Terms of Reference for Your Assignment in Vietnam, Stoneman to Kaufman (Federal Reserve Board), April 17, 1963, Folder: AID-7 Program Operations, Box 1, RG59 Vietnam Working Group, NARA.

127 Still his colleagues "felt the best course to follow would be to make an all-out effort between now and the end of the 1965, and then in 1966 work at stabilizing the economic situation." USAM/Viet-Nam Director's Staff Meeting, May 15, 1963, Folder: AID-7 Program Operations, Box 1, RG59 Vietnam Working Group, NARA.

128 "Economic Effects of Potential Decrease in Military Expenditures in Certain Selected Countries," Gordon to Kaysen, July 11, 1962, Folder: 1962, Box 362, NSF, Kaysen Papers, JFKL.

129 Trueheart, Saigon to Hilsman and Janow, May 28, 1963, Folder: June 1963 1–2, Box 11, Newman Papers, Research Materials, JFKL.

130 "Annual Report for 1962," Hohler, Saigon to Home, January 2, 1963, Reel 23: FO 371/166763. FO Files: The USA. Series Two: Vietnam 1959–1975, National Archives, Kew.

131 Transcript, NSC meeting, October 3, 1963: Tape 144/A49, Cassette 2/3, Folder: Fog of War, background and research materials, Box II:114, RSM Papers, LoC.

132 General Clay testimony in front of Senate Foreign Affairs Select Committee, April 25, 1963, Folder: President's Message, Rusk Statement and Legislation, 1963, Box 29, RG200, RSM Records, Defense Programs and Operations, 1961–67, NARA.

133 "FY65–69 MAP Plan for Republic of Vietnam," CINCPAC to Director of Military Assistance, OSD, July 31, 1963, Folder: July 1963 15–27, Box 13, Newman Papers, Research Materials, JFKL.

134 In a letter to State and AID, McNamara wrote that the "legal and practical feasibility of these transfers has not yet been fully considered with the Department of Defense." McNamara to Department of State/AID Administrator Bell, November 14, 1963, Folder: Reading File, October 1963, Box 119, RG200, RSM Records, Reading Files, NARA.

135 "Revisions in the Military Assistance Program Budget Presentation," McNamara to President Johnson, December 3, 1963, Folder: Defense Budget 1/2, Box 45, Sorensen Papers, Subject Files 1961–64, JFKL.

136 "Realignment of the MAP Program for FY1965," William Bundy to Bureau of Budget, State, AID, White House, November 22, 1963, Folder: Defense Budget 1/2, Box 45, Sorensen Papers, Subject Files 1961–64, JFKL.

137 Ibid.

Chapter 6

1 Michael Forrestal said that "Kennedy never got too discouraged about Vietnam, and felt despite all the difficulties, we had a good chance of making." (Research Notes for *A Thousand Days*, Folder: Vietnam, Research Notes and Memoranda, Box W-15, Schlesinger Papers, Memoranda to the President, JFKL.) In an oral history, William Bundy stated that "[withdrawal] was pegged to an optimistic view of the situation and I doubt very much that it was intended to apply if the situation had been going badly." (William P. Bundy Oral History Interview by William W. Moss, April 25, 1972, JFKL.)

2 Transcript NSC meeting, October 3, 1963: Tape 144/A49, Cassette 2/3, Folder: Fog of War, background and research materials, Box II:114, RSM Papers, LoC.

3 Ibid.

4 *Pentagon Papers*, Part IV.B.3, p. 9.

5 Although, in a revealing side note, he added, "McCone feels that it may be that the discouragement is not about how the war is going but about the setup in the American Military setup there in Viet Nam and its relations to CINCPAC and the JCS." Memorandum for the Record, Hilsman, April 27, 1962, Folder: April 1962, Box 6, Hilsman Papers, Memoranda of Conversations, JFKL.

6 "Status Report on Southeast Asia, Task Force Southeast Asia," October 3, 1962, Folder: October 1962 1–10, Box 9, Newman Papers, Research Materials, JFKL; "Developments in Viet-Nam between General Taylor's Visits: Oct 1961–Oct 1962" Brubeck to McGeorge Bundy, October 8, 1962, Folder: October 1962 1–10, Box 9, Newman Papers, Research Materials, JFKL.

7 Kattenburg to the Special Group (CI), October 22, 1963, Box 3, RG59 Vietnam Working Group, NARA; Honolulu Briefing Book (Part II), November 20, 1963, Folder: Vietnam, Honolulu Briefing Book, 11/20/62, Part II, Box 204, NSF, Countries Series, Vietnam, JFKL.

8 "US Policy on Viet-Nam: White House Statement," October 2, 1963. Retrieved online November 2, 2014, Mt. Holyoke Documents Relating to American Foreign Policy, Vietnam: www.mtholyoke.edu/acad/intrel/state63.htm.

9 Report of the McNamara–Taylor Mission to South Vietnam, 24 September–1 October 1963, Folder: Vietnam, McNamara–Taylor Report, 10/1/63, Box 4, Hilsman Papers, Memoranda of Conversations, JFKL.

10 In his optimism, Harkins had a powerful ally in Admiral Felt, who was the other field commander in charge of drafting the withdrawal plans. In response to an article written by David Halberstam that suggested the situation in the Delta had seriously deteriorated and in defense of Harkins, writing to the JCS in March 1963, Felt effused: "I believe the reasons for Harkins' optimism is: 1)

the inescapably evident fact of continuing US support and military aid; 2) the obvious fact that in both military and civilian efforts the people running things are getting organized and have gained a reasonably comprehensive understanding of the problem to be solved and have actually gone to work to solve the problem ... My overall comment is that improvement is a daily fact, thanks to the combined efforts of the RVN and the US the success of the counterinsurgency is attainable and we are confident of the outcome." CINC-PAC to JCS, March 9, 1963, Folder: February 1963 9–20, Box 11, Newman Papers, Research Materials, JFKL. Also, shortly before McNamara's visit, Felt reported to the JCS that the foundations for a solid program in the Delta had been laid and so victory could also be carried there. McNamara's notes from the trip pointed specifically to numerous failures and weaknesses in the Delta region. (CINCPAC to JCS, August 18, 1963, Folder: August 1963, Box 13, Newman Papers, Research Materials, JFKL.) Moreover, even after the transition to the Johnson administration when the CPSVN was quietly dropped, Felt still "stood by predictions that the war against the Vietcong will be completed successfully in three years." US Embassy, Taipei to McGeorge Bundy, December 1963, Folder: 1 Vietnam General, 1963, Box 128a, POF, JFKL.

11 Robert S. McNamara Interview by Brian Vandemark for "In Retrospect," December 7, 1993, Folder: Drafts and Notes, Box II:100, RSM Papers, LOC.

12 "Report on Trip to Far East with General Taylor, August 31–September 21, 1962," Folder: September 1961 1, Box 8, Newman Papers, Research Materials, JFKL.

13 *Pentagon Papers*, Part IV.B4, p. 5.

14 Harkins to Taylor, January 1963, Folder: January 1963 3–4, Box 10, Newman Papers, Research Materials, JFKL.

15 Transcript, NSC meeting, October 3, 1963: Tape 144/A49, Cassette 2/3, Folder: Fog of War, background and research materials, Box II:114, RSM Papers, LoC.

16 Research Notes for *A Thousand Days*, Folder: Vietnam, Research Notes and Memoranda, Box W-15, Schlesinger Papers, Memoranda to the President, JFKL.

17 "Discussion about Senator Mansfield's Visit to Vietnam with the Director of the Vietnam Working Group in the State Department, Mr. Wood," Forster, Washington to Williams, FO, January 25, 1963, Reel 27: FO 371/170110, FO Files: The USA, Series Two: Vietnam 1959–1975, National Archives, Kew.

18 Robert McNamara draft of "In Retrospect" with comments from McGeorge Bundy, undated, Folder: In Retrospect, Comments and Criticisms (pre-publication reviews), Box II:95, RSM Papers, LoC.

19 Ibid.

20 Gilpatric left the Pentagon in January 1964, so this recollection would have been solely from impressions gleaned during the Kennedy administration. (Roswell Gilpatric Oral History Interview by Ted Gittinger No. 1, November 12, 1982, LBJL.)

21 Transcript, NSC meeting, October 3, 1963: Tape 144/A49, Cassette 2/3, Folder: Fog of War, background and research materials, Box II:114, RSM Papers, LoC.

22 RGK Thompson, Report on Visits to Delta Provinces to Anderson, USMC, September 21, 1963, Folder: Vietnam Trip, Box 63, RG200, RSM Records, Defense Programs and Operations, NARA.

23 "Vietnam: Review of United States Aid and Policy towards Vietnam Following Senator Mansfield's Report" by Warmer, FO, April 3, 1963, Reel 27: FO 371/170110, FO Files: The USA, Series Two: Vietnam 1959–1975, National Archives, Kew.

24 "Thompson Visit," CINCPAC to JCS, March 26, 1963, Folder: March 1963 23–30, Box 11, Newman Papers, Research Materials, JFKL.

25 Revised Report from Thompson to Peck, FO, October 30, 1963, Reel 25: FO 371/170102, FO Files: The USA, Series Two: Vietnam 1959–1975, National Archives, Kew.

26 Harkins and most other military officers McNamara met during his visit to Vietnam in September 1963 insisted (despite receiving contradicting reports) that the Buddhist crisis had "not had an appreciable impact on the military situation to date." USMACV Headway Addenda to JCS et al., July 10–17, 1963, Folder: July 1963 15–27, Box 13, Newman Papers, Research Materials, JFKL.

27 "Report on Visits to the Delta Provinces over the Last 3 Months, and Interview with Cabot Lodge, United States Ambassador" Thompson to FO, September 18, 1963, Reel 25: FO 371/170102, FO Files: The USA, Series Two: Vietnam 1959–1975, National Archives, Kew.

28 McNamara handwritten notes, September 25, 1963, Folder: Trip Notes, Box 63, RG200, RSM Records, Defense Programs and Operations, NARA.

29 Peter Busch, "Killing the 'Vietcong': The British Advisory Mission and the Strategic Hamlet Programme," *Journal of Strategic Studies* 25:1 (2002): 152.

30 Ibid.

31 "Report on Visits to the Delta Provinces over the Last 3 Months, and Interview with Cabot Lodge, United States Ambassador" Thompson to FO, September 18, 1963, Reel 25: FO 371/170102, FO Files: The USA, Series Two: Vietnam 1959–1975, National Archives, Kew.

32 Report of the McNamara-Taylor Mission to South Vietnam, 24 September–1 October 1963, Folder: Vietnam, McNamara–Taylor Report, 10/1/63, Box 4, Hilsman Papers, Memoranda of Conversations, JFKL.

33 Robert S. McNamara Oral History Interview No. 2 by the OSD Historical Office, May 22, 1986, Folder: OSD OH 2, Box I:109, RSM Papers, LoC.

34 It saw "clear differences of opinion about the extent of GVN control" and complained that "Lodge has been told quite a different situation exists shown by MACV reports." McNamara handwritten notes, September 25, 1963, Folder: Trip Notes, Box 63, RG200, RSM Records, Defense Programs and Operations, NARA.

35 Report of the McNamara–Taylor Mission to South Vietnam, 24 September–1 October 1963, Folder: Vietnam, McNamara–Taylor Report, 10/1/63, Box 4, Hilsman Papers, Memoranda of Conversations, JFKL.

36 Also, McNamara's team on the trip reflected biases: William Bundy, the head of ISA, also oversaw the struggling MAP that financed operations; Forrestal had expressed anger at air power and the "militarization" of policy; Colby

had worried about the proliferation of militias; Krulak had complained of the military's inability to integrate counterinsurgency theory; and William Sullivan, the former Deputy Head of Mission in South Vietnam, had criticized Diem's leadership. Secretary McNamara's Instructions to Party Delivered aboard Plane, September 23, 1963, Folder: South Vietnam Trip, Box 63, RG200, RSM Records, Defense Programs and Operations, NARA.

37 McNamara handwritten notes, September 25, 1963, Folder: Trip Notes, Box 63, RG200, RSM Papers, Defense Programs and Operations, NARA.

38 Lodge to Rusk, September 30, 1963, Folder: South Vietnam Trip, Box 63, RG200, RSM Records, Defense Programs and Operations, NARA.

39 McNamara handwritten notes, undated, Folder: Trip Notes, Box 63, RG200, RSM Records, Defense Programs and Operations, NARA.

40 Victor H. Krulak Oral History Interview by William W. Moss, November 19, 1970, JFKL.

41 Research Notes for *A Thousand Days*, Folder: Vietnam, Research Notes and Memoranda, Box W-15, Schlesinger Papers, Memoranda to the President, JFKL.

42 *Pentagon Papers*, Part IV.B.4, p. 42.

43 William Knighton Jr., "McNamara and Taylor Feel US Can Withdraw Most of Troops from Vietnam by End of 1965," *Baltimore Sun* (October 3, 1963).

44 Tad Szulc, "Vietnam Victory by the End of '65 Envisaged by US"; "Officials Say War May Be Won if Political Crisis Does Not Hamstring Effort," *New York Times* (October 3, 1963): 1; "Text of Statement on Vietnam," *New York Times* (October 3, 1963): 4.

45 Logevall, for instance, has written that these plans were "primarily to pressure Diem." Logevall, *Choosing War*, 69.

46 NSC meeting, October 2, 1963, 6:05 p.m. meeting, Tape 144, Cassette 3, Presidential Recordings, JFKL.

47 *Pentagon Papers*, Part IV.B.4, p. 5.

48 Ledward, Washington to Warmer, FO, April 8, 1962, Reel 19: FO 371/166733, FO Files: The USA, Series Two: Vietnam 1959–1975.

49 "Record of a Meeting with General Maxwell Taylor on September 12," Thompson to Warmer, FO, October 9, 1962, Reel 17: FO 371/166723, FO Files: The USA, Series Two: Vietnam 1959–1975, National Archives, Kew.

50 "Mr. Thompson's Visit to Washington to Consult with US Officials: Report on His Discussions" Ledward, Washington, April 6, 1963, Reel 27: FO 371/170111, FO Files: The USA, Series Two: Vietnam 1959–1975, National Archives, Kew.

51 Telephone conversation between President Kennedy and McNamara, May 7, 1963, Tape 85, Presidential Recordings, JFKL.

52 "Public Affairs Plan for Reduction in Force," MACV to CINCPAC, September 15, 1963, Folder: September 1963 13–15, Box 14, Newman Papers, Research Materials, JFKL.

53 JCS to CINCPAC and MACV, October 5, 1963, Folder: Vietnam, General, September–November 1963, Box 519, Harriman Papers, LoC.

54 Memorandum for the Files of a Conference with the President, October 5, 1963, *FRUS, Vietnam August–December 1963*, vol. 4, doc. 179.

55 Transcript, NSC meeting, October 3, 1963: Tape 144/A49, Cassette 2/3, Folder: Fog of War, background and research materials, Box II:114, RSM Papers, LoC.

56 Memorandum for the Record, Meeting on McNamara–Taylor Mission to South Vietnam, September 23, 1963, Folder: September 1963 21–25, Box 15, Newman Papers, Research Materials, JFKL.

57 Memorandum of Conference with the President, September 11, 1963, Folder: Meetings on Vietnam, 9/11/63–9/12/63, Box 316, NSF, M&M Series, JFKL.

58 Memorandum for the Record, Meeting on McNamara–Taylor Mission to South Vietnam, September 23, 1963, Folder: September 1963 21–25, Box 15, Newman Papers, Research Materials, JFKL.

59 McNamara handwritten notes, September 25, 1963, Folder: Trip Notes, Box 63, RG200, RSM Records, Defense Programs and Operations, NARA.

60 Minutes of a Meeting in the Situation Room (without the President), October 3, 1963, Folder: October 1963 2–3, Box 15, Newman Papers, Research Materials, JFKL. Hilsman and Rufus Phillips were pushing the idea of a "psychological warfare campaign" most aggressively. Coming out of the NSC meetings, Hilsman wrote that the policy that had been "agreed upon" was "a policy of graduated pressure on the GVN." Neubert to Hilsman, October 18, 1963, Folder: Vietnam 10/6/63–10/31/63, Box 4, Hilsman Papers, Memoranda of Conversations, JFKL.

61 Report of the McNamara–Taylor Mission to South Vietnam, 24 September–1 October 1963, Folder: Vietnam, McNamara–Taylor Report, 10/1/63, Box 4, Hilsman Papers, Memoranda of Conversations, JFKL.

62 Memorandum for the Record, Meeting on McNamara–Taylor Mission to South Vietnam, September 23, 1963, Folder: September 1963 21–25, Box 15, Newman Papers, Research Materials, JFKL.

63 Proposal for a Memorandum from the South Vietnam Working Group to the Director of the CIA, September 30, 1963, Folder: Vietnam III, Box 4, Hilsman Papers, Memoranda of Conversations, JFKL.

64 Report of the McNamara–Taylor Mission to South Vietnam, 24 September–1 October 1963, Folder: Vietnam, McNamara–Taylor Report, 10/1/63, Box 4, Hilsman Papers, Memoranda of Conversations, JFKL.

65 Ibid.

66 Ibid.

67 Cooper, *The Lost Crusade*, 215–216.

68 *Pentagon Papers*, Part IV.B.4, p. 42.

69 Forrestal to McGeorge Bundy, November 7, 1963, Folder: Vietnam, General, 11/6/63–11/15/63, Memos and Miscellaneous, Box 202, NSF, JFKL.

70 US Embassy, Saigon to Rusk, November 7, 1963, Folder: Vietnam, General 11/3/63–11/5/63, State Cables, Box 201, NSF, Countries Series, Vietnam, JFKL.

71 McNamara and VanDeMark, *In Retrospect*, 79–80.

72 State Department to US Embassy, Saigon, October 4, 1963, Folder: Vietnam, Top Secret Cables, 10/63, Box 204, NSF, Countries Series, Vietnam, JFKL.

73 Hilsman to McNamara, October 3, 1963, Folder: October 1963, Box 6, Hilsman Papers, Memoranda of Conversations, JFKL.

74 Forrestal to McGeorge Bundy, November 7, 1963, Folder: Vietnam, General, 11/6/63–11/15/63, Memos and Miscellaneous, Box 202, NSF, JFKL.

75 Robert S. McNamara Oral History Interview No. 1 by Walt Rostow, January 8, 1975, LBJL.

76 McNamara and VanDeMark, *In Retrospect*, 80.

77 On this, see especially the following collection of recently declassified materials: John Prados, ed., "The Diem Coup after 50 Years," *National Security Archive Electronic Briefing Book* 444 (November 1, 2013). Retrieved online December 13, 2014: http://goo.gl/BCF20q.

78 "Notes of a Meeting with Professor Honey," September 25, 1963, Folder: Trip Notes, Box 63, RG200, RSM Papers, Defense Programs and Operations, NARA.

79 "Memorandum of a Conference with the President," August 29, 1963. Retrieved online November 4, 2014, GWU Online: http://goo.gl/xcB1IC.

80 David Kaiser, *American Tragedy: Kennedy, Johnson, and the Origins of the Vietnam War* (Cambridge, MA: Harvard University Press, 2000), 262.

81 For a relevant example of counterfactual reasoning on the Kennedy administration, see James G. Blight et al., *Virtual JFK: Vietnam If Kennedy Had Lived* (New York: Rowman & Littlefield, 2009).

Chapter 7

1 For a detailed analysis of Johnson's decision-making style, his search for consensus, and the way it influenced the JCS recommendations to him, see especially McMaster, *Dereliction of Duty*; Logevall, *Choosing War*; Robert Dallek, "Lyndon Johnson and Vietnam: The Making of a Tragedy," *Diplomatic History* 20:2 (April 1996): 147–162; Berman, *Planning a Tragedy*; George C. Herring, *LBJ and Vietnam: A Different Kind of War* (Austin: University of Texas, 1996).

2 David C. Humphrey, "Tuesday Lunch at the Johnson White House: A Preliminary Assessment," *Diplomatic History* 8:1 (Winter 1984): 83.

3 George Herring in his seminal book on Vietnam, for instance, wrote: "The extent to which Kennedy was committed to withdrawal remains quite unclear, and there is not a shred of evidence to support the notion of a secret plan for extrication." George C. Herring, *America's Longest War: The United States and Vietnam*, 4th edn. (New York: McGraw-Hill, 2002), 114.

4 In Retrospect first draft, Folder: In Retrospect Drafts and Notes, 1993–1994, Box II:100, RSM Papers, LoC.

5 VanDeMark, *Into the Quagmire*, 7.

6 Larry Berman, *Planning a Tragedy: The Americanization of the War in Vietnam* (New York: W. W. Norton, 1984), 30.

7 *Pentagon Papers*, Part IV.B.4, p. 42.

8 MC LBJ Presidential Recordings: President Johnson and McNamara, February 25, 1964, WH 6402.21, Conversation 2191.

9 *Pentagon Papers*, IV B.4.

10 Sorensen to President Johnson, January 14, 1964, Folder: Vietnam, 10/2/63–1/14/64, Subject Files 1961–64, Box 55, Sorensen Papers, JFKL.

11 "Last Will and Testament: South Viet-Nam and Southeast Asia," Hilsman to Rusk, March 10, 1964, Folder: Chronological File – 1/64–3/64, Memoranda of Conversations, Box 6, Hilsman Papers, JFKL.

12 Lien Hang Nguyen, *Hanoi's War: An International History of the War for Peace in Vietnam* (Chapel Hill: University of North Carolina Press, 2012), 63–65; Ang Cheng Guan, "The Vietnam War, 1962–64: The Vietnamese Communist Perspective," *Journal of Contemporary History* 35:4 (October 2000): 612.

13 William Colby and Ellen Hammer, in particular, have emphasized Diem's leadership qualities as a nationalist leader who, if the United States had continued to support him, could have provided the stability and unity that was needed to "win" in South Vietnam. Ellen J. Hammer, *A Death in November: American in Vietnam, 1963* (Oxford: Oxford University Press, 1988); William C. Colby and James McCargar, *Lost Victory: A Firsthand Account of America's Sixteen-Year Involvement in Vietnam* (Chicago, IL: Contemporary Books, 1989), chapter 10 especially. For a discussion on more recent scholarship, see also Gary R. Hess et al., "Jessica Chapman, *Cauldron of Resistance*: Ngo Dinh Diem, the United States, and 1950s Southern Vietnam," *H-Diplo Roundtable Review* 15:12 (November 2013).

14 Colby, *Lost Victory*, 161.

15 "Vietnam Situation," McNamara to President Johnson, December 21, 1963. *Pentagon Papers*, Gravel edn., vol. 4: 494–496.

16 McNamara handwritten notes, December 22, 1963, Folder: South Vietnam trip, Box 63, RG200, RSM Records, Defense Programs and Operations, NARA.

17 Highlights of Discussions in Saigon, December 18–20, 1963, Folder: South Vietnam trip, Box 63, RG200, RSM Records, Defense Programs and Operations, NARA.

18 Transcript NSC meeting, October 3, 1963: Tape 144/A49, Cassette 2/3, Folder: Fog of War, background and research materials, Box II:114, RSM Papers, LoC.

19 Ibid.

20 Wilson (MAAG) to Harkins (MACV), October 17, 1963, Folder: October 1963, Box 16, Newman Papers, Research Materials, JFKL.

21 "Interview with the President, Hyannis Port, Massachusetts on CBS," September 2, 1963, *FRUS, Vietnam August–December 1963*, vol. 4, doc. 50.

22 Transcript, NSC meeting, October 3, 1963: Tape 144/A49, Cassette 2/3, Folder: Fog of War, background and research materials, Box II:114, RSM Papers, LoC.

23 This is not to say that this was a position shared by the entire administration. The sentence continues with: "It is also clear however that the elements of his position that a) the loss of SVN might not result in the loss of all SEA and the credibility of US guarantees elsewhere or b) if it would, after a reasonable effort, we could not be accused of preventing it at reasonable cost, had ever been explicitly countered and debated at the highest levels of government.

Even today, among the serving senior members of the Kennedy administration, I believe that there are strong differences of opinion on many of these events." McNamara handwritten notes for "In Retrospect," Folder: 1993, Box II:100, RSM Papers, LoC.

24 Logevall, *Choosing War*, 98.

25 Berman, *Planning a Tragedy*, 4.

26 VanDeMark Interview of Robert S. McNamara, September 10, 1993, Folder: In Retrospect First Draft, Ch. 5–8, Box II:100, RSM Papers, LoC.

27 MC LBJ Presidential Recordings: President Johnson and McNamara, March 2, 1964, WH 6403.01, Conversation 2301.

28 Logevall, *Choosing War*, 79.

29 Interview between Brian VanDeMark and Adam Yarmolinsky, April 1, 1993, Folder: Yarmolinsky 1993, Box II:104, RSM Papers, LoC.

30 MC LBJ Presidential Recordings: President Johnson and McNamara, January 6, 1964, WH 6401.06, Conversation 1195, and August 1, 1964, WH 6408.01, Conversation 4601.

31 Shapley, *Promise and Power*, 278–279.

32 McNamara and VanDeMark, *In Retrospect*, 98.

33 MC LBJ Presidential Recordings: President Johnson and McNamara, April 9, 1964, WH 6404.06, Conversation 2961.

34 MC LBJ Presidential Recordings: President Johnson and McNamara, April 27, 1964: WH6404.13, Conversation 3140.

35 MC LBJ Presidential Recordings: President Johnson and McNamara, March 21, 1964, WH 6403.13, Conversation 2584.

36 MC LBJ Presidential Recordings: President Johnson and McNamara, September 24, 1964: WH 6409.15, Conversation 5686.

37 CIA Director McCone's notes from the meeting chime with McNamara's on this meeting. Quoting Johnson, he wrote, "All too often when we engaged in the affairs of a foreign country we wanted to immediately transform that country into our image, and this, in [Johnson's] opinion was a mistake ... was anxious to get along, win the war – he didn't want as much effort placed on social reforms." Shapley. *Promise and Power*, 292. See also Logevall, *Choosing War*, 89.

38 McNamara and VanDeMark, *In Retrospect*, 102.

39 CBS, November 24, 1963. Retrieved November 24, 2013, online live coverage of President Kennedy's assassination on 50th anniversary: http://tinyurl.com/qg49yjp.

40 President Johnson to Taylor, December 2, 1963, Folder: December 1963 1–5, Box 17, Newman Papers, Research Materials, JFKL.

41 McNamara to Ambassador Lodge, US Embassy, Saigon, December 12, 1963, Folder: December 1963 9–16, Box 18, Newman Papers, Research Materials, JFKL.

42 Logevall, *Choosing War*, 91.

43 Ibid., 89.

44 "Report of the McNamara–Taylor Mission to South Vietnam, 24 September–1 October 1963," Folder: Viet Nam McNamara–Taylor report, 10/1/63, Memoranda of Conversations, Box 4, Hilsman Papers, JFKL.

45 MC LBJ Presidential Recordings: President Johnson and McNamara, February 25, 1964, WH 6402.21, Conversation 2191.

46 There is a debate about whether Johnson went on a limb here as John Newman contends (Newman, *JFK and Vietnam*, 89–92) or if he was "obviously acting on instructions" as the *Pentagon Papers* say (*Pentagon Papers*, Gravel edn., vol. 2, chapter 1, p. 9).

47 Paper prepared by the Vice President, undated, *FRUS, Vietnam 1961*, vol. 1, doc. 59.

48 Report by the Vice President, undated, *FRUS, Vietnam 1961*, vol. 1, doc. 60.

49 "Vietnam Situation," McNamara to President Johnson, December 21, 1963. *Pentagon Papers*, Gravel edn., vol. 4: 494–496.

50 McNamara to President Johnson, March 16, 1964, *FRUS, Vietnam 1964*, vol. 1, doc. 84.

51 "South Vietnam," McNamara to President Johnson, March 16, 1964. *Pentagon Papers*, Gravel edn., vol. 3: 496–499.

52 Ormsby-Gore to Caccia, March 6, 1964, PM's correspondence, PREM 11/4759, UK National Archives, Kew.

53 MC LBJ Presidential Recordings: President Johnson and McNamara, March 2, 1964, WH 6403.01, Conversation 2301.

54 McNamara handwritten trip notes, December 19, 1963 Saigon, Folder: 12/19–12/20 SVN Visit, Box 63, RG200, RSM Records, Defense Programs and Operations, NARA.

55 Rostow to Sullivan, February 26, 1964, Folder: SVN Feb–March 1964, Box 64, RG200, RSM Records, Defense Programs and Operations, NARA; William Bundy to Rostow, April 6, 1964, Folder: SVN Feb–March 1964, Box 64, RG200, RSM Records, Defense Programs and Operations, NARA.

56 McNamara handwritten notes on White House paper, February 1964, Folder: Questions and Schedule March 1964 Trip to Vietnam, Box 62, RG200, RSM Records, Defense Programs and Operations, NARA.

57 McNamara-annotated copy of "History of Air Force Involvement in South Vietnam," Folder: Vietnam Book May 1964, Box 62, RG200, RSM Records, Defense Programs and Operations, NARA.

58 Draft report, March 6, 1964, Folder: McNamara Notes Vietnam, Box 64, RG200, RSM Records, Defense Programs and Operations, NARA.

59 McNaughton handwritten notes, undated, Folder: Questions and Schedule March 1964 Trip to Vietnam, Box 62, RG200, RSM Records, Defense Programs and Operations, NARA.

60 McNamara instructions to trip, Folder: Instructions re 3/64 Mission, Box 62, RG200, RSM Records, Defense Programs and Operations, NARA.

61 MC LBJ Presidential Recordings: President Johnson and McNamara, March 2, 1964, WH6403.01, Conversation 2301.

62 RGK Thompson to McNamara, March 12, 1964, Folder: Misc. Reports – Vietnam Trip – March 1964, Box 63, RG200, RSM Records, Defense Programs and Operations, NARA.

63 McNaughton-annotated Memorandum for the President, March 5, 1964, Folder: SVN Feb–March 1964, Box 64, RG200, RSM Records, Defense Programs and Operations, NARA.

64 William C. Gibbons, *The US Government and the Vietnam War: Executive and Legislative Roles and Relationships, Part II* (Princeton, NJ: Princeton University Press, 1986), 244.

65 See also Shapley, *Promise and Power*, 298.

66 Logevall, *Choosing War*, 83; Kaiser, *American Tragedy*, 306.

67 "Vietnamese Situation," Mansfield to President Johnson, January 6, 1964, Folder: Vietnam, 10/2/63–1/14/64, Subject Files 1961–64: Box 55, Sorensen Papers, JFKL.

68 Ted Sell, "Rusk Sees Viet Victory Possible," *Washington Post* (March 4, 1964); Undated notes, Folder: SVN: McNamara Statements and Supporting Papers 1961–65, Box 61, RG200, RSM Records, Defense Programs and Operations, NARA.

69 Sullivan to Thompson, March 23, 1964, *FRUS, Vietnam 1964*, vol. 1, doc. 95.

70 "United States Policy in Vietnam," McNamara, March 26, 1964, Department of State Bulletin, April 13, 1964, *The Pentagon Papers*, Gravel edn., vol. 3: 712–715.

71 Gibbons, *The US Government and the Vietnam War, Part II*, 244.

72 MC LBJ Presidential Recordings: President Johnson and McNamara, March 21, 1964, WH 6403.13, Conversation 2584.

73 MC LBJ Presidential Recordings: President Johnson and McNamara, January 6, 1964, WH 6401.06, Conversation 1195.

74 Robert A. Caro, *The Years of Lyndon Johnson: The Passage of Power* (New York: Vintage Books, 2012), 413.

75 In a further indication of the animosity some of Kennedy's closest advisors felt toward Johnson almost immediately, he explained his decision to stay and help with Johnson's first State of the Union by saying: "I wanted to help commit LBJ to carrying on Kennedy's program for 1964, and Kennedy's legacy for the ages; and I wanted him to invoke these policies and words specifically as well as the late President's name." Ibid.

76 Preston, "The Soft Hawks' Dilemma in Vietnam"; Bird, *The Color of Truth*, 278–280.

77 Roger Hilsman Oral History Interview No. 1 by Paige E. Mulhollan, May 15, 1969, LBJL.

78 Rowland Evans and Robert Novak, "Inside Report: Intellectuals' War Criticism Roils Rusk," *Milwaukee Sentinel* (October 13, 1967): 9.

79 Maxwell Taylor Oral History Interview No. 1 by Elspeth Rostow, Robert F. Kennedy OH Collection, October 22, 1969, JFKL.

80 Roger Hilsman, "Vietnam: The Decisions to Intervene," in Jonathan R. Adelman, ed., *Superpowers and Revolution* (New York: Praeger, 1986).

81 "Hilsman Resigns Key Policy Post: US Advisor on Far East Plans Academic Career," *New York Times* (February 25, 1964): 1.

82 "Last Will and Testament: South Viet-Nam and Southeast Asia," Hilsman to Secretary of State Rusk, March 10, 1964, Folder: Chronological File – 1/64–3/64, Memoranda of Conversations, Box 6, Hilsman Papers, JFKL.

83 Busch, *All the Way with JFK*, 169–170.

84 Robert Thompson, *No Exit from Vietnam* (New York: David McKay, 1969), 29.
85 MC LBJ Presidential Recordings: President Johnson and McNamara, March 31, 65 WH6503.16, Conversation 7194.
86 Kelly, *US Army Special Forces*, 48.
87 See also Marilyn Young, *The Vietnam Wars: 1945–1990* (New York: Harper Collins, 1991); Francis Bator, "No Good Choices: LBJ and the Vietnam/Great Society Connection," *Diplomatic History* (June 2008): 309–340.
88 MC LBJ Presidential Recordings: President Johnson and McNamara, December 10, 1963, K6312.06.
89 Caro, *The Passage of Power*, 397.
90 Harris, *Economics of the Kennedy Years*, 234.
91 C. Douglas Dillon Oral History Interview by Paige E. Mulhollan, June 29, 1969, LBJL, p. 7.
92 Ibid., p. 14.
93 Report on the Balance of Payments to President Johnson, December 2, 1963, Folder: 2 of 2, November–December 1963, Box 35, Dillon Papers, JFKL.
94 On November 25, 1963, in a meeting with his top economic aides, the new President made clear that he wanted to reduce federal expenditures to around $100 billion. As the official OSD history notes, "Had he lived, Kennedy probably would have done the same. Treasury Secretary Douglas Dillon had reached an understanding with Kennedy that the budget would be under $100 billion, although Dillon thought that $99.5 billion was as low as it could go." On January 21, 1964, in his budget message to Congress, Johnson was able to announce planned federal expenditures for $97.9 billion for FY65. Kaplan et al., *The McNamara Ascendancy*, 479–481. See also Caro, *The Passage of Power*, 393–397.
95 C. Douglas Dillon Oral History Interview by Paige E. Mulhollan, June 29, 1969, LBJL, p. 10.
96 MC LBJ Presidential Recordings: President Johnson and McNamara, December 7, 1963, K6312.05. Congressional passage on the Defense Department's FY65 budget, coming in an election year, was particularly acrimonious with Democrats seeking to cut defense spending further and Republicans leveling a similar charge that Kennedy had against Eisenhower, namely that the administration was putting fiscal concerns ahead of national security. On this, see Kaplan et al., *The McNamara Ascendancy*, 487–489.
97 Harris, *Economics of the Kennedy Years*, 234.
98 James Reston in the *New York Times*, quoted in Kaiser, *American Tragedy*, 284.
99 Going against his CEA's Keynesian economic advice, Dillon recalled that Kennedy feared the inflationary pressures that might come with a tax cut and increased expenditures and that defense expenditures, which had formed the bulk of federal expenditure rises in the Kennedy administration, were due to level off by FY64 and then reduce moving into FY65. C. Douglas Dillon Oral History Interview No. 7 by Harvey Brazer, September 22, 1964, JFKL;

Kaplan et al., *The McNamara Ascendancy*, 460; Edward J. Drea, *McNamara, Clifford and the Burdens of Vietnam: 1965–1969* (Washington, DC: Historical Office OSD, 2011), 2.

100 McNamara and VanDeMark, *In Retrospect*, 56.

101 OSD OH, April 29, 1994, p. 17, Folder: OSD OH 1993–1998, Box II:118, RSM Papers, LOC; David G. Nes Oral History Interview by Ted Gittinger, November 10, 1982, LBJL, p. 8.

102 McNamara handwritten trip notes, May 14, 1964, Folder: Report to Pres 5/14/64–SVN 5/12/64, Box 63, RG200, RSM Records, Defense Programs and Operations, NARA.

103 MC LBJ Presidential Recordings: President Johnson and McNamara, April 30, 1964, 3220.

104 Carl Vinson to McNamara, May 13, 1964, Folder: Vietnam Book May 1964, Box 62, RG200, RSM Records, Defense Programs and Operations, NARA.

105 On Lodge as a political threat to Johnson and his campaign, see especially Anne E. Blair, *Lodge in Vietnam: A Patriot Abroad* (New Haven, CT, Yale University Press, 1995); Eugene Vasilew, "The New Style in Political Campaigns: Lodge in New Hampshire, 1964," *Review of Politics* 30:2 (April 1968): 131–152.

106 President Johnson press conference, February 28, 1964, Folder: SVN Feb–March 1964, Box 64, RG200, RSM Records, Defense Programs and Operations, NARA.

107 Undated notes, Folder: SVN: McNamara Statements and Supporting Papers 1961–65, Box 61, RG200, RSM Records, Defense Programs and Operations, NARA.

108 MC LBJ Presidential Recordings: President Johnson and McNamara, April 30, 1964. WH 6404.16, Conversation 3220. This is a recurring theme in the tapes. For instance, on the eve of the decision to send Marine forces to Da Nang, Johnson told McNamara to involve General Wheeler and the Joint Chiefs of Staff, adding, "I believe we haven't had enough of them and I'm worried that they're going to feel left out." MC LBJ Presidential Recordings: President Johnson and McNamara, February 26, 1965, WH 6502.06, Conversation 6887.

109 Robert Caro, in particular, has made a significant contribution to understanding Johnson's views on masculinity and how this contributed to him favoring "strong" positions on Vietnam but also during the Cuban Missile Crisis. During the Cuban Missile Crisis and throughout his career, Johnson regularly criticized President Kennedy specifically for his "weakness." In one particularly harsh line from their senator days, Caro quotes Johnson as describing Kennedy as "weak and pallid – a scrawny man with a bad back, a weak and indecisive politician, a nice man, a gentle man, but not a man's man." Caro, *The Passage of Power*, 33. See also Robert D. Dean, *Imperial Brotherhood: Gender and the Making of Cold War Policy* (Amherst: University of Massachusetts Press, 2002).

110 In a tape dated September 8, 1964, President Johnson quipped, "If there are any bigger fools than damn military men, I don't know who." MC LBJ

Presidential Recordings: President Johnson and McNamara, September 8, 1964, WH 6409.08, Conversation 5533.

111 As early as February 1964, Johnson was considering "send[ing] the Marines in there" and suggested that McNamara bring David Shoup, the Commander of the Marine Corps, with him to Vietnam and to the hearings in front of the Senate Foreign Relations Committee. He indicated that this would have value "from a psychological standpoint and from a political standpoint," that Shoup was "worth a dozen Averell Harrimans." MC LBJ Presidential Recordings: President Johnson and McNamara February 25, 1964, WH 6402.21, Conversation 2191.

112 MC LBJ Presidential Recordings: President Johnson and McNamara, April 30, 1964: WH640.4.16, Conversation 3220.

113 Galbraith to President Kennedy, May 31, 1962. Galbraith, *Letters to Kennedy*, 48.

114 Draft memorandum DOD to President, May 24, 1964, *FRUS, Vietnam 1964*, vol. 1, doc. 171.

115 Summary Record of NSC Executive Committee Meeting, May 24, 1964, *FRUS, Vietnam 1964*, vol. 1, doc. 172.

116 McGeorge Bundy to President Johnson, May 26, 1964. *FRUS, Vietnam 1964*, vol. 1, doc. 179.

117 Summary Record of NSC Executive Committee Meeting, May 24, 1964, *FRUS, Vietnam 1964*, vol. 1, doc. 172.

118 MC LBJ Presidential Recordings: President Johnson and McNamara, June 9, 1964, WH 6406.04, Conversation 3663.

119 Shapley, *Promise and Power*, 300.

120 McNamara handwritten trip notes, Folder: Questions and Schedule March 1964 Trip to Vietnam, Box 62, RG200, RSM Records, Defense Programs and Operations, NARA.

121 Lodge to President Johnson, May 14, 1964, Folder: RSM Trip Notes SVN 5/12/64, Box 63, RG200, RSM Records, Defense Programs and Operations, NARA.

122 Ellsberg, *Secrets*, 17.

123 MC LBJ Presidential Recordings: President Johnson and McNamara, June 18, 1964, WH 6406.10, Conversation 3767.

124 Ball Telcon with McNamara, August 3, 1964, Folder: Vietnam 1, Box 7, George Ball Papers, LBJL.

125 MC LBJ Presidential Recordings: President Johnson and McNamara, August 3, 1964, WH6408.03, Conversation 4633.

126 Ellsberg, *Secrets*, 9–10.

127 Summary Notes of the 538th Meeting of the NSC, August 4, 1964 *FRUS, Vietnam 1964*, vol. 1, doc. 278.

128 President Lyndon B. Johnson statement of the Gulf of Tonkin Incident, August 4, 1964. Retrieved online, May 13, 2018, US Embassy to Germany: goo.gl/vubZuM.

129 Text of Joint Resolution (the Tonkin Gulf Resolution), August 7, 1964, Department of State Bulletin, August 24, 1964. Retrieved online, May 13, 2018, American Presidency Project: https://bit.ly/2jTr3NZ.

130 Memorandum for the Record of a Meeting, Cabinet Room, White House, August 10, 1964, *FRUS, Vietnam 1964*, vol. 1, doc. 307.

131 "III: The Broad Options," Draft Paper by William Bundy, November 7, 1964, *Pentagon Papers*, Gravel edn., vol. 3: 604–606.

132 McNamara notes "issues raised by papers on SEA," November 24, 1964, Folder: SVN – Memo to Pres Dec '64, Box 63, RG200, RSM Records, Defense Programs and Operations, NARA.

133 Ibid.

134 McMaster, *Dereliction of Duty*, 183.

135 "Future US Actions in RVN," Westmoreland to Wheeler, November 27, 1964, Folder: SVN – Memo to Pres Dec '64, Box 63, RG200, RSM Records, Defense Programs and Operations, NARA; Draft instructions from President Johnson to Ambassador Taylor, November 30, 1964, Folder: SVN – Memo to Pres Dec '64, Box 63, RG200, RSM Records, Defense Programs and Operations, NARA.

136 "Bus re: JCS mtg," McNamara handwritten notes, November 1, 1964, Folder: SVN – Memo to Pres Dec '64, Box 63, RG200, RSM Records, Defense Programs and Operations, NARA.

137 Ibid.

138 Kinney WG VN to Thomson WH, November 9, 1964, Folder: Pol 1–2, Basic Policies 1964, Box 5, RG59 Vietnam Working Group, NARA.

Chapter 8

1 MC LBJ Presidential Recordings: President Johnson and McNamara, August 6, 1964, WH6408.08, Conversation 4773.

2 Daniel Ellsberg, phone interview by author, January 11, 2013.

3 MC LBJ Presidential Recordings: President Johnson and McNamara, March 1, 1965, WH6503.01, Conversation 7002.

4 Robert McNamara Oral History Interview 1 by the Secretary of Defense Historical Office, April 23, 1986, Folder: OH 1 for OSD, Box I:109, RSM Papers, LoC.

5 "Basic Policy in Vietnam," McGeorge Bundy to President Johnson, January 27, 1965, Folder: SVN: McNamara Statements and Supporting Papers 1961–65, Box 61, RG200, RSM Records, Defense Programs and Operations, NARA.

6 McGeorge Bundy to President Johnson, January 4, 1965, *FRUS, Vietnam January–June 1965*, vol. 1, doc. 2.

7 Telcon Dillon with McGeorge Bundy, January 27, 1965, Folder: 1 of 3, Jan. 65, Box 40, Telcon Series, Dillon Papers, JFKL.

8 Dillon to Bill Moyers, February 1, 1965, Folder: 1042, Box 35, Dillon Papers, JFKL.

9 Telcon Dillon with Gardner Ackley, February 4, 1965, Folder: Jan–March 65, 2 of 3, Box 40, Telcon Series, Dillon Papers, JFKL.

10 President Johnson, "Special Message to the Congress on International Balance of Payments," February 10, 1965. Retrieved online May 13, 2018, American Presidency Project: www.presidency.ucsb.edu/ws/index.php?pid=27352.

11 McNamara, "Remarks to Bankers at the White House" (speech, Washington, DC, February 15, 1965), Folder: Balance of Payments February 1965, Box 60, RG200, RSM Records, Defense Programs and Operations, NARA.

12 McNaughton to McNamara, February 7, 1965, Folder: In Retrospect Material Jan–April 1965, Box II:81, RSM Papers, LoC.

13 Kenneth H. Williams, ed., *LeMay on Vietnam* (Washington, DC: Air Force History and Museums Program, 2017), 16.

14 Dillon Memcon, January 27, 1965, Folder: 1 of 3, Box 40, Dillon Papers, JFKL.

15 McMaster, *Dereliction of Duty*, 256–257.

16 Ibid., 223.

17 McNamara to Service Secretaries, March 1, 1965, quoted in General Leonard B. Taylor, *Financial Management of the Vietnam Conflict, 1962–1972* (Washington, DC: Department of the 1974), preface. Retrieved online December 16, 2014, US Army Center of Military History: http://tinyurl.com/kmkcqzc.

18 Anthony S. Campagna, *The Economic Consequences of the Vietnam War* (New York: Praeger, 1991), 32.

19 Richard M. Miller, *Funding Extended Conflicts: Korea, Vietnam and the War on Terror* (Westport, CT: Greenwood Publishing Group, 2007), 45.

20 McNamara began this manipulation in the last month of the Kennedy administration. Campagna, *The Economic Consequences of the Vietnam War*, 32.

21 Morton H. Halperin, "The Decision to Deploy the ABM: Bureaucratic and Domestic Politics in the Johnson Administration," *World Politics* 25:1 (October 1972): 64.

22 MC LBJ Presidential Recordings: President Johnson and McNamara, March 30, 1965, WH 6503.15, Conversation 7182.

23 MC LBJ Presidential Recordings: President Johnson and McNamara, February 26, 1965, WH6502.06 Conversation 6887.

24 Minutes of a meeting in the Cabinet room, July 21, 1965, Folder: In Retrospect, 1965 July 1–29, Box II:92, RSM papers, LoC.

25 McGeorge Bundy to McNamara, June 30, 1965, *FRUS, Vietnam June–December 1965*, vol. 3, doc. 35.

26 McGeorge Bundy also received a copy, although he was not the document's intended recipient. McNaughton to McNamara, "Proposed Course of Action re: Vietnam," March 24, 1965, *Pentagon Papers*, Gravel edn., vol. 3: 694–702.

27 Memorandum for the Record, April 21, 1965, *FRUS, Vietnam January–June 1965*, vol. 2, doc. 266.

28 Trip notes and draft reports, Folder: Vietnam Hawai Meeting 4-6-65 PT A-J, Box 61, RG 200, RSM Records, Defense Programs and Operations, NARA.

29 McNamara to President Johnson, April 21, 1965, Folder: SVN: McNamara Statements and Supporting Papers 1961–65, Box 61, RG200, RSM Records, Defense Programs and Operations, NARA.

30 Minutes of a Meeting in the President's Office, May 16, 1965, Folder: In Retrospect Background, 1965 May, Box II:9, RSM papers, LoC.

31 SFRC hearings notes, March 11, 1965, Folder: Misc. Secret, Box 37, RG200, RSM Records, Defense Programs and Operations, NARA.

32 Drea, *McNamara, Clifford and the Burdens of Vietnam*, 29.

33 Ibid., 27.

34 Ibid., 32.

35 MC LBJ Presidential Recordings: President Johnson and McNamara, March 6, 1965. WH 6503.03, Conversation 7028.

36 Robert S. McNamara Oral History Interview by Walt W. Rostow for the LBJL Oral History Collection, January 8, 1975, Folder: Oral History for the Johnson Library, Box I:110, RSM papers, LoC.

37 John T. McNaughton diary, May 30, 1966.

38 "Program of Expanded Military and Political Moves with Respect to Vietnam," McNamara to President Johnson, June 26/July 1, 1965 draft, Folder: 7/65 SVN Trips and Memos – Misc Papers, Box 61, RG200, RSM Records, Defense Programs and Operations, NARA.

39 McGeorge Bundy response to McNamara report, June 30, 1965, Folder: 7/65 SVN Trips and Memos – Misc Papers, Box 61, RG 200, RSM Records, Defense Programs and Operations, NARA.

40 Enthoven, *How Much Is Enough?*, 270–275.

41 McNamara notes on "Program of Expanded Military and Political Moves with Respect to Vietnam," McNamara to President Johnson, June 26/July 1, 1965 draft, Folder: 7/65 SVN Trips and Memos – Misc Papers, Box 61, RG200, RSM Records, Defense Programs and Operations, NARA.

42 Jack Shulimson and Major Charles M. Johnson, *US Marines in Vietnam: The Landing and Buildup 1965* (Washington, DC: USMC History and Museums Division, 1978), 26.

43 Memorandum for the Record, July 21, 1965, Folder: In Retrospect July 1965, Box II:92, RSM papers, LoC.

44 "Why We Are in Vietnam," President Johnson press conference, July 28, 1965. Retrieved online May 13, 2016, American Presidency Project: www.presidency.ucsb.edu/ws/?pid=27116.

45 McNamara to Senator John C. Stennis, July 15, 1965, Folder: In Retrospect July 1965, Box II:92, RSM papers, LoC.

46 Drea, *McNamara, Clifford and the Burdens of Vietnam*, 38.

47 Robert S. McNamara Oral History Interview by Walt W. Rostow for the LBJL Oral History Collection, January 8, 1975, Folder: Oral History for the Johnson Library, Box I:110, RSM papers, LoC.

48 Memorandum for the Record, July 21, 1965, Folder: In Retrospect July 1965, Box II:92, RSM papers, LoC.

49 NSC meeting minutes, July 27, 1965, Folder: In Retrospect July 1965, Box II:92, RSM papers, LoC.

50 Memorandum for the Record, Minutes of an NSC/JCS meeting on Vietnam, July 21, 1965, Folder: In Retrospect July 1965, Box II:92, RSM papers, LoC.

51 Walter Isaacson and Evan Thomas, *The Wise Men: Six Friends and the World They Made* (New York: Simon & Schuster, 1997), 651–652.

52 Minutes of a meeting in the Cabinet room, July 21, 1965, Folder: In Retrospect, 1965 July 1–29, Box II:92, RSM papers, LoC.

53 "Comment on Mr. McNaughton's Draft of July 18, 1965," Lodge to McNamara, July 19, 1965, Folder: Vietnam Hawai Meeting 4-6-65 PT A-J, Box 61, RG 200, RSM Records, Defense Programs and Operations, NARA.

54 U. Alexis Johnson to McNaughton, July 19, 1965, Folder: Vietnam Hawai Meeting 4-6-65 PT A-J, Box 61, RG 200, RSM Records, Defense Programs and Operations, NARA.

55 Minutes of a meeting in the Cabinet room, July 21, 1965, Folder: In Retrospect, 1965 July 1–29, Box II:92, RSM papers, LoC.

56 McNamara to President Johnson, August 2, 1965, Folder: McNamara Statements and Supporting Papers 1961–65, Box 61, RG200, RSM Records, Defense Programs and Operations, NARA.

57 Campagna, *The Economic Consequences of the Vietnam War*, 34–38.

58 McNamara to President elect Kennedy, December 12, 1960, Folder: Secretary of Defense letter of acceptance, 1960, Box II:46, RSM Papers, LoC.

59 McNamara handwritten notes, October 7, 1965, Folder: Post-Defense, Box I:89, RSM papers, LoC.

60 John T. McNaughton diary, November 24, 1966.

61 Brock Brower, "Robert S. McNamara Interview," *Life Magazine* (May 10, 1968), Folder: Interview, Misc., Box I:108, RSM papers, LoC.

62 McNamara and VanDeMark, *In Retrospect*, 216–218.

63 John T. McNaughton diary, April 1, 1966. See also Hendrickson, *The Living and the Dead*.

64 December 2, 1965, presidential recording transcript, Folder: The Fog of War Background and research material, Presidential tapes transcripts, 1963–1965, Box II:114, RSM papers, LoC.

65 "Roger Hilsman's Crimes," McGeorge Bundy to President Johnson, September 30, 1965. Retrieved online November 2, 2014, Texas Tech University Center and Archive: http://tinyurl.com/n2ldfk4.

66 Hilsman to Yarmolinsky, November 18, 1965, Folder: Correspondence 1965, Box 66, Yarmolinsky Papers, JFKL.

67 At the time, Fall criticized the "desultory military effects" of bombing and supported a longer bombing pause. He had ominously added, "You can't let South Vietnamese weakness lead you into a large-scale war or a disaster; their threat to collapse on you if you talk to the North Vietnamese is phony and not real; either they are real and can stand negotiations; or they will collapse anyway." Johnson report to VN Working Group, June 8, 1965, Folder: POL 1 Memoranda of Conversations 1965, Box 8, RG59 Vietnam Working Group, NARA; Lewis Sorley, "To Change a War: General Harold K. Johnson and the PROVN Study," *Parameters* (Spring 1998): 93–109.

68 Yarmolinsky to Hilsman, Folder: Correspondence 1965, November 13, 1965, Box 66, Yarmolinsky Papers, JFKL.

69 John T. McNaughton diary, January 8, 1966.

70 Herring, *LBJ and Vietnam*, 93–94.

71 Notes of a meeting, December 18, 1965, *FRUS, Vietnam June–December 1965*, vol. 2, doc. 235.

72 John T. McNaughton diary, January 4, 1966.

73 Minutes of a meeting in Cabinet Room, December 18, 1965, Folder: In Retrospect July–December 1965, Box II:92, RSM papers, LoC.

74 Minutes of a meeting, December 17, 1965, Folder: In Retrospect July–December 1965, Box II:92, RSM papers, LoC.

75 After secret conversations with Richard Russell, Martin became alarmed at the administration's attempts to mislead him and the public about the costs of Vietnam. This precipitated his decision to raise interest rates over Johnson's pressure. Helen Fessenden, "1965: The Year the Fed and LBJ Clashed," *Econ Focus: Richmond Federal Reserve* (2016): 6.

76 Drea, *McNamara, Clifford and the Burdens of Vietnam*, 67.

77 McGeorge Bundy was McNaughton's former neighbor on Berkeley Street in Cambridge during their shared time at Harvard and shared the anecdote "between old Berkeley Street buddies." John T. McNaughton diary, January 5 and 6, 1966.

78 Ibid.

79 John T. McNaughton diary, January 7, 1966; Minutes of a meeting, December 17, 1965, Folder: In Retrospect July–December 1965, Box II:92, RSM papers, LoC.

80 John T. McNaughton diary, January 7, 1966.

81 Quoted in Drea, *McNamara, Clifford and the Burdens of Vietnam*, 69.

82 Isaacson and Thomas, *The Wise Men*, 669–670.

83 John T. McNaughton diary, January 29, 1966.

84 See also Herring, *LBJ and Vietnam*, 11–13.

85 "Basic Policy in Vietnam," McGeorge Bundy to President Johnson, January 27, 1965, Folder: SVN: McNamara Statements and Supporting Papers 1961–65, Box 61, RG200, RSM Records, Defense Programs and Operations, NARA.

86 John T. McNaughton diary, January 6, 1966.

87 Drea, *McNamara, Clifford and the Burdens of Vietnam*, 538.

Chapter 9

1 Meeting with Robert S. McNamara and OSD Historical Office, April 29, 1994, Folder: OSD 1993–1998, Box II:118, RSM papers, LoC.

2 See Kevin V. Mulcahy, "Walt Rostow as National Security Advisor, 1966–1969," *Presidential Studies Quarterly* 25:2 (Spring 1995): 223–236. Mulcahy contests that the position was downgraded under Rostow.

3 John T. McNaughton diary, January 31, 1966.

4 Ibid., April 1, 1966.

5 Ibid., May 18, 1966.

6 Ibid., March 25, 1966.

7 Caro, *The Passage of Power*, xiii.

8 John T. McNaughton diary, February 11, 1966.

9 Ibid.

10 McNamara hearing notes, undated, Folder: Points in Support of FY 67 MAP, Box 53, RG200, RSM Records, Defense Programs and Operations, NARA.

11 Misc. notes, Folder: McNamara Statements re: Objectives in SVN 1965–66, Box 62, RG200, RSM Records, Defense Programs and Operations, NARA.

12 Secretary's calendar 1966, Folder: Calendar 1966, Box II:68, RSM papers, LoC.

13 Oral history interview 5, Edward M. Kennedy by James Sterling Young, June 17, 2005, Edward M. Kennedy Oral History Project, p. 10–11. Retrieved online November 24, 2015, MC: http://goo.gl/Ww3xvi.

14 MC LBJ Presidential Recordings: President Johnson and McNamara, May 7, 1966, WH WH 6605.01, Conversation 10106.

15 MC LBJ Presidential Recordings: President Johnson and Hubert Humphrey, March 2, 1966, WH 9813.

16 See also Robert Mann, *A Grand Delusion: America's Descent into Vietnam* (New York: Basic Books, 2001), 495–497.

17 John T. McNaughton diary, March 3, 1966.

18 Remarks on the Effect of Shortages on SEA Operations, Folder: Senate Committee hearings, Box 53, RG200, RSM Records, Defense Programs and Operations, NARA.

19 MC LBJ Presidential Recordings: President Johnson and McNamara, May 7, 1966 WH 6605.01.

20 Campagna, *Economic Consequences of the Vietnam War*, 21–22.

21 MC LBJ Presidential Recordings: President Johnson and McNamara, May 7, 1966, WH 6605.01, Conversation 10106.

22 John T. McNaughton diary, April 8, 1966.

23 Ibid., April 4, 1966.

24 Ibid., April 8, 1966.

25 Ibid., May 18, 1966.

26 "Foreign Assistance Act, 1966," Robert S. McNamara hearings in front of Senate Committee on Foreign Relations, April 6, 1966, p. 183. Hearing ID: HRG-1966-FOR-0009, US Congressional Hearings Digital Collection Historical Archive, 1824–2003.

27 Memcon Harriman and McNamara, May 30, 1966, Folder: Nov. '65–Nov. '66, Box II:92, RSM papers, LoC; John T. McNaughton diary, May 30, 1966.

28 McNaughton to McNamara, April 5, 1966, Folder: In Retrospect Declassified Documents 1963–1967, Box II:100, RSM papers, LoC.

29 John T. McNaughton diary, April 4, 1966.

30 Ibid., May 22, 1966.

31 McNaughton to McNamara, April 12, 1966, Folder: In Retrospect Declassified Documents 1963–1967, Box II:100, RSM papers, LoC. McNaughton also appended a memo to McNamara where he repeated an observation that he had made to him in private in January: "I referred to Kennedy's distinguishing of Cuba – where Soviet vital interests were not involved, where we had conventional supremacy, and where even they recognized that the equities favored us. In Vietnam, I told McNamara, all 3 are by no means clear – indeed, to me it seems that some of the three, in open minds, may tip the other way." John T. McNaughton diary, January 18, 1966. He now concluded that all three "equities" were not in fact in the United States' favor and it should therefore withdraw.

32 John T. McNaughton diary, February 4, 1966.

33 Report to Secretary of Defense McNamara, March 16, 66, Folder: Defense Department Memoranda, Papers and report 1965–1966, Box II:65, RSM papers, LoC; Herring, *LBJ and Vietnam*, 47.

34 Jacob Van Staaveren, *Gradual Failure: The Air War over North Vietnam* (Washington, DC: USAF History and Museums Program, 2002), 279–284.

35 "Proposal for Barrier System," Wheeler to McNamara, September 17, 1966, Folder: SVN trip October 1966, Box 62, RG200, RSM Records, Defense Programs and Operations, NARA; JCS papers, January 16, 1967, Folder: Prairie Fire 1964– , RG59 State Department Bureau of East Asian and Pacific Affairs Political Files, NARA.

36 John T. McNaughton diary, January 29, 1966.

37 Ibid., May 22, 1966.

38 Arthur J. Schlesinger, *Journals: 1952–2000* (New York: Penguin, 2008), 250.

39 John T. McNaughton diary, June 10, 1966.

40 Andrew Preston, "Mission Impossible: Canadian Secret Diplomacy and the Quest for Peace in Vietnam," in Lloyd C. Gardner and Ted Gettinger, eds., *The Search for Peace in Vietnam, 1964–1968* (College Station: Texas A&M University Press, 2004), 131.

41 McNamara to President Johnson, May 9, 1966, Folder: Nov. '65–Nov. '66, Box II:92, RSM papers, LoC.

42 John T. McNaughton diary, June 24, 1966.

43 Notes of President Johnson's Meeting with the NSC, June 22, 1966, *FRUS, Vietnam 1966*, vol. 4, doc. 161.

44 MC LBJ Presidential Recordings: President Johnson and McNamara, June 28, 1966, WH 10266.

45 *Pentagon Papers*, Part VI.A.

46 Although new research suggests it may have been divisions, more than intransigence, that scuttled negotiations on the North Vietnamese side. See, for instance, Nguyen, *Hanoi's War*, 78–79; James G. Hershberg, *Marigold: The Lost Chance for Peace in Vietnam* (Palo Alto, CA: Stanford University Press, 2012).

47 John T. McNaughton diary, June 24, 1966.

48 Jonathan Colman, "The 'Most Distinguished Envoy of Peace': Averell Harriman and the Vietnam War in the Johnson Years," *International History Review* (February 2015): 75.

49 Memcon Harriman and McNamara, August 2, 1966 Memcon, Folder: RSM, Box 486, Harriman Papers, LoC.

50 John T. McNaughton diary, July 1, 1966.

51 Ibid., September 1, 1966.

52 Record of a conversation with McGeorge Bundy, Ibid., January 25, 1966.

53 MC LBJ Presidential Recordings: President Johnson and McNamara, March 4, 1966, 9829.

54 MC LBJ Presidential Recordings: President Johnson and George Aiken, March 4, 1966, 9830.

55 McNamara handwritten notes, Folder: Senate Foreign Relations Committee 4-20-66, Box 53, RG200, RSM Records, Defense Programs and Operations, NARA.

56 Robert S. McNamara, "Security in the Contemporary World," Address before American Society of Newspaper Editors, Montreal, Canada, May 18, 1966, Folder: Montreal, Box 30, Yarmolinsky Papers, JFKL.

57 Ibid.

58 President Lyndon B. Johnson, "Remarks at a Democratic Party Dinner" (speech, Chicago, IL, May 17, 1966). Retrieved online November 2, 2014, American Presidency Project: http://tinyurl.com/kajp2ca.

59 Richard Neustadt to Institute of Politics Members, Faculty Associates and Fellows, undated (November 1966), Folder: RSM Visit, Box 53, Yarmolinsky Papers, JFKL.

60 "Full Committee Hearings on Review of the Administration and Operation of the Selective Service System," Edward M. Kennedy hearings in front of Senate Committee on Armed Services, June 1966. Hearing ID: HRG-1966-ASH-0025, US Congressional Hearings Digital Collection Historical Archive, 1824–2003.

61 EWK Oral History Interview 5, p. 15.

62 "The Real McNamara," *New Republic*, 154:23, Issue 2689 (June 4, 1966): 7.

63 Ambassador Dean to Foreign Office, May 22, 1966, PREM 13/1258, National Archives, Kew.

64 Hoopes to Yarmolinsky, May 20, 1966, Folder: Subject File: RSM speech, Box 31a, Yarmolinsky Papers, JFKL.

65 Ambassador Dean to Foreign Office, May 22, 1966, PREM 13/1258, National Archives, Kew.

66 John T. McNaughton diary, September 7, 1966.

67 McNamara handwritten trip notes, Folder: SVN Trip October 1966, Box 62, RG200, RSM Records, Defense Programs and Operations, NARA.

68 Gibbons, *US Government and the Vietnam War*, part IV: 458–460.

69 Ibid., 442.

70 President Johnson, "Manila Summit Conference Declaration" (October 25, 1966). Retrieved online May 10, 2018, American Presidency Project: www.presidency.ucsb.edu/ws/?pid=27958.

71 John T. McNaughton diary, November 13, 1966. Within days, however, Johnson backtracked when Nixon criticized him for timidity. The position of mutual withdrawal, Nixon said, "simply turns back the clock two years and says let the South Vietnamese fight it out with the Viet Cong" and would necessarily fail. Alex Mashburn, "Manila Communiqué: Nixon's Comeback," Retrieved online May 10, 2018, Richard M. Nixon Presidential Library: goo.gl/oYuAF7. Asked about Nixon's comments in a press conference at the White House, Johnson criticized the former Vice President as a "chronic campaigner" but added, "We have explained that we would pull out just as soon as the infiltration, the aggression, and the violence ceases. We made that statement and we set a time limit on it." In other words, he reinstated the "and." President Johnson, "The President's News Conference" (Washington, DC, November 4, 1966). Retrieved online May 10, 2018,

American Presidency Project: www.presidency.ucsb.edu/ws/index.php?pid=27990.

72 John T. McNaughton diary, March 12, 1967.
73 Clark Clifford and Richard Holbrooke, *Counsel to the President: A Memoir* (New York: Random House, 1991), 457.
74 John T. McNaughton diary, December 11, 1966.
75 Memcon Harriman and McNamara, November 26, 1966, Folder: RSM, Box 486, Harriman Papers, LoC; "The Air War in North Vietnam, 1965–1968," *Pentagon Papers*, Gravel edn., vol. 4: 112–169.
76 Drea, *McNamara, Clifford and the Burdens of Vietnam*, 213.
77 Herring, *LBJ and Vietnam*, 56–57.
78 Ibid.
79 John T. McNaughton diary, January 22, 1967.
80 Ibid., December 16, 1966.
81 Ibid., March 3, 1966.
82 Ibid., November 13, 1966.
83 Evan Thomas, *Robert Kennedy: His Life* (New York: Simon & Schuster, 2000), 250.
84 Memcon McNamara and McGeorge Bundy, December 1966, Folder: Offers and Proposals for Post-Defense Service 1967–1968, Box I:89, RSM papers, LoC.
85 Report on FBI investigations concerning McNamara, Folder: FBI Investigations, Box II:69, RSM papers, LoC.
86 Drea, *McNamara, Clifford and the Burdens of Vietnam*, 222.
87 Minutes of Tuesday lunch, August 8, 1967, Folder: 5, Box II:94, RSM papers, LoC.
88 Draft Memorandum McNamara to President Johnson, May 19, 1967, *FRUS, Vietnam 1967*, vol. 5, doc. 177.
89 "The Air War in North Vietnam, 1965–1968," *Pentagon Papers*, Gravel edn., vol. 4: 112–169.
90 Drea, *McNamara, Clifford and the Burdens of Vietnam*, 139.
91 Ibid., 156.
92 Draft Memorandum McNamara to President Johnson, May 19, 1967, *FRUS, Vietnam 1967*, vol. 5, doc. 177.
93 "Kennedy's Plan: Quit Bombing, Negotiate Now," *New York Herald Tribune*, European Edition (March 2, 1967). Retrieved online May 10, 2018: https://goo.gl/LZwEfN.
94 John T. McNaughton diary, February 12, 1967.
95 Notes of meeting, September 26, 1967, Folder: 5, Box II:94, RSM papers, LoC.
96 President Johnson, "Address on Vietnam before the National Legislative Conference" (San Antonio, TX, September 29, 1967). Retrieved online May 10, 2018, American Presidency Project: https://goo.gl/N7d3NB.
97 Minutes of a Tuesday lunch, August 8, 1967, Folder: 5, Box II:94, RSM papers, LoC.
98 See, especially, Robert K. Brigham and George C. Herring, "The Pennsylvania Initiative, June–October 1967," in Lloyd C. Gardner and Ted Gittinger, eds.,

The Search for Peace in Vietnam, 1964–1968 (College Station: Texas A&M University Press, 2004).

99 Henry Kissinger to Rusk, September 13, 1967, Folder: Pennsylvania Initiative, Box II:94, RSM papers, LoC.

100 Clifford, *Counsel to the President*, 457.

101 McNamara to President Johnson, November 1, 1967, Folder: 1, Box II:94, RSM papers, LoC.

102 Drea, *McNamara, Clifford and the Burdens of Vietnam*, 222.

103 McNamara interview by Paul Warnke, March 28, 1994, Folder: 8, Box II:104, RSM papers, LoC.

104 Ambassador Dean to Foreign Office, November 30, 1967, FCO 7/758, National Archives, Kew.

105 Ibid.

106 Secretary's calendar 1967, Folder: Calendar 1967, Box II:68, RSM papers, LoC.

107 President Johnson, "Remarks upon Presenting the Medal of Freedom to Robert S. McNamara" (speech, Washington, DC, February 28, 1996). Retrieved online May 10, 2018, American Presidency Project: https://goo .gl/xHEUbq.

108 "The Fog of War: Eleven Lessons from the Life of Robert S. McNamara, Transcript." Retrieved online May 20, 2018, Errol Morris website: www .errolmorris.com/film/fow_transcript.html.

109 Ibid.

Conclusion

1 Westmoreland to Sharp, February 12, 1968, *FRUS, Vietnam January–August 1968*, vol. 6, doc. 68.

2 Robert M. Collins, *The Politics of Economic Growth in Postwar America* (New York: Oxford University Press, 2002), 88.

3 MC LBJ Presidential Recordings: President Johnson and McNamara, June 9, 1964, WH 6406.04, Conversation 3663.

4 James T. Currie, "The Army Reserve and Vietnam," *Parameters* 14:3 (1984): 75–85.

5 John T. McNaughton diary, February 11, 1966.

6 Alwyn H. King, *The Impact of the Vietnam Conflict on the Economy of the United States* (Carlisle, PA: US Army War College, 1980), 3–5.

7 Enthoven to McNamara, March 20, 1968, Folder: Defense Department, Balance of Payments, 1968, Box I:88, RSM papers, LoC.

8 Collins, *Politics of Economic Growth*, 69.

9 See, for instance: Lloyd Gardner, "Lyndon Johnson and Vietnam: The Final Months," in Robert A. Divine, ed., *The Johnson Years*, vol. 3: *LBJ at Home and Abroad* (Lawrence: University of Kansas Press, 1994), 198–238.

10 John T. McNaughton diary, February 28, 1966.

11 Lerner, *A Companion to Lyndon B. Johnson*.

12 Maxwell Taylor Oral History Interview No. 1 by Elspeth Rostow, April 12, 1964, JFKL.

13 "Department of Defense Reorganization Act of 1958," August 6, 1958. Retrieved online December 17, 2014, Government Printing Office: http://goo.gl/2GNiyN.

14 "The Real McNamara," *New Republic* 154:23, Issue 2689 (June 4, 1966): 5–7.

15 Nolting to Rusk, December 19, 1961, Folder: Vietnam, General, 12/19/61–12/23/61, Box 195a, NSF, JFKL.

16 CINCAPC to JCS, March 1962, Folder: Vietnam, General, 2/1/62–3/12/62, Box 196, NSF Files, JFKL

17 H. W. Brands, "Dean Rusk: Defending the American Mission Abroad (review)," *Journal of Cold War History* 4:2 (Spring 2012): 151.

18 Ambassador Dean to Clift, December 6, 1967, FCO 7/758, National Archives, Kew.

19 Hilsman, *The Politics of Policy Making*, 54, 158.

20 Adam Yarmolinsky, "The Military Establishment (or How Political Problems Become Military Problems)," *Foreign Policy* (January 1, 1971). Retrieved online December 16, 2014: http://goo.gl/swHbFo.

21 John T. McNaughton diary, April 4, 1966.

22 Hilsman to Rusk, November 18, 1963, Folder: Vietnam, General, 11/16/63–11/12/63, Memos and Miscellaneous, Box 202, NSF Files, JFKL.

23 Yarmolinsky to Kaufmann, September 9, 1965, Folder: Kaufman Defense, 2/2, Box 28, Yarmolinsky Papers, JFKL.

24 Yarmolinsky, "The Military Establishment (or How Political Problems Become Military Problems)."

25 Hilsman, *The Politics of Policy Making*, 45.

26 Yarmolinsky, "The Military Establishment (Or How Political Problems Become Military Problems)."

27 Adam Yarmolinsky in Richard M. Pfeffer, *No More Vietnams? The War and the Future of American Foreign Policy* (New York: Harper & Row, 1968), 102.

28 Palmer, *Summons of the Trumpet*, 2.

29 Kennedy, "After Two Years."

30 President John F. Kennedy, "Inaugural Address" (speech, Washington, DC, January 20, 1961). Retrieved online on November 2, 2014, JFKL: http://goo.gl/EFuLrL.

31 The present book suggests the concern was rather more inward-looking, that Kennedy was relatively more preoccupied with domestic economics than the hegemonic aspects of the international monetary system that Lundestad or Gavin have emphasized. See Gavin, *Gold, Dollars, and Power*; Geir Lundestad, *The United States and Western Europe since 1945: From "Empire" by Invitation to Transatlantic Drift* (Oxford: Oxford University Press, 2005).

32 Adam Yarmolinsky, interview by Brian Vandemark, April 1, 1993, Folder: Yarmolinsky 1993, Box II:104, RSM papers, LoC.

33 "His Business Is War," Stewart Alsop, May 21, 1966, Folder: Sec Def on Vietnam Book 5, Tabs 49–59, Box 179, RG200, RSM Records, NARA.

34 John T. McNaughton diary, April 6, 1966.

35 Vietnam War US Military Fatal Casualty Statistics. Retrieved online May 10, 2018, NARA: https://goo.gl/JLKbjx.

36 MC LBJ Presidential Recordings: President Johnson and McNamara, March 6, 1965, WH6503.03, Conversation 7028.

37 Hilsman to Yarmolinsky, November 18, 1965, Folder: Correspondence 1965, Box 66, Yarmolinsky Papers, JFKL.

38 On this, see especially Freedman, "Vietnam and the Disillusioned Strategist," 133–151.

39 Robert McNamara Oral History Interview 3 by the Secretary of Defense Historical Office, July 24, 1986, Folder: OSD OHs, Box I:109, RSM papers, LoC.

40 John T. McNaughton diary, March, 25, 1966,

41 Minutes of a meeting, October 4, 1967, Folder: Penn Meetings, Box II:94, RSM papers, LoC.

42 Yevgeny Yevtushenko, "The Main Thing Now Is to Stop Bloodshed," *Gordon English Edition* (16 February 2015). Retrieved online May 10, 2018: https://goo.gl/m3LRbp.

43 McNamara and VanDeMark, *In Retrospect*, 258–259.

Bibliography

ARCHIVES CONSULTED

Georgetown University Special Collections Research Centre, Washington, DC
    Paul C. Warnke Papers
Gerald R. Ford Presidential Library, Ann Arbor, MI
    Ambassador Graham Martin Files
    Melvin Laird Papers
    Subject Files, Vietnam, General
Harvard Business School Archives, Baker Library, Cambridge, MA
    Class notes, Robert S. McNamara
Hoover Institution Archives, Stanford, CA
    David M. Shoup Papers
John F. Kennedy Presidential Library, Boston, MA
    Advisors and Personal Papers
        George W. Ball
        McGeorge Bundy
        C. Douglas Dillon
        Bernard B. Fall
        Paul B. Fay
        John K. Galbraith
        Roger Hilsman
        Stanley Karnow
        Nicholas de B. Katzenbach
        William W. Kaufmann
        Carl Kaysen
        Lawrence O'Brien
        Kenneth O'Donnell
        Pierre Salinger
        Arthur M. Schlesinger
        Theodore C. Sorensen

James C. Thompson
Robert Thompson
Adam Yarmolinsky
John M. Newman Research Papers
National Security Files, Series
  Carl Kaysen Papers
  Chester V. Clifton
  Country
  Meetings and Memoranda
  Regional Security Studies
  Special Group (CI)
  Subject Files
  Trip and Conferences
Pre-Presidential Papers
  Richard E. Neustadt Papers
Presidential Office Files
  Countries File, Vietnam/Vietnam Security
  Departments and Agencies
  Staff Memoranda
  Presidential Recordings
  United States Agency of International Development Records
Library of Congress, Washington, DC
  Manuscript Room
    Joseph and Stewart Alsop Papers
    Averell Harriman Papers
    Curtis LeMay Papers
    Robert S. McNamara Papers
    Paul H. Nitze Papers
    Elliot L. Richardson Papers
    Neil Sheehan Papers
  Senate Room
    Congressional Hearings on Defense
    Congressional Hearings on Foreign Aid
National Archives and Records Administration, College Park, MD
  RG59   Records of the Vietnam Working Group
  RG59   Records of the Special Group (CI)
  RG200 OSD Files, Robert S. McNamara Papers
  RG218 Joint Chiefs of Staff
  RG263 Central Intelligence Agency
  RG330 Records of the Office of the Secretary of Defense Files
  RG334 Interservice Agencies
  RG472 United States Forces in Southeast Asia
National Archives, Kew, UK
  Cabinet (CAB) Files
  Foreign Office (FO/FCO) Files

Prime Minister's (PREM) Files
United States of America Microfiche Collection: Series 1 and 2
NATO Archives, Brussels, Belgium
    Annual Review and Defence Planning Multilateral Discussions
    Defence Planning and Policy
    North Atlantic Council: Council Memoranda, Summary and Verbatim Records
Naval Historical Center, Washington, DC
    Admiral Harry D. Felt Papers and Oral History
Rockefeller Archive Center, Sleepy Hollow, NY
    David Rockefeller Papers
    John D. Rockefeller III Papers
Roosevelt Study Center, Middleburg, Netherlands
    Oral History collections (Columbia University, JFKL as shown below)
    William C. Westmoreland Papers
    Public Papers of the President
Sciences Po Contemporary History Archives, Paris, France
    Wilfrid Baumgartner Papers
SOAS University of London Archives, London
    Patrick J. Honey Papers
United Nations Archives, New York, NY
    U Thant Papers
University of Virginia Archives, Charlottesville, VA
    Louis A. Johnson Papers

DIGITAL RESOURCES

The American Presidency Project, www.presidency.ucsb.edu/. Retrieved December 16, 2014.
Atomic Archive, www.atomicarchive.com/index.shtml. Retrieved December 16, 2014.
CBS news, www.cbsnews.com/news/schedule-of-cbsnewscoms-live-stream-of-jfk-assassination-broadcast-coverage/. Retrieved December 16, 2014.
CIA Freedom of Information Act Electronic Reading Room, www.cia.gov/library/readingroom/. Retrieved May 10, 2018.
Declassified Documents Reference System (DDRS), http://gdc.gale.com/products/declassified-documents-reference-system/. Retrieved December 16, 2014.
Defense Technical Information Center, http://dtic.mil/dtic/. Retrieved December 16, 2014.
Digital National Security Archive, George Washington University (DNSA), www2.gwu.edu/~nsarchiv/. Retrieved December 16, 2014.
Dissertations and Theses, http://search.proquest.com/pqdtft/index?accountid=9630. Retrieved December 16, 2014.
Errol Morris, *Fog of War* transcript, www.errolmorris.com/film/fow_transcript.html. Retrieved December 16, 2014.
Federal Reserve Bank of St. Louis, www.stlouisfed.org/. Retrieved December 16, 2014.

Federal Reserve History Resources, www.federalreservehistory.org. Retrieved December 16, 2014.

Frontline Diplomacy, http://adst.org/oral-history/. Retrieved December 16, 2014.

H-Diplo, https://networks.h-net.org/h-diplo. Retrieved December 16, 2014.

John F. Kennedy Presidential Library, www.jfklibrary.org/. Retrieved December 16, 2014.

Lyndon B. Johnson Presidential Library, www.lbjlib.utexas.edu/. Retrieved December 16, 2014.

LZ Center, www.lzcenter.com/Vietnam%20War%20Documents.html. Retrieved December 16, 2014.

Miller Center, University of Virginia, http://millercenter.org/. Retrieved December 16, 2014.

Mississippi Department of Archives and History, Digital Archives, http://mdah .state.ms.us/arrec/digital_archives/. Retrieved June 15, 2015.

National Bureau of Economic Research, www.nber.org/. Retrieved December 16, 2014.

National Public Radio, www.npr.org/. Retrieved December 16, 2014.

Old Colorado City Communications, www.oldcolo.com/. Retrieved December 16, 2014.

Open Society Online Archives, www.osaarchivum.org/. Retrieved December 16, 2014.

Open Vault Archives, http://openvault.wgbh.org

The Pentagon Papers, Gravel Edition, Mt. Holyoke, www.mtholyoke.edu/acad/ intrel/vietnam.htm. Retrieved December 16, 2014.

The Pentagon Papers, US National Archives, www.archives.gov/research/penta gon-papers/. Retrieved December 16, 2014.

Texas Tech University: The Vietnam Center and Archive, www.virtual.vietnam .ttu.edu/. Retrieved December 16, 2014.

Tom Paulin: John T. McNaughton – Find a Way Out blog, http://jtmcnaugh tonfindawayout.blogspot.co.uk/2011/02/epilogue.html. Retrieved December 16, 2014.

US Air Force Historical Agency, www.afhra.af.mil/documents/oralhistorycata logue.asp. Retrieved December 16, 2014.

US Army Center of Military History, www.history.army.mil/. Retrieved December 16, 2014.

US Congressional Hearings Digital Collection Historical Archive, 1824–2003, http://congressional.proquest.com.gate2.library.lse.ac.uk/congressional/ search/basic/basicsearch. Retrieved December 16, 2014.

US Department of Defense, www.dod.mil/pubs/foi/. Retrieved December 16, 2014.

US Department of Defense, Historical Office, http://history.defense.gov/. Retrieved December 16, 2014.

US Department of Justice, www.justice.gov/ag/rfkspeeches/. Retrieved December 16, 2014.

US Marine Corps, www.marines.mil/News/Publications.aspx. Retrieved December 16, 2014.

White House Historical Series, www.whitehouse.gov/sites/default/files/omb/ budget/fy2011/assets/hist.pdf. Retrieved December 16, 2014.

FILMS

The Fog of War. Directed by Errol Morris. Sony Pictures Classics, 2003. DVD.
Virtual JFK: Vietnam If Kennedy Had Lived. Directed by Koji Masutani. Sven Kahn Films, 2009. DVD.

ORAL HISTORY COLLECTIONS

Columbia University Oral History Collection
  General Lucius Clay
  Roger Hilsman
Frontline Diplomacy: The Foreign Affairs Oral History Collection
  Thomas L. Hughes
  Frederick E. Nolting Jr.
  David G. Nes
John F. Kennedy Presidential Library, Oral History Collection
  George W. Anderson Jr.
  Harold Brown
  McGeorge Bundy
  William P. Bundy
  Arleigh A. Burke
  General Lucius D. Clay
  Chester L. Cooper
  Council of Economic Advisers
  George H. Decker
  Paul B. Fay
  Roswell Gilpatric
  Albert Gore
  Roger Hilsman
  Carl Kaysen
  Robert Komer
  Victor H. Krulak
  Robert A. Lovett
  John A. McCone
  Robert S. McNamara
  Paul Nitze
  David M. Shoup
  Arthur Sylvester
  James W. Symington
  Maxwell D. Taylor
  Earl G. Wheeler
  Adam Yarmolinsky
  Eugene M. Zuckert
John F. Kennedy Presidential Library, Robert F. Kennedy Oral History Collection
  Maxwell Taylor
Lyndon B. Johnson Presidential Library, Oral History Collection
  George Ball

McGeorge Bundy
Roswell Gilpatric
Roger Hilsman
John A. McCone
Robert S. McNamara
David G. Nes
Adam Yarmolinsky
MIT Security Studies Program Oral History Program
  Carl Kaysen
Presidency Project, Miller Center, University of Virginia
US Office of the Secretary of Defense Oral History Collection
  Robert S. McNamara
  General Maxwell Taylor

INTERVIEWS

Professor Graham Allison, Cambridge, MA, September 11, 2012.
Dr. Daniel Ellsberg, telephone, January 11, 2013.
Professor Alain C. Enthoven, Stanford University, former DASD and ASD for
  Systems Analysis, telephone, January 17, 2013.
Errol Morris, London, March 18, 2014, and Cambridge, MA, July 23, 2014.
Thomas S. Paullin, telephone, November 22, 2012.

NEWS SOURCES

Baltimore Sun
Boston Globe
Chicago Daily Tribune
Christian Science Monitor
Florida Times
Gordon
The Guardian
Harvard Crimson
Life Magazine
Look Magazine
Los Angeles Times
Milwaukee Sentinel
New Republic
New York Herald Tribune
New York Review of Books
New York Times
St. Petersburg Times
Sunday Times
Time Magazine
Wall Street Journal
Washington Post
Washington Star

PUBLISHED PRIMARY MATERIAL

Allen, George W. *None So Blind*. Chicago, IL: Ivan R. Dee, 2001.

Ball, George. *The Past Has Another Pattern*. New York: Norton, 1982.

Blight, James G., and Janet M. Lang. *The Fog of War: Lessons from the Life of Robert S. McNamara*. Oxford: Rowman & Littlefield, 2005.

Califano, Joseph A. Jr. *The Triumph and Tragedy of Lyndon Johnson: The White House Years*. New York: Simon & Schuster, 1991.

Clifford, Clark, and Richard Holbrooke. *Counsel to the President: A Memoir*. New York: Random House, 1991.

Colby, William, and James McCargar. *Lost Victory: A Firsthand Account of America's Sixteen-Year Involvement in Vietnam*. Chicago, IL: Contemporary Books, 1989.

Cooper, Chester. *The Lost Crusade: America in Vietnam*. New York: Dodd, Meade, 1970.

Ellsberg, Daniel. *Secrets: A Memoir of Vietnam and the Pentagon Papers*. New York: Penguin, 2003.

Enthoven, Alain C. *Defense Planning and Organization*. Santa Monica, CA: RAND, 1961.

"Reason, Morality and Defense Policy." *America* 108:14 (April 13, 1963): 494–502.

"Tribute to Charles J. Hitch." *OR/MS Today* 22:6 (December 1995). Available online: www.orms-today.org/orms-12-95/hitch-tribute.html. Retrieved December 16, 2014.

Fall, Bernard. *Last Reflections on a War*. Garden City, NY: Doubleday, 1967.

Fay, Paul B. *The Pleasure of His Company*. New York: Harper & Row, 1966.

Galbraith, John K. *Ambassador's Journal: A Personal Account of the Kennedy Years*. St. Paul, MN: Paragon House, 1988.

Letters to Kennedy. Cambridge, MA: Harvard University Press, 1998.

Gillette, Michael. *Launching the War on Poverty: An Oral History*. New York: Twayne, 1996.

Halperin, Morton H. "The Decision to Deploy the ABM: Bureaucratic and Domestic Politics in the Johnson Administration." *World Politics* 25:1 (October 1972): 62–95.

Harris, Seymour E. *Economics and the Kennedy Years and a Look Ahead*. New York: Harper & Row, 1964.

Hoopes, Townsend. *The Limits of Intervention: How Vietnam Policy Was Made – and Reversed – During the Johnson Administration*. New York: W. W. Norton, 1973.

Hoopes, Townsend, and Douglas Brinkley. *Driven Patriot: The Life and Times of James Forrestal*. Annapolis, MD: Naval Institute Press, 1992.

Kennedy, Caroline, and Michael Beschloss, eds. *Jacqueline Kennedy: Historic Conversations on Life with John F. Kennedy*. New York: Hyperion Audio Books, 2011.

Kennedy, John F. *Why England Slept*. London: Hutchinson, 1940.

Kissinger, Henry. *The White House Years*. Boston: Little, Brown, 1979.

Lodge, Henry Cabot. *As It Was: An Inside View of Politics and Power in the '50s and '60s*. New York: Norton, 1976.

Macmillan Cabinet Papers, 1957–1963. London: Adam Matthew Publications, 1999. CD-ROM.

McNamara, Robert S. *The Essence of Security: Reflections in Office*. London: Hodder & Stoughton, 1968.

    Out of the Cold: New Thinking for American Foreign and Defense Policy in the Century. London: Bloomsbury, 1989.

McNamara, Robert S., and James G. Blight. *Wilson's Ghost: Reducing the Risk of Conflict, Killing and Catastrophe in the 21st Century*. New York: Public Affairs, 2001.

McNamara, Robert S., and Brian VanDeMark. *In Retrospect: The Tragedy and Lessons of Vietnam*. New York: Vintage Books, 1995.

McNamara, Robert S., James G. Blight and Robert K. Brigham. *Argument without End: In Search of Answers to the Vietnam Tragedy*. New York: Public Affairs, 1999.

Mecklin, John. *Mission in Torment: An Intimate Account of the US Role in Vietnam*. Garden City, NY: Doubleday, 1965.

Millis, Walter Millis, ed. *The Forrestal Diaries*. New York: Viking, 1951.

Nolting, Frederick. *From Trust to Tragedy: The Political Memoirs of Frederick Nolting, Kennedy's Ambassador to Vietnam*. Westport, CT: Praeger, 1988.

O'Donnell, Kenneth P., David F. Powers and Joe McCarthy. *Johnny, We Hardly Knew Ye*. Boston: Little, Brown, 1970.

Palmer, David R. *Summons of the Trumpet: US-Vietnam in Perspective*. San Rafael, CA: Presidio Press, 1978.

The Pentagon Papers, Gravel edition. Boston: Beacon Press, 1971.

Public Papers of the Presidents of the United States. Available online: www.gpo.gov/fdsys/browse/collection.action?collectionCode=PP. Retrieved December 16, 2014.

Roosa, Robert. *The Dollar and World Liquidity*. New York: Random House, 1967.

Rostow, Walt W. "The Case for the Vietnam War." *Times Literary Supplement* (June 9, 1995).

Rusk, Dean. *As I Saw It*. London: Tauris, 1990.

Salinger, Pierre. *With Kennedy*. Garden City, NY: Doubleday, 1966.

Schlesinger, Andrew, and Stephen Schlesinger. *The Letters of Arthurs Schlesinger*. New York: Random House, 2013.

Schlesinger, Arthur M. Jr. *A Thousand Days: John F. Kennedy in the White House*. New York: Greenwich House, 1983.

Schlesinger, Arthur M. "What Would He Have Done?" *New York Times* (March 29, 1992).

    Journals: 1952–2000. New York: Penguin, 2008.

Sharp, U. S. Grant. *Strategy for Defeat: Vietnam in Retrospect*. San Rafael, CA: Presidio Press, 1978.

Sorenson, Theodore C. *Kennedy*. New York: Smithmark Publications, 1965.

Taylor, General Maxwell D. *Swords and Plowshares*. New York: Da Capo Press, 1972.

The Uncertain Trumpet. Westport, CT: Greenwood Press, 1974.

Thompson, Robert. *Defeating Communist Insurgency*. London: Chatto & Windus, 1967.

No Exit from Vietnam. New York: David McKay, 1969.

US Department of Commerce. *The Balance of Payments and the United States*. Washington, DC: US Government Printing Office, 1990.

US Department of State, Office of the Historian. *Foreign Relations of the United States (FRUS)*, vol. I: *Vietnam, 1961*. Washington, DC: Government Printing Office, 1988.

Foreign Relations of the United States (FRUS), vol. III: *Vietnam, January–August 1963*. Washington, DC: Government Printing Office, 1991.

Foreign Relations of the United States (FRUS), vol. IV: *Vietnam, August–December 1963*. Washington, DC: Government Printing Office, 1991.

Foreign Relations of the United States (FRUS), vol. I: *Vietnam, 1964*. Washington, DC: Government Printing Office, 1992.

Foreign Relations of the United States (FRUS), *1961–1963*, vol. IX: *Foreign Economic Policy*. Washington, DC: Government Printing Office, 1995.

Foreign Relations of the United States (FRUS), *1964–1968*, vol. II: *Vietnam, January – June 1965*. Washington, DC: Government Printing Office, 1996.

Foreign Relations of the United States (FRUS), *1964–1968*, vol. III: *Vietnam, June–December 1965*. Washington, DC: Government Printing Office, 1996.

Foreign Relations of the United States (FRUS), *1964–1968*, vol. IV: *Vietnam, 1966*. Washington, DC: Government Printing Office, 1998.

Foreign Relations of the United States (FRUS), *1964–1968*, vol. V: *Vietnam, 1967*. Washington, DC: Government Printing Office, 1998.

Foreign Relations of the United States (FRUS), *1964–1968*, vol. VIII: *International Monetary and Trade Policy*. Washington, DC: Government Printing Office, 1998.

US Office of the Secretary of Defense. *Report of the Office of the Secretary of Defense Vietnam Task Force*. Washington, DC: 1967. Available online: archives.gov/research/pentagon-papers. Retrieved December 16, 2014.

Westmoreland, William C. *A Soldier Reports*. New York: Doubleday, 1976.

White, Theodore H. *The Making of the President, 1960*. Cutchogue, NY: Buccaneer Books, 1961.

Yevtushenko, Yevgeny. "The Main Thing Now Is to Stop Bloodshed." *Gordon English Edition* (February 16, 2015). Available online: https://goo.gl/m3LRbp. Retrieved May 10, 2018.

OTHER PRIMARY SOURCES

Unclassified Personal Diary of John T. McNaughton, January 1, 1966–April 22, 1967. Thomas S. Paullin.

SECONDARY SOURCES

Ahern, Thomas Jr. *CIA and the Generals: Covert Support to Military Government in South Vietnam*. Washington, DC: CIA, 1998. Available online: foia .cia.gov. Retrieved December 16, 2014.

CIA and the House of NGO. Washington, DC: CIA, 1998. Available online: foia.cia.gov. Retrieved December 16, 2014.

CIA and Rural Pacification in South Vietnam. Washington, DC: CIA, 1998. Available online: foia.cia.gov. Retrieved December 16, 2014.

Allison, Graham T., and Philip Zelikow. *Essence of Decision: Explaining the Cuban Missile Crisis*. New York: Longman, 1999.

Anderson, David L. *The Human Tradition in the Vietnam War*. Wilmington, DE: Scholarly Resources, 2000.

Anderson, James E., and Jared E. Hazleton. *Managing Macroeconomic Policy: The Johnson Presidency*. Austin: University of Texas Press, 1986.

Asselin, Pierre. "Kimball's Vietnam War." *Diplomatic History* 30:1 (2006): 163–169.

Hanoi's Road to the Vietnam War, 1954–1965. Berkeley: University of California Press, 2013.

Barnet, Richard. "The Men Who Made the War." In Ralph Stavins, Richard Barnet and Marcus Raskin, eds., *Washington Plans an Aggressive War*. New York: Vintage, 1971.

Basset, Lawrence J., and Stephen E. Pelz. "The Failed Search for Victory." In Robert J. McMahon, ed., *Major Problems in the History of Vietnam War*. Lexington, MA: D. C. Heath, 1990.

Bator, Francis. "The Political Economics of International Money." *Foreign Affairs* 47:1 (October 1968): 51–67.

"No Good Choices: LBJ and the Vietnam/Great Society Connection." *Diplomatic History* (June 2008): 309–340.

Berman, Larry. *Planning a Tragedy: The Americanization of the War in Vietnam*. New York: W. W. Norton, 1984.

Lyndon Johnson's War: The Road to Stalemate in Vietnam. New York: Norton, 1989.

Bernstein, Irving. *Guns or Butter: The Presidency of Lyndon B. Johnson*. New York: Oxford University Press, 1996.

Bertram, Eva, "Democratic Divisions in the 1960s and the Road to Welfare Reform," *Political Science Quarterly* 126:4 (Winter 2011–2012): 579–610.

Bird, Kai. *The Color of Truth. McGeorge Bundy and William Bundy: Brothers in Arms*. New York: Simon & Schuster, 1998.

Bischak, Gregory A. *Towards a Peace Economy in the United States*. London: Macmillan, 1991.

Blair, Anne E. *Lodge in Vietnam: A Patriot Abroad*. New Haven, CT: Yale University Press, 1995.

Blight, James G., Janet M. Lang and David A. Welch. *Virtual JFK: Vietnam If Kennedy Had Lived*. New York: Rowman & Littlefield, 2009.

Bordo, Michael, and Barry Eichengreen, eds. *A Retrospective on the Bretton Woods System*. Chicago, IL: University of Chicago Press, 1993.

Boyle, Kevin. "The Price of Peace: Vietnam, the Pound, and the Crisis of American Empire." *Diplomatic History* 27:1 (January 2003): 37–72.

Bradley, Mark Philip, and Marilyn B. Young. *Making Sense of the Vietnam Wars: Local, National and Transnational Perspectives*. Oxford: Oxford University Press, 2008.

Brands, H. W. "Dean Rusk: Defending the American Mission Abroad (Review)." *Journal of Cold War History* 4:2 (Spring 2012): 150–153.

Brigham, Robert K., and George C. Herring, "The Pennsylvania Initiative, June–October 1967." In Lloyd C. Gardner and Ted Gittinger, eds., *The Search for Peace in Vietnam, 1964–1968*. College Station: Texas A&M University Press, 2004.

Brinkley, Douglas. "The Stain of Vietnam: Robert McNamara, Redemption Denied." *Foreign Affairs* (Summer 1993). Available online: www.foreignaf fairs.com/articles/48974/douglas-brinkley/the-stain-of-vietnam-robert-mcna mara-redemption-denied. Retrieved December 16, 2014.

"Eisenhower the Dove." *American Heritage* 52:6 (September 2011): 58–65.

Bundy, William P. *The Path to Vietnam: A Lesson in Involvement*. London: Twentieth Century Press, 1967.

Busch, Peter. "Killing the 'Vietcong': The British Advisory Mission and the Strategic Hamlet Programme." *Journal of Strategic Studies* 25:1 (2002): 135–162.

All the Way with JFK: Britain, the US, and the Vietnam War. Oxford: Oxford University Press, 2003.

Buzzanco, Robert. *Masters of War: Military Dissent and Politics in the Vietnam Era*. New York: Cambridge University Press, 1996.

Cable, Larry E. *Conflict of Myths: The Development of American Counterinsurgency Doctrine and the Vietnam War*. New York: New York University Press, 1988.

Callahan, David. *Dangerous Capabilities: Paul Nitze and the Cold War*. New York: Edward Burlingame, 1990.

Calleo, David P. "De Gaulle and the Monetary System: The Golden Rule." In Robert O. Paxton and Nicholas Wahl, eds., *De Gaulle and the United States*. Oxford: Berg, 1994.

Campagna, Anthony S. *The Economic Consequences of the Vietnam War*. New York: Praeger, 1991.

Campbell, Craig. "Kennedy's International Legacy: Fifty Years On." *International Affairs* 89:6 (2013): 1367–1378.

Caro, Robert A. *The Years of Lyndon Johnson: The Passage of Power*. New York: Vintage Books, 2012.

Casey, Steven. *Selling the Korean War: Propaganda, Politics and Political Opinion in the United States 1950–1953*. New York: Oxford University Press, 2008.

Catton, Philip E. *Diem's Final Failure: Prelude to America's War in Vietnam*. Lawrence: University Press of Kansas, 2003.

Cha, Victor D. *Alignment despite antagonism: The US–Korean–Japan Security Triangle*. Stanford, CA: Stanford University Press, 1999.

Chapman, Jessica M. *Cauldron of Resistance: Ngo Dinh Diem, the United States, and the 1950s Southern Vietnam*. Ithaca, NY: Cornell University Press, 2013.

Chivvis, Christopher S. "Charles de Gaulle, Jacques Rueff and French International Monetary Policy under Bretton Woods." *Journal of Contemporary History* 51 (2006): 701–720.

Clarfield. Gerard. *Security with Solvency: Dwight D. Eisenhower and the Shaping of the Military Establishment*. Westport, CT: Praeger, 1999.

Clarke, Jeffrey. *US Army in Vietnam. Advice and Support: The Final Years, 1965–1973*. Washington, DC: US Army Center of Military History, 1988.

Cohen, Eliot A. *Supreme Command: Soldiers, Statesmen, and Leadership in Wartime*. New York: Anchor Books, 2002.

Collins, Robert M. *The Politics of Economic Growth in Postwar America*. New York: Oxford University Press, 2002.

Colman, Jonathan. "The 'Most Distinguished Envoy of Peace': Averell Harriman and the Vietnam War in the Johnson Years." *International History Review* (February 2015): 1–22.

Costigliola, Frank. *France and the United States: The Cold Alliance since World War II*. New York: Twayne, 1992.

Cuddy, Edward. "Vietnam: Mr. Johnson's War – Or Mr. Eisenhower's?" *Review of Politics* 65:4 (September 2003).

Currie, James T. "The Army Reserve and Vietnam," *Parameters* 14: 3 (1984).

Dallek, Robert. "Lyndon Johnson and Vietnam: The Making of a Tragedy." *Diplomatic History* 20:2 (April 1996).

Flawed Giant: Lyndon Johnson and His Times. New York: Oxford University Press, 2000.

John F. Kennedy: An Unfinished Life, 1917–1963. London: Allen Lane, 2003.

Despres, Emile, Charles P. Kindelberger and Walter S. Salant. *The Dollar and World Liquidity: A Minority View*. Washington, DC: Brookings Institution, 1966.

Divine, Robert A. "Historiography: Vietnam Reconsidered." *Diplomatic History* 12 (Winter 1988): 79–93.

Dockrill, Saki. *Eisenhower's New-Look National Security Strategy, 1952–61*. New York: St. Martin's Press, 1996.

Dorwart, Jeffrey M. *Eberstadt and Forrestal: A National Security Partnership, 1909–1959*. College Station: Texas A&M University Press, 1991.

Drea, Edward J. *McNamara, Clifford and the Burdens of Vietnam, 1965–1969*. Washington, DC: US Government Printing Office, 2011.

Dumbrell, John. *Rethinking the Vietnam War*. New York: Palgrave Macmillan, 2012.

Eichengreen, Barry. "From Benign Neglect to Malignant Preoccupation: US Balance-of-Payments Policy in the 1960s." In George L. Perry and James Tobin, eds., *Economic Events, Ideas, and Policies: The 1960s and After*. Washington, DC: Brookings Institution Press, 2000.

Globalizing Capital: A History of the International Monetary System, 2nd edn. Princeton, NJ: Princeton University Press, 2008.

Eisenberg, Carolyn. "The New Cold War." *Diplomatic History* 29:3 (June 2005): 423–427.

Elliot, Mai. *RAND in Southeast Asia: A History of the Vietnam War Era.* Santa Monica, CA: RAND, 2010.

Enthoven, Alain C., and K. Wayne Smith. *How Much Is Enough? Shaping the Defense Program, 1961–1969.* New York: Harper & Row, 1971.

Fall, Dorothy. *Bernard Fall: Memoirs of a Soldier-Scholar.* Dulles, VA: Potomac Books, 2006.

Farris, Scott. *Kennedy and Reagan: Why Their Legacies Endure.* Guilford, CT: Lyons Press, 2013.

Federal Bank of St. Louis. "The United States Balance of Payments, 1946–1960." *Monthly Review* 43:2 (March 1961). Available online: https://fraser .stlouisfed.org/docs/publications/frbslreview/rev_stls_196103.pdf. Accessed December 16, 2014.

Fessenden, Helen. "1965: The Year the Fed and LBJ Clashed." *Econ Focus: Richmond Federal Reserve* (2016): 6–10.

Fieleke, Norman S. "The Buy-American Policy of the United States Government: Its Balance of Payments and Welfare Effects." *New England Economic Review* (July/August 1969): 2–18.

"Unilateral International Transfers: Unrequited and Generally Unheeded." *New England Economic Review* (November/December 1996): 27–39.

Fitzgerald, Frances. *Fire in the Lake: The Vietnamese and the Americans in Vietnam.* New York: Back Bay Books, 2002.

Freedman, Lawrence. "Vietnam and the Disillusioned Strategist." *International Affairs* 72:1 (1996): 133–151.

Kennedy's Wars: Berlin, Cuba, Laos, and Vietnam. New York: Oxford University Press, 2000.

Friedberg, Aaron L. *In the Shadow of the Garrison State: America's Anti-Statism and Its Cold War Grand Strategy.* Princeton, NJ: Princeton University Press, 2000.

Fulbright, William J. *The Arrogance of Power.* London: Penguin, 1966.

Futrell, Robert F., and Martin Blumenson. *The US Air Force in Southeast Asia: The Advisory Years to 1965.* Washington, DC: Office of Air Force History, 1981.

Gaddis, John Lewis. "The Emerging Post-Revisionist Synthesis on the Origins of the Cold War." *Diplomatic History* 7 (Summer 1983): 171–190.

The Landscape of History: How Historians Map the Past. Oxford: Oxford University Press, 2002.

Strategies of Containment. Oxford: Oxford University Press, 2005.

Galbraith, James K. "Exit Strategy." *Boston Review* (October/November 2003). Available online: http://new.bostonreview.net/BR28.5/galbraith.html. Retrieved December 16, 2014.

Galbraith, John K. *How to Control the Military.* Garden City, NY: Doubleday, 1968.

Gallucci, Robert L. *Neither Peace nor Honor: The Politics of American Military Policy in Viet-Nam.* Baltimore, MD: Johns Hopkins University Press, 1975.

Gardner, Lloyd C. "Lyndon Johnson and Vietnam: The Final Months." In Robert A. Divine, ed., *The Johnson Years*, vol. 3: *LBJ at Home and Abroad*. Lawrence: University of Kansas Press, 1994: 198–238.

Pay Any Price: Lyndon Johnson and the War in Vietnam. Chicago, IL: Ivan R. Dee, 1995.

Gardner, Lloyd C., and Ted Gittinger. *Vietnam: The Early Decisions*. Austin: University of Texas Press, 1997.

The Search for Peace in Vietnam, 1964–1968. College Station: Texas A&M University Press, 2004.

Garofano, John. "Tragedy of Choice in Vietnam? Learning to Think Outside the Archival Box." *International Security* 26:4 (Spring 2002): 143–168.

Gavin, Francis. "The Gold Battles within the Cold War: American Monetary Policy and the Defense of Europe, 1960–1963." *Diplomatic History* 26:1 (2002): 61–94.

Gold, Dollars, and Power: The Politics of International Monetary Relations, 1958–1971. Chapel Hill: University of North Carolina Press, 2004.

Nuclear Statecraft: History and Strategy in America's Atomic Age. Ithaca, NY: Cornell University Press, 2012.

Gavin, Francis J., and Erin Mahan. "Hegemony or Vulnerability? Giscard, Ball and the 1962 Gold Standstill Proposal." *Journal of European Integration History* 6 (2000): 61–84.

Gelb, Leslie H., and Richard K. Betts. *The Irony of Vietnam: The System Worked*. Washington, DC: The Brookings Institution, 1979.

Gibbons, William C. *The US Government and the Vietnam War: Executive and Legislative Roles and Relationships, Part II*. Princeton, NJ: Princeton University Press, 1986.

The US Government and the Vietnam War: Executive and Legislative Roles and Relationships, Part III. Princeton, NJ: Princeton University Press, 1989.

The US Government and the Vietnam War: Executive and Legislative Roles and Relationships, Part IV. Princeton, NJ: Princeton University Press, 1995.

Gibson, James William. *The Perfect War: Technowar in Vietnam*. Boston: Atlantic Monthly Press, 1986.

Giglio, James N., ed. *The Presidency of John F. Kennedy*. Lawrence: University of Kansas Press, 1991.

Goldstein, Gordon M. *Lessons in Disaster: McGeorge Bundy and the Path to War in Vietnam*. New York: Henry Holt, 2008.

Gray, Colin S. "Strategy in the Nuclear Age: The United States, 1945–1991." In Williamson Murray, MacGregor Knox and Alvin Bernstein, eds., *The Making of Strategy: Rules, States and War*. Cambridge: Cambridge University Press, 1994.

Guan, Ang Cheng. "The Vietnam War, 1962–64: The Vietnamese Communist Perspective." *Journal of Contemporary History* 35:4 (October 2000): 601–618.

The Vietnam War from the Other Side: The Vietnamese Communists' Perspective. London: RoutledgeCurzon, 2002.

Halberstam, David. *The Best and the Brightest*. New York: Ballantine Books, 1969.

Hammer, Ellen J. *A Death in November: American in Vietnam, 1963.* Oxford: Oxford University Press, 1988.

Harrison, Benjamin T., and Christopher L. Mosher. "John T. McNaughton and Vietnam: The Early Years as Assistant Secretary of Defense, 1964–1965." *History* 92:308 (October 2007): 496–514.

Heath, Jim F. *John F. Kennedy and the Business Community.* Chicago: University of Chicago Press, 1969.

Hendrickson, Paul. *The Living and the Dead: Robert McNamara and Five Lives of a Lost War.* New York: Vintage Books, 1996.

Herring, George C., ed. *The Secret Diplomacy of the Vietnam War: The Negotiating Volumes of the Pentagon Papers.* Austin: University of Texas Press, 1983.

"The Strange 'Dissent' of Robert S. McNamara." In Jayne Warner and Luu Doan Huynh, eds., *The Vietnam War: Vietnamese and American Perspectives* London: M. E. Sharpe, 1993.

"The Wrong Kind of Loyalty: McNamara's Apology for Vietnam." *Foreign Affairs* (May/June 1995). Available online: www.foreignaffairs.com/articles/50985/george-c-herring/the-wrong-kind-of-loyalty-mcnamara-s-apology-for-vietnam. Retrieved December 16, 2014.

LBJ and Vietnam: A Different Kind of War. Austin: University of Texas Press, 1996.

America's Longest War: The United States and Vietnam, 4th edn. New York: McGraw-Hill, 2002.

Hershberg, James G. "Collateral Damage? 'Marigold,' Franco-American Relations and Secret Vietnam Peace Diplomacy, 1966–1967." *Diplomacy & Statecraft* 28:3 (2017): 403–430.

Marigold: The Lost Chance for Peace in Vietnam. Palo Alto, CA: Stanford University Press, 2012.

Herspring, Dale R. *The Pentagon and the Presidency: Civil-Military Relations from FDR to George W. Bush.* Lawrence: University Press of Kansas, 2005.

Hess, Gary R. "The Military Perspective on Strategy in Vietnam." *Diplomatic History* 10:1 (January 1986): 91–106.

"The Unending Debate: Historians and the Vietnam War." *Diplomatic History* 18:2 (Spring 1994): 239–264.

"Jessica Chapman. Cauldron of Resistance: Ngo Dinh Diem, the United States, and 1950s Southern Vietnam." *H-Diplo Roundtable Review* 15:12 (November 2013). Available online: http://h-diplo.org/roundtables/PDF/Roundtable-XV-12.pdf. Retrieved December 16, 2014.

Hilsman, Roger. *The Politics of Policy Making in Defense and Foreign Affairs.* New York: Harper & Row, 1971.

To Move a Nation: The Politics of Foreign Policy in the Administration of John F. Kennedy. New York: Doubleday, 1964.

"Vietnam: The Decisions to Intervene." In Jonathan R. Adelman, ed., *Superpowers and Revolution.* New York: Praeger, 1986.

Hitch, Charles J., and Roland N. McKean. *The Economics of Defense in the Nuclear Age.* Santa Monica, CA: RAND, 1960.

Hogan, Michael J., and Frank Costigliola. *America in the World: The Historiography of American Foreign Relations since 1941*. Cambridge: Cambridge University Press, 2013.

Hogan, Michael J., and Thomas G. Paterson, eds. *Explaining the History of American Foreign Relations*, 2nd edn. Cambridge: Cambridge University Press, 2004

Humphrey, David C. "Tuesday Lunch at the Johnson White House: A Preliminary Assessment." *Diplomatic History* 8:1 (Winter 1984): 81–101.

Hunt, David. "Dirty Wars: Counterinsurgency in Vietnam and Today." *Politics & Society* 38:35 (2010): 35–66.

Hunt, Michael H. *Lyndon Johnson's War: America's Cold War Crusade in Vietnam, 1965–1968*. New York: Hill and Wang, 1996.

Huntington, Samuel P. *The soldier and the State: The Theory and Politics of Civil-Military Relations*. Cambridge, MA: Harvard University Press, 1957.
  "American Ideals versus American Institutions." *Political Science Quarterly* 97:1 (Spring 1982): 1–37.
  "Defense Organization and Military Strategy." *The Public Interest* 75 (Spring 1984): 20–46.

Huntington, Samuel P., and Andrew J. Goodpaster. *Civil-Military Relations*. Washington, DC: American Enterprise Institute, 1977.

Information Office of the US Navy. *The Navy in Vietnam*. Washington, DC: US Government Printing Office, 1968.

Isaacs, Arnold *Without Honor: Defeat in Vietnam and Cambodia*. Baltimore, MD: Johns Hopkins University Press, 1983.

Isaacson, Walter, and Evan Thomas. *The Wise Men: Six Friends and the World They Made*. New York: Simon & Schuster, 1997.

Ives, Christopher. *US Special Forces and Counterinsurgency in Vietnam: Military Innovation and Institutional Failure, 1961–1963*. London: Routledge, 2007.

Jacobs, Seth. *American's Miracle Man in Vietnam: Ngo Dinh Diem, Religion, Race and US Intervention in Southeast Asia*. Durham, NC: Duke University Press, 2004.

Jauvert, Vincent. *L'Amérique contre De Gaulle: histoire secrète, 1961–1969*. Paris: Seuil, 2000.

Jervis, Robert. "The Impact of the Korean War on the Cold War." *Journal of Conflict Resolution* 24:4 (December 1980): 563–592.
  "The Politics of Troop Withdrawal: Salted Peanuts, the Commitment Trap, and Buying Time." *Diplomatic History* 34 (2010): 507–516.

Johnson, Griffith. "Western Europe and the American Balance of Payments." *Annals of the American Academy of Political and Social Science* 246 (July 1963): 110–120.

Jones, Douglas N. "Economic Aspects of Military Assistance." *Air University Review* 16:1 (November/December 1964): 42–46.

Jones, Howard. *Death of a Generation: How the Assassinations of Diem and JFK Prolonged the Vietnam War*. Oxford: Oxford University Press, 2003.

Kaiser, David. *American Tragedy: Kennedy, Johnson, and the Origins of the Vietnam War*. Cambridge, MA: Harvard University Press, 2000.

Kamps, Charles T. "The JCS 94-Target List: A Vietnam Myth That Still Distorts Military Thought," *Aerospace Journal* (Spring 2001).

Kaplan, Lawrence S. "McNamara, Vietnam and the Defense of Europe." In Vojtech Mastny, Sven G. Holtsmark and Andreas Wenger, eds., *War Plans and Alliance in the Cold War: Threat Perceptions in the East and West.* Oxford: Routledge, 2006.

Kaplan, Lawrence S., Ronald D. Landa and Edward J. Drea. *History of the Office of the Secretary of Defense,* vol. V: *The McNamara Ascendancy: 1961–1965.* Washington, DC: US Government Printing Office, 2006.

Karnow, Stanley. *Vietnam: A History.* New York: Penguin Books, 1991.

Kaufmann, William W. *The McNamara Strategy.* New York: Harper & Row, 1964.

Kelly, Brendan. "Lester B. Pearson's Temple University Speech Revisited: The Origins and Evolution of the Proposal for a Bombing Pause." *American Review of Canadian Studies* 47:4 (November 2017): 373–384.

Kelly, Francis John. *Vietnam Studies: US Army Special Forces, 1961–1971.* Vol. CMH Publication 90-23. Washington, DC: Department of the Army, 1989.

Khong, Yuen Foong. *Analogies at War: Korea, Munich, Dien Bien Phu and the Vietnam Decisions of 1965.* Princeton, NJ: Princeton University Press, 1992.

Kinnard, Douglas. "Eisenhower and the Defense Budget." *Journal of Politics* 39:3 (August 1977): 596–623.

The Secretary of Defense. Lexington: University Press of Kentucky, 1980.

The Certain Trumpet: Maxwell Taylor and the American Experience in Vietnam. McLean, VA: Brassey's, 1991.

The War Managers. Annapolis, MD: Naval Institute Press, 2007.

King, Alwyn H. *The Impact of the Vietnam Conflict on the Economy of the United States.* Carlisle, PA: US Army War College, 1981.

Knock, Thomas J. "George C. McGovern and Mr. Johnson's War: A Liberal Democrat Dissents." In Lloyd C. Gardner and Ted Gittinger, eds., *The Search for Peace in Vietnam, 1964–1968.* College Station: Texas A&M University Press, 2004.

Kolko, Gabriel. *Vietnam: Anatomy of War, 1940–1975.* London: Allen & Unwin, 1986.

Krepinevich, Andrew F. *The Army and Vietnam.* Baltimore, MD: Johns Hopkins University Press, 1986.

Kunz, Diane B. *Butter and Guns: America's Cold War Economic Diplomacy.* New York: Free Press, 1997.

Langguth, A. J. *Our Vietnam: The War 1954–1975.* New York: Simon & Schuster, 2000.

Lary, Hal B. *Problems of the United States as World Trade and Banker.* New York: Columbia University Press, 1963. Available online: www.nber.org/chapters/c1908.pdf. Retrieved December 16, 2014.

Lawrence, Mark A. *Assuming the Burden: Europe and the American Commitment to War in Vietnam.* Los Angeles: University of California Press, 2005.

Leffler, Melvyn P. *A Preponderance of Power: National Security, the Truman Administration and the Cold War.* Stanford, CA: Stanford University Press, 1992.

"Defense on a Diet: How Budget Crises Have Improved US Strategy." *Foreign Affairs* (November/December 2013). Available online: http://fam.ag/132TXkn. Retrieved November 2, 2014.

Lerner, Mitchell B. *A Companion to Lyndon B. Johnson.* Oxford: Wiley-Blackwell, 2012.

Lewy, Guenter. *America in Vietnam.* New York: Oxford University Press, 1978.

Logevall, Fredrik. *Choosing War: The Lost Chance for Peace and the Escalation of War in Vietnam.* Berkeley: University of California Press, 1999.

Embers of War: The Fall of an Empire and the Making of America's Vietnam. New York: Random House, 2012.

Lundestad, Geir. *The United States and Western Europe since 1945: From "Empire" by Invitation to Transatlantic Drift.* Oxford: Oxford University Press, 2005.

Mahan, Erin. *Kennedy, De Gaulle and Western Europe.* London: Palgrave Macmillan, 2002.

Mann, Robert. *A Grand Delusion: America's Descent into Vietnam.* New York: Basic Books, 2001.

Martin, Gareth. *General de Gaulle's Cold War: Challenging American Hegemony, 1963–1968.* New York: Berghahn Books, 2013.

McFarland, Keith D., and David L. Roll. *Louis Johnson and the Arming of America.* Bloomington: Indiana University Press, 2005.

MacGregor, Morris J. *Integration of the Armed Forces, 1940–1965.* Washington, DC: Department of the Army, 1985.

Masure, Matthew. "Exhibiting Signs of Resistance: South Vietnam's Struggle for Legitimacy, 1965–1960." *Diplomatic History* 33:2 (April 2009): 292–313.

May, Ernest R. "The US Government, a Legacy of the Cold War." *Diplomatic History* 16:2 (1992): 269–277.

May, Ernest R. ed. *American Cold War Strategy: Interpreting NSC 68.* Boston: Bedford/St. Martin's, 1993.

McAllister, James. "Who Lost Vietnam? Soldiers, Civilians, and the US Military Strategy." *International Security* 35:3 (Winter 2010/2011): 95–123.

McGrath, John J. *The Other End of the Spear: The Tooth-to-Tail Ratio (T3R) in Modern Military Operations.* Fort Leavenwroth, KS: Combat Studies Institute Press, 2007.

McMaster, H. R. *Dereliction of Duty: Lyndon Johnson, Robert McNamara, the Joint Chiefs of Staff, and the Lies That Led to Vietnam.* New York: HarperCollins, 1997.

Mearsheimer, John J. "McNamara's War." *Bulletin of Atomic Scientists* 49:6 (July/August 1993). Available online: http://mearsheimer.uchicago.edu/pdfs/A0020x1.pdf. Retrieved December 16, 2014.

Mecklin, John. *Mission in Torment: An Intimate Account of the US Role in Vietnam.* Garden City, NY: Doubleday, 1965.

Melson, Charles D., and Wanda J. Renfrow. *Marine Advisors: With the Vietnamese Marine Corps.* Quantico, VA: USMC History Division, 2009.

Meltzer, Allan H. *US Policy in the Bretton Woods Era.* St. Louis, MO: Federal Reserve Bank of St. Louis, 1991.

Mikesell, Raymond. *The US Balance of Payments and the International Role of the Dollar*. Washington, DC: American Enterprise Institute, 1970.

Miller, Edward. *Misalliance: Ngo Dinh Diem, the United States, and the Fate of South Vietnam*. Cambridge, MA: Harvard University Press, 2013.

Miller, Richard M. *Funding Extended Conflicts: Korea, Vietnam and the War on Terror*. Westport, CT: Greenwood, 2007.

Miller, Robert H. "Vietnam: Folly, Quagmire, or Inevitability?." *Studies in Conflict & Terrorism* 15 (April 1992): 99–123.

Milkis, Sidney. "How Great Was the Great Society?" In Mitchell B. Lerner, ed., *A Companion to Lyndon B. Johnson*. Oxford: Wiley-Blackwell, 2012.

Moyar, Mark. *Triumph Forsaken: The Vietnam War, 1954–1965*. Cambridge: Cambridge University Press, 2006.

Mrozek, Donald J. *Air Power and the Ground War in Vietnam: Ideas and Actions*. Maxwell Air Force Base, AL: Air University Press, 1988.

Mulcahy, Kevin V. "Walt Rostow as National Security Advisor, 1966–1969." *Presidential Studies Quarterly* 25:2 (Spring 1995): 223–236.

Nardi, Major Philip P. "The Foreign Military Sales Policy of the Kennedy Administration." *DISAM Journal* (Winter 1995/1996): 67–77.

Newman, John M. *JFK and Vietnam: Deception, Intrigue, and the Struggle for Power*. New York: Warner Books, 1992.

Nguyen, Lien Hang. *Hanoi's War: An International History of the War for Peace in Vietnam*. Chapel Hill: University of North Carolina Press, 2012.

Novick, Peter. *That Noble Dream: The Objectivity Question and the American Historical Profession*. Cambridge: Cambridge University Press, 1988.

Odell, John S., ed. *US International Monetary Policy: Markets, Power and Ideas as Sources of Change*. Princeton, NJ: Princeton University Press, 1982.

Olson, James C. *Stuart Symington: A Life*. Columbia: University of Missouri Press, 2003.

Palmer, Gregory. *The McNamara Strategy and the Vietnam War*. Westport, CT: Greenwood Press, 1978.

Parker, Jay M. *The Colonels' Revolt: Eisenhower, the Army and the Politics of National Security*. Newport, RI: Naval War College, 1994.

Paterson, Thomas G. *Kennedy's Quest for Victory*. New York: Oxford University Press, 1992.

Perry, George L., et al. *Economic Events, Ideas and Policies: The 1960s and After*. Washington, DC: Brookings Institution Press, 2000.

Pfaff, William. "Mac Bundy Said He Was 'All Wrong.'" *New York Review of Books* (June 10, 2010).

Pfeffer, Richard M. *No More Vietnams? The War and the Future of American Foreign Policy*. New York: Harper & Row, 1968.

Piller, Geofrrey. "DOD's Office of International Security Affairs: The Brief Ascendancy of an Advisory System." *Political Science Quarterly* 98:1 (Spring 1983): 59–78.

Pool, Walter S. *The JCS and National Policy, 1950–1952*. Washington, DC: Office of Joint History, 1998.

Prados, John. "Phoenix and the Drones." *Passport* 43:3 (January 2013): 36–39.

Preble, Christopher. *John F. Kennedy and the Missile Gap*. DeKalb: Northern Illinois University Press, 2004.

Preston, Andrew. "The Soft Hawks' Dilemma in Vietnam: Michael V. Forrestal at the National Security Council, 1962–1964." *International History Review* 25:1 (March 2003): 63–95.

"Mission Impossible: Canadian Secret Diplomacy and the Quest for Peace in Vietnam." In Lloyd C. Gardner and Ted Gittinger, eds., *The Search for Peace in Vietnam, 1964–1968*. College Station: Texas A&M University Press, 2004.

The War Council: McGeorge Bundy, the NSC, and Vietnam. Cambridge, MA: Harvard University Press, 2006.

"Review: Virtual JFK: Vietnam If Kennedy Had Lived." *Michigan War Studies Review* 19 (May 2011). Available online: www.miwsr.com/2011-019.aspx. Retrieved December 16, 2014.

Rabe, Stephen G. *The Most Dangerous Area in the World: John F. Kennedy Confronts Communist Revolution in Latin America*. Chapel Hill: University of North Carolina Press, 1999.

RAND Corporation. *Report: Limited War Patterns, Southeast Asia*. Santa Monica, CA: RAND, 1962.

Rearden, Steven L. *History of the Office of the Secretary of Defense*, vol. I: *The Formative Years: 1947–1950*. Washington, DC: OSD Historical Office, 1984.

Reeves, Richard. *President Kennedy: Profile of Power*. New York: Simon & Schuster, 1994.

Rockoff, Hugh. *America's Economic Way of War*. Cambridge: Cambridge University Press, 2012.

Roherty, James. *Decisions of Robert S. McNamara: A Study of the Role of Secretary of Defense*. Coral Gables, FL: University of Miami Press, 1970.

Rosenzweig, Phil. "Robert S. McNamara and the Evolution of Modern Management." *Harvard Business Review* (2010): 87–93.

Rovere, Richard H., and Arthur Schlesinger Jr. *The MacArthur Controversy and American Foreign Policy*. New York: Farrar, Straus & Giroux, 1965.

Ruiz-Palmer, Diego. "Big Lift." *AirFan: Le magazine de l'aéronautique militaire internationale* 419 (October 2013): 16–25.

Ryan, David. *US Collective Memory, Intervention and Vietnam: The Cultural Politics of US foreign Policy since 1969*. London: Routledge, 2014.

Schandler, Herbert Y. *The Unmaking of a President: Lyndon Johnson and Vietnam*. Princeton, NJ: Princeton University Press, 1977.

Schwab, Orrin. *Defending the Free World: John F. Kennedy, Lyndon Johnson and the Vietnam War, 1961–1965*. Westport, CT: Praeger, 1998.

A Clash of Cultures: Civil-Military Relations during the Vietnam War. Westport, CT: Praeger, 2006.

Selverstone, M. J. "It's a Date: Kennedy and the Timetable for a Vietnam Troop Withdrawal." *Diplomatic History* 34:3 (2010): 485–495.

Shapley, Deborah. *Promise and Power: The Life and Times of Robert McNamara*. New York: Little Brown, 1993.

Sheehan, Neil. *A Bright Shining Lie*. London: Picador, 1990

Shulimson, Jack, and Charles M. Johnson. *US Marines in Vietnam: The Landing and Buildup*. Washington, DC: USMC History and Museums Division, 1978.

Sohmen, Egon. "International Monetary Problems and the Foreign Exchanges." *Special Papers in International Economics* 4 (April 1963). Available online: www.princeton.edu/~ies/old_series-win.htm. Retrieved December 16, 2014.

Sorley, Lewis. "To Change a War: General Harold K. Johnson and the PROVN Study." *Parameters* (Spring 1998).

A Better War: The Unexamined Victories and Final Tragedy of America's Last Years in Vietnam. New York: Mariner Books, 2007.

Spanier, John W. *The Truman-MacArthur Controversy and the Korean War* Cambridge, MA: Harvard University Press, 1959.

Spector, Ronald H. *Advice and Support: The Early Years, the US Army in Vietnam*. Washington, DC: US Government Printing Office, 1983.

Stanton, Shelby L. *The Rise and Fall of the American Army: US Ground Forces in Vietnam, 1965–1973*. Novato, CA: Presidio Press, 1995.

Stavins, Ralph, Richard Barnet and Marcus Raskin. *Washington Plans an Aggressive War*. New York: Vintage, 1971.

Stuart, Douglas T. *Creating the National Security State: A History of the Law That Transformed America*. Princeton, NJ: Princeton University Press, 2008.

Summers, Harry G. *On Strategy: The Vietnam War in Context*. Honolulu, HI: University Press of the Pacific, 2003.

Sutherland, R. J. "Cost-Effectiveness and Defence Management; Mr. McNamara's Pentagon." Paper presented at the ORD Informal Paper, Ottawa, 1966. Available online: http://publications.gc.ca/collections/collection_2008/forces/D12-11-11-1E.pdf. Retrieved December 16, 2014.

Taylor, Leonard B. *Financial Management of the Vietnam Conflict, 1962–1972*. Washington, DC: Department of the Army, 1974.

Tertrais, Hugues. *Le piastre et le fusil: le cout de la guerre d'Indochine, 1945–1954*. Paris: Comité pour l'histoire économique et financière de la France, 2002.

Thayer, Thomas C. *Systems Analysis View of the Vietnam War: 1965–1974*, vols. 1–12. Fort Belvoir, VA: Defense Technical Information Center, 1975.

Thomas, Evan. *Robert Kennedy: His Life*. New York: Simon & Schuster, 2000.

Thompson, Nicholas. *The Hawk and the Dove: Paul Nitze, George Kennan, and the History of the Cold War*. New York: Henry Holt, 2009.

Trachtenberg, Marc. *Between Empire and Alliance: America and Europe during the Cold War*. Lanham, MD: Rowman & Littlefield, 2003.

Trewhitt, Henry L. *McNamara*. New York: Harper & Row, 1971.

Triffin, Robert. "Sterling, the Dollar, de Gaulle and Gold." *Challenge* 13:4 (1965): 19–23.

US Department of Army. *Vietnam Studies: US Army Special Forces, 1961–1971*. CMH Publication 90–23. Washington, DC: US Army, 1973.

US Department of the Navy. *The Marines in Vietnam, 1954–1973: An Anthology and Annotated Bibliography*. Washington, DC: USMC, 1985.

Vaisse, Maurice. *La grandeur: politique étrangere du General de Gaulle 1958–1969*. Paris: Fayard, 1998.

Van Atta, Dale. *With Honor: Melvin Laird in War, Peace, and Politics.* Madison: University of Wisconsin Press, 2008.

Van Creveld, Martin. "Why Iraq Will End as Vietnam Did." November 18, 2004. Available online: www.lewrockwell.com/2004/11/martin-van-creveld/why-iraq-will-end-as-vietnam-did/. Retrieved December 16, 2014.

Van Staaveren, Jacob. *USAF Plans and Policies in South Vietnam: 1961–1963.* Washington, DC: USAF Historical Liaison Office, 1965.

Gradual Failure: The Air War over North Vietnam. Washington, DC: USAF History and Museums Program, 2002.

Vasilew, Eugene. "The New Style in Political Campaigns: Lodge in New Hampshire, 1964." *Review of Politics* 30:2 (April 1968): 131–152.

Webb, Clive. *Rabble Rousers: The American Far Right in the Civil Rights Era.* Athens: University of Georgia Press, 2010.

Weidenbaum, Murray L. *Economic Impact of the Vietnam War.* Washington, DC: Center for Strategic Studies Special Report No. 5 (June 1967).

Weidman, Steven J. *Resurrecting Phoenix: Lessons in COIN Operations* Newport, RI: Naval War College, 2006.

Wells, Samuel F. Jr. "Sounding the Tocsin: NSC68 and the Soviet Threat." *International Security* 4 (Spring 1979): 116–158.

Willbanks, James H. *Abandoning Vietnam: How America Left and South Vietnam Lost Its War.* Lawrence: University of Kansas Press, 2008.

Winters, Francis X. *The Year of the Hare: America in Vietnam, January 25, 1963– February 15, 1964.* Athens: University of Georgia Press, 1997.

Woods, Randall B. "Dixie's Dove: J. William Fulbright, the Vietnam War and the American South." *Journal of Southern History* 60:3 (August 1994): 533–552.

Shadow Warrior: William Egan Colby and the CIA. New York: Basic Books, 2013.

Yarmolinksy, Adam. *Case Studies in Personnel Security.* Washington, DC: Bureau of National Affairs, 1955.

"Book Review: The Oppenheimer Case by Charles Curtis." *Harvard Law Review* 69 (1956): 1345–1352.

The US Military and Foreign Policy. Chicago, IL: Centre for Policy Study, 1967.

"Bureaucratic Structures and Political Outcomes." *Journal of International Affairs* 23:2 (1969): 225–236.

"The Strength of Government by McGeorge Bundy." *Policy Sciences* 1:1 (Spring 1970): 152–154.

The Military Establishment: Its Impacts on American Society. New York: Harper & Row, 1971.

"The Military Establishment (Or How Political Problems Become Military Problems)." *Foreign Policy* 1 (January 1971): 78–97.

"Some Lessons of Vietnam." *The Round Table* 62:245 (1972): 85–91.

"Civilian Control: New Perspectives for New Problems." *Indiana Law Journal* 49:4 (Summer 1974): 654–672.

"Cold War Stories." *Foreign Policy* 97 (Winter 1994/1995): 158–170.

Yarmolinsky, Adam, and Gregory D. Foster. *Paradoxes of Power: The Military Establishment in the Eighties.* Bloomington: Indiana University Press, 1983.

Yarmolinsky, Adam, Ernest May and Graham Allison "Limits to Intervention." *Foreign Affairs* 48 (January 1970): 245–261.

Yergin, Daniel. *Shattered Peace: The Origins of the Cold War and the National Security State*. New York: Penguins Books, 1980.

Young, Marilyn. *The Vietnam Wars: 1945–1990*. New York: Harper Collins, 1991.

    Bombing Civilians: A Twentieth-Century History. New York: W. W. Norton, 2009.

Zeiler, Thomas W. "The Diplomatic History Bandwagon: A State of the Field." *Journal of American History* 95:4 (March 2009): 1053–1073.

Ziemke, Caroline F., "Richard B. Russell and 'Lost Cause' in Vietnam, 1954–1968." *George Historical Quarterly* 72:1 (Spring 1998): 30–71.

UNPUBLISHED SECONDARY SOURCES

Barlow, Jeffrey G. "President John F. Kennedy and the Joint Chiefs of Staff." PhD dissertation, University of South Carolina, 1981.

Klimas, Joshua E. "Balancing Consensus, Consent, and Competence: Richard Russell, the Senate Armed Services Committee and Oversight of America's Defense, 1955–1968." PhD dissertation, Ohio State University, 2007.

McMaster, H. R. "Distrust, Deceit, and Disaster: Lyndon Johnson, Robert McNamara, the Joint Chiefs of Staff and the Americanization of the Vietnam War." PhD dissertation, University of North Carolina, 1996.

Young, Stephanie C. "Power and the Purse: Defense Budgeting and American Politics, 1947–1972." PhD dissertation, University of California, Berkeley, 2009.

Index